BLACKBIRD'S SONG

Portrait of Andrew J. Blackbird, circa 1890.

BLACKBIRD'S SONG

Andrew J. Blackbird and the Odawa People

Theodore J. Karamanski

Michigan State University Press
East Lansing

♾ The paper used in this publication meets the minimum requirements of ANSI/NISO Z39.48-1992 (R 1997) (Permanence of Paper).

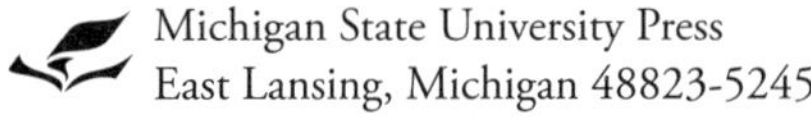
Michigan State University Press
East Lansing, Michigan 48823-5245

Printed and bound in the United States of America.

18 17 16 15 14 13 12 1 2 3 4 5 6 7 8 9 10

LIBRARY OF CONGRESS CATALOGING-IN-PUBLICATION DATA
Karamanski, Theodore J., 1953-
Blackbird's song : Andrew J. Blackbird and the Odawa people / Theodore J. Karamanski.
p. cm.
Includes bibliographical references and index.
ISBN 978-1-61186-050-4 (pbk. : alk. paper) 1. Blackbird, Andrew J., b. 1810. 2. Ottawa Indians—Michigan—Biography. 3. Indian authors—Michigan—Biography. 4. Ottawa Indians—History. 5. Ottawa Indians—Social life and customs. I. Title.
E99.O6B534 2012
[B]
977.4004'973360092—dc23

2011050490

Book design by Scribe Inc. (www.scribenet.com)
Cover design by Erin Kirk New

Front cover art is *Mackadepenessy/Andrew J. Blackbird* by Jane Cardinal, Harbor Springs, Michigan, and is used courtesy of the artist.
Back cover art is of Andrew Blackbird's home in Harbor Springs where he and his wife Elizabeth raised their four children, and is used courtesy of Jane Cardinal.

green press INITIATIVE Michigan State University Press is a member of the Green Press Initiative and is committed to developing and encouraging ecologically responsible publishing practices. For more information about the Green Press Initiative and the use of recycled paper in book publishing, please visit www.greenpressinitiative.org.

Visit Michigan State University Press at www.msupress.org

For the elders who have gone before—
we walk in your light.
And the dear ones whom we mourn, ever
in our hearts they live.

Contents

Acknowledgments

Eventually, all things merge into one, and a river runs through it. —*Norman Maclean*

THE RIVER THAT RUNS THROUGH THE HEART OF MY CAREER HAS BEEN public history. Most books and articles I have written began as projects in which an individual, corporation, or government agency needed help with an issue of historic preservation, heritage interpretation, or legal history. Exploring the historical background of other people's questions is hardly the typical way of doing history. It has been, however, very rewarding to do work that has an immediate and practical application. Public history work with the National Park Service first brought me to the beautiful section of northwest Michigan that is the homeland of the Odawa people. Later Alan Newell of Historical Research Associates approached me to work on history issues in northern Michigan with the Michigan Department of Natural Resources. It was Alan who first saw there was a book lurking in the weeds of our client-based work; although this might not be the book he initially had in mind, his advice and support made what is here possible.

My interest in the Odawa people and their struggle to protect their homeland was stimulated by litigation support research dealing with Odawa and Ojibwe treaty rights. Andrew Blackbird emerged from my research as a particularly eloquent source documenting aspirations of the Odawa people. While working on the treaty rights project, I benefited from the comments and criticism of historians and anthropologists working with Historical Research Associates; Emily Greenwald, Vice President at HRA; Paul Dribben of Lakehead University; James Davis of Illinois College; and especially Lawrence C. Kelly, University of North Texas, and Anthony G. Gulig, University of Wisconsin, Whitewater. Richard A. Rhodes of the University of California, Berkeley—thanks for your help with Odawa linguistics. Thanks are also due to attorneys Deirdre Boggs, Loretta S. Crum, John Wernet,

Marie Shamraj, Todd B. Adams, and Chris Dobyns. Their probing questions and open minds represented the best blending of the law and history. Dr. Dan O'Reilly generously shared his knowledge of internal medicine and reviewed materials regarding William Blackbird's mysterious death. Special thanks are reserved for historians who read various versions of this biography, particularly Alan Newell and Anthony Gulig.

Research on Blackbird's life has taken me to just about every research library in the Great Lakes region and to quite a few farther afield. I would especially like to thank Scott Forsythe of the National Archives, Great Lakes Branch; Brian Dunnigan of the Clements Library, University of Michigan; Karen Jania, Marilyn McNitt, and Diane Bachman at the Bentley Historical Library, University of Michigan; Harry Miller at the Wisconsin Historical Society; and Kevin Cawley for access to the superbly organized Diocese of Detroit records at the University of Notre Dame Archives. I also gratefully acknowledge the help of staffs at the Western Reserve Historical Society, the American Philosophical Society, the Newberry Library, Chicago Historical Museum, Clarke Historical Library at Central Michigan University, the Detroit Public Library's Burton Collection, Indiana University's Great Lakes Ethnohistory Archive, the Library and Archives of Canada, the Harbor Springs Historical Society, the Little Traverse Historical Museum, the Library of Congress, and the National Archives in Washington, D.C.

Eric Hemenway, Little Traverse Bay Band Repatriation Specialist, helped me locate Andrew Blackbird materials held by the band. I would also like to thank Yvonne Keshick of the Little Traverse Bay Band Archives, Research, and Collections Department for access to Blackbird material in the Obermiller Collection. Maria Davis, Archivist at Eastern Michigan University, graciously made available to me the scant records of Andrew Blackbird's academic career at Michigan State Normal School. Joyce Shagonaby provided me access to Blackbird letters held by the Andrew J. Blackbird Museum in Harbor Springs, Michigan.

My study of Blackbird's life was greatly assisted by a fine master of arts thesis written in 1964 by Grace Walz at Western Michigan University. Her excellent research included interviews with a number of individuals who knew Andrew, providing a tenuous oral connection to Blackbird's generation. Like many others who have worked on late nineteenth-century Michigan Indian history, I am indebted to Bruce Alan Rubenstein for his fine 1974 dissertation on Indian-white relations in the state. James M. McCluken's 1988 dissertation on Ottawa-American political contests was another important research aid for this project.

Working on this project brought me back to topics and issues that occupied my attention as a student and young historian and made me appreciate as never before the fine training in Indian history provided by my mentor and friend Professor Robert W. McCluggage at Loyola University Chicago. I also appreciate David R. Miller and the incomparable Helen Hornbeck Tanner at the Newberry Library's D'Arcy McNickle Center for the History of the American Indian, who many years ago, over many afternoons, shared sherry, nuts, and sage advice.

This book was begun at a very dark time for my home institution, Loyola University Chicago. Thanks to President Michael J. Garanzini, S.J., the university has never been stronger and more vital. I am indebted to the university for providing a marvelous and supportive base for doing public history and in particular for awarding me a paid leave of absence to complete this volume. My colleagues in the Department of History have set a high standard for both teaching and research that I hope this book will help to sustain. I am grateful also for the many fine students of public and Indian history whose class comments and office conversations have shaped my thinking, especially Bethany Hirt Fleming, Ryan Booth, and Melissa Cushing-Davis.

I would also like to acknowledge the careful assistance of the staff of Michigan State University Press in bringing this manuscript to press, particularly Project Editor Kristine M. Blakeslee. Thanks are also due to Jane Cardinal whose lovely painting of Andrew Blackbird graces the cover of this volume and to the Andrew Blackbird Museum for their permission to use the painting.

I am fortunate that the river that runs through my life also led me to the door of my dear wife and occasional coauthor, Professor Eileen M. McMahon. Whenever my canoe threatens to tip, her steady hand and wise ways keep me stable. My sons Ted and Joe are also in these pages, having shared in some of the research travels and more importantly having grown up amid the surf and sand of Andrew Blackbird's Lake Michigan homeland. "Eventually," Norman Maclean reminds, "all things merge into one." What I want for my sons, Andrew Blackbird wanted for his, and I hope for theirs. Over the divide of years, across the gulf of culture, we all share the same fears and live in the same hope.

Introduction

A GRAY-HAIRED MAN SAT AT A TABLE, PEN IN HAND. HE WROTE SEVERAL lines then paused, looking up from the white page and out the adjacent window. In the pale, dull light of a winter afternoon he stared at the still, leafless limbs of lifeless trees. This had always been a good time of year to tell the old stories. Perhaps he remembered what the grandmothers of the village used to say when he and his friends broke the rule that stories were to be saved for winter telling: "Ha! This person is telling a story. Now a toad will sleep with him!"[1] It had been on winter evenings, huddled close to the fire, that he had first thrilled to the adventures of the hero, Nanabojo. He could close his eyes and hear the Ottawa words of his father flow smooth and sonorous amid the flickering shadows of the rush mat lodge. The wood frame house in which he wrote was so very different. It was bigger and brighter, but not necessarily warmer. More striking were his four children, not one of whom had experienced a winter hunting camp, and who could not even understand the Ottawa language. It was not merely a good time of the year to tell once more the old stories, it was time to record in writing the history of a people who were rapidly changing.

With small and nimble hands he wrote on the page, "it seems desirable that the history of my people should not be lost, like that of other tribes who previously existed in this country, and who have left no record of their ancient legends and their traditions."[2]

Andrew Jackson Blackbird wrote those words in his 1887 book *History of the Ottawa and Chippewa Indians of Michigan: A Grammar of Their Language, and the Personal and Family History of the Author.* The book succeeded in its stated purpose and it is today one of the most important sources of information concerning the Indians in the Great Lakes region. An unstated goal of the book was to provide a stream of income for an old man no longer able to sustain himself or his family through farming or government work. In this the book was a disappointment. Andrew Blackbird continued to live in genteel poverty, his house encumbered by unpaid debts until 1908, when he was taken to the Emmet County Poor Farm, where he died. It was a sad end for a man whose life had been a model of what American Indians could achieve as citizens of the State of Michigan. It was a poignant and strange end for the son of an Ottawa chief, estranged from the love and care of extended family, to die alone among the detritus of rugged individualism. Perhaps it was a fitting end for a man who made the American journey from community to self-accomplishment, to failure.

This book is a cultural biography of Andrew Blackbird. The history of the Ottawa Indians of northwest Michigan is as much the focus as the actual life of Andrew Blackbird. His writings provide an intimate point of entry into an interesting and complex Indian community that has largely been seen only from the perspective of European-American sources. As a cultural biography the book looks at Blackbird's life as a means to understand how individual Ottawa confronted the challenges of a traumatic time in their history. The gaps and contradictions in Blackbird's own writing, the muted voices of his Ottawa contemporaries are particular challenges to this Indian biography. All biographers grope in the dark *terra incognito* of an individual's inner life. Native American biography brings the added challenges of confronting a culture that is imperfectly understood save for the fact that it was undergoing rapid change. There is, for example, no book-length ethnography of the Ottawa.[3] In spite of the prominence of this people in the history of the Great Lakes region much of what can be said about their historic lifeways has to be inferred from studies of their closely allied and more numerous neighbors, the Chippewa. In trying to document and imagine Andrew Blackbird's life I have tried to respect the otherness of his times and his cultural background, while trying to reach across the years to a fellow resident of Lake Michigan's shores—a man who shared a life of aspiration, love, frustration, accomplishment, and resignation.

Indian biography is almost always written in the tragic key. But here that tone would be too somber to accurately depict the life of a man who never participated in violence and whose people largely avoided the massacres, forced removals, and bleak reservations that fill the pages of American Indian histories. The frustrated aspirations of Andrew Blackbird and the Ottawa people of his generation were not a tragedy according to the sorry standard set by United States Indian policy. Blackbird's life, however, was a betrayal of the implicit promise of American life. Blackbird's experience and the fate of his people in the nineteenth-century Midwest was a sad case of arrested development. The Ottawa sought both to become part of American society and to preserve their unique identity, only to have their efforts circumscribed by racism and indifference. They became Christians, landowners, and citizens, yet like African-American freedmen in the Reconstruction South, they suffered the fate of people in a democratic society who cannot marshal political power. At their moment of crisis, Andrew Blackbird tried and failed to protect his people from the abuse of the law, and they were relegated to the status of a despised minority group in their homeland.

Andrew Blackbird came of age in a revolutionary time for the Indians of the Great Lakes region. The end of the War of 1812 announced the conclusion of the long period of Indian and European mutual dependence and cooperation in the region, an era that historian Richard White has famously dubbed "the Middle Ground."[4] That era had begun in the 1640s and had lasted through tribal wars, trade crisis, and the fall of the French and British empires in North America. At its core was the reality that on the Great Lakes frontier the Europeans were too weak to be able to dominate the Indians. Mutuality of economic and political interests was maintained by both peoples through careful negotiations. Personal relationships, particularly the marriage of Indian women to European men, played an important role in cultivating the peaceful landscape of the middle ground. Historians know that the forced withdrawal in 1815 of the British from the United States side of the Great Lakes marked the end of the middle ground era. Yet that judgment would have seemed much less certain to the United States officials and Indian leaders who faced each other uneasily in the wake of the Treaty of Ghent. What was clear was that native people of the Great Lakes region had to shape a new relationship with the emerging American nation.

In some ways this book may be seen as a coda to Richard White's middle ground. The Blackbird story not only illustrates what followed the demise of that regime of compromise, it demonstrates that the relationships formed in that long era continued to shape the perceptions of whites and Indians, most notably in the Ottawa embrace of Catholicism as a vehicle of civilization.

To enter into the world of the Ottawa and Chippewa people in the wake of 1815, we need to remember the old adage, "Men make history, but they can never know the history they are making."[5] A generation of Indian leaders in the Great Lakes region devised political and economic strategies for their people. They did so with a clear notion of their past relations with Europeans in the middle ground era. To understand their actions we must suspend the dismal history of United States Indian policy that we know lay in front of them, and open our minds to the vastly different futures that were still contingent on individual action. Andrew Blackbird's father and his uncles were critical to the formulation of a bold strategy of cultural reinvention adopted by the Ottawa and Chippewa people. Blackbird himself and the men and women of his generation were the ones charged with trying to make real the promise of their fathers' revolution.

This book is the story of founding fathers and sons. Two generations were necessary to conceive and carry out the Ottawa's cultural change. Andrew Blackbird's father, Mackadepenessy, was one of the leading figures that moved the Ottawa from resisting the Americans to accommodation. The accommodation and transformation begun by Mackadepenessy was carried forward by his son. This relationship between fathers, sons, and cultural change was not unique to the Ottawa, but a necessity of a dangerous era. Contemporaries of Mackadepenessy and Blackbird, who led their people on a similar path of accommodation, were Leopold and Simon Pokagon among the Potawatomi; Waishkee and his sons, founders of the Bay Mills Chippewa community; and Blackbird's uncle and cousin, Jean Baptiste Assiginack and Francis Assiginack, who founded a Catholic Ottawa community on Manitoulin Island.

The story of Mackadepenessy, Andrew Blackbird, and the Ottawa counters the popular image of the warrior chief as the paragon of Indian leadership. The Ottawa leaders described below did not lead their people in "heroic" battle; rather, they were ordinary individuals who made deals and traded land for time. Yet the survival, persistence, and renaissance of native America has been the work of men and women who pursued the frustrating path of peace. Education and Christianity, the tools adopted by Blackbird and his father, have been of more good in preserving and protecting the core of Indian culture than any military resistance. While history remembers the tragic end of warriors such as Black Hawk, Little Crow, or even Sitting Bull, it would do better to honor the success of Mackadepenessy or the Pokagons in protecting families and preserving homelands. Blackbird's story joins those of other Great Lakes Indian peace leaders described by Edmund Danziger, Rebecca Kugel, and Jane Chute. In choosing accommodation they opened the door for the continued evolution of their unique culture and set the stage for more effective resistance in the courtroom by later generations.[6]

Late in his life Blackbird was generally referred to by his white neighbors as "the last chief of the Ottawa." In spite of his lineage of notable tribal leaders, Blackbird was never a "chief" or leader in a traditional sense. His claim to leadership was based not on traditional Ottawa values or virtues, but on his knowledge of the larger American society. He shaped his people's future through his service as a treaty councilor, legislative lobbyist, and member of the federal Indian bureaucracy. By the late nineteenth century and all across the broad sweep of Native America individuals like Blackbird—teachers, interpreters, and tribal business committee members—were making themselves the new face of Indian leadership. Confronted with a United States Indian policy designed to be, in Teddy Roosevelt's inimitable words, "a mighty pulverizing engine to break up the tribal mass," the new generation of Indian leaders faced a daunting task. Even the self-styled "Friends of the American Indian" alternately patronized and ignored them. While these new Indian leaders were products of European-American education, they were also believers in the future of their people. Individuals such as Charles Eastman, Sarah Winnemucca, Arthur Parker, and Andrew Blackbird were frustrated by federal Indian policy, but acted as intercultural brokers, protectors of tribal traditions and voices of Indian identity. Blackbird expressed his understanding of his transitional leadership role when he described his long advocacy for Indian boarding schools as "my war-song."[7]

Blackbird's dedication to boarding schools as a means of advancing Indian education discomforts the traditional historical narrative that polarizes resistance and assimilation. Like so many Indian leaders of the post-treaty era, Blackbird's leadership was based on the education he received at a boarding school, immersed in a European-American cultural environment. Throughout his life Blackbird championed this approach to Indian education, if not for all young people, certainly for those who would aspire to a leadership role. Blackbird and his contemporary activist, Carlos Montezuma, believed such an experience was necessary in order to produce a generation of Indian leaders who would, in Blackbird's words, take their place "in the halls of [the] Legislature and in the halls of Congress to protect the rights of their beguiled race." In this way Blackbird was a voice of both assimilation as well as resistance.[8]

Blackbird's lifelong dedication to self-determination fits more comfortably in standard notions of Indian resistance. While modern Indian nations emphasize sovereignty in their relationship with federal and state authorities, nineteenth-century Indian leaders had the more modest goal of self-determination, the basic right to live where and how they chose. Sovereignty, complete political authority over a discreet territory, for the Ottawa community in the 1830s would have been illusory political goal, and self-determination for Ottawa men and women offered a way to protect the core of their culture. Self-determination is what Blackbird's father and other elders exercised when they initiated the Ottawa program of accommodation with the United States. It was also what Blackbird sought for his people when he pressed for Indian citizenship in Michigan and later for the protection of their property rights. In his personal life, Blackbird was very much his own man. He blazed his own course in seeking education, in the torturous path of his faith history, in his political party allegiance, and in his marriage to a white woman. Blackbird acted as he saw fit, and he sought that autonomy for the Ottawa. In this regard, perhaps Blackbird was, after all, a warrior.

Like many who have studied Indian history. I have encountered nineteenth-century American Indians as individuals only when their names have appeared in government records, their spellings often torturously anglicized by a translator, and signed with the letter "X." Andrew Jackson Blackbird is one of those names that appear on an Indian treaty. Unlike the majority of his contemporaries, he left a record of what he saw and what he thought, and I have used him as a point of imaginative entry into the world of Great Lakes Indians. This book is not a textual study of Blackbird's writings, nor is it a cultural study. I have employed Blackbird's literary productions in the same way I have used his contemporary correspondence as sources of historical evidence to be weighed, evaluated, and utilized as tools to move beyond the silence that surrounds the names of nineteenth-century native people. I have attempted to interpret and contextualize what Blackbird wrote and experienced with respect for the integrity of his words and his lived experience.

This book is an attempt to use the life of Andrew Blackbird to understand a neglected chapter in American Indian history. In trying to preserve the history and legends of the Ottawa Indians Andrew Blackbird presented also a history of his life and his family's experience in antebellum Michigan. No other source presents in such detail the Indian perspective on the era of transition, when the middle ground of the fur trade yielded to the rise of the industrial commonwealth of Michigan. Too often Indian lives are seen as distinct from the main course of American history. Yet Blackbird and the Ottawa and Chippewa people of Michigan grappled with the most American of questions, one that is both personal and national: "Who am I?" Caught between the old ways of tradition and an uncertain future, with a mixture of urgency and improvisation, he and many of his people embraced the chance to exercise choice. This book is the story of a man, his writings, and his people. It is, like so many American stories, a journey of discovery for an individual, an exploration of the limitations of a society, and a reflection on the possibilities of its future.

AUTHOR'S NOTE

Throughout this book I refer to Andrew Blackbird's people as the Ottawa. The modern Little Traverse Bay Bands government prefers the spelling Odawa. Both names are derived from the word *adaawe*, meaning "to trade." A people have the right to be known by the name they choose; however, the term Odawa was seldom used historically. I have reluctantly chosen to use the English derivative Ottawa because this was the term always used by the United States government and it was the spelling used by Andrew Blackbird in his *History of the Ottawa and Chippewa.* For the same reason I have used the term Chippewa as opposed to the synonyms Ojibwa or Ojibwe. The Ottawa and Chippewa lived in close proximity to each other and were close cultural relatives. When referring to both groups, common interests or values I use the term *Anishnabeg,* or when referring to an individual, *Anishnabe.*

1

A Forest Youth

A SON IS BORN TO MACKADEPENESSY

BEFORE HE WAS BORN, BEFORE HE WAS EVEN CONCEIVED, THE SOUL of Andrew Blackbird had been placed by the Great Manitou in his mother's womb. In a dome-shaped wigwam the body and the soul became one when his mother, kneeling on a mat of woven reeds, her arms clutching the smooth wooden pole of the delivery rack, pushed the infant boy out into the world. The women attending the birth took the baby and washed him in a murky bath of hot water, herbs, and ash. With relief the weary mother looked at the well-formed baby boy bawling over his unceremonious entrance into the world. For months both she and her husband had tried to avoid the sight of any deformed people or animals for fear of transmitting an abnormality to their child. She smiled with pride on the healthy child that would join his six brothers and four sisters as the newest member of the family. He was given the name Penesswiquaam, which can be roughly translated to mean Big Bird.[1]

Like most Indians of his time and place Andrew Blackbird never knew the exact year of his birth. In 1884 he told the compilers of a commercial biographical and local history volume that he was "born south of the Traverse Region about 1820." Sixteen years later in one of his own writings Blackbird wrote, "The first remembrance I have of seeing a white man is more than 80 years ago, or soon after the war of 1812." How soon after 1815 this encounter was Blackbird could not be certain. He confessed in 1900, "I don't know just how old I am, as my parents did not remember."

The best approximation of when he was born that can be obtained is his own estimate of "about 1820."[2]

Andrew Blackbird was born and spent the first months of his life in the thick forests of the upper Muskegon River valley. Every day his father and brothers took their guns and set out in pursuit of game. Beaver and raccoon were hunted for their furs; deer, elk, and bear for their meat. Andrew's mother and sisters were kept perpetually busy by the laborious process of scrapping and drying the hide of furs destined for trade. At night in the wigwam Mackadepenessy and his older sons, while puffing on pipes, recounted their success and failures in the day's hunt. Their accounts of tracking deer through the winter forest or of treeing raccoons, told amid the blue haze of wood smoke and the glow of campfire, were the boy's first lessons on what was expected of him as a man.[3]

Hunting camp stories also taught the boy to be proud of his lineage. The men of the Blackbird family were unique among the Ottawa in that they were said to descend from a people known as the "Undergrounds." Generations before they had come to the tribe as prisoners captured by far-ranging war parties. Their name came from "their habitations in the ground" and they likely were *Panis,* Indian slaves found among most Great Lakes Indian peoples. The name derived from the French term for the plains-dwelling Pawnee Indians, who did live in earth lodges. By Andrew's time the "Undergrounds," through merit and intermarriage with their captors, were in his words "the best counselors, best chieftains, and best warriors among the Ottawa."[4]

Late in life when Andrew Blackbird wrote his history he took pains to present his family as "closely connected with the royal families" of the Ottawa. His mother's brother was the famed warrior Shaubena, an Ottawa who had married into the Illinois Potawatomi, and rose to a position of eminence. During the War of 1812, Shaubena was a strong supporter of Tecumseh's Indian alliance and he fought alongside the Shawnee leader until the latter's death at the Battle of the Thames. Thereafter, Shaubena became an advocate of peaceful coexistence with the United States, and in 1832 he won praise from white settlers for keeping the Potawatomi from joining Black Hawk's tragic "war." On his father's side was Ningegon, known to the Americans as Wing, the leading chief of the Mackinac Straits Ottawa. Wing earned the trust and friendship of the Americans for his anti-British position during the War of 1812. Pungowish, Andrew's great-grandfather, first brought the family to northern Michigan from the Detroit area. Pungowish in short order became an important leader among the Ottawa of the Straits region and according to family tradition he played a key role in obtaining Ottawa and Chippewa approval for the British to build a fort on Mackinac Island.[5]

HUNTING CAMP DAYS

To appreciate the changes embraced by the Ottawa during his lifetime, it is useful to review in detail how Andrew Blackbird spent his early life. For at least the first eight years of Blackbird's life the family returned each winter to the Upper Muskegon country. Here was the family's designated and exclusive winter hunting and trapping ground. Large mammals such as deer, elk, and bear were hunted for food for the family and to trade at Mackinac Island. Fur-bearing animals were also trapped for trade. Commercial hunting provided the Ottawa with the ability to purchase firearms and other manufactured items, the most important of which were cotton and wool cloth. The winter hunting camp was one phase of a seasonal subsistence cycle that was adapted to exploiting widely separated ecological niches. While most European-Americans lived rooted on a family farm or village shop, the Ottawa lived mobile lives, sometimes working as farmers, fishermen, hunters, trappers, or craftsmen as the season dictated.

The subsistence round began each year at the end of August, when most families would leave the great summer village near Little Traverse Bay and canoe down the east shore of Lake Michigan. As Andrew later recorded:

> In navigating Lake Michigan they used long bark canoes in which they carried their whole families and enough provisions to last them all winter. These canoes were made very light, out of white birch bark, and with a fair wind they could skip very lightly on the waters, going very fast, and could stand a very heavy sea. In one day they could sail quite a long distance along the coast of Lake Michigan. When night overtook them they would land and make wigwams with light poles of cedar which they always carried in their canoes. These wigwams were covered with mats made for that purpose out of prepared marsh reeds or flags sewed together, which made very good shelter from rain and wind, and were very warm after making fires inside of them. . . . After breakfast in the morning they are off again in the big canoes.[6]

From early fall until the long winter was over, the family would hunt in the interior, isolated from other Ottawa.

As the snow began to melt, Andrew's father, Chief Mackadepenessy, directed the family to decamp for their sugar bush. There at a fine stand of maple trees Blackbird's family set to work tapping the sweet sap and processing it into granulized sugar. This was happy work. The isolation of the winter was replaced with the conviviality of the sugar camp, where many families would come together for several weeks and cooperate in a festive atmosphere. Sugar was the Ottawa's principle condiment and they used it as freely as the European-Americans employed salt. It was also a lucrative trade item, valued by the Mackinac traders desperate for bit of sweetness on the frontier.

When the last *makuks* of sugar were loaded onto their canoes, it was time to once more head for the shore of Lake Michigan. In his *History* Blackbird wrote:

> Early in the spring we used to come down this beautiful stream of water (Muskegon River) in our long bark canoes, loaded with sugar, furs, deer skins, prepared venison for summer use, bear's oil, and bear meat prepared in oil, deer tallow, and sometimes a lot of honey, etc. On reaching the mouth of this river we halted for five or six days, when all the other Indians gathered, as was customary, expressly to feast for the dead. All the Indians and children used to go around among the camps and salute one another with the words, "Ne-baw-baw-tche-baw-yew," that is to say, "I am or we are going around as spirits," feasting and throwing food into the fire—as they believe the spirits of the dead take the victuals and eat as they are consumed in the fire.[7]

The feast would take place at a traditional burial ground where family members who had perished during the winter would be formally laid to rest and the memories of long-departed loved ones would be celebrated.

After the Feast of the Dead, all the Ottawa who had wintered in the Muskegon basin would form a flotilla of canoes and paddle back up the Michigan shore. After many days hard travel, the canoes, by tradition, stopped at Big Rock Point, the entrance to Little Traverse Bay. Here the lead canoes were honor bound to wait for the slower paddlers, so they could all arrive home together. When the canoes were halfway across the bay some of the men would hold their guns close to the water and fire, sending the sound to shore to alert the village folks. As the lodges came into sight the young men strained at their paddles, digging deep powerful strokes into the cold water to propel their canoe ahead of their friends and rivals. The bow of each canoe surged through the waves as moment by moment home gradually loomed closer and closer. Finally, through the clear water they could make out the lake bottom of stone and sand, which as the canoe glided forward, seemed to be rising up to meet them. Arms aching, the paddlers rested their blades on the gunnels of the craft and glided up to the beach, where the sweet sound of sand on the bow told them they were home.

Chief Mackadepenessy led his family to their wigwam in the village. This was a large dwelling, "sixty or seventy feet long" and twenty-five feet wide, that would be used by the family year after year. The frame was made of wooden poles secured in the ground and bent to form a domed roof. Overlapping sheets of bark clad the structure and ensured, according to a French observer, that "no rain whatever gets into them."[8] Andrew lived in his father's wigwam with his brothers, sisters, and possibly with one of his uncles and his family. "I distinctly remember the time," he wrote in his history, "and I have seen my brothers and myself dancing around the fires in our great wigwam, which had two fireplaces inside it." The flickering light cast their large shadows on the wigwam walls as before the blazing fire the boys performed "grand medicine dances."[9] The rhythmic drumbeat and the cantabile chorus of voices rose up with whiffs of smoke through the chimney hole, where it joined with the sounds of celebration rising from hundreds of similar lodges spread out on the dark shore of the inland sea.

LAND OF THE CROOKED TREE

L'Arbre Croche had been the grand village of the Ottawa since 1742. To the Ottawa the village was known as *Waganagisi,* taking its name from a tall, crooked pine tree that overhung a high lakeshore bluff. However, it was the French name for the land of the crooked tree that became best known, L'Arbre Croche. In time the term referred to not simply a single collection of wigwams but the dense concentration of Ottawa families along the entire shore of Little Traverse Bay.

"In my first recollection of the country of Arbor Croche," Andrew Blackbird wrote in his history, "there was nothing but small shrubbery here and there in small patches, such as wild cherry trees, but the most of it was a grassy plain; and such an abundance of wild strawberries, raspberries and blackberries that they fairly perfumed the air of the whole coast with [the] fragrant scent of ripe fruit." Andrew, like the other boys, had free run of the village area. Some days they played ball games; others were devoted to footraces, wrestling, and frequently hunting squirrels and chipmunks with their little bows and arrows. The boys also learned to set nets for fish in the clear waters of Little Traverse Bay. Gill nets made from twine purchased from fur traders were set in the bay by means of sinker stones tied to the bottom and wooded floats attached to the top. Andrew would set his nets in the evening. When the boy returned in the morning, he remembered, "Your net would be so loaded with delicious whitefish as to fairly float."[10]

Blackbird's memory of his youth at L'Arbre Croche was clearly tinted by nostalgia. Writing in old age he recalled,

> Then I never knew my people to want for anything to eat or to wear, as we always had plenty of wild meat and plenty of fish, corn, vegetables, and wild fruits. I thought (and yet I may be mistaken) that my people were very happy in those days, at least I was as happy myself as a lark.[11]

Summer generally was a time of plenty for the Ottawa. Nor did Blackbird overstate the abundance of resources offered by the Little Traverse area during that beautiful yet brief time of year. It was very much an ideal setting for a young boy with a bow, a landscape of beaches and forests to explore, and a cohort of friends to do it with.

The sights and sounds of those long summer days at old L'Arbre Croche stayed with Andrew Blackbird and became for him a refuge, a place to which he could retreat in snug security during the years ahead. He took particular comfort in the memory of a small bird, a brown thrush.

> Early in the morning as the sun peeped from the east, as I would yet be lying close to my mother's bosom, this brown thrush would begin his warbling songs perched upon the uppermost branches of the basswood tree that stood close to our lodge. I would then say to myself, as I listened to him, "here comes again my little orator," and I used to try and understand what he had to say; and sometimes thought I could understand some of its utterances as follows: "Good morning, good morning! Arise, arise! shoot, shoot! Come along, come along!" etc., every word repeated twice. Even then, and so young as I was, I used to think that little bird had a language which God or the Great Spirit had given him, and every bird of the forest understood what he had to say, and that he was appointed to preach to other birds, to tell them to be happy, to be thankful for the blessings they enjoy among the summer green branches of the forest, and the plenty of wild fruits to eat.[12]

It was common for an Ottawa man to have a special relationship with an animal who has blessed him. It is likely that throughout his life Blackbird listened for the sound of the brown thrush's song and that its warbling soothed him by opening a window on a happy time of his life.

The beauty and plenty of L'Arbre Croche masked a history of tragedy and death that haunted the landscape. In his history, Andrew Blackbird later recounted how in times past a smallpox epidemic had killed much of the village's original and larger population. It may have been a story he was told in his youth, though it is likely one he embellished with his own details.

> The Ottawas were greatly reduced in numbers from what they were in former times, on account of the smallpox which they brought from Montreal during the French war with Great Britain. This small-pox was sold to them shut up in a tin box, with the strict injunction not to open the box on their way homeward, but only when they should reach their country; and that this box contained something that would do them great good, and their people! The foolish people believed really there was something in the box supernatural, that would do them great good. Accordingly, after they reached home they opened the box; but behold there was another tin box inside, smaller. They took it out and opened the second box, and behold, still there was another box inside of the second box, smaller yet. So they kept on this way till they came to a very small box, which was not more than an inch long; and when they opened the last one they found nothing but moldy particles in this last box! They wondered very much what it was, and a great many closely inspected to try to find out what it meant. But alas, alas! Pretty soon burst out a terrible sickness among them. The great Indian doctors themselves were taken sick and died. The tradition says it was indeed awful and terrible. Every one taken with it was sure to die. Lodge after lodge was totally vacated—nothing but the dead bodies lying here and there in their lodges—entire families being swept off with the ravages of this terrible disease. The whole coast of Arbor Croche, or Waw-gaw-naw-ke-zee, . . . was entirely depopulated and laid waste.

According to the story, the blame for this disaster lay with "the British people" who acted out of "hatred" to "kill off the Ottawas and Chippewas because they were friends of the French Government or French King, whom they called 'Their Great Father.'"[13]

This tragic tale was a mix of actual history and oral tradition, blended by Blackbird. It is very likely that L'Arbre Croche was hit by a smallpox epidemic during the time of the French and Indian War (1755–60). War parties frequently went east to participate in campaigns with the French army. European military encampments were seedbeds for all sorts of contagion. During the 1750s an influential war chief among the Ottawa was Charles Langlade, son of a French father and an Ottawa mother. He led Michigan Ottawa in routing the army of Edward Braddock in the famous ambush on the Monongahela. Two years later he was with the Ottawa, Menominee, and Potawatomi at Fort William Henry, the grisly encounter so famously depicted in the novel *Last of the Mohicans.* Smallpox had infected some of the surrendering British garrison, who spread it to the Indians when clothing and equipment were plundered. The victorious warriors inadvertently brought the disease back to the Lake Michigan country. Smallpox was reported that year among the Potawatomi villages along the

St. Joseph River and could well have hit L'Arbre Croche also. During the 1750s the region was hit by several waves of smallpox. Blackbird' s account of "nothing but dead bodies lying here and there in their lodges" is graphically accurate of the impact of the dreaded pox on Indian villages.[14]

During Pontiac's War against the British, field commanders did authorize the deployment of blankets from a smallpox ward in an insidious effort to spread the disease to warriors besieging Fort Pitt. Blackbird's tale of British biological warfare is mirrored in a Chippewa account of British commandant distributing infected gifts that were not to be opened until the pillager Chippewa returned to their Minnesota home. Both stories reflect the Indian's correct association of smallpox with the European colonialists and the decline of indigenous populations.[15]

The denuded landscape around L'Arbre Croche during Andrew Blackbird's youth need not have indicated, as he implied, a reduced population at all. Somewhere between 1,000 and 1,200 people lived along Little Traverse Bay in the 1820s.[16] At that time the village had been located in the same place for eighty years. The demands for building materials and firewood were the likely reason there were so few trees in the area. Rather than being, as Andrew Blackbird described it, "a continuous village some fifteen or sixteen miles long," the shore along Little Traverse Bay was occupied intermittently by clusters of Ottawa lodges.

The prosperity of the L'Arbre Croche Ottawa rested in part on their association with the great fur-trading entrepôt at Mackinac Island. Even going back to the French regime the area where Lake Michigan and Lake Huron joined was a major distribution center for trade goods. The Europeans' need to maintain a large year-round base at this location made them dependent on the Ottawa for food supplies and canoes. The Ottawa's ability to bargain astutely made some European traders resentful, as a Frenchmen from the early 1700s revealed when he wrote:

> The savages who dwell there do not need to go hunting in order to obtain all the comforts of life. When they choose to work, they make canoes of birchbark, which they sell two at three hundred livres each. They get a shirt for two sheets of bark for cabins. The sale of their French strawberries and other fruits produces means of procuring their ornaments, which consist of vermilion and glass and porcelain beads. They make a profit on everything.[17]

The Ottawa farms of L'Arbre Croche produced corn, cabbage, turnips, squash, cucumbers, and melons for the fur traders. Without this agricultural produce, together with dried meat and fish, the Mackinac traders would not have been able to dispatch brigades of fur traders each year into the far reaches of the Great Lakes and Upper Mississippi region. Long before the United States of America was created, the Ottawa had shaped for themselves a lifestyle based on commercial exchanges and an international market in furs.[18]

MACKADEPENESSY: THE WAY OF THE HUNTER

There was a tremendous gap of experience between the world in which Mackadepenessy, Andrew Blackbird's father, grew up in and that which would be known by his son. It is necessary to understand the world of the father to appreciate the challenges faced by the son. Mackadepenessy matured in an era when the time-honored roles of hunter and warrior still defined male identity. Yet it would be a mistake to call Mackadepenessy's youth "traditional." Ottawa life had long responded dynamically to the changing world around them, most notably during the Iroquois Wars of the mid to late seventeenth century, when they were forced to temporarily seek refuge west of Lake Michigan. Mackadepenessy's youth in the late eighteenth century coincided with the expansion of the international fur trade from the Great Lakes region into the far northwest of what is now Canada. The expansion was not simply the action of European fur companies but also a westward movement of Great Lakes Indian peoples, pushing on the frontiers of their homeland.

Many times Andrew Blackbird heard his father relate tales of his life in the western fur trade. With pride Blackbird recorded in his history that his father was "noted as one who was most daring and adventurous in his younger days." Mackadepenessy initially went west to what is now Manitoba with his father on an extended trapping expedition and he spent much of his early life in the far northwest.[19]

The first Ottawa and Chippewa may have gone west to act as hunters for European or Canadian fur traders. Others simply followed the lakes and streams west of Lake Superior into what is now Manitoba in pursuit of better trapping. By the 1790s there was a genuine migration of Chippewa to the prairie west. In time, these western Chippewa were known as the Bungee. The Ottawa went west in smaller numbers than the Chippewa but there was a close association between the two *Anishnabeg* groups. In 1799 a Hudson's Bay Company explorer reported "Bungees and Ottoways" wintering together west of Lake Winnipeg. These people extended their hunts far up the Saskatchewan River valley into what is now northern Alberta.[20] Groups of Chippewa and Ottawa hunters and their families would travel to new country in brigades of canoes, sometimes comprising as many as forty canoes. The Cree and the Assiniboine people who inhabited the region initially harbored few resentments regarding the *Anishnabeg* expansion. A major smallpox epidemic in the 1780s may have significantly reduced their population in the area and made the newcomers seem less like a burden. The Ottawa and Chippewa offered something else, a bulwark against attacks by the Dakota (Sioux). The Chippewa had previously expanded into Dakota territory along the Upper Mississippi River and were well respected for their ability to best Dakota in battle.[21]

In addition to adventure the Ottawa went west because of the ready availability of beaver. These prized pelts were much easier to obtain in the far northwest than along Lake Michigan's shores. After several years hunting in the west, a young man could return equipped with the finest firearms and adorned with new woolen coats, cotton shirts, and trade silver jewelry.

According to Andrew Blackbird, Mackadepenessy was "about twenty years in the county of Manitoba with his brother Wa-ke-zoo, among other tribes of Indians and white fur-traders in that section of country."[22] Late in life Andrew amused children with a story of his father's boyhood pet in Manitoba, a baby moose. Mackadepenessy raised the orphan ungulate. As the moose grew in size, it was loaded like a packhorse when ever they had to move their camp. Unfortunately, the moose had made a habit, ever since it was a calf, of each night following the Ottawa into their wigwam. This was no problem at first, but gradually the moose's long legs began to crowd out the tired hunters. The story ended sadly for the moose: "They were obliged to dispose of him & eat the meat & use the skin for [a] mat."[23]

It is unclear if Mackadepenessy had been in Manitoba continuously since his boyhood, or if he returned there periodically. What is clear is that the experience of his time in the far northwest stayed with the chief and was passed down to his son. Mackadepenessy was very much struck by what he regarded as fur traders' abuse of the Indians. He told Andrew of

> liquor sold to Indians measured with a woman's thimble, a thimbleful for one dollar; one wooden coarse comb for two beaver skins; a double handful of salt for one beaver skin—and so on in proportion in everything else; the poor Indian had to give pile upon pile of beaver skins, which might be worth two or three hundred dollars, for a few yards of flimsy cloth.

The details of this description are not creditable. Traders in the northwest at the time neither sold liquor by the thimbleful or for denominations of

American currency. A bottle of diluted rum would have more likely sold for two beaver skins.[24] The Chippewa and Ottawa who came to the northwest were experienced traders and they enjoyed the increased buying power the superior hunting conditions allowed. Fur trader David Thompson described the western Ottawa as "rich." The "Women and Children, as well as the Men, were covered with silver brooches, Ear Rings, Wampum, Beads and other trinkets. Their mantles were of fine scarlet cloth as all was finery and dress."[25]

The negative picture of the northwest fur trade Andrew Blackbird heard from his father was exaggerated in its specifics, but it nonetheless conveyed Mackadepennesy's disapproval of the way the fur trade was conducted. The period of the 1790s and early 1800s was a time of intense competition between rival fur traders. The Hudson's Bay Company based in London was locked into a furious rivalry with the Montreal-based Northwest Company and numerous smaller partnerships. Desperate competition bred unscrupulous methods. Rum and high wines flowed freely when trade was conducted, and a hunter merely shopping his furs for the best price might, after several drinks, find himself settling for considerably less than he deserved. Cutthroat competition eroded bonds of kinship or trust that on the Great Lakes continued to mark much of the dealings between trader and trapper.

According to Blackbird, Chief Mackadepenessy was particularly offended by the degrading treatment of Indian women that was occasioned by the bitter competition for furs. Kinship ties were traditionally an important means by which fur traders established stable commercial relations with Indian peoples. In Michigan Ottawa or Chippewa women who married fur traders played an important role as cultural mediators. The willingness of merchants to join *Anishnabeg* society was a crucial step in the formation of the middle ground. This practice was also present in parts of the northwest, but during the early 1800s economic and demographic instability eroded the values behind stable relationships. In his history Blackbird recorded Mackadepennesy's complaint that "Englishmen and Frenchmen who went there to expressly traffic with the Indians . . . would take Indian wives." What bothered Mackadepenessy was that "when they left the country, they would leave their Indian wives and children there to shift for themselves."[26]

Mackadepenessy later told Andrew Blackbird, "There are in this region thousands of half breeds, most beautiful men and women, but they are as savage as the rest of the Indians." The prominence of the mixed-blooded offspring of fur trade marriages and liaisons was not a distinctive feature of the Manitoba region. At established fur trade enters such as Mackinac Island and Sault Ste. Marie mixed bloods were also present. The tradition in the Great Lakes region had been to describe these people as being

"French" or "Indian," as their choice of lifestyle indicated. Mackadepenessy was in the northwest at a moment of what historians have called "ethnogenisis," the birth of a distinct cultural group known as the "Métis" that considered itself neither Indian or European. Seeing the emergence of this new people out of a chaotic period of the fur trade may have affected Mackadepenessy's later thinking regarding the place of the Ottawa in the United States.

Blackbird attributed to his father's negative experiences in the northwest a profound lack of trust for "white men." One particular incident reported by Blackbird underscores that lesson.

> My father was once there left to perish on a lonely island by the fur traders, not because he had done any crime, but simply from inhuman cruelty and disregard of Indians by these white men. He was traveling with these traders from place to place in a long bark canoe, which was the only means of conveyance on the water in those days. It appears that there were two parties, and two of these long bark canoes were going in the same direction, one of which my father was paddling for them. He was not hired, but simply had joined them in his travels. But these two parties were thrown into a great quarrel about who should have my father to paddle their canoe. Therefore they landed on this little island expressly to fight amongst themselves; and after fighting long and desperately, they left my poor father on this little island to die, for they concluded that neither of them should take him into their canoe. He was left to die![27]

This incident reflects the opportunity and danger for individual Indians interacting in the European-American fur trade.

The story as it is related by Blackbird seems senseless and brutal, yet it is not completely out of character with the experiences of the many Ottawa and Chippewa who went west during this period. In 1799, for example, a groups of Chippewa hunters approached the Lac la Biche trading post when a Canadian trader reportedly ordered his men "to rush into the water and took every thing from [them] . . . by force."[28] In this incident and others traders clearly dashed any chance of a long-term trade relationship in favor of beating the opposition out of the furs at hand. An Indian hunter alone with two groups of competitive traders, as Mackadepenessy was, was even more vulnerable to their excesses.

In his account Andrew Blackbird portrays his father as not merely a victim, but a man of greater natural moral character than the "civilized" and Christian traders.

> What must be the feelings of this poor Indian, to whom life was as sweet as to any human creature? What revenge should he take upon those traders? He had a gun, which he leveled at them as they started off in their canoes. His fingers were on the trigger, when suddenly a thought flashed across his mind—"Perhaps the Great Spirit will be displeased." So he dropped his gun, and raised a fervent prayer to the Almighty ruler for deliverance from this awful situation. After being several days on this little island, when almost dying from starvation, fortunately deliverance came. He spied a small canoe with two persons in it within hail. They came and took him off from his dying situation. It was an Indian woman with her little son who happened to travel in that direction who saved my father's life.

The lesson that Mackadepenessy learned in his years participating in the northwest fur trade, one that he conveyed unmistakably to Andrew Blackbird, was not to place confidence in a white man. "He told us to beware of them, as they all were after one great object, namely to grasp the world's wealth," Blackbird recorded in his history; "and in order to obtain this, they would lie, steal, rob, or murder, if it need be; therefore he instructed us to beware how the white man would approach us with very smooth tongue, while his heart is full of deceit and far from intending to do us any good."[29]

It is impossible to chart Mackadepennesy's movements in the west. Blackbird reported that he enjoyed many adventures during those years. "Many times he has grappled with and narrowly escaped from the grizzly bear and treacherous buffalo which were then very numerous in that portion of the country," he wrote. The memoir of John Tanner, a young white man who was adopted into the Ottawa, sheds some light on their actions. Tanner encountered Mackadepenessy and his brother Wakezoo in the fall of 1813. Mackadepenessy was described as a notable man from L'Arbre Croche. His brother Wakezoo was a band leader and Tanner spent most of a winter with the brothers. According to Tanner, Mackadepenessy had "arrived from Lake Huron, to call us all home to that country." The occasion for the mission was the outbreak of the War of 1812. The time had come for the Ottawa hunters to once more become warriors. War between Great Britain and the United States was an unparalleled opportunity for the Ottawa to keep the rising American tide from washing against the shores of their Lake Michigan homeland.[30]

MACKADEPENESSY: THE WAY OF THE WARRIOR

According to Andrew Blackbird his father "left the Manitoba country about 1800, or about the time when the Shawnee prophet, 'Waw-wo-yaw-ge-she-maw,' who was one of Tecumseh's own brothers, sent his emissaries to preach to the Ottawas and Chippewas." In his history, Andrew Blackbird prefaced his version of his father's adventures in the west by noting: "My father was a very brave man. He has led his warriors several times on the warpath." It is possible that Mackadepenessy returned to L'Arbre Croche in time to participate in the war with the United States. Andrew Blackbird boasted that two of his uncles, Wing and Shaubena, had been friends of the United States during the War of 1812. He said nothing about Mackadepenessy posture during the conflict.[31]

If Mackadepenessy had returned to the Lake Michigan country in 1807, he would have found a vastly altered political environment. The United States government finally had established its presence in northern Michigan in 1796 when its army occupied the fort on Mackinac Island. The British, who had been the allies of the Ottawa since the 1760s, were forced to withdraw just over the international border to St. Joseph Island, only forty miles away from Mackinac. The growing military power of the young republic had first been made clear to the Ottawa at the 1794 Battle of Fallen Timbers, where Chippewa and Ottawa from northern Michigan served as part of a coalition of warriors determined to stop the Americans' advance in distant Ohio. Chiefs from northern Michigan had been forced to sign the humiliating Treaty of Greenville that necessitated the cession of Mackinac Island to the United States. Mackadepenessy may have gone west in the wake of the defeat at Fallen Timbers. It is also possible that Mackadepenessy may have been inspired by what he heard of the Shawnee Prophet's message to return to L'Arbre Croche.

The man known to history as the Shawnee Prophet was known to his followers as Tenskwatawa, "Open Door." He was a drunken wastrel the Master of Life had raised literally from the grave to lead Indian people to spiritual salvation and cultural renewal. He was in many ways a voice of tradition calling Indian people back to time-tested social ethics, respect for elders, care for the widowed, and abstinence from liquor. Less popular were his teachings that firearms were only to be used in self-defense and that hunting should take place with the stone-tipped arrows of the ancestors and that women should eschew the use of European metal cookware. The Prophet condemned the technology of the "Long Knives," as the Americans were called, because unlike the British and French, they were a people born of an evil spirit. Tenskwatawa was a revolutionary of the most profound kind. In the dark shadows that followed the defeat of the Indian alliance at Fallen Timbers, he fashioned a vision of the future that assured a revitalization of a Native American world under siege. His teachings borrowed heavily from Christianity, not the least in the evangelical fervor with which he reached out beyond the Shawnee to all Indian people. He rejected the world of property and military power that was encroaching on Indian peoples and offered spiritual power as an antidote to bitter pills the "Long Knives" had forced down their throats. Backed by the military and diplomatic prowess of his brother Tecumseh, Tenskwatawa's message spread rapidly throughout the Great Lakes region.[32]

Among the Ottawa who heard the Prophet's message was a warrior from L'Arbre Croche named Le Maigouis, The Trout. Early in 1807 he journeyed to Tenskwatawa's village in Ohio where he received the tenets of the new religion from the Prophet's own lips. He returned to Lake Michigan later that year filled with a desire to spread the message of revival among the northern Indians. Like the prophet himself Trout challenged the Ottawa to make a major change in the way they lived their lives. "You complain that the animals of the Forest are few and scattered," he challenged them. "How could it be otherwise? You destroy them yourselves for their Skins only and leave their bodies to rot or give the best pieces to the Whites." The Great Spirit warned the Ottawa and Chippewa, "I am displeased when I see this, and take them back to the Earth that they may not come to you again. You must kill no more animals than are necessary to feed and cloathe you."[33] This message may well have resonated with Mackadepenessy after his negative experiences with the fur traders of the northwest. It certainly swept through L'Arbre Croche and across the Upper Peninsula of Michigan. At the large summer gatherings of the Ottawa and Chippewa, Trout and his message were omnipresent. Some of the *Anishnabeg* were filled with a missionary spirit and they took the message farther west. In Manitoba John Tanner received one of these missionaries in 1812 and he was dismayed when all of his Chippewa neighbors adopted the Prophet's strict code.[34]

Trout's message of Indian renewal swept through the villages of the upper Great Lakes region. "All the Ottawas from L'arbe au Croche adhere strictly to the Shawney Prophets advice," a fur trader reported in September 1807; "they do not wear Hats Drink or Conjure." The suddenness with which the Ottawa and Chippewa turned away from the use of alcohol dismayed the fur traders. They tried offering free gallons of the formerly lucrative trade article only to have the Indians refuse "it with distain."[35] At Michilimackinac Captain Josiah Dunham of the United States army garrison repeatedly tried to silence Trout, yet when he finally snared the preacher, so insistent were the protests of the Ottawa chiefs, he was forced to release him almost immediately. Dunham contented himself by sending a message to the Ottawa and Chippewa villages of the region warning them that Trout was a "Dog" who "has taken great pains to avoid me, by creeping round behind the island," and that he was the messenger of "a great Imposter." Undeterred, Trout crossed over to the Upper Peninsula and took his creed to the Chippewa of Lake Superior.[36]

By 1808 hundreds of Ottawa and Chippewa had left their homes on the upper Great Lakes to journey to Prophetstown, on the banks of the Tippecanoe River in what is now northwest Indiana. Prophetstown was a large, multiethnic village that lacked the extensive agricultural fields that could support a large population through the winter. The flour, fowl, and swine found in the villages of Indian bands friendly to the United States were forbidden by the Prophet. When the winter of 1808–9 set in, the people of Prophetstown began to starve. They ate their horses and then they ate their dogs. Weak and vulnerable to infection, they were hit by disease. These calamities weakened the tenuous bonds of unity that brought Shawnees, Kickapoos, Miami, and Wyandot together with Ottawa and Chippewa. The coughing sickness devastated the lodges of the latter but seemed to pass over the Shawnee. Before the epidemic ended more than 150 Ottawa and Chippewa lay in their graves, while only five Shawnee yielded to disease. The survivors muttered to themselves that Tenskwatawa was a false prophet. They claimed that he would hide "himself in a hollow oak" and then "assert that he has been to the spirit land and communed with the master of life."[37]

The surviving Ottawa returned to Michigan convinced that the Prophet was at best a fraud, and at worst a practitioner of witchcraft. So great was their disillusionment that they would likely have sent war parties against Prophetstown, had not their intention become known to General William Hull in Detroit, who, ironically, offered Tenskwatawa American military protection.[38]

The loss of more than a hundred people left L'Arbre Croche in a much weakened and badly shaken condition. In his history, Andrew Blackbird offered a garbled account of the rise and fall of Tenskwatawa's influence over the Ottawa. Chronologically he locates the event "about 1800." He accurately describes the Shawnee Prophet's fundamentalist message but he adds to it the injunction that believers were instructed to "go west, and there to worship the Great Spirit according to the old style as their forefathers did." According to Blackbird, the Prophet's successful forecast of an earthquake convinced many wavering residents of L'Arbre Croche to follow his teachings. "At the earthquake," Andrew Blackbird wrote, "many Indians were frightened, and consequently many more believed and went west; but nearly all of them died out there because the climate did not agree with them." He concluded his account by observing, "This was the second time that the Ottawas were terribly reduced in numbers in the country of Arbor Croche."[39]

There is no evidence of a mass migration of Ottawa inspired by Tenskwatawa. If anything the Prophet wanted his followers to unite in defense of their existing homelands. Andrew Blackbird may have been conflating his father's return from the west with the rise of the Prophet. But Blackbird was correct that the land of L'Arbre Croche suffered a severe population loss at the beginning of the nineteenth century. In 1799 smallpox spread from Canada to Lake Michigan. According to a report made two decades later, as many as half of the people of L'Arbre Croche were lost. The fact that the epidemic occurred following a visit by the missionary Father Gabriel Richard made many Ottawa see the calamity as either stemming from the Christian's bad medicine or the Great Spirit's displeasure with the missionary's visit. The devastating epidemic may have helped to prepare the ground for Trout's evangelization in 1807. But when hunger and sickness seemed to single out the Ottawa who had gone to stay with the Prophet the memory of the 1799 epidemic together with a second major loss of family and loved ones pushed the Ottawa to reject the Prophet.[40]

Whatever the long-term causes, the tragic events of the spring of 1809 set in motion a precipitous decline in the Prophet's influence among the Ottawa and Chippewa; however, it is likely that pockets of support for his creed endured. The United States government unwittingly bolstered support for Tenskwatawa and his brother Tecumseh by arranging a series of land cession treaties with the Ottawa and Chippewa. In 1807, for $10,000 in goods and cash, the Indians of the Detroit region ceded the lands between Lake Erie and Lake Huron. A year later the United States was after these same people for a second cession, this time for a right-of-way for a road through the remaining Indian lands in southeast Michigan. These cessions established the unmistakable fact that the native land base was eroding—replicating the same process that had pushed the Shawnee and the Delaware to the point of disinheritance. The lands of L'Arbre Croche were as yet unaffected, but for how much longer?[41]

After 1809 the Ottawa, and to a lesser extent the Chippewa, were divided in their opposition to the Americans. While many repudiated the Prophet's spiritual doctrine, his call for a united front was viewed as a necessary step if their homelands were to be preserved. Therefore, it was

Tecumseh, the Prophet's brother, who became the more prominent figure in leading Indian resistance. He was able to offer very tangible proof of his power, in the form of military supplies from the British. When war finally broke out between the British and the Americans in the summer of 1812, hundreds of Indians from the western Great Lakes joined the English attack on the American garrison at Fort Michilimackinac. Hopelessly outnumbered and cut off from reinforcements, the Americans surrendered without a fight. The Ottawa, however, seemed cool to this initial call to rally to the Union Jack. Several hundred warriors assembled, but rather than joining the attacking force they remained a few miles away, waiting to see if the British assault would succeed.[42] Captain Charles Roberts, who led the attacking force, condemned the Ottawa as treacherous and unreliable. But the fact was the Ottawa were determined to fight or remain at peace according to their own understanding of what was right and in accordance with their own schedule. The decision was a personal one, made by each warrior for himself. Friends and families were sometimes divided by the need to choose sides in the war.

What role Mackadepenessy played in these events is sketchy at best. His older brother Ningegon, known to the Americans as Wing, was a staunch friend of the United States.[43] Early in the war one of Wing's sons fell fighting for the Americans near Detroit. After the fall of that town there was little Wing could do for the American cause. Nonetheless, he rejected the appeals of the British and defiantly flew a small American flag in his village. Because he resided just across the Straits from Mackinac Island, Wing's action was rightly regarded as a provocation by the British, but it was one that they had to suffer for fear of rupturing ties with the bulk of the Ottawa, who although they had no love of the United States, respected Wing. Years later, at the time of the negotiation of the 1836 Treaty of Washington, the Ottawa and the Americans agreed to a clause that granted a annuity of $100 to Wing, "because he was a firm friend of the American Government, in that quarter, during the late war, and suffered much in consequence of his sentiments."[44]

It is likely Mackadepenessy took a very different line during the war. Instead of following Wing's example he seems to have been inspired by another brother, Assiginack. Born in 1768 at L'Arbre Croche, it is probable that Assiginack was much closer in age to Mackadepenessy than either one was to Wing. They shared a love of adventure and travel as well as a curiosity about the ways of the white man—a curiosity that was mixed with a mounting sense of dread of the growing power of the Americans in their homeland. Both of the brothers also possessed the gift of rhetorical eloquence, which propelled them to positions of leadership among their people. Assiginack fought with the British along the Niagara frontier and he was regarded by the commandant at Michilimackinac as among the most important warriors at L'Arbre Croche.[45] At the beginning of the war, when many of the Ottawa wavered in their support of the British cause, it was Assiginack who prodded them to action. According to oral tradition he delivered a celebrated oration that lasted from sunrise to sunset. He stirred the hearts of the young Ottawa warriors and inspired them to take up the hatchet against the "Long Knives," as the Americans were called.[46] While Assiginack led the warriors of L'Arbre Croche into battle, his brothers Mackadepenessy and Wakezoo seem to have been given the job of recruiting reinforcements among the Ottawa in Manitoba.

The journey required they winter in the west and by the time Mackadepenessy returned to Michigan the war had taken a turn for the worse. The victory of United States naval forces on Lake Erie in the fall of 1813 had forced the British to withdraw from Detroit. Many Indian warriors abandoned Tecumseh's banner at this point. The Shawnee warrior, however, refused to give up the fight and retreated into British territory, where he was attacked and defeated in the Battle of the Thames. During the battle Tecumseh was killed and his followers, who included a number of Michigan Ottawa and Chippewa, were routed. The news was a bitter blow to Indians who believed that united action was the only way to protect their homelands from American expansion. Although the Indian cause was severely weakened, the dream of successful military resistance persisted as long as the British were willing to wage war on the United States. Despite the fall of Detroit in 1813 the British and Indian alliance managed to fend off an American attempt to retake Fort Mackinac in 1814 and even strengthened their hold on the northwest by capturing from the Americans the strategic trading center of Prairie du Chien on the Mississippi River. At both battles, Ottawa and Chippewa from Lake Michigan played a prominent part and it is likely that Mackadepenessy and his brother Assiginack served as war leaders.[47]

As the year 1814 drew to a close Indians such as Mackadepenessy who opposed American expansion could take heart that the northern lakes region remained secure from the armies of the United States. But unbeknownst to the *Anishanbeg* their British allies had already agreed to a peace treaty that would return American power to the Ottawa homeland. On Christmas Eve 1814 British and American peace commissioners in Ghent concluded a treaty that restored the prewar status quo to the region. Word of the agreement did not reach the United States until February 1815, and

Great Lakes frontier remained in the dark even longer. The Potawatomi and Ottawa allies of the British continued to send out war parties. Mackadepenessy joined his brother Assiginack in one of these final sorties of the war.

The war party was led by Mokomanish, Little Knife, and it departed L'Arbre Croche in a canoe. Mackadepenessy, Assiginack, and a handful of picked warriors paddled over lake and stream until they reached the upper Wabash River in what is now Indiana. There they ambushed a United States Army patrol, killing nine soldiers. Mokomanish was wounded in the attack and they managed to take a single soldier prisoner. The other members of the war party "reproached" Mokomanish for not revenging his wound by slaying the prisoner. Instead, the man was taken back to Fort Mackinac and turned over to the British. In June 1815 the British commander there presented Mokomanish with silver-mounted sword "in testimony of my great approbation of his conduct upon this occasion, which will be gratifying to the King, his great father, and to encourage similar acts of mercy to the unresisting and vanquished."[48]

Lieutenant Colonel Robert McDonall had good reason to be gracious in his praise of Mokomanish's mercy. When the latter's war party returned home to Michigan they heard the shocking news that the war was already over. As late as mid-April 1815, McDonall had boldly proclaimed that his government would never stop fighting until the Americans recognized the complete independence and sovereignty of the Indian nations.[49] Only a few days later he was forced to retract that boast. He advised the Ottawa and Chippewa of the region to stop all hostile actions against the United States and prepare for the return of the "Long Knives" to Michilimackinac. Reconciling the Ottawa and Chippewa to this bitter fact was no easy task. In May Colonel McDonall held a council with the chiefs of L'Arbre Croche. Many Indians undoubtedly drew the conclusion, as the Indians had discovered in 1794, following their defeat in the Battle of Fallen Timbers, that the British were inconsistent allies in war. McDonall, however, tried to counter this opinion by portraying the Treaty of Ghent as merely an armistice in the continuing struggle with the Americans. His troops would only withdraw to Drummond Island, a few miles from Mackinac Island. He proposed that the Ottawa and Chippewa continue to look upon the British king as their "Great Father" and he promised them generous gifts of blankets and guns when they visited Drummond Island. Thanks in part to Assiginack's warm support, the Ottawa leaders, in McDonall's words, "behaved nobly on the occasion."[50] Assiginack was so unwavering in his support of the British that he took on the thankless task of journeying down the shore of Lake

Michigan and officially notifying other Ottawa and Chippewa that the war was over.[51]

However stoic the Ottawa response to McDonall's news, the reality of the return of the Americans to Fort Mackinac was deeply demoralizing to all *Anishnabeg,* with the exception of Wing and his band. McDonall himself believed that the Indian's "brighter hopes, to look forward to happier days" were "about to be immolated on the altar of American vengeance." So strong was the sentiment against the "Long Knives" that for several years after the war ended Americans on the upper Great Lakes would be the mark for covert rifle musket volleys and the subjects to verbal threats of violence.[52]

Such latent hostility could not disguise the fact that after the trials of campaigns in distant places and the deaths of numerous young men, United States power would once more be in place at Fort Mackinac. The way of the warrior had been tried and it had failed. Even in 1815–16 some chiefs may have suspected the truth, that the Ottawa had just lost their last, best chance to maintain control of their destiny. While his older brother Wing basked in the attention lavished on him as America's only true friend among the Ottawa, and Assiginack relocated to Drummond Island to work for the return of the British, Mackadepenessy's response was more typical of the Ottawa. He retreated to his hunting grounds, to trap, to hunt, to think about the future of his family and his people. Near the Big Rapids on the Muskegon River he wintered in despair.

2

The Crisis

IN THE FALL OF 1835 ON THE SHORES OF LITTLE TRAVERSE BAY, NEAR the present city of Harbor Springs, Michigan, a large group of Ottawa gathered on the warm sands of the beach. The old women, draped in bright red blankets, had their hands in front of their faces, vainly hiding tears. The men tried to busy themselves with the matter-of-fact tasks of preparing a canoe for a long journey, speaking little, thinking much.

Andrew Blackbird looked down on the somber scene. He was at the awkward adolescent stage of life, more than a child and less than a man. He did not feel it was his place to be with the adults on the beach. Instead, he had joined "my little chums" at a favorite playing spot. High up on the sandy terrace overlooking the beach two cedar trees had grown together and leaned precipitously toward the lake. They had become, in Blackbird's words, "almost like a staircase projecting far out into the bay." Andrew was "clear at the top of those trees." He was a witness but apart from the scene on the beach. He watched "our people as they were about going off in a long bark canoe, and as we understood, they were going to Washington to see Great Father, the President of the United States, to tell him to have mercy on the Ottawa and Chippewa Indians of Michigan, not to take all the land away from them." The men, who included his cousin Augustin Hamlin and perhaps his father, Mackadepenessy, entered the canoe and secured their paddles in front of them. They then took off their broad dark hats and "crossed themselves and repeated the Lord's prayer; at the end of the prayer, they crossed themselves again, and then away they went towards the Harbor Point." Andrew stayed on his high perch watching the canoe as it smoothly rose and fell on the swells of the big lake, slowly getting smaller, until at last "they disappeared in rounding the point."[1]

Andrew shimmied down the tree as the gathering on the beach dispersed. The people walked back to the village deep in thought concerning "their future destinies respecting their possession of the land." It had taken sixteen years, but the full price of military defeat was about to be paid. By the fall of 1835 the Ottawa were in the midst of a crisis that affected every aspect of their lives, economic, political, social, and environmental. It was a challenge less violent than the Iroquois attacks of the mid-1600s, but one that threatened their very existence as a people just as surely.[2]

Much had changed in the condition of the Ottawa since the depressing days following the end of the War of 1812. The Ottawa of Michigan had a new "Great Father." He lived in a white house and his white children had an enormous appetite for land—a sad fact that necessitated the delegation to the capital. New also were the prayers to the Christian God. Where sixteen years before there might have been an offering of tobacco or even a dog to the spirits of the lake, that autumn day the men said the Lord's Prayer. Together with that fundamental change was the alteration in their lifestyle. Not just a single canoe should have been departing L'Arbre Croche that fall. In the past, most families would have already taken to their canoes in order to safely reach their winter hunting grounds before the snow flew. But by 1835 many residents of the village had abandoned their winter hunts for a more sedentary lifestyle.

Over too was the way of the warrior. Unlike his fathers before him, Andrew was poised on the cusp of adult life with no clear cultural guidance as to how he should live his life. The two principle standards by which young men had been measured, their prowess as hunters and their bravery as warriors, no longer seemed relevant. The decades of the 1820s, 1830s, and 1840s were a period of crisis for the Ottawa. It was a time when a venerable and successful culture was challenged to pioneer a new way. To find a path of peace and yet still protect their identity and homeland would prove more difficult than any military battle Ottawa warriors of old had ever fought. It was a time that demanded the cool-blooded reason of elders and the creativity of a rising generation of young men and women who, like Andrew Blackbird, knew their place neither in the changing world of L'Arbre Croche nor in the onrushing, alien world of the white man.

THE RETURN OF THE *CHEMOKMON*

In 1815 the United States cautiously reasserted itself in the Great Lakes region. The Treaty of Ghent restored to the Americans what they could neither hold nor take back in war; this stark reality bred insecurity and a desire to purge the frontier of all possible pro-British elements. To this effect Congress banned foreigners from engaging in the fur trade within United States territory, a right previously guaranteed by treaty.

Quite consciously this action threatened to sunder the middle ground system of carefully constructed personal relationships between English, French-Canadian, and *Anishnabeg* that undergirded the Great Lakes fur trade. From the 1670s to the return of the Americans in 1815, this intercultural system was based upon mutual support in time of war and commerce cemented by kinship ties. It was a flexible ordering of relationships between culturally diverse people who were equal in their power and their need for each other. French and then later English officials and traders married into the families of *Anishnabeg* notables, making personal an important public connection. Gift giving, annual trade fairs, and sometimes recruitment of war parties all grew out of well-established personal and political relationships. United States policy took its "long knife" to this web of relationships first when it forced British officials to the other side of the border and again when it prohibited their traders from operating on the American side of the lakes.

Historian Richard White dates the demise of the old middle ground to the 1815 return of the Americans.[3] The Americans in 1815, however, were too weak on the frontier to completely revolutionize the social and economic organization of the Great Lakes region. What followed the War of 1812, therefore, was a period of transition that lasted at least a decade in which Americans, after excising the British from the middle ground, contented themselves to occupy their erstwhile opponent's former niche.

American fur companies replaced British or Canadian companies, but they were careful to incorporate in their operations individuals related to the Ottawa and Chippewa. John Jacob Astor's American Fur Company, for example, brought into partnership Magdelaine Laframboise, a woman trader of Ottawa-French ancestry, who operated on the Grand River. Also continuing was Therese Marcot Lasaliere Schindler, yet another woman trader. She was a Métis with family ties to L'Arbre Croche. Even where new faces were seen, the Americans gave every indication of playing by the established rules of the middle ground. In 1816 Edward Biddle, the son of a prominent Pennsylvania family, came to Mackinac Island with the intention of entering the fur trade. Within a few years he married Agatha, the stepdaughter of a French-Canadian trader and a full-blooded Ottawa woman. Her connections with the people of L'Arbre Croche were as lucrative to her husband as they were reassuring to the Ottawa.[4]

For a time even the actions of representatives of the United States government appeared to demonstrate the enduring power of the middle ground. In the summer of 1817 the wedding of Josette Laframboise, granddaughter of an Ottawa chief, to Captain Benjamin K. Pierce, brother of a future president of the United States, was celebrated at a festive party that featured guests arrayed in a unique mixture of Ottawa, Métis, American, and military fashion.[5] In 1823 Henry Rowe Schoolcraft, the Indian agent in Sault Ste. Marie wed Jane Johnston, daughter of a prominent Chippewa woman and an Irish fur trader. In 1824 John Tanner became the interpreter for the Indian agent at Mackinac. Tanner, the former war captive who lived most of his life as an *Anishnabe,* was well known to Wakezoo and Mackadepenessy and he brought a familiar face to the Indian agency.[6]

Such hopeful signs, however, did not fully reconcile the Ottawa to the control of the Americans. They would treat with American agents and trade with American merchants, but the *Anishnabeg* continued to cultivate warm relations with the British. For more than a decade after the end of the war, the Ottawa at L'Arbre Croche undertook a summer canoe journey to Drummond Island, where they received ample presents from the British Indian Department. Even Chief Wing, who had been so staunchly pro-American during the war, was unable to prevent his people from making the pleasant canoe trip to Drummond Island and cashing in on British generosity. As a face-saving measure he falsely told his people that he had personally received permission from governor of the Michigan Territory, Lewis Cass, for them to make the journey.[7]

When the Michigan Ottawa arrived at Drummond Island they were greeted by a familiar face. Assiginack, the former war chief from L'Arbre Croche, had been retained by the British as the official interpreter for the Indian Department. Assiginack adhered to the British banner in the vain hope that the Peace of Ghent that ended the War of 1812 might prove to be no more than a temporary truce. He was no doubt heartened by the success of the Indian Department in attracting to the island as many as 4,500 Indians each year. Among those who visited Drummond Island was Assiginack's brother, Mackadepenessy. The L'Arbre Croche leader was carefully courted by the British. One of their officials reported that Mackadepenessy was a distinguished orator who "complains bitterly of the state of slavery to which his tribe are reduced since the war."[8]

It would be overreaching to say the Ottawa were consciously trying to triangulate a policy of survival between the antagonisms of the competing British and American empires. It would be closer to the truth to suggest that in an unsettled and uncertain time, they were trying to pursue a course that adhered as much as possible to the status quo. The British offered needed goods and extended the hand of an established, if not altogether reliable, ally in time of war. The Americans, after 1816, offered the continuation of fur trade commerce through established and expanded kinship networks. Both represented short-term accommodations that were compatible with the practices of the 150-year-old middle ground. Neither, however, held out a flattering prospect for the future. No Ottawa or Chippewa leader articulated a strategy that addressed the long- term challenge of adapting to an American Republic whose appetite for land seemed insatiable.

Andrew Blackbird's earliest memory dates from around 1825 and concerned a family visit to Drummond Island. It was the first time the boy, then about five years old, saw white men, and he found their strange appearance such that "I would run away fast, as soon as I would get sight of them." This reaction had been prompted by having heard many times his father's warnings about the treachery of white men. Blackbird later remembered feeling quite different, however, about the handful of white women at the British base. "I thought they were very charitable; God's queens of the earth." As Blackbird and his little niece were exploring the area around the fort, they happened to pass a British house and noticed "two beautiful women" sitting by the window. When the ladies saw the wide-eyed Indian children, they invited them into the house. Blackbird sat on a chair, perhaps for the first time, and carefully examined what appeared to be food placed on a plate in front of him. "I wondered and wondered what pie was," he recalled, "a preserve inside of the bread, which was indeed delicious to taste. This was the first that I ever saw or tasted such food."[9]

LOSING THE GREAT SPIRIT'S FAVOR

When Mackadepenessy and Assiginack reunited on Drummond Island, the brothers no doubt reminisced about past accomplishments and discussed concerns for the future. Assiginack had a striking memento of their warrior days to show his brother, an intricately carved wooden model of the men and canoe that composed Mokomanish's 1815 war party. Perhaps Mackadepenessy closely inspected the wooden figures that represented himself and Assiginack. That raid had now become part of history. They could not then have known that they had participated in what was likely the last war party the Ottawa would ever send against the white man. They did know that over the years *Anishnabeg* warriors from northern Michigan had won many victories against the Anglo-Americans, often fighting far from home to keep their enemies at bay. Their string of triumphs had begun in 1754 when their bullets shredded the red-coated columns of General Edward Braddock near the Monongahela River and continued through the humiliation of the British at Fort William Henry in 1757, and the capture of Fort Michilimackinac in 1763. In the 1790s they had joined with the Ohio tribes to oppose the United States and rejoiced in many stunning victories. In the War of 1812 they had swept the Americans from the northern lakes. Yet, while *Anishnabeg* warriors had won much glory and many battles, war had done little to slow the spread of white settlers and the growing power of the United States government.[10]

The way of the warrior had not worked in the past when the American settlements were far from Lake Michigan, and they knew it had little chance now that the *Chemokmon* occupied Fort Mackinac and the white canvas or black smoke of their ships blighted every horizon. The Ottawa needed access to a power greater than a warrior's muscled right arm. The Shawnee Prophet's path to such power had excited Mackadepenessy as a young man, but in the end proved false. Yet perhaps the Prophet had been correct when he warned the Indians that they had lost the favor of the Great Spirit. The Prophet had cited the abuse of alcohol as an example of his people's failings. That problem had only grown worse since the end of the war. The use and abuse of this substance through the fur trade was more of a problem during the era of American control because of an increase in the number of traders and because access to the Great Lakes region became easier over time. United States government sanctions against the sale of alcohol in Indian country were easily circumvented and Indian people paid the penalty.

The result of large amounts of alcohol at trading posts was the shaming of otherwise good and competent people. Lacking the social conventions that had developed over centuries of European use of alcohol, some Indians engaged in binge drinking. Such drinking bouts were usually limited to occasional encounters with fur traders, but what started as a libation often ended in violent struggles with fellow inebriants or staggered individuals falling into the fire. Small quarrels or all-but-forgotten slights would become inflamed during a drinking bout. The normal generosity of Ottawa society became perverted by drink. While only one hunter might have furs, his purchase of a keg of whiskey would be shared with many others in the band. Tragically, mothers with cradleboards on their backs would sometimes become staggered with drink and kill their infants with a fall.[11] In 1834 the missionary Frederic Baraga wrote about the Grand River Ottawa.

> It is a terrible sight to see an Indian drunk, but especially the women. They are then real furies. One finds here very many Indian woman who have no nose.

> When I first came here and noticed this I did not know the reason for it. I made inquiries and learned that, when drunk, they attack each other like raging wolves and bite off each other's noses. Others miss fingers on their hands, which they have lost in similar bacchanalian battles.[12]

Compounding these social ills was the economic drag of drunkenness. Furs traded for whiskey could not be used to purchase the blankets, clothing, and hunting supplies required by Indian families. In this way the use of alcohol accelerated the rise of indebtedness among the Ottawa.

There is no evidence of Mackadepenessy, Andrew Blackbird's father, abusing alcohol. The problem, however, was widespread and it was for a time a dark shadow over his brother Assiginack's life. During his first few years on Drummond Island, he drank heavily. Bitter over the late war and anxious about the future, he was not a happy inebriant. The artist Paul Kane reported that during these years Assiginack was known for his "continual habit of drinking to excess," a habit made much worse because when in his cups he became "a perfect maniac." Renowned for his "Herculean strength," Assiginack as a drunk was a great danger to his friends and associates. Therefore, "It was the custom of his attendants to increase the amount of the stimulus, and ply him with it until he became insensible, rather than expose themselves to danger from his ungovernable violence."[13]

This pattern of behavior eventually tried the patience of Thomas Anderson, the British Indian agent on Drummond Island. One day when he came across Assiginack "in a state of drunken stupor," Anderson set about giving the interpreter a humiliating lesson. He "bound him hand and foot with strong cords, placing a sickly decrepit boy to watch over him." When Assiginack awoke he "furiously demanded his instant liberation." Anderson told him that he had been bound by his orders, and for hours he had been "exposed to the derision of the whole camp." Assiginack was "greatly mortified at the degraded position in which he had placed himself" and he promised Anderson "he would never again taste ardent spirits." Assiginack's pride in his position of importance with the British, his pride in being respected as a great warrior, his pride in being a strong and capable man were all affected by the incident. Alcohol had reduced him from the state of honored leader to that of "brute beast," and he ever after was an enemy of the distribution of liquor to the Ottawa.[14] In 1837 the Irish traveler Anna Jameson witnessed Assiginack lead a "canoe full of stout men" to an American sailing ship attempting to land a cargo of whiskey on Manitoulin Island. The whiskey was thrown into the lake as the chief "declared his enmity to the 'dealers in firewater.'"[15]

Leadership among the *Anishnabeg* rested in part on being born into a family of chiefs, as the brothers Mackadepenessy, Assiginack, Wakezoo, and Wing had been. But just as important was the personal example set by the leader. As a violent drunk Assiginack would never had had the prestige to return to L'Arbre Croche and assume the leadership of a reform movement, nor would he have been able to eventually form his own Ottawa community at Manitoulin Island, as he later did. Assiginack's immediate and categorical disavowal of alcohol was a testament to his strength of will and his desire to lead. It was also, however, an exceptional act by an exceptional man. Many Ottawa in the 1820s and 1830s, like people locked in substance abuse today, recognized the destructive features of alcohol, but on their own lacked the means to break with strong drink. In European-American communities, Christian congregations and the temperance associations they formed provided ordinary people with the means avoid or beat substance abuse.

Assiginack was unique among the Ottawa leaders of his generation in that he had received a Christian education. In his youth he had been a student at the Sulpician mission school at Lake of the Two Mountains in what is now Quebec. There he learned basic literacy and converted to Catholicism. It is possible that for a limited time Mackadepenessy also attended school with his brother, but Andrew Blackbird's father was not an early convert to Christianity. Assiginack's Christianity may have helped him break with alcohol. Faced with a political threat from the rising American nation and the socially disorganizing impact of substance abuse, Ottawa people were in search of a renewal of spiritual power. If they looked to Christianity for this renewal, they had in the exiled warrior and orator Assiginack a role model and potential leader.[16]

CIVILIZATION OR RUIN

For the people of L'Arbre Croche the need to find a new way to respond to American power was given emphasis by the visit of an official United States delegation to Little Traverse. Lewis Cass, the governor of the Michigan Territory, specifically planned the expedition to the frontier to carry the American flag "into those regions where it has never been borne by any person in a public station." L'Arbre Croche fit that description. The Ottawa may have had high expectations when the visit was first proposed. The British usually brought a lavish supply of presents for such formal councils, sometimes giving each warrior a woolen blanket or cotton shirt.[17] But instead the governor brought with him only a proposal and a missionary.

The proposal was that the Ottawa agree to sell to the United States the St. Martin Islands. It is hard to say how the Americans became interested in these two small islands, located a couple of miles north of Mackinac. From the beginning of the Cass expedition, an investigation of the islands was proposed. Henry Rowe Schoolcraft, who would later be the Ottawa's Indian agent, accompanied Cass as a mineralogist and he conducted a hasty survey of the isles. He concluded that they possessed abundant deposits of gypsum—a superior source of plaster. So taken were the Americans with this resource, that when they proposed buying the islands they told the Ottawa: "Their Great Father the President wanted these islands for his children, not for their soil, or timber, but for the Plaster—and this he intended to give to his children." To this proposal an Ottawa elder sagely suggested, "If our Father does not want the soil, nor the timber of these islands, but the Plaster only, we will keep the soil and timber, and he shall be welcome to the Plaster."[18] But the Americans did not want a mineral easement, they wanted complete title and they obtained it in exchange for "a quantity of goods."[19] For fewer goods than the British gave as gifts, the Americans took possession of a small portion of the *Anishnabeg* estate.

It is possible that Mackadepenessy participated in these negotiations. He was the son of a chief, a successful warrior, a noted hunter, and he was now old enough to be regarded as a man of experience. Among the chiefs who signed the treaty was "Cuddimalmese, or Black Hawk, Ottawa chief." In his history Andrew Blackbird argued that "Black Hawk," not "Blackbird," was the proper translation of his father's name, which suggests that Mackadepenessy did make his mark on the agreement but that the interpreter, Henry Gravereat, mangled the anglicanization of his name. Whether he signed the treaty or merely participated in discussions regarding the cession, it is likely Mackadepenessy was familiar with the ominous implications of the treaty. No matter how small, even eccentric, the cession was, it was also a reminder that the Americans were very different than the British and French who had come before them. They came not bearing gifts but with proposals and contracts. They did not just want to dwell in *Anishnabeg* territory to trade furs. They had instead a broader, deeper interest in the land. When they made agreements about mother earth, they were not satisfied with mere access to resources, they wanted the right to possess the land. Equally alarming was a treaty Governor Cass forced on the Chippewa at Sault Ste. Marie. That agreement gave the United States control of a tract of land near the St. Mary's rapids on which they could build a new fortification for their army. The Americans were most definitely in *Anishnabeg* territory to stay.[20]

If the Americans were greedy for land and stingy with gifts, they were very free with words. Unsolicited advice flowed from them like water from a spring. Accompanying Governor Cass's expedition to Little Traverse was Jedidiah Morse, a leading Congregational minister, a prominent intellectual, and the official representative of John C. Calhoun, the secretary of war. Morse had been commissioned by Calhoun to inspect the "actual condition" of the Indians of the United States in order to "devise the most suitable plan to advance their civilization and happiness." Morse had heard much about the size and importance of L'Arbre Croche, and he was determined to present to the Ottawa his plans for "civilization" through Christianity.[21]

Knowing nothing of the importance of horticulture in the traditional Ottawa subsistence system, Morse saw L'Arbre Croche's extensive fields of corn, potatoes, and pumpkins as a sign that the Ottawa wanted to adopt European-American practice. He wrote, "these Indians are much in advance in point of improvement. . . . of all Indians I have visited." As he approached the council grounds, he observed, "The women and children, who were apart by themselves, had a cleanly appearance; in countenance and manners, intelligent and modest." He then approached the warriors, "who occupied a separate station" and who in Morse's opinion "would appear well on any of our military parades. They are a tall, strait, fine-faced band of men." Morse studied the band leaders while they were in council with Governor Cass, describing them as "shrewd, sensible, well behaved men, most of them advanced beyond middle age, and of venerable appearance."[22]

The business of the St. Martin Islands cession dominated the council and served, no doubt, to put the Ottawa chiefs on edge. After they had acceded to Governor Cass's demands and the cession was completed, Indian agent George Boyd attempted to introduce the Reverend Morse. But the "principal speaker" among the chiefs rose and said that "they had received some information from Mackinac, of the object" of Morse's visit and that they had considered the subject "and concluded not to accept the proposals of the Government. They were contented and happy in their present situation." Morse, however, refused to believe they had "correct information" regarding his proposals, and he abused the Ottawa's hospitality by proceeding to deliver his address.[23]

While Jedidiah Morse committed a breach of etiquette, his words would have a significant impact on the future of L'Arbre Croche. He began by presenting the papers of his official commission from the president of the United States and several missionary societies. That few if any of the Ottawa leaders could read the markings on the paper underscored the gulf between them and the Americans. He then informed the chiefs that "a glorious day is dawning." The "christian white people" were "praying to God for their red brethren" and "devising plans for your happiness." After every few sentences, Morse paused and Henry Gravereat, a New Yorker who learned his Ottawa from his mixed-blood wife, translated the minister's message to the chiefs. In typical fire-and-brimstone fashion Morse used all his eloquence to make the Ottawa see what he regarded as their dire circumstances. "Your game is already diminishing, and e'er long will be gone, and you will waste away, and perish, as hundreds of tribes of your brethren in the country east of you, have successively perished before you." White settlers, Morse warned, were coming to the Ottawa's homeland. "They are now spread over a wide extent of the country of your fathers; and are spreading still more and faster over other parts of it; purchasing millions of acres of your good land; leaving for you and your children, *Reservations* here and there, small indeed, compared with the extensive hunting grounds you once possessed." A terrible future lay before the Ottawa, one of "idleness, ignorance, and drunkenness." According to Morse, even many of the "wisest" Indians believed that the Great Spirit "is angry with the red people, and is destroying them, while he prospers the white people."[24]

The president of the United States, Morse related, held out a different future for the Ottawa, one in which they would learn the language, "modes of life," and religion of the whites; "to have one government, the same laws, equal rights and privileges." The single most important step in making this change possible, Morse intoned, was for the Ottawa to embrace Jesus Christ and the Bible. "This book causes the wide difference which exists, as you see, between the white man and the Indian." The alternative before them was the stark choice between "*Civilization* or *ruin*." Morse closed by saying that Christian missionaries could be sent to teach them and that he would give the elders of L'Arbre Croche three weeks to contemplate his words. "*Children*," he concluded, "attend to what I have said. Lay it up in your memories, and in your hearts."[25]

What did Mackadepenessy and the other chiefs made of this bleak and insulting pronouncement of their imminent demise as a people? Certainly as a warrior and champion of his people, Mackadepenessy must have bristled at Morse's arrogant tone and condescending concern. Yet, as angry as he must have been, Mackadepenessy listened "patiently and respectfully." Proper decorum at a council required it, and it was the duty of all the chiefs to carefully weigh all that was said, to sift through the words, to fully understand their import. He and the other chiefs had seen with their own eyes the degraded condition of once powerful Indian peoples such as the Delaware, Huron, and Shawnee. It was also true that the settlements of the whites, while still far from Little Traverse, were growing larger each year. Only recently the Ottawa of the Maumee, in northwest Ohio, had been reduced to begging their kinsmen for permission to settle in northern Michigan—an offer they had to rebuff because of the depleted condition of their own hunting grounds.[26] Drunkenness was becoming a bigger problem for the Ottawa. But to become a *Chemokmon*, to live, think, and act like them must have seemed a repugnant notion.

For Morse's part he was delighted the message had been "received with much civility." He expected an answer from them prior to his departure for Washington in three weeks. The weeks passed, but there was no response from the Ottawa chiefs.

For all his hubris Morse considered himself a friend of the Indian. His dark prophecies of Ottawa doom were based on the sad history of American Indian policy. The good reverend was one side of the American Republic's Janus-faced Indian policy. On one hand were the men like Morse and his fellow "friends" of the American Indian, Thomas Jefferson and James Monroe, who believed that Indians were equal to European-Americans in their capacity to reason and learn. Christianity and education were all that stood between the Indian and a state of full equality with white citizens. Morse never for a moment considered that a person capable of social and political equality might also be inclined to use their power to reason to hold close to their own culture. But for all of its blind assumptions, Morse and men of his ilk presented a less menacing face to the Ottawa than that presented by Lewis Cass, who came to their village with a politely worded demand for a territorial cession. This was the other side of American policy, one that did not look at the Ottawa as potential citizens but merely as obstacles that needed to be removed. In separating the Indian from his land, the United States government was serving the interests of its rapidly growing population of existing citizens. American policy was two faced because it was caught between its hopes for the future and the demands of the present, between its idealism and its pragmatic needs. The 1820 council at L'Arbre Croche brought the Ottawa nose to nose with the Janus face of the United States.

For a year the chiefs ruminated on Morse's dire prophecy of "*Civilization* or *ruin*" for the Ottawa. At winter hunting camps and around the bubbling maple sugar kettles the elders shared their growing anxiety for the future. Then came an unmistakable warning that the prophecy had validity. The Ottawa of L'Arbre Croche were invited to a treaty council in Chicago to discuss the cession of their Michigan lands.

In 1821 the United States government determined "to treat for the extinction of Indian title within the Territory of Michigan." Accordingly

Ottawa, Chippewa, and Potawatomi from all across the territory were invited to Chicago to meet with treaty commissioner Lewis Cass. The summons to Chicago, sent out in the spring of that year, must have aroused the dread of most Ottawa. There is no evidence of what took place in the councils of the L'Arbre Croche elders. They may have simply failed to achieve a consensus on what to do. It is possible, however, they may have designed a risky Fabian strategy of passive resistance to the *Chemokmon*'s attempt to take their lands. What is known for certain is that when the *Anishnabeg* delegates met with Lewis Cass in Chicago that August, there were no representatives from L'Arbre Croche present.[27]

If the Ottawa of Little Traverse did simply turn their back on the treaty as a strategy, it was one fraught with risk. The United States government had been known to impose cessions on Indian people not represented at council. Lewis Cass had been charged to "procure a Cession of all the aboriginal claims" in Michigan. Fortunately, on this occasion Cass exercised better judgment. He explained to the secretary of war that "other portions of the same tribe were present, yet as they lived in different quarters of the Country no proposition for a cession of this land could be made to them. Indians of the same tribe are divided into various political communities, with separate interests & separate rights. The inhabitants of one village are unwilling to cede the land of another, and when distances are considerable, they feel rather as independent bodies, than as members of the same nation."[28] Instead, Cass focused his attention on securing the cession of the "nearer and more important" lands in southern Michigan.

The Treaty of 1821, save for a few small reservations, eliminated the last of the Potawatomi claims to land in Michigan. It also secured the cession of the lands the Ottawa shared with the Potawatomi south of the Grand River. These were lands seldom visited by the people of L'Arbre Croche, but which had long been used by the Grand River Ottawa. In return for the cession, the Grand River Ottawa received a $1,000 annuity to be paid for ten years and a $1,500 annual "civilization" appropriation to be used to support the purchase of livestock and farming equipment, blacksmith services, a teacher, and an experienced farmer.[29]

Eight Ottawa chiefs signed the 1821 Treaty of Chicago. This group included Kewagoushcum, one of the leading Ottawa along the Grand River. But the Chicago council had been spurned by the most important Grand River chiefs, among them Makatoquet (Black Cloud), Cocoosh (Old Hog), Muckatosha (Black Skin), and most notably, Noaquageshik (Noon Day). Kewagoushcum with the other Ottawa present, nonetheless, approved the treaty. This action earned him the enmity of many of his people. He was gradually striped of his authority as a chief and, thereafter, lived in fear of his fellow Ottawa. Indeed, white settlers in the Grand valley reported that he was eventually murdered for signing the session. The Ottawa leaders who had not gone to Chicago complained that they "considered the sale of their country illegal." However, the United States fully intended to enforce the treaty.[30]

The 1821 treaty demonstrated two things to the Ottawa of L'Arbre Croche. On one hand they saw plainly the ability of the United States to obtain the lands it wanted. They may well have sensed what Cass had told Secretary of War Calhoun, that the lands in northern Michigan could be "easily acquired" at any time. Clearly, in the future a strategy of ignoring treaty councils would be foolhardy, as the Grand River Ottawa discovered. The United States could and would impose its will upon the Ottawa. On the other hand, as ominous as treaties were, the Chicago council brought to the Grand River Ottawa assets that would allow them to adapt to the new era. By signing the treaty, Kewagoushcum secured for the Grand River valley a blacksmith shop that allowed Indian hunters to extend the life of their existing guns and traps. And for those who were interested in exploring a bolder adaptation to American rule, the treaty brought teachers of European-American farming techniques and a missionary anxious to spread the gospel of Christianity. If the choice before them was, as Jedidiah Morse put it, "*Civilization* or *ruin,*" then a treaty with the United States could be a vehicle, albeit a risky one, for embarking on the new path.

That at least some Ottawa at L'Arbre Croche were interested in treading that new path was apparent by the summer of 1823. On August 12 of that year a remarkable letter was sent to the president of the United States by Ottawa seeking to explore the Christian road of civilization.

> We, the undersigned, chiefs, heads of families, and others, of the tribe of Ottawas, residing at Arbre Croche, on the east bank of Lake Michigan, take this means to communicate to our father, the President of the United States, our requests and wants. We thank our father and Congress for all the efforts they have made to draw us to civilization, and the knowledge of Jesus, redeemer of the red man and white. Trusting in your paternal goodness, we claim liberty of conscience, and beg you to grant us a master or minister of the gospel, belonging to the same society as members of the Catholic Society of St. Ignatius, formerly established at Michilimackinac and Arbre Croche by Father Marquette and other missionaries of the order of Jesuits. They resided long years among us. They cultivated a field on our territory to teach us the principles of agriculture and Christianity.

Since that time we have always desired similar ministers. If you grant us them, we will invite them to live on the same ground formerly occupied by Father Du Jaunay, on the banks of Lake Michigan, near our village of Arbre Croche.

If you grant this humble request of your faithful children, they will be eternally grateful, and will pray the great Spirit to pour forth his blessings on the whites.

In faith hereof, we have set our names this day, August 12, 1823.

Hawk,	Crane,	Bear,
Fish,	Eagle,	Stag,
Caterpillar,	Flying-Fish.[31]	

The timing of the letter is suggestive. The summer before the letter was sent the first of the missionaries Jedidiah Morse had requested for northern Michigan arrived on Mackinac Island. The Reverend William M. Ferry established a Presbyterian congregation among the Anglo-American elements on the island. In 1823, after returning east to marry, he and his wife founded a mission school for Indian children. In time some of the Ottawa would send children to the Ferrys' school, but the 1823 memorial to the president was a clear statement of preference for the Catholic version of Christianity. But how and why did the Ottawa come to express a denominational preference for a religion that was still largely alien to them?

It is likely that the memorial was written by Father Gabriel Richard, the Michigan Territory's first Catholic priest. This remarkable man had, along with Morse, helped to lay the foundation for the Ottawa's interest in Christianity. He was a native of France and a member of the Sulpician order who fled the Old World when the promise of the French Revolution was betrayed by violence and ambition. He had a strong desire to build on the Michigan frontier a community that was both an expression of Enlightenment idealism and the Catholic faith, something most Protestant Americans, and even other Catholics clerics, would have found incongruous. Richard's fingerprints on the memorial can be seen in the attention the document devotes to establishing the priority of the Catholic Church in the mission fields of Lake Michigan. There is more in the memorial about the activities of Jesuit missionaries in the 1600 and 1700s than there was about the Ottawa's actual interest in Jesus. We know Richard was in contact with the people of L'Arbre Croche well before Morse's visit. The tireless priest first visited the Ottawa in 1799 and paid a return visit to L'Arbre Croche in 1819. It is likely that he had subsequent discussions with the Ottawa regarding the reestablishment of a mission near Little Traverse. The trouble was that the Catholic Church lacked the money and the personnel to send missionaries to the Ottawa on its own. In 1823 Richard was elected Michigan's territorial delegate in Congress, so he was very familiar with the political milieu of United States Indian policy. Since 1819 Congress authorized a "civilization fund" to promote Indian education. The Ottawa memorial was Richard's attempt to draw upon federal funds to reestablish a Catholic mission at L'Arbre Croche. The use of phrases such as "we claim liberty of conscience" were a calculated attempt to induce the president to look past anti-Catholic prejudice and answer the Ottawa's request.

While the language of the memorial was Richard's, the intent behind the call for a missionary originated with the Ottawa. The memorial, in fact, is the first clear sign of a strategy for survival that appears to have evolved out of the deliberations of the elders at L'Arbre Croche. Throughout the postwar period, the people of L'Arbre Croche looked for ways to develop a rapprochement with the *Chemokmon.* In May 1816 they petitioned the United States for economic assistance for "cows, Hogs, Fowls," and a "blacksmith to make repair their farm utensils, Traps, guns, etc. and that he may instruct them to build houses and live as whites live."[32] At the same time they made clear to their Indian agent that they had completely rejected the nativist message of the Shawnee Prophet and that they were willing to hereafter "tender their assistance to the American Government."[33] Nothing came of these early overtures of cultural and political alliance with the Americans, but they reflected a savvy recognition by the chiefs of L'Arbre Croche that it might be best to bend before the strong wind blowing from the east.

Jedidiah Morse's challenge of "*Civilization* or *ruin*" came after three years of official American silence in response to the Ottawa's own offer to "live as whites live." What was new was Morse's emphasis upon Christianity as the path to become "companions and equals with your white brethren." In Morse's words Christianity was "the best, the only *effectual,* means of making you truly happy."[34] It is only natural then that Ottawa leaders would look to the sacred sphere as the primary step in building a new relationship with the Americans. Sacred power was essential to any successful strategy, whether economic, political, or social. It was sacred power that allowed an Ottawa canoe to cross the broad expanse of Little Traverse Bay safe from sudden lake squalls, it was sacred power that matured the corn crops that the women so laboriously planted and tended, it was sacred power that brought the lake trout to the gill nets set in the bay by the fishermen. It was sacred power that guided the councils of the elders. The rituals of the *Midewiwin* were practiced to access sacred power or to influence supernatural beings. But the growing number of *Chemokmon* soldiers, traders, and missionaries was a clear sign that the Ottawa required access to greater or even new spiritual power.

That the Ottawa chose Catholicism, the Christian denomination held in the lowest regard by the American mainstream, as their vehicle to acquire sacred power reveals the degree to which the "civilization program" was formulated and led not by missionaries but by the Ottawa themselves. Jedidiah Morse functioned as a spur, prodding the people of L'Arbre Croche to move more aggressively in their search for sacred power. But the Protestant divine was not responsible for the Ottawa's the first steps toward Christianity. Like most peoples forced to move in a new direction, the Ottawa sought a familiar guides.

The Ottawa had a historical memory of Catholicism to draw upon. Under the French regime the Ottawa had hosted Jesuit missionaries as early as 1660. Accepting missionaries had been part of the etiquette of the middle-ground relationship with the French. While there were some genuine converts made, the religion cannot be said to have really taken root among the Ottawa. What growth had taken place withered after the fall of New France in 1760 and the suppression of the Society of Jesus in 1764. Peter du Jaunay, S.J., the last Jesuit missionary, left L'Arbre Croche by 1765. Two generations later Catholicism was barely a memory. A handful of aged folk could point out beaten path where du Jaunay had walked his breviary.[35] When Richard visited the Ottawa in 1799, he was told there remained only a single Catholic convert, a seventy-five-year-old man who had been baptized as a child.[36] The choice of Catholicism, had less to do with historical memory, however, than it did with the example of contemporary Ottawa.

OTTAWA EVANGELISTS

According to Andrew Blackbird's history, sometime in the early 1820s an Ottawa man long removed from L'Arbre Croche returned to his home.[37] His name was Andowish. He appears to have spent many years among the Mahican Indians at the Catholic mission settlement of St. Francis, in Quebec.[38] During his time in the east, Andowish became a devout Catholic and upon his return, according to Blackbird, "he began to teach some of his own relatives the faith of the Catholic religion, which some of them were very ready to receive." There were, however, real limits to how far Andowish could go in introducing them to the faith. Under Catholic doctrine he could not baptize them into the Church let alone acquaint them with the other sacraments. What Andowish did succeed in doing was to stimulate the interest of several leading Ottawa in Catholicism as a means of accommodating the Americans and tapping into a new source of sacred power. Among the chiefs who spoke with Andowish was Apokisigan, the leading man among the Ottawa who dwelled near Seven-Mile Point. This was among the most densely inhabited portions of the L'Arbre Croche coast and Apokisigan had considerable influence among all the Ottawa of the Little Traverse region. It is from his conversations with Andowish that Apokisigan, in concert with Mackadepenessy and perhaps some other leading men, developed his idea of seeking a rapprochement with the Americans based on a conversion to Catholicism. In confronting a Janus-faced American Indian policy, they chose to embrace the face that offered civilization and Christianity as a way of avoiding the face that threatened loss of land and removal.[39]

In developing this strategy, Apokisigan and Mackadepenessy also drew upon their kinship connections to the European-American community at Michilimackinac. They took their canoe up the coast to the island where they consulted leaders of mixed French and Ottawa blood. These were people who knew the customs and beliefs of the Ottawa and with whom the Ottawa had long-established commercial relations. There is some irony in the Ottawa going to the Métis of Michilimackinac for advice on how to gain a missionary for L'Arbre Croche. The French-Canadian and Métis Catholic community of the Michilimackinac region had also been without a regular priest since 1765, and they had unsuccessfully petitioned the Church for a pastor many times. The want of consistent spiritual direction left many of the fur traders Catholic in name only. Apokisigan and Mackadepenessy might have sought out Magdelaine Laframboise and Therese Marcot Lasaliere Schindler, Ottawa women and fur traders who were respected as among the most devout of the lax collection of Catholics on Mackinac Island. It may have been at their initiative that Father Richard was contacted and the petition to the president was drafted.[40]

The consultation with Métis relations was in keeping with the traditions of the middle ground. In becoming Catholics and in attempting to move toward a greater involvement in market agriculture, the Ottawa were not so much as embarking on a new path as they were moving further down a path they already knew. The Christian worldview was alien to the Ottawa, but in embracing Catholicism they were at least choosing a path that had been sanctioned by their past. In seeking advice on how to access Christian sacred power, they could have could consulted the Indian agent, George Boyd. Had they done so it is unlikely that Boyd would have recommended requesting a Catholic missionary. Boyd had a record of being supportive of Protestant missionaries, but he was suspicious of the Catholic Church.[41] Instead, the Ottawa ignored the official representative of the United States and worked through family connections. Mackadepenessy and Apokisigan also spurned the opportunity to meet directly with the Protestant minister sent west by Jedidiah Morse. The Reverend William Ferry was in residence on Mackinac Island as part of a formal plan, sanctioned by the United States government, to bring Christianity to the Ottawa and Chippewa. But rather than even meet with Ferry, the chiefs preferred to initiate a lengthy petition process to the president of the United States. Part of their motivation was an instinctive reach toward that which was familiar. They remembered little of what the *Mekateokwin-iwieg,* or black robes taught a century before, but they did recall a Jesuit proverb, "*Wewitegoji anawiewin gwaiakosing ititwawin*" (The French faith is the true religion).[42] Catholicism was a conservative way to carry out the bold "civilization" program thrust on them by the United States.

Mackadepenessy was an important, if not a dominant influence, behind the Catholic strategy. Although he was a warrior and a patriot, Mackadepenessy also had extensive experience from his time in the northwest working and interacting with European-Americans. It is also possible that he had been exposed to a Christian education sometime during his youth or when he was involved in the western fur trade. Writing a half-century after the fact, Andrew Blackbird related that his father had the ability to read and write, although in all of his official dealings with the United States government there is no hint of Mackadepenessy's literacy. In the August 1823 petition to President Monroe, for example, Mackadepenessy's signature is the drawing of a hawk next to which is written "*Macate Binesse* in person." In that document all of the Ottawa leaders "signed" by drawing a pictograph of their name. Mackadepenessy is described in the document as "the main chief of Larborcroche." Did he hide his ability to write his own name out of solidarity with the other chiefs? In addition, several white men signed the petition, which suggests they may have had a hand in either writing it or obtaining the signatures.[43]

In the winter of 1823, four months after the petition had been sent to President James Monroe, Mackadepenessy addressed a second memorial to the American leader. He wrote on behalf of the "chiefs, fathers of families, and other Ottawa, residing at Arbre Croche." He appealed to President Monroe as "the greatest Chief of the United States" and a "Renowned Father, to obtain for us a Black-robe (priest) like those who instructed the

Indians in the neighborhood of Montreal." If the government did obtain a "Man of God of the Catholic religion" for the Ottawa, Mackadepenessy promised, "we will give land for cultivation to the Minister of the Great Spirit whom thou shalt send to instruct us and our children." He further promised the Ottawa would "do our very best to please him and follow his good advice." The text of this second and personal appeal by Mackadepenessy was published in the *Annales De L'Association De La Propagation De La Foi,* a French publication series that promoted Catholic overseas missions. It is likely that Gabriel Richard is responsible for forwarding the text of the message to Paris, where it served the purpose of reminding European Catholics of the continuing needs of the North American missions.[44]

This second appeal brings into sharper focus Mackadepenessy's leading role in the Catholic conversion strategy, but like the initial petition, this appeal fell on deaf ears in Washington, D.C. Federal officials were no doubt cool to the idea of having Catholic priests from the British territory near Montreal working with Indians on the edge of the American frontier. By way of an excuse, American officials responded that all civilization funds available for the Ottawa were being expended on a Baptist mission on the Grand River, several hundred miles from L'Arbre Croche. Nor did the Catholic Church have the manpower or financial resources to establish a mission. Only a handful of priests were available for the whole of the Michigan Territory; however, it was difficult for the Church to completely ignore such an earnest and unsolicited appeal for instruction in the Catholic faith. For this reason in 1825 the Catholic bishop for the northwestern region dispatched Father Vincent Badin to spend the spring and summer seasons traveling to Catholic communities in the upper Great Lakes region.[45]

On July 19 Badin's canoe arrived off Nine Mile Point, the site of one of the largest concentrations of L'Arbre Croche lodges. Apokisigan, whom Badin referred to as "the grand chief of the Indians," and Mackadepenessy took charge of the long-awaited visitor. He was led up a hill overlooking the blue waters of Lake Michigan, where under a canopy of hardwood trees the Ottawa had built a log chapel. Badin recorded that it measured twenty-five feet by seventeen feet and that it had been built in the Indian manner, with bent poles and a cedar bark exterior, without the use of a single nail. In this chapel Badin said the mass, accompanied by Ottawa men and women singing Catholic hymns in their own language. Andowish, the Catholic Ottawa, had done his work so well that Badin found the singing uplifted his soul and was the rival of anything he had ever heard in Europe. The wigwam-style church, in Badin's opinion, was "the equal to the Temple of Solomon."[46]

Father Badin's visit was an opportunity for the civilization faction at

L'Arbre Croche to lobby for a full-time pastor. In addition to the beautifully prepared chapel, the priest encountered many examples of a deep interest in Christianity, including a married man who offered to leave behind his family so that he could be trained as a priest, and a torchlight funeral for a child, baptized in her last moments of life. The Ottawa also escorted the priest to the site of the old mission, where Badin was introduced to a venerable old man, the last living Ottawa who had been baptized by the Jesuits.[47]

Badin performed many baptisms while at L'Arbre Croche. Among those brought into the Church were Mackadepenessy's ten children. The eldest son, Pungowish, who was renowned a hunter, was given the name of Peter. Petawanequot, a bright and inquisitive middle son, was baptized William. Their younger sister was baptized Margaret. The future historian, Andrew, who could have been no more than four or five years old, on this occasion was also given a new name. "I was small," he later wrote, "but I distinctly remember having the water poured over my head and putting some salt in my mouth, and changing my name from Pe-nesswi-qua-am to Amable."[48] The chief himself took a Christian name upon his baptism. Perhaps Badin chose this new name to reflect the active role Mackadepenessy had played calling the Church to his people; in any event the man known as Blackbird was given the name Gabriel.[49]

Badin made another visit to L'Arbre Croche in October, at which time he was presented with yet another petition from Mackadepenessy. This missive was addressed not to the president of the United States but to Gabriel Richard, "the chief Blackrobe at Rome" and the "highly celebrated Father of the French, the King of France." Perhaps Mackadepenessy hoped to reopen the old channels of communication, when the French king was honored as a "father" of the Great Lakes Indians, or he may have meant the letter much more pragmatically to be used by the French Association for the Propagation of the Faith to attract support for a mission at Little Traverse. In any event, this letter was more explicit regarding the political and economic problems faced by the Ottawa than Mackadepenessy's earlier appeals to President Monroe. "There are now so many hats [white people] in the country, we cannot kill enough game to support our children." Mackadepenessy was particularly concerned with the escalating problem of drunkenness. "There is too much whiskey here," he wrote, "and we are reduced to extremes. We want a French priest to teach us temperance and the way to salvation."[50]

Meanwhile, Mackadepenessy's appeals to the United States were finally making an impact. Gabriel Richard, who was at this time a delegate to Congress, used his position to lobby the secretary of war to appropriate a portion of the Civilization Fund for a Catholic mission. Secretary John C. Calhoun and President Monroe were both impressed with Richard's republican spirit and knowledge of the northwest frontier. The government pledged to pay half the cost of constructing mission buildings and to appropriate twenty dollars for every child educated in the mission school. Unfortunately, the appeals of Badin and Mackadepenessy were unable to convince the Society of Jesus to once more send a missionary to L'Arbre Croche. For the next two years the Church's inability to find a mission priest retarded the development of the Ottawa "civilization" program.[51]

The Ottawa, however, did not simply wait for action from the Catholic Church or the United States government. Sometime after 1825 Mackadepenessy's brother, Assiginack, returned from to L'Arbre Croche and began to act as a lay minister. Since the end of the War of 1812 he had remained at Drummond Island, loyal to the British. During Father Badin's sojourn in the region he visited Drummond Island and met with Assiginack, whom he called "*le grand chef*." It is likely that Assiginack had kept in touch with developments in Michigan through summer visits to Drummond Island by his brothers. But the meeting with Badin seems to have inspired in him a desire to uplift the people of his home village. He probably returned to Little Traverse sometime in 1826, but he was certainly there by 1828. In September of that year he tendered his resignation from the British Indian Department.[52]

According to Andrew Blackbird's history, when Assiginack "learned that his people had joined the Catholic faith, he left his home at Drummond's Island and came to Arbor Croche expressly to act as missionary in the absence of the priest. Every Sunday he preached to his people and taught them how to pray to God and to the Virgin Mary and all the saints and angels in heaven." Prior to his return, Assiginack had carried out this role of lay minister, a role that was unsanctioned by the Catholic Church, for the Ottawa at Drummond Island. His eloquence, which was in high repute among all the Ottawa, his fame as a warrior, his position of trust in the British Indian Service, even his personal triumph over drunkenness all contributed to the Assiginack's success as an evangelist at his old home on Little Traverse Bay. He was the embodiment of traditional Ottawa virtues as well as a role model of how those characteristics could be adapted to challenges of the antebellum world.[53]

Andrew Blackbird's memory of Assiginack's preaching emphasized saints, angels, and Marian devotion. These were all strong features of the folk Catholicism of French Canada, where Assiginack had first been exposed to Christianity. These were also features that helped to adapt the new religion to sensibilities of a people who had been brought up in a world where there was a Great Spirit, and hundreds of other manitou influencing all aspects of the world around them. Before the people of L'Arbre Croche had ever been exposed to regular instruction in Catholic doctrine, they were afforded several years to assimilate Christianity with their own worldview and traditional practices. Through the work of first Andowish and later Assiginack, the Ottawa came to Catholicism by an indigenous path. They learned the gospel not through the translated words of a missionary, but through the filter of men who shared the experience and culture of the converts and who could adapt religious concepts and practices to best suit their sensibilities. Years later Andrew Blackbird would state with pride that his people became Christian because of the work of their own evangelists, "although everybody supposes that some white people or missionary societies brought the Christian religion among the Ottawa tribes of Indians at Arbor Croche."[54]

Assiginack's return stimulated both the spiritual side of the Ottawa "civilization" program and its educational thrust. Andrew Blackbird's 1887 history is the sole source for the efforts of Assiginack and Mackadepenessy to bring literacy to the Ottawa. Prior to his brother's return, Blackbird remembered, "My father was the only man who was friendly to education."

> When I was a little boy, I remember distinctly his making his own alphabet, which he called "Paw-pa-pe-po." With this he learned how to read and write; and afterwards he taught other Indians to read and write according to his alphabet. He taught no children, but only the grown persons. Our wigwam, which was about sixty or seventy feet long, where we lived in the summer time, was like a regular school-house, with my father as teacher of the school, and they had merry times in it. Many Indians came to learn his Paw-pa-pe-po, and some of them were very easy to learn [*sic*], while others found learning extremely difficult.

When Assiginack returned home he brought with him hymn and prayer books "from Montreal" that Blackbird later contended were printed in a "dialect of the Ottawa and Chippewa languages." These books, Blackbird said, "could be quite intelligently understood by the Ottawas."[55]

Blackbird's contention that his father invented "Paw-pa-pe-po" is problematic, not the least because of a lack of evidence of Mackadepenessy's literacy. In the early 1830s a Baptist missionary working in Kansas, Robert Simmerwell, developed a syllabary writing system for the Potawatomi language that became known as "Ba-be-bo-bu." His work was greatly elaborated upon in the late 1830s and early 1840s by Father Christian Hoecken and Father Maurice Gailland, two Jesuits also working in Kansas.[56] "Ba-be-bo-bu" remained in limited use among the prairie Potawatomi until the 1960s. "Paw-pa-pe-po" sounds suspiciously like "Ba-be-bo-bu." In any event there is no other recorded evidence for a writing system called Paw-pa-pe-po. Ethnologists working with the Ottawa in the 1940s interviewed people who remember using a syllabary. Because both Assiginack and Mackadepenessy had earlier lived in Canada, it is most likely that the Indian writing system they introduced to Michigan was learned there.[57] The books brought by Assiginack likely came from the Lake of the Two Mountains mission, which was regarded by the Catholic Church as "the cradle" of the western missions. There the Sulpicians prepared catechisms, hymnals, and prayer books.[58]

In his history Andrew Blackbird presents the reader with a picture of life at L'Arbre Croche in the late 1820s that included books, prayers, hymns, and schools. At the center of each of these innovations was the initiative of a member of Blackbird's own lineage. Family pride played a major part in his motivation to write the first history of his people. Andrew Blackbird's filiopietism is by and large sustained by the documentary record, which makes clear the commitment of both Assiginack and Mackadepenessy to the education of their people. In addition to his work at L'Arbre Croche, Assiginack later supported mission schools on Manitoulin Island. In 1840 he sent his sixteen-year-old-son Francis Assiginack to Upper Canada College (the future University of Toronto), where he studied English, Latin, and Greek.[59] Mackadepenessy lobbied United States officials to bring educational programs to L'Arbre Croche. When Presbyterians established a mission school at Mackinac Island, Mackadepenessy sent his son William. Later, a daughter attended the school. Another daughter, Margaret, attended Catholic schools at L'Arbre Croche, Detroit, and Cincinnati. Mackadepenessy sent his children to schools, both Catholic and Protestant, near and far, in order that they would be prepared for the job of leading their people. The involvement with education and Christianity of the brothers Mackadepenessy and Assiginack, for their time and place, was extraordinary. They were the driving force in Ottawa cultural transformation.[60]

Mackadepenessy's commitment to education cost him the life of a bright and promising son. William, his middle son, was one of the few children to whom Mackadepenessy taught his Paw-pa-pe-po. The boy mastered it easily and his intellectual curiosity was remarked upon by the entire family. "He was quick to learn," Andrew Blackbird wrote of his older brother, "and very curious and interesting questions he would often ask of his father, which would greatly puzzle the old man to answer." When William was about eight or nine years old, well before he was baptized, an incident occurred that shaped the boy and his entire family. While the family was at their sugar camp near the Muskegon River, William took his bow and arrow and went into the forest.

> At sundown, our parents were beginning to feel very uneasy about their little boy, and yet they thought he must have gone to some neighboring sugar bush, as there were quite a number of families also making sugar in the vicinity. Early in the morning, my father went to all the neighboring sugar camps, but William was nowhere to be found. So at once a search was instituted. Men and boys were out in search for the boy, calling and shooting their guns far and near, but not a trace of him anywhere could be found.

Distraught with "anxiety and fear," Mackadepenessy searched tirelessly for the boy. For three days friends and relations joined him in combing the forest.[61]

By the dawn of the fourth day, hope for the missing child's survival began to fade. There was no snow on the ground, but it was still very cold. A child without food or shelter would not last long. The forest was leafless and the searchers had excellent visibility, but even though they were skilled hunters and trackers they found no trace of the boy. One of those helping with the search was a cousin named Ogemawwenene. He climbed to the top of a hill and loudly called the boy by his Ottawa name, Petawonequot. To his surprise he heard his cousin shout back "Wau," the Ottawa equivalent for "What?" Looking up to where he heard the voice, he saw William sitting on the limb of a tree. The boy had been up there looking to see the way home to the sugar camp. When he scrambled down, his overjoyed cousin offered him something to eat. Surprisingly the child said he had just finished eating.

> "Ah, you have been fed then. Who fed you? We have been looking for you now over three days." The boy replied, "I had every thing that I wanted to eat in the great festival of the 'Wa-me-te-go-zhe-wog,'" which is "the white people." "Where are they now?" asked our cousin. "That is just what I would like to know, too," said the boy; "I had just come out of their nice house between the two hills, and as I looked back after I came out of their door I saw no more of their house, and I heard no more of them nor their music."

As William retold what had happened many times in the days that followed, he never deviated from his version: "Those Wa-me-te-go-zhe-wog came to our sugar camp and invited me to go with them, but I thought it was very close by. I thought we walked only just a few steps to come close to their door."[62]

The mysterious experience was much discussed among Mackadepenessy's family. William's story had many of the earmarks of a traditional adolescent spirit fast. Boys of William's age would often go off into the forest for several days, abstain from eating, and commune with the spirit world. That his cousin found him in a tree is telling, as boys going into the woods to fast often built platforms in the limbs of trees where they would sleep during their time away. The spring season was a common time for a young man to go on such a fast. Of course, it was typical for children to inform their parents they were undertaking a spirit fast. William's departure was unexpected. Mackadepenessy and his family did not regard William's disappearance as a spirit fast. Instead, they accepted the validity of his dream as he related it. Andrew Blackbird recalled that "it is firmly believed by all of our family and friends that he was cherished and fed three days in succession by angelic beings."[63]

The incident, which seems to have occurred sometime in the early 1820s, may have affected Mackadepenessy as well as his son. It is possible that his son's vision made him more interested in the religion of the white man. It was about this time that he participated in the writing of a memorial to the president of the United States requesting a Catholic missionary. The vision marked William as the child best suited to explore the world of European-American education. When he was twelve years old, Mackadepenessy sent this quick, inquisitive boy to the mission school of the Presbyterian minister William Ferry. According to family lore, "After being there less than a year, he was going around with his teachers, acting as an interpreter among the Indian camps at the Island of Mackinac." Andrew Blackbird recalled, "I was perfectly astonished to see how quick he acquired the English language." Later William attended for two years the Catholic mission school that was established at L'Arbre Croche. He so excelled at his lessons that he was selected by Bishop Frederic Rese to go to Detroit for more advanced training.[64]

It was the bishop's plan to take three of the brightest Ottawa students and train them for a life of holy orders as missionaries to their people. Along with William the bishop selected his sister Margaret, and Augustin Hamelin, Jr. The latter was William's cousin, the mixed-blooded son of a Mackinac fur trader and an Ottawa woman. After a time studying in the household of Bishop Rese in Detroit, the three young Ottawa were sent to Cincinnati. There Bishop Edward Dominic Fenwick had just opened a new three-story Catholic academy. William and Augustin studied here for two years, living with the priests and faculty. William did his share of teaching as well as learning. Frederic Baraga, the future linguist of the Ojibwe language and then newly arrived from Europe, received his first lessons in Ottawa from William.

In 1832 the boys were admitted into the Urban College of the Propaganda Fide, in Rome. Margaret remained in Cincinnati, living and studying with the nuns until 1835, when she returned to northern Michigan to begin a career as a teacher. William was received by the pope and was introduced to some of the leading families of Rome, yet, in the end, neither William nor Augustin became missionary priests. William, only nineteen years old, died shortly before his ordination and Augustin returned to the United States without taking vows. At L'Arbre Croche there was suspicion that somehow the Americans had a hand in the promising boy's death. After William's death the Church approached a greatly dispirited Mackadepenessy to see if he would allow another of his sons (Andrew) to go to Rome and be educated in William's stead. "No," the distraught man said, "they have killed one of my sons after they have educated him, and they will kill another."[65]

Long before the loss of William there was a distrust of United States policy among the leading Ottawa of Little Traverse. When Assiginack returned home he brought with him political as well as religious ideas. Although he had left British territory, Assiginack remained a firm supporter of the Ottawa-British alliance. He appreciated the "friendship and kindness" of many of the officials in the Indian Department. He also continued to regarded the British monarch as his "Great Father." He was only too aware of the dangers of overt resistance to United States authority so he did not counsel a return to military resistance. Nonetheless, he recognized the Ottawa needed help to undertake a cultural and economic transition, and his experience told him that the British were both more generous than the tight-fisted Americans, and also they were, relatively speaking, more trustworthy. Assiginack advised the Ottawa elders at Little Traverse to consider looking to the British for assistance.[66]

In July 1828 Mackadepenessy journeyed to Drummond Island. Unlike previous visits, when he contented himself with the receipt of "presents" from the British, Mackadepenessy requested an audience with Colonel William McKay, head of the British Indian Department. Through the agent at Drummond Island Mackadepenessy sent the following message:

> Tell McKay my Father I want to see our Great Fathers Great Fire & that I must see it I believe my Great Father at Quebec will not object to my going in one of his great wooden canoes. I only love one path & by that I would prefer going but tell McKay to ask my Great Father at Quebec if he will assist me to cross the great salt lake & enable me to return home again for I cannot buy a place in a great Canoe.

Mackadepenessy concluded his letter by noting that if the British government would not assist him, "I will try & go myself in the Spring." He was, he said, "determined to hear news with my own ears & to see for myself."[67]

This request, while less formal than his letter to President Monroe, was also the product of mature consideration. At least three intertwined desires surface in the note to Colonel McKay. First, at the heart of the request was a desire to cut through the many layers of imperial administrative filters and to determine what, if anything, the English Great Father could do for the Ottawa. As a warrior and a hunter Mackadepenessy was a man of action. He was frustrated by years of rumors, promises, and uncertainty. The British officials had promised military assistance on many occasions, but it never arrived. The American government had promised to send assistance for "civilization," but it also never arrived. In the thirteen years of empty British promises and seven years of American and Catholic Church inaction, Mackadepenessy was growing old and his people's situation was becoming more precarious. What he hoped to get from a trip to Canada and England was certainty regarding the British. Second, it is also likely that Mackadepenessy still had the desire for adventure. A trip across the "great salt lake" and a visit to the fire of the English king would have been a marvelous adventure. Third, Mackadepenessy and some of the other chiefs at L'Arbre Croche may have been aware of how limited their understanding was of European-American life. They were embarking on a cultural change for their people, but they knew little of American or Canadian life beyond Mackinac Island and Detroit, neither of which were much more than fur-trading centers. Mackadepenessy told the British, "Perhaps I will come back thro' the Big Knives Settlements. I wish to see and hear all."[68]

It was Mackadepenessy's plan to bring five or six men with him. One of these he hoped would be his brother Assiginack, who had greater experience with the British officials than he and who could act as an interpreter. British Indian officials quickly approved Mackadepenessy's request, promising passage for an Ottawa delegation "in a Public Vessel next year." But the English trip never occurred. The following spring the Ottawa civilization program suddenly began to bear new fruit.[69]

BREAKING WITH THE PAST

In May 1829 L'Arbre Croche finally was assigned a resident priest. Father Pierre S. DeJean, a French diocesan priest who had only recently come to the United States, first visited to L'Arbre Croche in 1827 as part of a summer mission to the upper Great Lakes region. He met with Assiginack and baptized his catechumens, thereby raising the number of Catholics there to more than 150 souls. The priest also heartily approved of the temperance society the Ottawa had founded. Two mixed-blooded Catholic women from Mackinac Island began to teach school. In 1829 DeJean returned to Little Traverse in the company of Bishop Fenwick. As their canoe neared the shore they saw a procession of several hundred Ottawa headed by Assiginack come down to the beach. It was evening and the sun had begun to sink into the broad expanse of Lake Michigan. The bishop rose in the canoe to offer his benediction to the Ottawa, who knelt in the sand with bowed heads to receive it. Assiginack then led the company to the chapel on the hill for evening prayers. Bishop Fenwick was greatly impressed by all that he saw. With little more than encouragement by the Church, a Catholic community had taken root on the shores of Little Traverse Bay. The visit by Bishop Fenwick, however, marked a change. Father DeJean was made pastor of the community, establishing for the first time ecclesiastical control over the Ottawa Catholics.[70]

The Catholic movement was by no means embraced by all of the people of the L'Arbre Croche coast. Three leaders, Apokisigan, Mackadepenessy, and Assiginack, had had made a collective decision, a decision that was both deeply personal as well as publically political. Their decision to seek greater sacred power through the Church of Rome was a decision that had a major impact on the community. That impact, however, was limited by the traditions of Ottawa society. None of the Catholic chiefs was in a position to impose his will on the any other members of their band. The chiefs could explain their reasons for converting to Catholicism and they could attempt, by their example, to persuade others it was the proper course, but that was the limit of their authority. No leader could impose his will on an unwilling band member. Bands relied upon the consensus of people joined by kinship and like minds to exercise social discipline. Therefore, as the formal presence of the Catholic Church grew on the shores of Little Traverse Bay, tensions arose between those who embraced the new religion and those who clung to the traditional *Anishnabeg* beliefs. One of the unhappy effects of the Catholic movement was to create a schism in the

Ottawa community at a time when those people were already under great political and economic stress.

Even before Bishop Fenwick's visit the religious traditionalists objected to the actions of the Catholics. When DeJean visited L'Arbre Croche in 1827, three chiefs gave up their medicine bags as a sign of their commitment to Christianity. Medicine bags were a deeply personal item, containing rocks, animal parts, or other items that conveyed a special spiritual power to the owner. It was uncommon, even dangerous for a person to allow someone to see what was in his medicine bag. The contents of the bag were in many ways a collection of relics that reflected the bearer's spiritual biography. Yet there was also a public side to the medicine bag; it was an overt expression of community spiritual solidarity. All Ottawa had a medicine bag. When a chief surrendered his sacred bundle, he was breaking an implicit connection with the world of the manitou. It was one thing to go to Christian services or sing Christian hymns—that anyone could do and still hold close to traditional beliefs. To burn a medicine bag was not only to surrender your private cache of spiritual power, but also to anger the very spirits who had heretofore been your special protectors. Such a step could only be taken by someone who had surrendered the traditional *Anishnabeg* worldview. Jesus, the Virgin Mary, the communion of saints, replaced (or at least were seen as more powerful than) the spirits of the trees, rocks, animals, and the lakes. In this way Christian converts looked out at a different world through different eyes than their traditionalist brothers and sisters.

Some sense of the psychological trauma that converts confronted can be glimpsed in the account of Father Samuel Mazzuchelli, who in 1831 visited L'Arbre Croche. During the course of three days, he baptized an old woman. She came to Mazzuchelli's lodge "carrying a rough wooden box about a foot and a half wide, containing some red feathers and an eagle's beak." The priest threw these items into the fire. "The old woman wept unrestrainedly at the sight of the consuming flames," observed the missionary. So deep was her grief that the priest's interpreter asked her "if she regretted giving to the fire these charms once so dear to her." One can easily imagine the flood of memories the burning objects must have released in the woman, who had held close those feathers through a lifetime's joys and tragedies. But in her reply she discounted her attachment to the medicine bundle. "Oh no, I weep because now I realize my past ignorance. See how the fire burns up the things I once thought had divine power!" Although this woman made no mention of the fear of isolation from the community of tradition that bound all Ottawa to each other, converts could face a real and dispiriting isolation. During this same visit Mazzuchelli also encountered "a melancholy young

Indian." The man was a Christian convert who had fallen into "deep and constant sadness" because of "the obstinate refusal of all his nearest relatives to be converted to the divine faith."[71]

It is likely Mackadepenessy was one of the chiefs who surrendered his medicine bag to Father DeJean in 1827. That three chiefs were reported to have done so suggests the action of Mackadepenessy, Apokisigan, and Assiginack, as this was the first report of medicine bags being surrendered to the Catholic Church at L'Arbre Croche and they were the leaders of the Catholic movement. This action would have sent shock waves through the community. Mackadepenessy's decision must have been a difficult one for himself, but it also greatly affected his sons. Pungowish, his eldest, was already a full-grown man who made his own decisions. He accepted the Christian name of Peter and baptism, but that is a far cry from breaking spiritually with Ottawa tradition. William, who would later go on to study for the priesthood, was old enough to have started his own medicine bundle. At some point in the years before he left L'Arbre Croche, it is likely that he followed his father's example and surrendered his bag to the Church. In some ways it would have been Mackadepenessy's youngest son, the boy baptized Amable (the future Andrew Blackbird), who was most affected by his father's action. He was just approaching the age when a boy would go off for his first spiritual fast. It is likely that he was too young to have begun his medicine bag. Instead of growing up within the spiritual traditions of the *Anishnabeg,* the boy's earliest memories of spiritual life would have been Christian. He would have thought, perhaps, of a guardian angel, not of a personal manitou, who came to him during a vision quest in the woods. He would have heard of the *Midewiwin,* but he would have grown up practicing the sacraments of the Church. Much more so than his older brothers and sister, Andrew Blackbird grew up outside of the practices of traditional Ottawa spirituality. In this sense, he would always be in some way alienated from that part of his own culture.

The outlook of those Ottawa who were reluctant to fully embrace Christianity is well expressed in an anecdote relayed in memoir of John Tanner, the white captive who grew up living with an Ottawa family. In the story a baptized Indian dies and goes to the gates of the white man's heaven to seek admittance. But there is a gatekeeper there who refuses to allow any Indian to enter. "Go," he tells the Christian Indian, "for to the west there are the villages and the hunting grounds of those of your own people who have been on the earth before you." The Indian did as he was told and in due time arrived at a village of Ottawa. But the chief of the village barred him from entering. "You have been ashamed of us while you lived," the chief said. "You have chosen to worship the white man's God. Go now to his village, and let him provide for you." The Christian Indian, in the view of the teller, forfeited that which made him an Indian, yet did not gain acceptance in the white man's world. Implicit in the story is the assumption that it was impossible to be both Indian and Christian.[72]

The Tanner story is particularly revealing of the tensions that wracked L'Arbre Croche because the person who told Tanner the anecdote was Wakezoo, Mackadepenessy's brother. In 1813 in present-day Manitoba Wakezoo spoke derisively of "a missionary who had come among the Ottawwas of Wa-gunukkezie [L'Arbre Croche]."[73] In this, he may have recalled the 1799 visit of Father Gabriel Richard to the village. At that time the Ottawa refused Richard's offer to find a missionary to live among them. In 1813, when the leadership of Tenskwatawa and Tecumseh still held promise, when the prospect of military victory over the Americans was possible, Wakezoo's dismissal of Christianity likely reflected the sentiments of most of the Ottawa. Mackadepenessy himself had shown no interest in the white man's religion prior to the end of the War of 1812. But did Wakezoo continue his disdain for the white man's religion into the 1820s? While the movement to bring a Catholic missionary to L'Arbre Croche brought Mackadepenessy closer to his brother Assiginack, religion may have been a wedge between him and Wakezoo. The evidence does not allow us to see more clearly how conversion may have caused a family rupture, but it does make clear that the divisions caused by the growth of Catholicism among the Ottawa were real.

It was in part because of "pagan" Ottawa complaints about the presence of a priest in their village that the Catholic converts moved to establish their own community. In a European or American community, a break with religious orthodoxy was also seen as a threat to the social order and the cause of deep political divisions. Even in the liberal nineteenth century, religious difference in Ireland or eastern Europe was seen as a political threat. The Americans had their openness to religious freedom challenged by the rise of the Mormons, whose distinctive brand of Christianity was seen as threat to local communities in Ohio, Missouri, Illinois, and Michigan. Both in Europe and America violence was often the result of religious conflict. Among the Ottawa, the division over Christianity did not lead to violence. Both the coverts and the traditionalists maintained the very Ottawa value that individuals chose their own path in life. No one could or even should try to impose a way of life upon another person. When people disagreed over fundamental issues, the Ottawa way was for them to separate, to leave the band. This is what Catholics did sometime in 1827 or 1828 when they moved as a group from the village near Nine Mile Point to a small inlet twenty miles farther south on the shore of Little Traverse Bay. They called their settlement New L'Arbre Croche.[74]

According to Andrew Blackbird, when Mackadepenessy left Nile Mile Point for New L'Arbre Croche, he was acting very much on his own. Most of the people of the band of which he was chief chose not to make the move. Indeed the title of chief devolved to his brother Kawmenotea. At the time of Mackadepenessy's move there were only a handful of Ottawa settled at the new site. There were several log cabin homes built by the converts, Peter Shomin, Joseph Ausawgon, and, of course, Assiginack. A church and a rectory had also been built, but otherwise the site of the future city of Harbor Springs, Michigan was an empty bay shore.[75]

What attracted Mackadepenessy to the new village, what seems to have made him leave behind the people of his band, was the Catholic school that Father DeJean established. Mackadepenessy wanted his children, especially William, Margaret, and Amable (Andrew) to learn to read and write. The move also coincided with a major change in the domestic economy of Mackadepenessy's household. About 1828 he stopped relocating the family each fall to his hunting ground on the upper Muskegon River. Taking children hundreds of miles away from L'Arbre Croche for five to six months of the year was a clear impediment to their education. It is, therefore, likely that the creation of a school at the village was a factor in convincing Mackadepenessy and other Ottawas to forgo the journey to distant hunting grounds. He would continue to hunt, but his activities would be restricted to the less profitable lands near Little Traverse Bay.

The decision to adopt a sedentary lifestyle at New L'Arbre Croche had political and economic repercussions. In embracing Catholicism Mackadepenessy and other leading Ottawa may also have committed themselves to an economic change that would bring them closer to the practices of European-American settlers. In 1816, at the time of the Ottawa's first request for "civilization" assistance from the United States, they solicited funds for "cows, Hogs, Fowls."[76] Since the 1740s the Ottawa had been raising corn along the L'Arbre Croche coast for sale in the Michilimackinac market. In moving to a sedentary lifestyle they obviously were hoping to increase their agricultural productivity. This move might also help their political position because it would make them more like European-Americans.

At the same time there is reason to believe that the Ottawa who abandoned the winter hunting camps were also making a shrewd economic evaluation. The fur trade was clearly in decline. "When our young men go out," the *Anishnabeg* of the Straits region complained in an 1834 petition, "they can not see any animals."[77] While such statements made to the government often exaggerated Indian misery in hopes of gaining assistance, the fact was the fur trade no longer was as secure a means of gaining trade goods as it had been a generation earlier. The Christian converts may have seen the possibility of transforming other traditional subsistence activities into marketable commerce. For people residing full time along the shores of Little Traverse Bay, maple sugar production and fishing were two forms of subsistence that could be effectively expanded for the market. Since early in the eighteenth century the Ottawa had provided fish and sugar, as well as corn, for use by the fur traders and the military garrisons at Michilimackinac. What was new was the scale of production and the significance of this trade for Ottawa domestic economy. The expansion of agriculture, fishing, and sugaring was the economic basis for the move to sedentary residence at New L'Arbre Croche.

A HOLE IN THE HEART OF THE FAMILY

Tragedy marred Mackadepenessy's family as they took their first steps on the path of this new domestic economy. "The first winter we lived at Little Traverse as a permanent home was in the year 1828," Andrew Blackbird wrote in his history, "and in the following spring my own dear mother died very suddenly, as she was burned while they were making sugar in the woods." Although sugar making was usually an enjoyable time of year, for the Ottawa severe burns often occurred while the maple syrup was being boiled. The large kettles, which were kept bubbling night and day, could suddenly shift on the fire and spill. There was also danger when the thickened syrup was transferred from the hot copper kettles to the granulating trough. However the accident happened, Mackadepenessy's wife was "burned so badly that she only lived four days after."[78]

Those two sentences are all that is known of the circumstances of Andrew Blackbird's mother's death. Even his mother's name is not known. To Andrew she likely had always been *Gachi,* mother, simply and completely. The record is silent on what was done to treat her burns in the days that followed the accident. Was Mackadepenessy tempted to call for the services of a *Mide* priest? The *Midewiwin* were often the best-informed Ottawa regarding the use of herbs to heal wounds and ease pain. Did he blame the *Mide* for the evil spirit that might have caused the accident, or did he, perhaps, reproach himself for having abandoned the manitou that had hitherto protected the members of his family? An *Anishnabeg* traditionalist might have offered a sacrifice to the Great Spirit to help the medicines of the *Mide* work more effectively. Did Mackadepenessy go to the little Catholic chapel and light a candle to signify his prayer for recovery? That she lingered on in pain for four days at least ensured that she was able to leave each of her children, from Pungowish, her eldest, to Andrew, her youngest son, a few last words of love.

For Andrew Blackbird the death of his mother shattered the emotional cocoon of his large family. "I was small, but I was old enough to know and mourn for my dear mother. I felt as though I had lost everything dear to me and every friend," he wrote nearly sixty years later. Such language was not merely a figurative statement of emotional loss. His mother's death was followed by the breakup of the family household in which he previously had spent each night of his life. His brother William and his sister Margaret shortly afterward departed for Catholic school in Cincinnati, leaving him without the older siblings who might have provided him with the succor he had previously received from his mother. His oldest brother, Pungowish, and at least one other older sister, to whom he was almost a stranger, had households of their own, in locations far removed from New L'Arbre Croche. This made Andrew and a younger sister particularly dependent upon his father. Yet Mackadepenessy was, for some reason, incapable of giving the boy the emotional and physical security the vulnerable child required. Andrew wrote, "There was no one that I could place such confidence in, not even my own father. So my father's household was broken up: we were pretty well scattered after that."[79]

In part it may have been because Mackadepenessy and his wife had a monogamous relationship that the household was broken up. It was not uncommon for successful men such as Mackadepenessy to have more than one wife. Had that been the case, Andrew would have had a second maternal figure upon whom he could have relied and Mackadepenessy would have had a women in his lodge upon whom he could depend for cooking, clothing, sugaring, and farming. Ironically, it was the "progress" that the Ottawa had made on the road of "civilization," monogamy and sedentary living, that made it difficult for him to maintain a household without a wife to make her vital market contributions to the household economy.

Andrew Blackbird remembered this traumatic moment in his life as something forced upon Mackadepenessy. "He could not very well keep us together," was the way he put it. But in another portion of his history, when Andrew describes the death of his brother William in 1833, he mentions that people came "to our dwelling" to console Mackadepenessy, which indicates that at least at that time he did still live with his father.[80] There is in

Andrew Blackbird's brief discussion of these troubled years a suggestion that his father was incapable of performing his family duties. At some point Mackadepenessy did wed again and in later years Andrew referred to this second wife as "my mother," but she does not seem to have performed that role during the formative years of the 1830s.[81] In fact, for at least the next ten years Mackadepenessy does not seem to have been a significant presence in Andrew's life. It is perplexing that during these years Andrew made no mention of his uncles, Wakezoo, Kawmenotea, Wing, and Assiginack. The latter had a log cabin home at New L'Arbre Croche. Assiginack also had a young son, Francis, who was roughly Andrew's age, yet there is no indication that Mackadepenessy's boy moved to his uncle's household.[82]

For the young boy, his life spinning out of control, school seemed to provide a steadying influence. He attended class in a log schoolhouse. Part of the building was devoted to a residence hall for the boys and girls. It is unclear if Andrew Blackbird was a residential student. "The larger boys and girls were taught household duties and to cook for the scholars," he remembered. "The children were kept quite clean." The academic program was led by Joseph Letourneau, a member of the French Canadian community at Detroit, and it was conducted completely in the French language. Most of the students, upwards of sixty in number, were Ottawa, although Andrew attended class with two of the sons of George Boyd, the federal Indian agent at Mackinac Island. The school taught spelling, reading, and writing as well as manual skills. The girls received lessons in needlework, while the boys received instruction in agriculture. Tuition for the school was collected each spring in the form of a large mocock of sugar weighing between eighty and one hundred pounds. Sale of the sugar provided the mission with the funds necessary to secure school supplies and clothing for the children. Andrew seems to have enjoyed his classmates, especially James and George Boyd, whom he later described "very great friends to the Indians." Another favorite at school was "an old nun whose real name I never learned, and only knew as 'Sister.'" From the nun the boy received a bit of the maternal attention he so dearly missed. "She was exceedingly kind to Indian children," he wrote, "and we all liked her very much."[83]

The school program, however, like everything else in Blackbird's troubled young life, was also thrown into flux. Father DeJean, who was not a young man, was not up to the rigors of a missionary's life. Near the end of 1830 he received permission from the bishop to leave L'Arbre Croche and return to his native France. Father Frederic Baraga, who replaced DeJean in May 1831, changed the orientation of the curriculum. The study of French was gradually phased out and most students were instructed in their native language and the boarding school was closed. Andrew Blackbird remembered the change from DeJean to Baraga with deep regret. Baraga, he contended, "did not give as good care to the children as his predecessor." Baraga would go on to be the most successful Christian missionary in the upper Great Lakes region, but L'Arbre Croche was his first mission and he was guilty of missteps. The educational program could only have suffered when Baraga undertook long journeys evangelizing at Manistique, Beaver Island, or Grand River. Andrew Blackbird was particularly affected when Baraga, faced with a financial shortfall, closed the dormitory for students. By doing so the missionary may have taken a secure home from young Andrew. After four years of mission school, Andrew ceased attending classes.[84]

In his history he described the general life of the Ottawa at L'Arbre Croche at this time in optimistic terms. "I thought my people were very happy in those days, when they were all by themselves and possessed of a wide spread of land, and no one to quarrel with them as to where they should make their gardens, or take timber, or make sugar." The boy provided for his own subsistence by means of fishing. "A hook anywheres in the bay," he wrote, "and at any time of year, would catch Mackinaw trout, many as one would want." Fishing by hook and net, unrestrained by paternal expectations, the boy might have found the years between 1831 and 1836 a happy time had it not been for the feeling there was no one he could truly trust. Long after he had matured into a man he regretted the lack of a friend or loved one "that I could place such confidence in." These were years in which, in the words of his history, "I became a perfect wild rover."[85]

There is an image of vigor and energy as well as of loneliness and emptiness in those words. A boy between the ages ten and fourteen is in the process of shaping his sense of self. A typical Ottawa boy of Andrew's age would have explored his identity, his place in the world, through long days of reflection and fasting in the woods. In addition to this emerging spiritual power, Andrew should have gained confidence in his future role from the daily example of his father and the other men around him. Andrew lacked an intimate relationship with his father and seemingly with any man during these years. This lack of a secure emotional base made the transition through puberty all the more difficult for Andrew.

Compounding his problem was the cultural transition that was then sweeping through Ottawa life. The freedom, danger, and prestige that came with war and the hunt was being replaced with agriculture, an activity that had previously been the sphere of women's work. Alternative models of male behavior based on finding new avenues for market exchanges were rising at a time when the honored roles of hunter and warrior were being eclipsed.

Andrew saw in his village men who were respected and worthy of emulation; their conduct, however, was not necessarily sanctioned by tradition. It was, rather, emerging and contingent. The boy was not presented with well-understood role models. Before him lay not a blazed way through the forest but an indistinct game trail, that might or might not lead to honor and respect. In this way neither family nor village could give the young man the clear course in life that so many young people need. Andrew Blackbird drifted through the formative years of puberty.

One potential role model, Andrew's uncle Assiginack, left L'Arbre Croche in 1832. He was never completely comfortable in American territory and with his evangelical work complete, he returned to the British side of the lakes, where he again became an influential figure mediating between the Ottawa and Crown officials. The move left Andrew further isolated and insecure.[86]

Andrew may well have resented his uncertain status in the village. His brother, cousin, and sister had been selected by his father for educational opportunities abroad. But Andrew was not afforded any special opportunities for education or advancement. In 1832 four more Ottawa boys were selected to go to Cincinnati, where Bishop Fenwick was to arrange for them to learn valuable trades, from blacksmith to carpenter. The Ottawa rightly saw these skills as critical to successfully building a new life and the boys who were chosen were marked for future positions of influence. Unlike all of the previous overtures to the Church, Mackadepenessy appears to have had nothing to do with this plan. His name does not appear among the Ottawa who petitioned the bishop. The son of Joseph Nawimashkote, listed on the petition as "head-chief of Old Arbre Croche," was among those selected. While others were being given the opportunity to contribute to a new life for Ottawa, Andrew may have been frustrated by being left directionless between the old and the new.[87]

Nor was Andrew's bond to the Catholic Church strengthened when he received the jarring news that his brother William, who was studying for the priesthood in Rome, had died suddenly. Andrew had followed William's successful educational career with great interest and perhaps envy. Learning English had come easily to William and he had a remarkable ability to adapt himself to the exotic circumstances of living in the European-American world. When he went to study at the Dominican school in Cincinnati, he assimilated quickly to an almost monastic lifestyle, with each day beginning at five in the morning with the prayer bell and all meals taken in common by the priests and the ecclesiastical students. In Rome he attended a college in which the language of instruction was Latin, a necessity because the students came from thirty-one different language backgrounds. William, nonetheless, excelled in this diverse setting. He was, of course, something of a novelty and he was received in the homes of many of the nobles of Rome. He participated in torchlight devotions in the depths of Rome's ancient catacombs. "Perhaps our countrymen would not believe," he wrote home, "that there was such a place as that place which I saw with my own naked eyes." He seems to have enjoyed the pomp and color of the Roman Church's administrative center. He attended the pope's Easter Sunday High Mass and participated in the ceremonies that elevated one of the college faculty to status of cardinal. The Church recognized in this successful student the makings of "a very eloquent and powerful orator." On the Feast of the Epiphany he addressed a convocation of students and faculty in the Ottawa language. It was because of his obvious talents and the loss of so promising a leader that Andrew, and indeed all of the Ottawa of L'Arbre Croche, were stunned to learn in the summer of 1833 that young William was dead.[88]

Church authorities informed the Catholic bishop in Detroit that William died from a ruptured artery in his breast. In the days prior to his death he had "complained of an internal pain" that the bishop attributed to "an accident that happened to him in America, when a wheel passed over his breast." On the morning of June 25 William was found in his room suffering from the rupture. The loss of blood "reduced him within a short time to the extreme and took him from this life."[89] This account is partially supported by a letter from William to his sister Margaret in Cincinnati. The letter was printed by Andrew Blackbird in his history. On April 17, 1833, he wrote, "I think of you often: perhaps I shall never have the pleasure of seeing you again." He went on to say, "I have been unwell ever since I came to this country. However, I am yet able to attend my school and studies. I hope I will not be worse, so that I may be unable to follow my intention."[90]

Presumably the Church's account of William's death was conveyed through Father Frederic Baraga, the missionary at L'Arbre Croche, to Mackadepenessy and his family. Yet in his 1887 history Andrew Blackbird told a very different story of William's death. Looking back on the events of the 1830s through the lens of fifty years of painful experience for himself and his people, Andrew linked the death of his brother with the loss of tribal lands. "He was slain, it has been said," he wrote, "because it was found out that he was counseling his people on the subject of their lands and their treaties with the Government of the United States." He went on to suggest that the murder was likely committed "by some of the American students from a secret plot originating in this country to remove this Indian youth who had attained the highest pinnacle of science and who had become their equal in wisdom, and in all the important questions of the day, both in temporal and spiritual matters." Andrew believed that following his ordination his brother had planned to meet with the president of the United States and find a way to save his people from removal. "His death deprived the Ottawa and Chippewa Indians of a wise counselor and advisor, one of their own native countrymen." Suspicion that the young man's death was the result of "a wicked conspiracy" was reinforced when the trunk containing his books and clothing, which had been sent from Rome, was lost upon arrival in Detroit."[91]

It is understandable that William's death so far from home became the subject of suspicion and wild theories. A bright and promising young man was dead and initially there were few details. The Church was aware of the speculation that William Blackbird's death would engender. In writing to Bishop Rese in Detroit, Cardinal Carlo M. Pedicini, the prefect of the school, advised that the bishop "stress the accident phase of the death" so that the "parents of the young man and those others who may be concerned" would not "be distressed." Nearly a year later, in May 1834, Augustin Hamlin, who was with William in Rome, returned to L'Arbre Croche. Hamlin had spoken with William the night before he died, and the next morning, when he heard of his cousin's death, he rushed to the room. At that time William's body was being "taken out, wrapped up in a cloth." Allegedly when Hamlin went in and inspected the room, he "saw at once enough to tell him that it was the work of the assassin." Such an observation no doubt refers to the presence of blood in the room, which was consistent with a ruptured artery. That Blackbird cited Hamlin suggests that upon the latter's return from Rome he too entered into the speculation regarding William's death. In 1835 Margaret returned home to begin her career as a teacher. Both she and Hamlin knew that William had not been well prior to his death and they were in a position to quiet speculation about his fate. Hamlin consciously chose to act otherwise. His account of seeing William's body taken out of his room "wrapped up in cloth" is not consistent with Church officials' statement that William lingered for a time after the rupture, before dying from the loss of blood. Mackadepenessy, in his understandable grief, may have been among those who thought William was murdered. When Mackadepenessy rejected a proposal that Andrew be sent to Rome to finish the course of study that William began, he said, "They have killed one of my sons."[92]

The death of William Mackadepenessy was a severe blow to Andrew and the entire family. That William occupied a large place in Andrew Blackbird's later history indicates how much he admired his older brother. The loss of so talented and loved a sibling robbed Andrew of a trusted counselor and guide at a vulnerable period of his life. But even in death

William did function as a role model for Andrew. Although his father's anguish prevented Andrew from being sent to Rome to study, he would in time find a way to follow in his brother's path. Unfortunately, it would take years for his feet to find that path, and when he did, it would not lead him to Rome and the heart of the Catholic Church, but to a more individual and American approach to God.

According to Andrew, the death of his brother was not simply a family loss but an event that touched the entire community. "When news reached Little Traverse," he wrote, "all the country of Arbor Croche was enveloped in deep mourning, and a great lamentation took place among the Ottawa."[93] William's knowledge of the white man's language and society, his position in the Catholic Church, all would have made him a vital resource in the crisis that was looming between the United States and the Ottawa. At L'Arbre Croche Apokisigan, Mackadepenessy, and other elders had developed a strategy to form a new middle ground in the upper Great Lakes region. By 1833 they had only just begun to change their society, yet a period of testing was nonetheless thrust upon them.

TRADING LAND FOR TIME

Prior to 1836 the United States had made few territorial demands upon the people of L'Arbre Croche. The cession of the St. Martin Islands in 1820 and the cession of the land around the Straits of Mackinac in 1795 were the limit of their territorial losses. In contrast, the Grand River Ottawa had already been forced into a much more significant cession in 1821, losing nearly half of their territory. In 1830 the United States government fully committed to a policy of removing American Indians from the area east of the Mississippi River. Like so many policies that would be disastrous for Native Americans this policy had emerged from a meeting of minds among those whites who believed they had the best interests of the Indians at heart, and those who callously cared only about separating Indian people from their land.[94] From 1783 to 1830 the government had explored the notion of "civilizing" Indian peoples, as preparation for their integration with American society. The Ottawa both at Grand River and at L'Arbre Croche had used this policy to demonstrate their ability to adapt to new conditions and to show their willingness to explore cultural and economic integration with the European-American world.

Unfortunately, the civilization policy began to lose favor in Washington,

D.C. For one thing, the program was a long-term solution to what, on the frontier, was often an immediate political problem. Educational programs were deemed the key to civilization, but that was a method, even in the most optimistic view, that would take at least a generation to be effective. In the meantime, many state governments, particularly in the South, wanted tribal lands opened to settlers immediately. A second problem was the enduring Achilles heel of Indian policy, execution. The Congress appropriated $10,000 for the education of all eastern and midwestern Indians. As the L'Arbre Croche Ottawa had found out the Civilization Fund was hard to access and when money came it was too little to have a major impact. More effective at bringing schools to the Indians were treaties of cession in which the Indians could dedicate the money they received for their land to support schools. The potential good work of schools, however, was undercut by the failure of the government to either supervise or set standards regarding the curriculum. This failure of execution was matched by the government's inability to enforce its laws governing trade with the Indians. These laws forbade the sale of alcohol, but merchants made their violation a matter of course. As alcohol abuse accelerated in Indian country many of the very missionaries engaged in the civilization program began to despair of the efficacy of their efforts.[95]

The Removal Act of 1830 was designed to open up a vast amount of Indian land to white settlers and at the same time "save" the Indian from the abuse of alcohol by removing them from proximity with European-American merchants. Removal had been discussed as a policy toward the eastern Indians since 1803 when the Louisiana Purchase first brought the trans-Mississippi region under United States control. In 1825 President James Monroe had proposed it as a policy alternative, and under Andrew Jackson removal became federal law. The plight of the Cherokees and the demand by the state of Georgia for their removal was at the heart of the Removal Act, but the act was also intended as a broad statement of policy. Lewis Cass, who as governor of the Michigan Territory had negotiated treaties with the *Anishnabeg,* was an early proponent of the act. Because of this, he was in 1831 appointed by Andrew Jackson to be the new secretary of war, the Cabinet post charged with the management of Indian affairs. Cass was, however, not a doctrinaire man, and while he supported removal in principle, he did not believe that Indians should be forced to move west against their will. It was the secretary's humane and pragmatic, if nonetheless ethnocentristic, views on Indian affairs that provided the Ottawa with room to try to avoid being swept up by the removal policy's big broom.[96]

Two things pushed the Ottawa and the United States toward a treaty of cession. The first was the rapid influx of white settlers into the Michigan Territory. During the period between 1825 and 1835, the *Anishnabeg* went from being the dominant population in the Michigan Territory to being an isolated minority. Michigan had largely been bypassed by the initial wave of European-American settlement that surged into the Midwest following the War of 1812. Illinois and Indiana swelled with newly founded farmsteads and by 1818 both had attained statehood. It was the opening of the Erie Canal in 1825 that directed the flow of emigrants to the Michigan Territory. The canal provided a water link between New York City and the Great Lakes, and it quickly became the preferred route west for settlers.[97] The approximately 5,500 Ottawa and Chippewa who lived in the unceded areas of northwestern Michigan were not directly affected by this demographic revolution. The European-American settlers were restricted to the lands that had been ceded in 1821 and through earlier treaties. Yet when land offices in those areas were recording as much as $70,000 in land sales per day the demand for more land was inevitable.[98]

The second thing that worked to create an impetus toward a treaty was implementation of the removal policy in southern Michigan. In 1833 at Chicago, United States representatives negotiated a treaty with the Potawatomi that set the stage for the cession of their remaining lands near Lake Michigan. That same year the United States Army bungled the forced removal of the Potawatomi from eastern Illinois. These events sent shock waves northward to the Ottawa. Hundreds of refugee Potawatomi, some seeking shelter in northern Michigan, others on their way to asylum in British territory, put a tragic face on this arresting news. Catholic missionaries who had been active with the Potawatomi in southern Michigan lobbied the United States that their flock be allowed to stay behind because of the progress they were making toward civilization. In Detroit Bishop Frederic Rese hatched a plan to resettle the Catholic Potawatomi near Little Traverse. In 1834 he sought permission from the Ottawa. While there was sympathy for the Potawatomi, however, the Ottawa did not feel they were in a position to absorb the refugees. "Why should these poor Indians," wrote a missionary at L'Arbre Croche, "desire to lose a part of their livelihood, when they have not enough for themselves and are forced to go to distant places for it." In rejecting the bishop's plan, Assiginack reminded the white men that just prior to the War of 1812 the people of L'Arbre Croche had rejected the appeal of the Ottawas of Maumee, Ohio, to settle in northern Michigan. As for the Potawatomi, Assiginack asked rhetorically, "Shall we receive them, when we refused our brethren, who are more nearly related to us? I think not." These events did, however, underscore the degree to which the Ottawa themselves were now imperiled by United States Indian policy. The people of L'Arbre Croche were forced to accelerate their efforts to reach rapprochement with the Americans.[99]

In the tradition of Indian-white relations in the Great Lakes region, the so-called middle ground, when one party felt anxious or aggrieved a council was arranged, with the Great Father himself or with his leading deputies. It is, therefore, natural that as the Ottawa became concerned about the prospect of removal, they sought to arrange a face-to-face meeting with American decision-makers. In November 1833 the Ottawa of L'Arbre Croche approached Henry Rowe Schoolcraft, the agent at Mackinac Island, with a request to send a delegation to Washington to meet with President Andrew Jackson. Such was the state of feeling among the Ottawa that their missionary, Frederic Baraga, reported that the lodges of L'Arbre Croche were rife with reports that as early as the following summer American troops would be sent to drive them from Michigan.[100]

The Ottawa had every reason to expect their request for a meeting to be granted but the response by United States officials was indifferent, if not negligent. George Porter, who had replaced Cass as governor of the Michigan Territory, received the Ottawa request from Schoolcraft, but promptly lost it. When he came across it again, he simply sent it on to the commissioner of Indian affairs in Washington, D.C. Commissioner Elbert Herring, having received no advice on the urgency of events in Michigan from Porter, dismissed the request for a council by noting there was no money "to defray the expenses of such an object."[101]

The Ottawa were confused and perhaps insulted by the Americans' indifference. They suspected that Henry Rowe Schoolcraft had not sent their request to Washington. In February 1834 eight Ottawa men made an arduous snowshoe trip from their Little Traverse villages to Mackinac Island. Their spokesman was Assiginack. Schoolcraft recorded the meeting in his *Memoirs.*

> The reasons for such a visit arose from a desire to see the President, on the subject of their lands. Many of these lands were denuded of game. . . . They were poor and indebted to the traders. The settlements would soon intrude on their territories. Wood was now cut for the use of steamboats and not paid for. They had various topics to confer about.

Perhaps in an effort to warm the Americans to the Ottawa's proposed visit, Assiginack held out the prospect of selling Drummond Island, the former British stronghold. The island in northern Lake Huron had been

Assiginack's home for over thirteen years, but since a United States–British boundary survey determined that it was in United States territory, it had been abandoned by both the British and the Indians.[102]

For more than 150 years the Ottawa had been dealing with a succession of European-American powers, first the French, later the British, and finally the Americans. Through this process their chiefs developed a method of conducting diplomatic relations. In the tradition of the middle ground they addressed the leader of the European or American power as their "Great Father," and through such usage, they emphasized their own weak or wretched condition. They did this because it comported with *Anishnabeg* social norms. Fathers were not figures of authority—as Ottawa children were seldom disciplined. Nor was the term "father" used exclusively to refer to one's male parent, but it was often used to address uncles or a revered elder of the band. By presenting themselves to the "Great Father" as poor and needy, the *Anishnabeg* were, according to their social ethics, creating an obligation on the president's part to bestow a gift or boon upon them. At the same time, they understood many critical aspects of the European-American system of managing government and organizing the land. In trying to maneuver the United States government to address their concern over their future status in Michigan, the Ottawa employed both the traditions of the middle ground and their knowledge of the American government. An example of the way the Ottawa leaders blended traditional notions with a savvy understanding of American law is illustrated by a council that was held at Mackinac Island in August 1834.

Instead of the invitation to Washington and a meeting with the president, the best the Ottawa overtures yielded was a grand council of Ottawa and Chippewa to meet with Schoolcraft at Mackinac. The large gathering included leading men from most of the important bands in northwestern Michigan. Schoolcraft called the council to explain that for budgetary reasons the United States was closing blacksmith shops it had previously operated for the Indians as a gesture of goodwill. Also to be eliminated were funds for small gifts of provisions to Indians who arrived at Mackinac Island without food. In the past, such gifts had been given because *Anishnabeg* notions of hospitality required the agent as the "friend" of the Indians to provide some assistance. Schoolcraft also wanted them present when a federal surveyor marked out the lines of a cession of land at the Straits of Mackinac made by the Ottawa and Chippewa to the United States. The cession had been made in 1795 at the Treaty of Greenville and included all of Mackinac Island and portions of the mainland. Because almost forty years had passed between the time the cession had been made and when its boundaries were being surveyed, Schoolcraft wanted to be sure the *Anishnabeg* understood that the action was in accordance with the earlier treaty.[103]

After the agent made his explanations, the Indians withdrew to hold a private discussion among themselves. When they finished, the council resumed. Pabanmitabi, a respected elder of L'Arbre Croche, rose to speak on behalf of all of the *Anishnabeg* present. "You will listen to us while we speak our minds," Pabanmitabi said in an authoritative tone that carried throughout the council grounds. "We have consulted on these subjects and I am to declare our sentiments." He then noted how the French king "as a mark of his friendship" provided blacksmith services to the *Anishnabeg*, as had the English after them. But if the Americans no longer wished to do so he asked that they take the trouble to teach "one of our young men" the smith's trade. Pabanmitabi then made the point that his people did not need to be reminded of their treaty obligations. "It is 40 winters since we first saw the Americans, When we first shook hands with you and smoked the pipe of peace with you, at Greenville Gen. [Anthony] Wayne the Chief who led your soldiers drew lines across our lands, and they were agreed to. . . . we have not forgotten the grant. Some of the men are yet living who were at the treaty And we have been told, by our old men of the terms of it." The Ottawa and Chippewa did not object to the surveyor making his lines upon the ground; in fact, said Pabanmitabi, "We will send men to go with the surveyor." The *Anishnabeg* would obey the treaty made a generation before, and they challenged the Americans to do the same. "We have but one request to make. It is when the lines are run, the white men will keep within them and we will promise not to go over them." Since the Americans no longer would offer hospitality, the Ottawa and Chippewa would do the same. "If any wood is cut upon our land hereafter, we should be paid for it." Pabanmitabi realized that the military garrison at Mackinac Island, the civilian population, and the steamboats that serviced the American settlement all relied upon wood cut from unceded Indian lands. Without access to Indian resources, "You could not live on the Island." "Were our means ample we would not ask remuneration. But we are impoverished in many ways."[104]

If the Americans were going to squeeze them economically, *Anishnabeg* would squeeze back. Pabanmitabi closed his address by bringing up the request of his own L'Arbre Croche people to meet with the president. "We have twice asked you in council to go and see the President, but it has not been granted." He then pointedly told Schoolcraft, "We request you to be the interpreter of our wishes to him."[105]

At the Mackinac council the Ottawa and Chippewa bands each with unique and diverse interests were nonetheless able to agree to a common response to the United States. As relations with the United States moved toward a crisis, however, the process of consensus formation was impeded by the differing interests and traditional independence of the bands. In June 1834, for example, a formal council was held between the Ottawa of L'Arbre Croche and the Ottawa of the Grand River valley. Both branches of the Ottawa nation had been alarmed by the prospect of removal, and chiefs gathered to address the danger. The meeting was held near the present city of Grand Rapids, Michigan, "in a small round valley which has the form of a large amphitheater." The council grounds were prepared by the building of several large fires over which were hung large kettles filled with maple sugar water, a favorite refreshment. The meeting was a chance for a variety of voices to be heard, although the elders pushed the delegates toward a common ground of understanding. At this meeting, the point of consensus, Father Baraga reported, was the commitment "not to cede their lands to the United States, and not to make themselves and their children unhappy." While this was, no doubt, a heartfelt sentiment, it obscured the differing interests of the Grand River and L'Arbre Croche bands. The Grand River bands had made the 1821 treaty with the United States, and from that agreement, they were already receiving annuities and educational assistance. But they were also directly in the path of rapidly expanding American settlements. The L'Arbre Croche bands were more removed from actual American farmers, and some of the band's leaders sought resources to help the ongoing transformation their society. Therefore, the bands differed significantly in their openness to a new treaty with the United States. For the L'Arbre Croche Ottawa a treaty was a way to gain federal recognition of their civilization program and to secure their tenure on the shores of Little Traverse Bay. The Grand River Ottawa, having already surrendered much of their land, saw any further treaty negotiations as a threat to their persistence in Michigan.[106]

Neither the federal nor the Michigan territory officials were particularly aggressive in pushing for a treaty. Secretary of War Lewis Cass informed Schoolcraft there would be no Ottawa meeting with President Jackson, let alone a treaty, "as their lands are not required at *present*."[107] Henry Rowe Schoolcraft the Agent at Mackinac, however, persisted in searching for some type of accommodation. Since he was the one who had explained the federal budget cuts that all but eliminated any gifts and services to the Indians, he was particularly anxious to find a way to restore the prestige of the United States in the region. Schoolcraft believed that a cession of *Anishnabeg* land would be a means to secure annuities for the Indians of the upper Great Lakes. Regular payments by the United States to the Ottawa and Chippewa would, in Schoolcraft's opinion, gradually reconcile those people to American rule. The fact that most *Anishnabeg* still made the annual journey to British territory to receive gifts and pensions from the War of 1812 helped to underscore the reputation of the president of the United States as a parsimonious father and reinforced the loyalty of the Indians to Great Britain. Schoolcraft reminded his superiors that the Ottawa and Chippewa were still "the largest and most unfriendly and warlike of the tribes." He saw in their increasing economic vulnerability, however, an opportunity for the United States to secure its control over a people who had hitherto remained independent of its influence. Schoolcraft also saw in a treaty a chance to increase his personal prestige in the Jackson administration.[108]

In June 1835 Schoolcraft tried to wet Washington's appetite for a treaty by reporting that Ottawa from Manitoulin Island had offered to sell Drummond Island to the United States. Schoolcraft in transmitting the offer to the commissioner of Indian affairs implied that the time was ripe for a treaty because many of the Indians of the upper Great Lakes region were migrating from United States to British territory. More than a month after receiving this notice Commissioner Elbert Herring gave Schoolcraft his permission to explore the Drummond Island offer as well as to "ascertain if the Indians residing north of the Grand River are willing to part with any portion of their lands, and if they are, to what extent, and upon what terms." Schoolcraft already had terms for a treaty in mind. In September he went so far as to advise the Sault Ste. Marie Chippewa that they "offer" to sell their lands between that place and Mackinac Island. "Reservations might perhaps in the event of its acceptance be assented to including their villages," Schoolcraft instructed, "and the right to hunt and live on the tract until it is required." In return for the cession, the Chippewa could expect annuities and renewed access to a blacksmith shop. During the fall of 1835 these draft terms—a cession with reservations for villages and a temporary right to live on the ceded lands in exchange for annuities and civilization assistance—were circulated by Schoolcraft to most of the *Anishnabeg* bands.[109]

By October 1835 the Ottawa along Little Traverse Bay had heard Schoolcraft's draft treaty terms. This, however, was not good news to the L'Arbre Croche Ottawa. They were deeply suspicious of Schoolcraft. For the past three years they had solicited permission to visit Washington, D.C., but never had they received a formal reply. Nor had Schoolcraft been particularly supportive of their civilization program. At the heart of their distrust of Schoolcraft was a denominational dispute. In the early 1830s the little community of Mackinac Island had been rocked by a religious controversy occasioned by the establishment of a strong Presbyterian congregation and a revival of the Catholic Church on the island. Priests and ministers formally debated the merits of each denomination. Schoolcraft, a leading member of the Presbyterian congregation, was accused of using his position in the government to favor the Protestants at the expense of the Catholic Church's mission activities. Ottawa distrust of the agent boiled to the surface at a formal L'Arbre Croche council.[110]

Schoolcraft sent William Johnston, a federal subagent, to present the draft treaty terms. Johnston was Schoolcraft's brother-in-law and an Irish-Chippewa mixed blood. The Ottawa listened respectfully to what Johnston had to say. Their reply came not from one of the elders but young Augustin Hamlin, the former Catholic seminarian who had returned from Rome and was living at L'Arbre Croche. Hamlin rose to his feet and launched into a heated assault on Schoolcraft's integrity. The agent, Hamlin contended, was in league with real estate speculators and his goal was to secure Ottawa land "for nothing" and then sell it to incoming farmers at a high price. Hamlin announced that the Ottawa were tired of working through agents. As an agent Schoolcraft had failed to get Ottawa messages to President Jackson. Besides, as Hamlin complained, "Agents all steal; even the English agents steal from the Indians." Hamlin announced the Ottawa would ignore Schoolcraft and his proposed treaty terms and send representatives to Washington, D.C., to consult the Great Father directly.[111]

Hamlin represented something new in the United States government's dealings with the Ottawa. Although he was a very young man, probably no more than twenty-two, he had a unique experience of the European-American world. He had lived in Cincinnati, studied in Rome, and had a good understanding of French, Ottawa, English, and Latin. He had returned from abroad to live with the Ottawa, and in 1835 he served as a teacher at the L'Arbre Croche Catholic school. Hamlin gave the Ottawa leaders a new pair of eyes with which to see far beyond the Lake Michigan horizon. He gave them a voice with which to speak their words in the language of the Great Father.

As early as May 1835 the elders had united to invest in this young man the role of spokesman for the Ottawa. Hamlin, whose father had been a mixed-blooded trader based in St. Ignace, Michigan, had enough personal ambition and genuine concern for the Ottawa that he embraced the opportunity. His mother had been the daughter of Kiminichagan, one of the most prestigious chiefs of L'Arbre Croche, and he lived most of his life as an Ottawa. In an attempt to formalize his position, which was in truth a role without precedent in *Anishnabeg* political structure, Hamlin drafted what amounted to a power-of-attorney document.

> Know ye, that placing special trust and confidence in the integrity, ability and learning of Augustin Hamelin, Jr., of our said tribe of Ottawas, and in consideration that his grandfather, Kiminichagan, was during his life, head chief of our said tribe, we therefore do unanimously appoint the said Augustin Hamelin, Jrs., head chief of our said bands resident as foresaid, and do hereby empower him to execute and perform all the duties pertaining to that appointment, and we hereby engage to ratify all his doing as such.

In order to have their choice of spokesman known in the white community, this document was signed by an impressive list of chiefs from the Straits of Mackinac in the north to Grand River in the south, and it was certified by Mackinac County clerk.[112]

The document was most likely written by Hamlin himself and self-serving phrases such as the chief's pledge to "ratify all his doing" tell us more about the young man's own insecurity than it does about how the Ottawa elders perceived his authority. New challenges demand new solutions, but like most people, then and now, the Ottawa found within their traditions the clay to shape something previously unknown. The elders appear to have folded two traditional leadership roles together to make use of Hamlin's unique talents. Chiefs, or as the Ottawa called them *ogima,* led largely by example. Their main job was to council with other elders and forge, if possible, a consensus among the people. *Ogima* were generally from special families. When one chief died the honor would be bestowed on one of this brothers, and only after them to the son. For that reason the power-of-attorney documents states that Hamlin was descended from a line of great chiefs and he was fit for a place of esteem. He was, however, still a very young man of unproven judgment and so it was doubtful the Ottawa would ever have recognized him as "head chief." Yet, there were another class of leaders known as *Kigdonine.* They were assistants to the chief, like an executive secretary. They were appointed by a chief and one of their main jobs was to do the chief's public speaking for him. The *Kigdonine*'s function was rhetorical; he was not a policymaker. It is likely that Hamlin was commissioned by the leading chiefs of northwestern Michigan to be a closely controlled spokesman, not the "head chief."[113]

Hamlin's rapid rise to prominence, from fatherless boy to honored counselor of the elders, proved to be a telling lesson for Andrew Blackbird. The twenty-two–year-old Hamlin owed his position to one thing, education. With the ability to read and write the white man's language, Hamlin possessed skills that were rare among his people. More important than the knowledge to translate, however, was his ability to interact with

European-Americans and to understand their social and political norms. This was a role of importance that may have excited the imagination of young Andrew Blackbird. As the boy grew to be a man, the example of Augustin Hamlin, and the memory of his brother William, offered lessons of a life he might lead.

Hamlin's first actions as "leader" of the Ottawa revealed his inexperience. He tried to freeze out of the councils of the Ottawa the fur trader John A. Drew. Drew, with his partner Edward Biddle, was the most active merchant along the Little Traverse coast. He had a kinship connection to the Ottawa through his marriage to an *Anishnabe* woman from nearby Cheboygan Rapids. Biddle and Drew had a deep interest in any prospective treaty between the Ottawa and the United States. The partners claimed that the Ottawa and Chippewa owed them $50,000 in unpaid credits for goods advanced to Indian hunters. This vested interest may have inclined Hamlin to resent Drew's involvement in Ottawa affairs, but the young man made a potent enemy in the veteran trader. Drew used his long relationship with Ottawa leaders to sow distrust of Hamlin's judgment. "Christians and heathens," a Catholic missionary reported, "disagree more than ever, because they are secretly influenced by Drew, who has made them suspicious of treachery from Hamlin." Rather than patching relations with Drew, Hamlin inflamed things further by attempting to recruit a young Catholic trader to set up a post at L'Arbre Croche. Drew skillfully squashed that threat by prevailing upon Henry Schoolcraft to refuse to grant the man a trading license.[114]

In the end it was Schoolcraft who was the biggest obstacle before Hamlin. The agent refused to deal with Hamlin as the official spokesman of the Ottawa or to even accept him as a useful cultural broker. Schoolcraft dismissed Hamlin as "a mere youth, the son of a French half breed trader."[115] If anyone was going to broker a deal between the *Anishnabeg* and the United States, Schoolcraft was determined he would. He regarded it as his primary job to be the interpreter of the Indian's needs to Washington and to be the one to reconcile the Ottawa and Chippewa to United States policy.

Hamlin and Schoolcraft should have been friends. The Indian agent was deeply interested in *Anishnabeg* culture and history. He was engaged in the arts and sciences. Hamlin was one of the best-educated men in the upper Great Lakes region and he shared Schoolcraft's interest in languages. But Schoolcraft's haughty demeanor played upon Hamlin's insecurity as a young mixed-blooded man. More importantly, Schoolcraft's paternalistic confidence that he knew what was best for the *Anishnabeg* clashed with the Ottawa's determination to manage their own affairs. From the beginning Hamlin and Schoolcraft worked at cross-purposes. This was particularly apparent in the fall of 1835 when Hamlin's speech against Schoolcraft helped to turn the L'Arbre Croche council against Schoolcraft's treaty overtures.

At the fall council Hamlin did more than denounce Schoolcraft as a dishonest obstructionist; he also announced that he had his own plan of action. "I wish to help you and not see you imposed upon," Hamlin assured the council. Skillfully playing his role as cultural broker, he recommended making use of another influential white man to help the Ottawa open direct communication with Washington, Bishop Frederic Rese of the Detroit diocese. "Whatever I say and do for you, I am aided in it by the Bishop," he told the council. "He is strong, he is great." More importantly the bishop had agreed to intervene to assure the survival of his most successful Indian mission. With great self-satisfaction Hamlin informed the council, "He will furnish us with seven hundred dollars, if you will go with me to see your Great Father."[116]

This news produced an immediate effect. The Ottawa's long-delayed plans to deal directly with the president suddenly became possible. A delegation consisting of Apokisigan, Mackadepenessy, and Hamlin was selected to visit the bishop in Detroit and to open direct communication with the president. There must have been considerable discussion among the Ottawa leaders concerning their negotiating strategy.

A memorial sent to the secretary of war, Lewis Cass, in December 1835 reflects the aims of the Ottawa mission to Washington. Their first and foremost goal was to dispel the dark cloud cast by the United States' removal policy. "It is a heart-rending thought to our simple feelings to think of leaving our native country forever," Hamlin wrote for the chiefs, "the lands where the bones of our forefathers lay thick in the earth; the land which has drank, and which has been bought with the price of, their native blood, and which has been there after transmitted to us." The treasured scenes of the Little Traverse shore, Hamlin wrote, "make the *soul shrink with horror* at the idea of rejecting our country forever—the mortal remains of our deceased parents, relations, and friends, cry out to us as it were, For our compassion, our sympathies and our love."[117]

But as much as the Ottawa loved their land of lakes and forests, they understood from long experience that goodwill from the Americans came at the price of land. "We do not wish to sell all the lands claimed by us and consequently not to remove to the west of the Mississippi." However, Hamlin continued, "if the government wishes, we might sell some Islands on Lake Michigan, and also our claims (with some reservations) on the North side of the Straits of Michilimackinac, a tract of land beginning somewhere near the Menominees on the west and terminating at Pt de Tour on the east." The Ottawa elders likely regarded this offer as only an opening wager in the negotiations. As for the offer of the land north of Mackinac, the Ottawa had no right to make such an offer, as the territory was almost entirely inhabited by Chippewa bands. Nonetheless, the offer indicates the Ottawa's willingness to enter into a discussion on land cessions.[118]

The reason why the Ottawa were willing to negotiate for a cession was their desire to have the time to continue undisturbed on the path of cultural change that they had initiated with their Catholic missionaries. Hamlin bluntly wrote, "We Indians cannot long remain peaceably and happily in this place where the tribe is at present if we persist in preserving that way and manner of life which we have hitherto loved," because that lifestyle was "incompatible with that of civilized man: and therefore we would wish to exchange the former for the latter." Having started on the "pleasing path" of "civilized" life, the Ottawa planned to "advance more and more on it." The boldest feature of the Ottawa's plan for the future was their vision of eventually becoming citizens of the United States. "With these things in view, we propose to submit ourselves to the Laws of that country within whose limits we reside." The Ottawa, however, understood the implications of the Michigan Territory's impending statehood and its potential impact on their government-to-government relations with Washington. They added to their pledge to work toward citizenship the caveat that although the Ottawa were not at present ready to "submit themselves to the laws of that State," they were "confident . . . that when the benefits of civilization would become generally diffused among them they would embrace those salutary regulations with cheerfulness."[119]

A key goal for the Ottawa in any negotiations with the United States was to "obtain some assistance from the government" in completing the transformation they had already begun. To do this they needed "implements of husbandry, and a fund for procuring things in this line." They also sought expanded aid "in the education of our young people and children in the necessary and useful branches of arts and sciences."[120]

In sum, the Ottawa of L'Arbre Croche had developed a strategy for coping with American expansion and to implement that strategy they were seeking to enter into treaty negotiations with the government of President Andrew Jackson. The Catholic Ottawa were behind the formation of a delegation to go to Washington, but it is unlikely that this action was taken without the general concurrence of most of the Ottawa leaders, Catholic and non-Catholic alike. Simply put, the Ottawa needed more time to adapt to the changed circumstances of the Great Lakes region. For some Ottawa, time was needed to simply make an economic change, away from the fur trade and toward a greater reliance on farming and fishing. For others, time was needed to continue a more fundamental change that would incorporate aspects of European-American culture. The only way to buy more time for both groups was to cede land. The delegation sent to Washington in the fall of 1835 was entrusted with the awful responsibility to trade beloved land for dearly needed time.

Embarking on that mission Apokisigan, Mackadepenessy, Augustin Hamlin, and the young men accompanying them as paddlers could easily be mistaken for one of the war parties that had in the past set out from L'Arbre Croche each fall. Instead of seeking honor and captives in a raid upon the Dakota, this group were warriors for peace who hoped to bring educational assistance and the promise of citizenship back to their people. There were no war cries heard on the beach that day; rather the men bowed their heads and said out loud the Lord's Prayer. Around them were a small circle of family and friends who, with tears in their eyes, crossed themselves at the prayer's end. The Ottawa were finally going to meet the American Father. Mackadepenessy must have been more than a bit apprehensive. Before him was a journey on the often stormy autumnal inland seas into the heart of the white American world. With so much on his mind, did Mackadepenessy look for his wild young son among those saying good-bye? The boy was there, but typically he was apart. Andrew Blackbird "was clear up at the top" of a tree that overlooked the departure point. He clung to his precarious perch for more than an hour watching, the canoe becoming smaller with each paddle stroke, the shape of his father less distinct, "until they disappeared in rounding the point."[121]

3

A New World

On March 14, 1836, Mackadepenessy finally met the "American father." He and twenty-three other *Anisanabeg* were ushered into the White House, where they were received by Andrew Jackson. White haired, grave, and tall, the president in his black suit cut an impressive figure. Mackadepenessy knew little about Jackson's record as an "Indian fighter" and probably had only a vague understanding of his administration's fierce adherence to the policy of Indian removal. What Mackadepenessy had long appreciated was that Jackson was the man who could speak with final authority for the Americans, and that he was the one with whom the Ottawa had to build a bond of friendship, such as that they had known in the past with the "French father" or the "British father."

The meeting with Jackson reinforced Mackadepenessy's growing understanding of how numerous and prosperous the Americans were. This was something he had been told and it is something that he had known intellectually, but seeing the centers of American power for himself brought a deeper and perhaps more depressing realization. The long journey east had taken him through scores of towns and cities any number of which exceeded the entire Indian population of the Michigan Territory. The power disparity between the Ottawas and the Americans, which was apparent even on the remote Great Lakes frontier, was awesomely realized by Mackadepenessy when he entered the American capital. The imposing buildings of stone, the bustle of pedestrians on the muddy streets of Washington, D.C., and the constant cacophony of carriages, crowds, and construction was new and disturbing. He had traveled widely in the West, but Mackadepenessy never knew the power of the Americans until he visited the "Great Father's" village. He and the other chiefs were as voyageurs entering a new world. The treaty negotiation that brought them to the capital would go far toward determining their place in that new world.[1]

"The President received them handsomely," an observer noted. Mackadepenessy and the other delegates each shook hands with Andrew Jackson. One of the *Anishnabeg* delegates, probably Augustin Hamlin, then delivered a formal speech to the president. His remarks were deemed an "eloquent address," unfortunately; no record was made of what was said. At that point the president terminated the audience. Mackadepenessy may have been disappointed that there would be no negotiation with Jackson. Instead of negotiating with the president or even his respected secretary of war, Lewis Cass, the Indian delegates from Michigan were forced to accept that the treaty process would begin the next day under the supervision of Henry Rowe Schoolcraft. For Mackadepenessy, Apokisigan, and the other Ottawa present the long-awaited meeting with the president was as deflating as it was brief. Their presidential audience made clear that there would be no bond of trust established between the Ottawa and the "American father." Unlike the British and the French, the Americans did not see the *Anishnabeg* as allies and partners. They did not care what was in Indian hearts, only how much land would be ceded. The Ottawa had journeyed all the way to Washington only to be forced to negotiate with a man from Michigan they did not trust. It was a sad indication of where they stood with the United States government.[2]

THE TREATY OF 1836

The 1836 Treaty of Washington was the most important agreement the Indian peoples of western and northern Michigan ever made with the United States. It was the contradictory document that both set the stage for their potential removal from Michigan and at the same time was the basis for their eventual persistence in the state. It was a deeply flawed agreement that was fated to be very shortly undermined by events on the ground, yet paradoxically it proved to be the legal taproot of tribal rights for the Ottawa and Chippewa people well into the twenty-first century. Like so many agreements between the United States and the native people of the Great Lakes region, this treaty was an instrument of European-American hegemony whose primary purpose was to separate Indian people from their land. At the same time, this treaty also provided a legal framework and political opportunity so that Ottawa and Chippewa people could continue to live within their culture.

To the disgust of the Ottawa, Henry Rowe Schoolcraft was the key man in making the treaty. Schoolcraft stood with one foot in the eroded middle ground of the frontier and the other in the dynamic world of Jacksonian America. Since 1820 he had lived on the northern fringe of the Michigan Territory. He served as Indian agent first at Sault Ste. Marie and later at Mackinac Island. The Chippewa were more than his job, however; they were also part of his extended family. In 1823 he married Jane Johnston, the mixed-blood child of a union between an Irish fur trader and the daughter of a distinguished Chippewa chief. Through Jane, Schoolcraft learned the customs, traditions, and language of the Chippewa. In Schoolcraft the old tradition continued of a blood relationship binding the *Anishnabeg* and their European-American interlocutors. Yet for all that, Schoolcraft was very different than the frontier intermediaries of the past. He was firmly rooted in the American world, serving not only as a federal official, but from 1828 to 1832 in the Michigan Territorial Legislature. He was a successful author with aspirations for a scientific and literary career and a staunch Democrat with hopes for bureaucratic advancement. Ambition pushed him to lead an exploring party in 1832 to the source of the Mississippi River as well as to maintain an extensive correspondence with scientists from throughout the United States and Europe and to send a steady stream of unsolicited policy papers to politicians in the capital. Schoolcraft was well aware of the importance of what he was doing for both his Chippewa in-laws and his career.[3]

Schoolcraft convened the *Anishnabeg* delegates on March 18 in Washington, D.C.'s old Masonic Hall. Located near Capitol Hill, the hall had often been used to house government meetings. The Chippewa leaders were seated together in a row of chairs; facing them were Mackadepenessy and the Ottawa chiefs. "There were about twenty-five Indian chiefs," a journalist noted, "a few of them old, but the greater part of them young men, the length of the journey having in general, deterred most of the old chiefs from coming in person." While the government had purchased new clothes for most of the delegates, the Ottawa chose to appear, as one of their number was described, in "full Indian costume, with his face painted, and his hair queerly arranged." Apokisigan, the baptized Catholic, was described as "so very unchristian that a dozen Chiefs like him would frighten an army of grenadiers with mustaches." Comparing the two groups of Indians, one American wrote: "Any one would have supposed the Ottawas a far more destitute, degraded, and neglected race than the Chippewas, who are even dressed (one of them in particular) more *buckish* than a New York beau."[4] Between the Ottawa and Chippewa delegations was a table upon which was a map of the Michigan Territory. At the front of the room, clearly presiding over the two delegations, sat Henry Rowe Schoolcraft and the interpreter,

John Holiday. Also present were a handful of other white people, some from the War Department; most, however, were men and women from Michigan with a stake in the treaty. The "negotiation" was a public proceeding and throughout the council members of the citizenry drifted in and out of the hall, gawking at the Indian dignitaries or simply observing firsthand the workings of American expansion. At one point, a school group was ushered into the hall to give the youngsters a chance to see real western Indians.[5]

Throughout the treaty council the atmosphere in the Masonic Hall was tinged with bluish clouds of tobacco smoke. The council began with the ceremonial smoking of the peace pipe and all through the deliberations the *Anishnabeg* councilors kept their pipes burning. Tobacco was more than an indulgence for them. It was also a substance blessed with sacred power. Therefore, for the same reasons the United States Congress began its sessions with a formal prayer, the Ottawa and Chippewa began all important meetings with the smoking of a pipe.

Rising in the smoke-filled room, Henry Rowe Schoolcraft, the treaty commissioner, began the council by outlining the terms proposed by the United States government. "You have heard the voice of your great father the President, and shaken hands with him," Schoolcraft began. "You perceive his kind feelings for you, and your families." He then went on to declare that the United States proposed that they cede all of their lands on the Lower Peninsula of Michigan north of the Grand River and continuing westward across the Upper Peninsula as far as the Chocolate River—near present-day Marquette, Michigan. "For such cessions as you may agree to make, I am authorized to make you the most liberal offer." This would include money to pay the Indians' debts to fur traders and funds for agricultural assistance. The Ottawa and Chippewa bands could determine to create reservations for themselves within the ceded territory, although Schoolcraft announced that the personal reservations to individual Indian leaders or to white friends of the Indians that had often been the feature of past treaties would not be accepted by the United States in this treaty. The *Anishnabeg* would also be granted the "usual" temporary right to reside upon and hunt on the ceded lands "till they are wanted." Schoolcraft instructed the *Anishnabeg,* "How much you will cede, depends upon your wisdom. Deliberate on the subject with calm minds, and with kind feelings towards each other and do not let one party cast blame on the other. It is only noble minds which can rise above little things." The Indian delegates requested three days to deliberate on the government's proposal.[6]

The basic outline of the treaty as proposed by Schoolcraft did not surprise the Ottawa and Chippewa leaders. During the months prior to their arrival in Washington, these terms had been presented to the chiefs by federal officials in Michigan. But knowing the terms and accepting them were two different things. The three days that followed the opening treaty session were marked by a furious round of lobbying and negotiation. These acrimonious sessions were likely held at the Indian Queen Hotel, a large rambling establishment located midway between the Capitol Building and the White House. Named for its large swinging sign that bore a colorful depiction of Pocahontas, the hotel was one of the Office of Indian Affairs' preferred locations to house its delegations of visiting Indians.[7] Hanging to the belts of the official delegations, however, were scores of uninvited interested parties who did their best to influence the Ottawa and Chippewa and bend the treaty to their personal benefit.

As the Ottawa and Chippewa leaders attempted to discuss Schoolcraft's proposed treaty, they were constantly interrupted. Fur traders John Drew and Rix Robinson, men appointed by the government to conduct delegations of *Anishnabeg* to the capital, participated in the deliberations as trusted advisors. John Holiday, an American Fur Company fur trader who served as the treaty's official interpreter, was also likely present when the Ottawa and Chippewa attempted to reach agreement. In addition to these "official" participants, however, were the other white fur traders who broke into the private councils and, as Augustin Hamlin later complained, "often called out [of the room] sometime one,—then two and as many as *six* had been called at one time." The chiefs button-holed in this manner were pressed to insist upon treaty provisions such as private reservations of land for various fur traders and mixed-blood relations or the full payment of all unpaid debts claimed against the Indians.[8]

Past Indian treaties had provided a financial windfall for fur traders by appropriating from the money Indians were awarded for the sale of their lands funds for the payment of all debts incurred by the Indians in the course of their participation in the fur trade. Fur traders with the longest and largest involvement in the trade had the biggest interest in seeing these debt claims paid in full. Smaller traders or traders now moving into other areas of economic activity had less money at stake and were more concerned with quickly receiving the treaty windfall. Therefore, the white "councilors" were divided in their advice to the Indians. They all wanted the treaty of cession to eventually be made, but the large traders, men such those involved with the giant American Fur Company, were willing to stall the negotiations indefinitely if they could not get the treaty terms they wanted. The smaller, independent traders, some of whom were also in Washington, wanted a treaty at all costs, as soon as possible. The American Fur Company was particularly opposed to Schoolcraft's offer because it included a threatening innovation in Indian treaty terms. Instead of the traders simply being paid the debts they claimed, the United States proposed that all debts be reviewed by an independent commission. Debts that could not be documented or those incurred in the sale of illegal items such as alcohol were likely to be rejected. With more than $30,000 at stake the American Fur Company pressed the Indian leaders very hard to reject the offer.[9]

The Ottawa and Chippewa leaders did not view the whites simply as self-interested or greedy. Most of the fur traders were kinsmen who had families who were both American and Indian. They were also men with whom they had conducted a valuable, life- sustaining trade for many years. As the *Anishnabeg* looked to a future in which they would interact more with Americans, old friends who knew both worlds would be more valuable than ever. When the traders advised rejecting Schoolcraft's offer and holding out for better terms, Mackadepenessy was among those who accepted their advice.

The Indians themselves were as divided as the traders were regarding the proposed treaty. The L'Arbre Croche Ottawa and the Sault Ste. Marie Chippewa were committed to making a major land cession in order to avoid removal and to attain the economic benefits offered by Schoolcraft. The Grand River Ottawa, however, were opposed to a land cession. Their villages were on the edge of the advancing line of American settlements and rightly they feared being dispossessed of their homeland. They, however, were not united in their approach to the treaty. Some of the Grand River Ottawa were affiliated with the Baptist mission of the Reverend Leonard Slater. Others were communicants of the rival Catholic mission founded by Father Fredric Baraga. The Grand River Christians, as devoted as they were to their lands, were vulnerable to the temptation of economic assistance a treaty could offer.

The lobbying of the fur traders and the divisions among the Indians surfaced when the treaty council was reconvened on March 18, 1836. The first speaker was the Grand River Ottawa leader Muckatosha. He was a pragmatic man straining to protect his people's best interests, yet he was painfully aware that the onrush of European-American settlements required creative leadership. He personally explored the Christian doctrines introduced by Leonard Slater and Father Baraga, attending at various times services at both missions. He was anxious to tell Schoolcraft that he and the other Grand River leaders were opposed to sale of their lands. Pointing to the map of the Michigan Territory before them, Muckatosha said, "When we look on the map of our country it appears very small and we conclude not to part with any of our lands." The Grand River chiefs had only come to Washington because "they had been called by their Great Father" and because they were deeply suspicious of what the L'Arbre Croche Ottawa had proposed to the Americans. Yet for all that, Muckatosha did not really believe that he could prevent a treaty of cession. He betrayed this sentiment when he complained to Schoolcraft about the government's refusal to make land grants to Indian's mixed-blood relatives and their white friends.

> One reason why we do not wish to dispose of our lands, is this, we fear the whites, who will not be our friends, will come into our country and trouble us and that we shall be able to know where our possessions are. If we do sell our land, it will be our wish that some of our white friends have lands among us and associated with us.

Another Grand River chief, Megiss Ininee, quickly seconded Muckatosha, objecting to the participation of the Chippewa in the conference, complaining about the lack of land grants to "white friends," condemning the L'Arbre Croche leaders for precipitating the cession, and concluding with a firm affirmation "not to sell any" land.[10]

This second Grand River complaint about the L'Arbre Croche Ottawa did not sit well with Apokisigan. He and Mackadepenessy had led the earlier delegation to Washington about which the Grand River chiefs had expressed such suspicion. He was unashamed that he was in favor of trading land to avoid removal and to receive financial assistance. He rose to his feet and responded to Megiss Ininee indirectly by saying to Schoolcraft: "I wish to say that some chiefs present have sold lands and have benefited, but as for myself and my people, we have not received so much as one pipe of Tobacco." In this way Apokisigan reminded the Grand River Ottawa that they had already ceded half their lands at the 1821 Treaty of Chicago and that they had the benefit of educational and technical assistance unknown to the L'Arbre Croche band. Apokisigan went on to say that he was fully "satisfied" with the government's proposals.[11]

Apokisigan's rebuttal, however, lost all of its bite when Mackadepenessy unexpectedly rose to his feet and disagreed with his longtime friend. For thirteen years Mackadepenessy and Apokisigan had cooperated on transforming Ottawa society and religion. Although he had earlier been a supporter of the plan to trade land for time, he declared to the council that "he was opposed to the sale of their lands." Mackadepenessy offered no explanation for this stunning reversal and closed by saying, "At another time he would say more on this subject." The announcement must have surprised

Treaty Commissioner Schoolcraft. Mackadepenessy's defection threatened the possibility that he could acquire all of the lands north of the Grand River. The L'Arbre Croche Ottawa's willingness to make a deal had been the engine behind the treaty. When Schoolcraft heard Mackadepenessy's words he must have detected the sound of that engine sputtering and he scrambled to restore the treaty's momentum.

Forcefully he chastised the Ottawas. With words dripping with condescension Schoolcraft accused them of having rejected the president of the United States' plan "to do them good" and because of that it was "uncertain when he would listen to them again." Turning to the Chippewa, Schoolcraft asked them if they would accept or reject the president's terms. "Your Father has thought of you," he said; "he knows your situation, that you are poor, that but little game is to be found, and that you obtain less and less every year, notwithstanding your country is of little value, yet feeling a desire to benefit you, he thinks your lands may be of some value to him, on these account a proposition will be made to the Chippewa on Tuesday next at this place to purchase their lands in the north Peninsula." The commissioner guaranteed that he would accept no cession except from "the rightful owners of the soil." The Ottawa, said Schoolcraft, could likewise have the weekend to reconsider their rejection of the treaty. He closed by asking rhetorically if the Ottawa would "not feel ashamed at seeing their Chippewa brothers, in possession of many goods, and much money and themselves entirely destitute and very poor." This appeal to intertribal rivalry was clever, particularly because Schoolcraft knew the Chippewa delegation—led by his wife's uncle—was committed to making a treaty of cession.[12]

The prospect of the Ottawa being frozen out of the treaty settlement was too much for Augustin Hamlin to bear. He had worked for more than a year to make such an agreement. Speaking to Schoolcraft in English, a language most of the Indian leaders did not understand, Hamlin complained that "the words the Commissioner had just heard from the Chiefs, were not their words, not the feelings of their hearts—but the words of white men who wanted reservations, and have dictated to them what to say." The chiefs, according to Hamlin, had never been left alone to properly deliberate on the proposed treaty terms. Instead white men "instructed" them to "say *No,* once, twice, and thrice in order that they might obtain more for their lands." Hamlin pledged that if the *Anishnabeg* were left undisturbed in their councils, they would readily agree to a cession. These words were then translated for the benefit of the Indian leaders. The council was adjourned till March 22 and the Indians were provided with private rooms for their deliberations.[13]

There is no record of what was said among the Ottawa and Chippewa during the long weekend that followed. It would seem that the acrimony and suspicion among the bands subsided and slowly the traditional commitment to consensual action began to assert itself. It is likely that in conjunction with trusted whites invited into the council chambers, the chiefs began to work out the likely practical impact of Schoolcraft's treaty provisions. They no doubt hoped that the cession of their vast lands in upper and lower Michigan would be appreciated as a gesture of friendship to the United States. The opportunity to choose reservations for their own future use ensured their persistence in Michigan and served as a guarantee against the dreaded prospect of forced removal. The financial payments from the cession were a chance to pay their fur trade creditors. With the debts removed traditionalists could use the payments to subsidize their continued involvement in the fur trade and the seasonal round. Those *Anishnabeg* interested in changing their culture and economy could use the treaty payments for that purpose. It is very likely that at this time some of the *Anishnabeg,* perhaps after discussions with missionaries, also began to consider the use of treaty money to purchase land as private citizens. Another important provision of the government's treaty offer was a clause common in Indian land cession treaties that allowed the Indians to continue to occupy the ceded lands until they were needed for white settlement. This meant that save for a few villages in the Grand River valley that were located in the path of the advancing farmer's frontier, few Ottawa or Chippewa would be affected by the cession for several years to come. The Ottawa and Chippewa leaders understood the dire long-term prospects of the cession, but they were attracted by its promise of much-needed immediate assistance.

There were also external factors that also likely influenced the chief's decisions. It had not been the government's initial intention to have them come to Washington, D.C., but in the end the large bustling city with its array of busy public buildings may have been the government's best argument for the treaty. While the Ottawa were in the city, the Senate debated the controversial Treaty of New Echota. This was a removal treaty that the United States had forced upon the Cherokee people. It had to be a disturbing backdrop for the *Anishnabeg* delegates. It certainly was a reminder, as was the city itself, of the vast power of the American nation and how easily that power could be turned against them. Another issue of which the chiefs were aware was the fierce debate in Congress over Michigan's impending statehood. White Americans were already in the process of creating a new government for Michigan's future, which could only have impressed upon the Ottawa and Chippewa their own need to come to terms with the United States.

When the council reconvened, the Ottawa and Chippewa leaders had formed a united position. They would cede their lands to the United States in return for sizable reservations. Schoolcraft proposed that they agree to 100,000 acres "to be located in two places, by the Chiefs after their return home." The Ottawa, however, wanted to know exactly what land would be reserved, and at their insistence the negotiation continued for four more days during which each band marked out their reserve. As a result the amount of land reserved more than doubled and included a 50,000-acre tract on Little Traverse Bay. Apokisigan, Mackadepenessy, and the other Ottawa leaders achieved a great coup by pressing that this matter be dealt with in detail, for from those details came a major increase in their reservations. Mackadepenessy could now return home having guaranteed Ottawa title to their treasured home along the L'Arbre Croche coast as well as access to rich financial benefits.[14]

On March 28, 1836, the Indian leaders signed the draft treaty. According to a newspaper report the Indian leaders were in high spirits. Perhaps as a release from the tension and anxiety of the past weeks, they began to exchange jokes with the Americans present. The Americans, the *Anishnabeg* confessed were, privately referred to by the name "the people with hats." Interspersed with the jocularity were small requests by some chiefs for gifts. Gesturing to a group of bonneted white ladies observing the treaty process from the gallery, one of the Indian men joked that "the people with hats ought to present each of the young men with a squaw!" This was regarded by the newspaper correspondent as a "piece of fun."[15]

THE UNRAVELING OF THE TREATY OF 1836

Back in Michigan, on the wave-washed shores of Little Traverse Bay, relief mixed with apprehension in the wake of Mackadepenessy and Apokisigan's return. The Ottawa understood that the treaty they had signed was just a piece of paper until it was approved by the United States Senate. As spring gave way to summer disturbing rumors wafted from lodge to lodge at L'Arbre Croche, carried on the cool Lake Michigan breeze from Mackinac Island. The Senate, it was said, had rejected the Washington treaty and a forced removal to the west was being planned by the Americans. Missionary Father John DeBruyn wrote to his bishop of rumors that "the Indian agreement will not obtain the sanction of the Senate, and so the Indians will, within 20 days, meet at Mackinac where it will be proposed that they, after

50 days depart from the territory." DeBruyn requested Bishop Rese prepare to intervene on the Ottawa's behalf. So powerful was the rumor that some L'Arbre Croche residents began to plan to relocate to the British side of the border to avoid forced removal by the United States.[16]

The rumor of removal may well have been a calculated manipulation, floated by American officials to panic the *Anishnabeg*. The Senate had in fact approved the treaty, but not before drastically altering it. The Committee on Indian Affairs had used to the Senate's power to "advise and consent" on treaties to change the status of the reservations set aside for the Indians. Instead of those lands being reserved in perpetuity for Ottawa and Chippewa use, they were to be held for a mere five years. Where the original document offered voluntary removal at federal expense to *Anishnabeg* who wished to move to forested lands west of Lake Superior, the revised treaty specified the arid plains of Kansas as the "place for the final settlement of said Indians." The Senate revisions changed the agreement from one that guaranteed the Ottawa persistence in their homeland to one that set the stage for removal to an alien environment.[17]

Mackadepenessy and the other Ottawa delegates must have felt shocked and betrayed. Only in comparison to the rumors of removal at bayonet point in a matter of weeks, could the *Anishnabeg* view Senate revisions optimistically. Schoolcraft himself was dismayed by the changes. He complained the revisions "violated the very principle" on which the cession had been made. In truth, however, the revisions brought the treaty in line with the Jackson administration's removal policy. The disconcerted Schoolcraft was forced to call for a convocation of Ottawa and Chippewa band leaders to be held on Mackinac Island in mid-July. Here the revised treaty was explained and the *Anishnabeg* leaders were asked to assent to or reject the treaty.[18]

Not surprisingly, Schoolcraft found most of the chiefs "strenuously opposed" to the Senate's insistence that they give up their reservations after five years. Apokisigan, a leader of the Catholic Ottawa, left Mackinac Island disgusted with Schoolcraft and complaining of the perfidy of the United States government. Some Ottawa were angered enough to quit American territory altogether, and they made plans to relocate to the British side of the Great Lakes borderland. Mackadepenessy, however, stayed and for two days he debated with the other remaining leaders how they might salvage something from the treaty process.[19]

The revised agreement still contained a provision that they could live on all ceded land until it was "required for settlement." Since the frontier of white settlement was still very far from L'Arbre Croche, this offered indefinite protection from removal. The treaty still offered $600,000 in annuities to be paid out over the next twenty years. Those funds would be key to educating the rising generation of Ottawa and to complete the "civilization" program already begun. Annuity payments also offered another avenue to secure their continued residence in northern Michigan. The Ottawa could purchase land and protect their homeland as private property owners. There is no evidence that this prospect was discussed at Mackinac Island, but landownership was something that some Ottawa had already begun to explore.[20]

Among the leaders Mackadepenessy consulted with at Mackinac was his nephew Ogemainini, known to the Americans as Joseph Wakaso.[21] Young Wakaso was the leader of an Ottawa band of fifty families that spent their summers at the Little Traverse settlement of Middle Village and wintered a couple hundred miles to the south in Allegan County, probably along the Black and Kalamazoo rivers. At the time of the debate over the revised treaty, Wakaso was deeply involved in plans to secure private title to the wintering grounds. In April 1836 he sent a petition to the president and Congress requesting a grant of public land for his band. He carefully explained that he did not want a reservation, because "we will be obliged to sell at some future time, whether we wish or not." Instead he wanted the federal government to give title to a portion of the public domain in Allegan County, "so that we can feel secure of maintaining our rights in Courts of Justice, as the White Man, who holds the President's patent on his farm." According to Chief Wakaso all the members of his band were "unanimous" in their desire to hold private title to their land as well as to have "Schools, Churches, and Roads." Only in this way, he wrote, will "the poor Indian at last feel that he has a home, and that he may lay his bones where he will feel that the bones of his descendents for ages to come will." This petition was endorsed with the signatures of seventy white settlers of Allegan County who welcomed making the Ottawa band permanent residents of their community.[22]

At the treaty council Wakaso and Mackadepenessy supported accepting the revised treaty since it offered a path to secure their homes as property owners under the "Laws, Government, and Jurisdiction of the United States."[23] Property would carry with it rights that could not be taken away at the whim of Indian agents or the Senate. It would not be until 1839 that Wakaso was successful in obtaining land for his people. When he acquired land it was by cash purchase, using annuities, at the General Land Office in Ionia, Michigan. By that time the people of L'Arbre Croche also had money set aside to begin a large program of land purchase.[24] The fact that most of the Ottawa and Chippewa bands used their annuities to make land purchases in the 1840s, when the lands became available for sale, supports this interpretation of why so many *Anishnabeg* leaders embraced the revised

1836 treaty. What is known for certain is that Wakaso (Ogemainini) and Mackadepenessy both signed the government's Articles of Assent, accepting the treaty for their people.[25]

The ability of the Ottawa and Chippewa to resist the treaty was undermined by a series of hardships between late 1835 and the summer of 1836. Poor hunting, crop failures, and disease stalked the *Anishnabeg.*[26] By August hungry Indian families began to set up their wigwams on the rocky beaches of Mackinac Island in anticipation of the delivery of $150,000 in "goods and provisions" secured by the treaty. As was so often the case in future years, the government was late in forwarding the funds and supplies to the Michigan frontier. Families were forced to wait for several weeks, in some cases an entire month. Initially a number of Mackinac traders sought to cash in on the anticipated payment by plying the Ottawa and Chippewa with liquor. Offered on credit to each newly arriving family, the liquor produced "scenes of rioting and drunkenness." To their credit Schoolcraft and many of the Indian leaders who had made the treaty sought to moderate the abuse and they succeeded in stopping the sale of alcohol. A New Yorker visiting the island contended that in the final two weeks before the payment was made "not an instance is known of a drunken Indian."[27]

The 1836 treaty payment brought to Mackinac Island the largest gathering of Indian peoples in the history of the storied Straits region. Schoolcraft estimated 4,000 Ottawa and Chippewa people, including children. The government provided $2,000 worth of flour, corn, rice, and pork to keep the multitude fed during their stay. All the Indians had "free access" to the stores and shops of Mackinac. The treaty allotted up to $300,000 to pay the accumulated debts of the *Anishnabeg,* so new credit was eagerly extended by all merchants. When the payment was finally made the heads of households stepped forward to claim their share of the $42,000 cash annuity that was divided on a per capita basis. Men such as Mackadepenessy, who were recognized by the Americans as chiefs, received an additional payment. All of these payments were made in silver coin, a rare commodity on the frontier where barter had long been the standard of exchange. On top of the cash payments, the treaty stipulated that 6,500 pounds of tobacco was to be distributed to the Indians and a staggering $150,000 worth of goods and provisions.[28]

In fact, too much wealth was placed into the hands of a people who had in recent years only known increasing poverty. The excess led to waste and a sense in young Andrew Blackbird of a patrimony squandered. Writing years after the great convocation of his people, Andrew Blackbird recorded that the chiefs complained that "there was a great deal of waste in distributing the goods among them, as there were lots of remnants, and much of it left after the distribution which they never knew what became of." According to Blackbird, the chiefs held a council and determined to ask Schoolcraft to stop the full distribution of the $150,000 in goods, as it was much more than was needed. In the *Anishnabeg's* opinion, $10,000 in goods was more than enough for a single payment and the rest should have been held back for the future or converted to cash. Blackbird left the payment suspicious that Schoolcraft and other government officials "had appropriated to themselves some of these dry goods and given away freely to their white friends and relatives."[29] Not surprisingly Schoolcraft's *Memoirs* recorded a different outcome. "The Indians went away with their canoes literally loaded with all an Indian wants, from silver to a steel trap."[30]

THE NEW WORLD: BLACKBIRD, THE OTTAWA, AND THE GREAT LAKES FRONTIER

For the Catholic community of L'Arbre Croche, the 1836 treaty included crucial benefits. For the next twenty years the bands covered by the treaty were to split a $5,000 annual education fund, a $3,000 annual missionary subsidy, $10,000 in annual agricultural assistance, and 500 wooden barrels a year to assist in making the transition to commercial fishing. These were the resources that Mackadepenessy and Apokisigan had sought to sustain the transition toward "civilization" they had initiated through their outreach to the Catholic Church.

In the wake of the treaty, priests and lay leaders in the L'Arbre Croche region sought to use these new resources to expand the education program. Government funds were used to operate schools at the core villages of La Croix (Cross Village), Middle Village (Good Hart), and New L'Arbre Croche (Harbor Springs). In addition to these establishments, the missionaries used personal and church funds to launch *Anishnabe* schools at Manistee, Grand Traverse, and Cheboygan.[31] The emphasis of instruction in all of these schools was on teaching the Ottawa and some Chippewa to read and write a European alphabet version of their own language. The primary goal of the missionaries was to allow their congregations to read the Catholic prayer book and sing hymns at mass. Therefore, most instruction was in the Ottawa language, a tongue the Catholic missionaries took much greater pains to learn than their Protestant rivals. In the words of François Pierz, who headed the L'Arbre Croche mission between 1839 and

1852, the goal was conservative, not liberal, education "to teach the children to read and write in the language of their fathers, and also the prayers and catechism." Young girls were also taught manual skills such as sewing. Only a handful of students, the unusually gifted and a number of adults, were taught French or English.[32] The result of this program was that a large number of young people were taught the fundamentals, such as their ABCs, and were able to read at a basic level. Yet, because instruction was in Ottawa it was difficult for students to advance farther because only a handful of prayer books and catechisms were available in that language. The strategy of teaching reading and writing in Ottawa was in accord with the 1836 treaty, which reserved some of the annual educational fund for "books in their own language." Secular books, however, were never produced. Nonetheless, the emphasis on written Ottawa ensured that literacy spread more quickly through the society, and it was not limited to a handful of gifted youngsters who could master English. By the 1840s the L'Arbre Croche schools were able to rely upon Ottawa men and women to assume some of the teaching duties. Ottawa taught Ottawa, and the "civilization" program at L'Arbre Croche grew from within the community. Education was not something that separated parents from their children, and literacy was not an alien practice imposed from outside the community.[33]

The "civilization" program's educational track broke down, however, when the time came for the students to move from learning to read and write Ottawa for religious reasons to learning English for political and economic advancement. Father François Pierz, who headed the mission, and his assistant Ignatius Mrak, while proficient in Slovene, German, Latin, French, and eventually Ottawa, were slow to learn English. They, like so many of the Catholic priests who labored in the Great Lakes missions, were immigrants from the Austrian Empire. As young men in Central Europe they had learned a number of languages, but as missionaries they struggled with learning both English and Ottawa, and understandably they put their emphasis on learning Ottawa. The Church had difficulty finding men and women who were proficient in English to teach at the isolated Indian schools. Augustin Hamlin had been educated in Rome for this purpose, but he clashed with Pierz. The missionary complained that Hamlin was a "good for nothing" who was "lazy" and lax in holding his classes in a regular manner. The fact that Hamlin demanded a higher wage for the heavy teaching load expected of him particularly angered Pierz, who regularly spent the bulk of his personal salary to pay teachers. Both men believed that federal officials starved them for funds, while providing lavish funding for the handful of Protestant mission schools. In 1850 Pierz, with some exaggeration, complained to his superiors that the Catholic missions on Lake Michigan had converted 3,000 Indians, while the most the Protestants could claim was 300 converts. The Catholics harbored deep suspicions that Protestant cliques in the government withheld from them their just share of the 1836 treaty monies.[34]

The shortcomings of the Catholic Church's "civilization" program gradually became apparent to parents and leaders at L'Arbre Croche. As early as 1839 some Ottawa parents started to take their children out of the local Catholic schools in search of English-language instruction. When Father Pierz exhorted them not to give up on learning, the parents shot back that "their children learn very little." The missionary was left to ruefully admit, "It is a pity there are no books [in Ottawa] to give the savages."[35] One of the reasons Wakaso's band relocated permanently from L'Arbre Croche to the Black River was because of their dissatisfaction with the Catholic teaching program and its slow approach to "civilization."[36]

When Mackadepenessy returned from the treaty negotiations in Washington, he was confronted with a challenge from the Catholic Church. The chief's relationship with the Church, which during the 1820s had been very strong, seems to have cooled following the death in Rome of his son William. His daughter Margaret had also been given to the Church for an education and after several years in a Cincinnati convent, she had returned to L'Arbre Croche, where she began a career as a teacher. During the spring of 1836 Margaret clashed with Magdelaine Laframboise, the redoubtable matriarch of Mackinac Island. Laframboise was a Ottawa-French-Canadian mixed blood who formerly had operated her own fur-trading business, and in her retirement had devoted herself to Catholic evangelical work. As a pillar of Mackinac society and as an indispensable supporter of Roman Catholicism, Madame Laframboise was not someone whom the missionaries could afford to cross. For unknown reasons Margaret Mackadepenessy felt that she was "wrongly handled by Madame LaFramboise." At the time Margaret was teaching the young girls of L'Arbre Croche, so it may have been a simple matter of the older woman disapproving of Margaret's classroom style. In any event Margaret, in what the priest called a moment of "youthful petulance," quit her teaching position and went to Mackinac Island to live with her sister. Mackadepenessy was dragged into the affair because the sister Margaret sought refuge with was living at the Presbyterian mission on the island. The Mackinac Mission of William and Amanda Ferry was an anathema to Catholic priests, but Mackadepenessy had respect for the Ferrys. His son William, prior going away for Catholic study, had learned English at the Mackinac boarding school. Father John DeBruyn tried to enlist Mackadepenessy to force Margaret to return to work at the Catholic school.[37]

When he pressured the chief to intervene, Father DeBruyn demonstrated that he seriously misunderstood both Mackadepenessy's relationship with his daughters and the traditional authority of an Ottawa father. The children of Mackadepenessy lived their own lives and he had no inclination to interfere. The daughter on Mackinac Island was a thirty-two-year-old woman who had been given the imposing mission name of Electa O. Hastings. She had attended the Ferrys' school from 1827 to 1832. Unlike most of the students, who were in their early teens, Electa was a full-grown woman. During her years as a student, she met and married the mission baker, Robert Gibson. With her marriage she became a member of the Mackinac white and mixed-blood community. When DeBruyn pressed Mackadepenessy, the latter let it be known that he intended "to give a section [of land] to his non-Catholic daughter and her non-Catholic husband."[38]

DeBruyn was deeply vexed by what he regarded as an affront to Church authority, although there was little he could do but "cite the father and daughter" from the pulpit. In time, Andrew Blackbird was drawn into the dispute. He had a boat that he used for fishing and trips up and down the lakeshore. Margaret, who was renowned for her personal warmth and generosity, was Andrew's favorite sibling. During her time at Mackinac, he visited her frequently. After DeBruyn failed to intimidate Margaret and Mackadepenessy, he "approached the brother of Margaret" and he demanded that the boy carry in his boat a load of "candles for the church" back to L'Arbre Croche. "Three times he refused," the priest reported, as much put out by the boy's independence as by the fact that his refusals were voiced openly "in front of Mr. [Edward] Biddle." DeBruyn speculated to the bishop that the boy "appeared to hide something," but it may have been no more than his anger at the priest.[39]

This incident of clerical intrusion into family business, coming when Andrew Blackbird was in his early teens, may have had major influence on the boy. The death of his much admired brother William and the lack of educational opportunities afforded him by the Catholic mission program may have turned Andrew away from the Roman Church. His sister Margaret soon patched things up with Father DeBruyn, who admitted the young teacher was "loved by many." She would remain a devout Catholic all her life. Andrew, however, began to explore other Christian denominations. It was at this time that Blackbird began to use the name Andrew Jackson. This entailed a rejection of Amable, the name given to him as part of his Catholic baptism. There is no way to know if this change was sparked by his feud with the Roman Church, or if it was spurred by a desire to be more strongly identified with the powerful United States government.

FARMER, FISHERMAN, SAILOR

His estrangement from one of the central institutions of his native village may have spurred Andrew Blackbird to leave home. It is likely that he made this move sometime in 1836 or 1837. In his history, he explained:

> At last I left Little Traverse when about 13 or 14 years age. I went to Green Bay, Wis., with the expectation of living with an older sister who had married a Scotchman named Gibson and had gone there to make a home somewhere in Green Bay. I found them, but I did not stay with them long.

For a boy of fourteen it must have been a lonely and intimidating journey. Blackbird wrote that his sister lived "somewhere in Green Bay" and that he "found them," which hints at what may well have been a trip of several anxious weeks. His arrival may not have been expected, nor may he have been entirely welcome, which would explain why he "did not stay with them long." This trip marked a bold departure in his life. It began a decade away from his L'Arbre Croche home. It was a time in which the boy who had lost his place in the village world of his ancestors explored the Anglo-American world.[40]

Andrew found his sister Electa living with her Scot in the little hamlet of Bay Settlement. The Gibsons were located among a group of French-Canadian and mixed-blood farmers, about six miles from Fort Howard, where the city of Green Bay would later rise. After a brief time living in the home of his sister, Andrew secured his first job. He signed on as a farm laborer for a man "whose name was Sylvester." With this step he entered the world of the seasonal Midwestern worker. Labor on the frontier was at a premium. Hired farmhands were in great demand at planting time and even more so at harvest. Hands were also sought in the summer by fishermen and ship captains to fill out crews on boats kept ever in motion during the brief period between spring and winter during which the Great Lakes were free of ice. The nascent lumber industry also used men seasonally, hiring loggers during the winter, rivermen (to drive the logs downstream) in the spring, and sawmill workers during the summer milling season. Men lacking land or families could be kept employed and in motion following the seasonal labor market. The traditional Ottawa subsistence system was also based on a mobile seasonal exploitation of differing resources and areas. One of the first steps in the missionaries' program of civilization was to induce Indians to abandon that lifestyle, even though thousands of young European-American settlers were living a variation of the native seasonal round.

It is unclear how long Andrew worked and boarded at the Sylvester farm. When he did leave, however, Andrew turned his back on agriculture, which may be an indication of how he regarded the drudgery of farm labor. He next tried his hand at working as a fisherman at Sturgeon Bay, Wisconsin, a small settlement on the Door Peninsula halfway down the shore of Green Bay. "I was persuaded by another man to go with him on the fishing ground," Blackbird wrote in his history. This reference hints at the young Ottawa's interactions with European-American workers. This other "man" may have been a fellow laborer at Sylvester's or he may have been someone Andrew met in Bay Settlement during his free time. Commercial fishing was just then beginning on the Door Peninsula. The work of sailing a Mackinac boat and setting and harvesting gill nets were tasks with which Andrew was very familiar. It was hard, cold, and dangerous work that he could have done as well on his own account at home as he could have done working for wages in the Wisconsin Territory. How long Andrew worked as a fisherman is unknown, but it is unlikely that it was for more than a season or two.[41]

"From there I sailed with Mr. Robert Campbell," he wrote. Andrew spent a summer before the mast. Campbell's ship was most likely a small schooner. At a time when steamboats made only rare visits to Green Bay, schooners and other sailing ships were the principal source of communication and supply for the isolated fishing villages and pioneer farming towns along the Wisconsin shore. Commercial vessels engaged in what was known as the "lakeshoring" trade, which simply amounted to a vessel moving from one site to another bartering with the locals and looking for cargoes that might turn a profit at Mackinac Island or Detroit. It was both financially and physically hazardous. Logbooks from the late 1830s and early 1840s reveal that vessels were engaged in constant sailing, trying to maximize the short summer season on the lakes, risking grounding, the loss of canvas, or rigging just to reach isolated island fishing stations that in the end had nothing to trade.[42] Such an outcome would usually be occasion for a schooner captain to let loose a string of verbal obscenity. Captain Robert Campbell, however, was in Blackbird's experience "a good man and Christian," which may have moderated his temper. Andrew's lack of experience as a sailor was no barrier to his joining Campbell's crew. While there were a smattering of "salt water men" who had genuine experience at sea, most of the crews of Great Lakes sailing ships in the late 1830s were landsmen such as himself who only brought to their tasks a desire for adventure and a need for wages. As a sailor Andrew would have been expected to work the capstan bars to raise the ship's anchor, hoist the heavy gaff set sails of the schooner's fore-and-aft rig, and most difficult of all, ascend the mast to a place high above the swaying deck where the topsails could be set. The high danger of working the topsails in heavy seas was balanced by the drudgery of loading and unloading cargo at each port.[43]

In September 1840 Andrew's time as a sailor came to end when Captain Campbell put into the harbor of Mackinac Island. The haven beneath the guns of the fort was full of bark canoes and along the isle's stony shores were scores of wigwams. Andrew recognized at once that the *Anishnabeg* had gathered for their annual treaty payment. In the village he met Mackadepenessy and most of his other relations. As he too was due a share of the payment, he determined to stay at Mackinac. Yet, instead of simply biding his time with his family, Andrew demonstrated his confidence in coping in the white man's world by hiring himself out at a store "to act as a clerk during the payment time." It was a remarkable decision that illustrated the changes in Andrew's life since he had left L'Arbre Croche. From his time in Wisconsin and working as a sailor, Andrew seems to have developed some ability if not fluency in English. That fall during the payment Andrew stood, as he was expected to do, with his kinsman as they waited patiently in line before Indian agent Henry Rowe Schoolcraft to receive his share of the annuities. Once the gold coins were in his pocket, however, he assumed the novel position of clerk behind the white man's counter. Here for the first time the Ottawa saw Andrew take on the role of an *Anishnabe* who could operate in the European-American world. Andrew was successful enough as a clerk that when the payment was concluded and his father and family returned to L'Arbre Croche, he stayed on in Mackinac with the intention of continuing his job at the store through the winter.[44]

Time spent working with whites as a farmer, fisherman, and before the mast had broadened Andrew Blackbird. Yet he had first gone to the Wisconsin Territory to live with his sister. He did not, however, find a home there. Back on Mackinac Island he did not feel drawn to join his father at L'Arbre Croche. He was in 1840 a rootless teenager, without the strong bonds to place that distinguished young Ottawa men or the commitment to moneymaking that drove many of his European-American coworkers. He was curious about the world that was dawning on the Great Lakes frontier, open to whatever opportunities might present themselves, and utterly uncertain as to his future. Without either expectation or attachment, he was that autumn like the yellow poplar leaves that fell upon the Mackinac beaches, detached and ready for the first breeze to carry him away.

Alvin Coe was the wind that lifted Blackbird off the Mackinac shore and eventually carried him far to the east of his Lake Michigan home. Coe was a Congregational missionary from Ohio who had a single-minded devotion to the education and evangelization of Indian youths. Beginning in 1816 he operated a school for Great Lakes Indians in the town of Greenfield, Ohio. During the late 1820s he took annual missionary trips through Indian country and he became acquainted with Mackadepenessy. Shortly after the 1840 payment the Reverend Coe arrived at Mackinac and encountered young Blackbird. Coe offered him the opportunity to return with him to Ohio and "go to school and receive an education like the white man." The offer both enticed and intimidated Andrew. "I told him I will go with him," he later wrote, "provided he will take an interest to watch over me, that no one would abuse me out there after getting into the strange country." The Reverend Coe eased Andrew's anxiety about traveling so far from his home by promising he would "do all he could to help me along to obtain my education."[45]

Unfortunately, Andrew stumbled at the first hurdle before him. Alvin Coe was scheduled to take a steamer to Detroit that night. Andrew left Coe to gather his belongs, pay off his lodgings, and quit his job as a clerk. In the course of doing so, he missed the night boat. In his *History of the Ottawa and Chippewa,* he later recorded the misadventure.

> He said he was going that night and I must be on hand when the boat arrived; but I failed to tell him my stopping place. So when the boat arrived I was too sound asleep to hear it. Poor old man! I was told that he felt disappointed to have to go without me. As I awoke in the morning I inquired if any boat had arrived during the night. I was told there was. I was also told there was an old man who seemed to be very anxious, and was looking for me all over the crowd on the dock, saying, "Tell my little boy, Jackson, son of the old chief Macka-de-be-nessy, of Arbor Croche, that I have gone on this boat."

Writing nearly fifty years after the event, Blackbird reflected, "Thus I was left, and missed the opportunity when I might have been educated while I was yet much younger."[46]

Over the years Andrew Blackbird genuinely regretted the lost opportunity offered to him by Reverend Coe. According to his account, the chance for an exciting journey into the unknown world of the Americans had been shipwrecked by an ill-timed slumber. He would have the reader pity the ambitious boy whose early chance for advancement was left marooned on a Mackinac wharf. But did the teenager who had spent the summer working as sailor simply sleep too soundly and miss the boat? If Andrew had anxiety about accepting Coe's sudden and unexpected offer, it is certainly understandable. His brother William had embraced his chance to secure a white man's education. He too had gone off with friendly black robes first to Detroit and eventually across the Atlantic to Rome. But William never returned. His death was a mystery to many Ottawa, with rumors of both accident and murder. As Andrew lay in his bed that night, with the prospect of his own departure from the familiar Lake Michigan world before him, his mind may have returned to bright and bold William's sad fate. A half-century later he recorded that he had asked Coe if the minister would "watch over me, that no one would abuse me out there after getting into a strange country." The statement, whether uttered by a boy in 1840, or constructed by an elderly man in 1887 when he wrote his history, points to a fear of how a young Ottawa would be treated in the European-American world. Rather than a contented young man sleeping too soundly that night, it is easier to imagine a teenager in his bed, eyes darting in the darkness as he hears the steamboat whistle its departure, his mind wracked with fear, relief, and regret.

The next morning Andrew went back to work at the store. In the light of day, with time to reflect, he likely felt remorse over the opportunity he had lost, and he was perhaps overly anxious to seize what chance might send his way.

THE BLACKSMITH'S ASSISTANT

The eager seldom need to wait long for an occasion to act. "A few days afterwards, as I walked out from the store one evening, I met two young men in the street, one of whom I frequently saw during the payment time, but the other was entirely a stranger to me." As Blackbird recalled, this latter fellow "was a most noble-looking and tall young man, but, behold, he spoke perfectly and freely the Indian language, saying to me, 'My boy, would you be willing to take us to that vessel out there?'" The speaker was a Chippewa-Irish mixed blood from Sault Ste. Marie and it seemed he also had missed his boat. Fortunately for him, however, the ship was a schooner not a steamer. After clearing the harbor, with all canvas set, the schooner had become becalmed and sat limply in the dark channel between Mackinac and Round Islands. Andrew and "another mate of mine" joined in rowing the boat. Years later Blackbird reconstructed the conversation that occurred as he rowed across the harbor.

"My boy," the mixed-blood man said, "would you like to come with us to Grand Traverse?" The surprised Blackbird was taken aback by the sudden offer. "I would like to see Grand Traverse, but am not prepared to go just now." "Would you not like to learn the blacksmith trade? This man is a government blacksmith in Grand Traverse," he said as he turned to his companion, "and he needs an assistant in the business. We will give you position as an assistant and a salary of $240 yearly, or $20 per month." "I will go," Andrew blurted out unhesitatingly, "for I would be very glad to find a chance to learn a trade and at the same time to get my living." With that he left behind his job in the store, his belongs, and his friend, who was left to row the boat back to Mackinac on his own while Blackbird and his two new companions boarded the schooner.

The young Ottawa must have felt a surge of excitement as he scrambled up the ship's ladder. Gone was the doubt and perhaps shame he had felt at missing the opportunity offered by the Reverend Coe. Just as suddenly a new chance had presented itself and Andrew, with no time for second thoughts, had seized the moment and found himself embarked on a new adventure. It was, however, an adventure in familiar surroundings. The schooner they had caught was none other than Captain Robert Campbell's ship on which Andrew had crewed most of the 1840 season. The boy liked and trusted Captain Campbell, and his presence may have steadied and assured him that the assistant blacksmith job with its guaranteed salary was indeed a fine opportunity.

Blackbird's new companions were John McDouall Johnston and Isaac George. The latter was the blacksmith employed by the Office of Indian Affairs to tend to the needs of the Chippewa of the Grand Traverse area. There were no native blacksmiths in the Great Lakes region. For Andrew to be offered the opportunity to learn the smith's trade was a significant opportunity. The apprenticeship of a number of *Anishnabe* boys as blacksmiths should have been the policy of the Jackson administration; instead the blacksmith's job was, like all the Indian agency positions, doled out to white men who were loyal to the Democratic Party.[47]

John McDouall Johnston's appointment to the agency underscored the workings of the patronage system. He was, as Blackbird noted, a fluent speaker of the Indian language. He grew up at Sault Ste. Marie in close contact with his Chippewa relations. His mother, Oshawguscodywayquay (aka Susan Johnston), spoke no English and raised her children to respect their Chippewa heritage. As a young man Johnston also had the benefit of a formal American education at a private school near Fredonia, New York. His multicultural background and education left him admirably suited to be an interpreter for the agency. Instead, he was there in a capacity as the government farmer, a position for which he had little qualification or inclination over and above its guaranteed salary. His job was to help the Chippewa of Grand Traverse learn the art of plow agriculture by operating a model farm and undertaking for them difficult agricultural tasks such as using a yoke of oxen to break the ground and plant. He had secured the position and its ample $500 annual pay in spite of his agricultural inexperience because his brother-in-law, Henry Rowe Schoolcraft, was the superintendent of Indian affairs for Michigan. His brother George Johnston was already at the Mission Point station in the capacity of carpenter and mechanic, a position for which he was hardly better suited than his brother. George's wife, Mary Rice Johnston, born and raised in Boston, completed the nepotistic circle when she secured the appointment as interpreter for the agency. Her knowledge of Chippewa rivaled her husband's skill at carpentry, but Schoolcraft's appointment kept another government salary in the family.[48]

No sooner did Captain Campbell steer his little schooner into the snug harbor at Mission Point than Blackbird was informed that he would not be allowed to take up his duties as assistant blacksmith.

"You have no commission yet to work in the shop," John Johnston informed him; "you will therefore have to go back to Mackinac with this letter which you will take to the Indian agent yourself and nobody else. Then come back at the first opportunity if he tells you to come." In other words, Johnston needed to have his brother-in-law Henry Schoolcraft's permission to hire Blackbird. Schoolcraft sat at the top of the Indian agency patronage pyramid in Michigan, and Johnston had acted in a characteristically impulsive manner in offering the position to Blackbird. Fortunately, Captain Campbell was taking his ship back to Mackinac and Andrew was able to present himself to Schoolcraft within a day. Schoolcraft must have known Andrew was the son of one of his biggest opponents among the Ottawa. Perhaps for this reason he validated Johnston's selection and issued Andrew his commission as the assistant blacksmith. In reporting his selection to Washington, Schoolcraft provided an interesting description of young Blackbird. "Jackson Blackbird," he wrote, "is an Indian of pure blood, eighteen years of age, of sober habits, speaks a little English, can read and write, is of an industrious turn of character, and will, it is thought, make a good workman."[49]

Schoolcraft's commission, however, did not fully settle the matter of the appointment. Upon his return to Grand Traverse, Blackbird discovered that the Chippewa from around the bay had gathered in council and that he was the reason for the convocation. "They were getting up remonstrances and petitioning the Government against my appointment, setting forth as reason of their complaint that I did not belong to that tribe of Indians, and was therefore, not entitled to the position, and they would rather have one of their boys belonging to the tribe put to this trade."[50]

John Johnston told Andrew "not to mind anything, but go about my business. The blacksmith shop had been established here for more than two years, and they should have thought of putting their boy in the shop long before this." Johnston's logic may have been flawed, but his advice was not. The Chippewa objections amounted to nothing. After all, their petitions were sent to Schoolcraft, who with his kinsman had decided on the appointment to begin with.

The Grand Traverse Indian agency had been established in 1839 due to the leadership of Peter Dougherty, a young minister sent to Michigan by the Presbyterian Board of Foreign Missions. He was a short, powerfully built, strong-willed man with luminous blue eyes and an unbounded energy. The way he moved industriously from task to task eventually prompted the Chippewa to name him Ma-koos, the beaver. In 1838 Dougherty toured the Lake Michigan basin looking for a likely location for a mission. His goal was to convert and educate the Ottawa or Chippewa.[51] It was Henry Rowe Schoolcraft who had advised Dougherty to select the Grand Traverse area as the site for the Presbyterian mission. In keeping with his strong advocacy of Protestant evangelization, Schoolcraft directed that an Indian service agency be established at the tip of the Mission Peninsula, a long slender finger of land that bisected Grand Traverse Bay. Dougherty, partially supported by treaty funds, eventually established his mission and school at this site. The settlement was an uneasy combination of the secular and the religious, government-funded and privately supported activities. Dougherty thought of Mission Point as his community, but he had no authority over the treaty-funded tradesmen, and limited influence over the Chippewa who settled in the area.

The agency employees were supposed to model European-American civilization for the Chippewa. Often what the Indians saw, however, were the expressions of jealousy and pettiness that marked the worst features of small-town life. The year before Blackbird came to Grand Traverse the agency carpenter, George Johnston, became embroiled in a dispute with the blacksmith, Isaac George. When the blacksmith claimed that Johnston was delinquent in paying him a $5 debt, the latter contended that his honor had been impugned. He took a gun to the blacksmith's shop and demanded that George apologize or "meet him like a man." The blacksmith refused and stayed holed up in his shop the entire day with George Johnston waiting outside, his gun cocked. Dougherty found them so situated that evening and he intervened, convincing Johnston to return to his home. Akosa, one of the leading chiefs in the area, was shocked at the confrontation and he asked Dougherty for an "explanation of the matter." The chief told Dougherty the Chippewa "could not understand how those that called themselves

Christians would thus try and shoot each other." Akosa slyly observed that for their part the Chippewa "lived in peace and they never saw any thing like that unless men were intoxicated."[52]

The family bonds between many of the whites at Grand Traverse did nothing to dampen resentments and rivalries. The brothers George Johnston and John Johnston worked at cross-purposes. It had been George Johnston who had incited the Chippewa against Andrew Blackbird's appointment as assistant blacksmith in spite of the fact that it was John who had recruited Blackbird for the post. In turn, both brothers were being undercut by their older brother, William Johnston. In March 1840 William journeyed to Washington, D.C., in order to formally lay before the commissioner of Indian affairs charges of nepotism and mismanagement against his brother-in-law, Henry Schoolcraft. Such accusations from William Johnston were ironic to say the least because he himself had long been employed in the Indian department by Schoolcraft. He turned against his brother-in-law only after Schoolcraft passed over William and gave the plum position of keeper of the Indian Dormitory on Mackinac Island to his own brother, James Schoolcraft. Nonetheless, the formal charges of nepotism, once publicly aired, were hard to deny and eventually cost both George Johnston and John Johnston their comfortable sinecures at Grand Traverse.[53]

Party politics and Indian policy were also behind the move to discredit Schoolcraft. The Indian agent had been a very active Democratic Party partisan during the 1840 election campaign in Michigan. When the Whig Party finally triumphed in the presidential race, its Mackinac supporters looked for an opportunity to bring down Schoolcraft. As a firm Jacksonian, Schoolcraft was a supporter of Indian removal. The Ottawa and Chippewa, however, were determined to remain in Michigan and they had the support of white merchants and missionaries. Both of these groups had supported the signing of the 1836 cession, but by 1840 they were at odds with Schoolcraft's interpretation of the treaty. As it had been amended by the Senate, the Ottawa and Chippewa held reservations for five years, after which time those lands were to be opened to white land purchases. Unexpectedly, however, the Panic of 1837 caused a devastating national depression which all but destroyed the demand for Michigan real estate. Instead of being obstacles to white settlement, the Indian tribes with their annual payments in gold coin were viewed in Michigan as vital elements in the local economy. Washington may have clung to removal as a necessary policy, but in Michigan it had lost its appeal. As a federal employee, Schoolcraft was caught between these conflicting views of Indian policy.

Peter Dougherty had once been Schoolcraft's friend and supporter, but by 1841 the two men had a falling out over the removal policy. Schoolcraft's 1840 report for the Michigan Superintendency openly called for the government, in the "best interests" of the Indians, to put in motion a formal removal to the Indian Territory. Dougherty knew the Chippewa would never agree to migrate to the area southwest of the Missouri River; he saw their future as a choice "between their going to Canada or purchasing land here [in Michigan]. I am clearly of the opinion the latter is the plan which promises the most benefit both temporal and spiritual to these people."[54]

Close contact with the Johnston brothers further soured Dougherty on Schoolcraft's stewardship of Indian affairs. After George Johnston was fired from the Indian service, he returned to the agency in the capacity of a private trader. The missionary and trader soon were locked in a series of disputes having to do with Johnston's alleged sale of liquor to the Chippewa. The other brother, John Johnston, also angered Dougherty when he held a Christmas Eve Party at his house in December 1840. This would have been Andrew Blackbird's first Christmas at Grand Traverse and he was undoubtedly among the guests at his friend's house. Jugs of whiskey were passed as the evening progressed, "as it was a custom with them to drink on Christmas eve." The ascetic teetotaler Dougherty was scandalized. "These are the men," Dougherty complained to his eastern sponsors, "Mr. Schoolcraft has sent here professing to wish to aid the Mission. The whole influence of the Govt. establishment is adverse to the Mission."[55]

Dougherty and the Chippewa at Mission Point were no doubt relieved to hear in the spring of 1841 that Henry Rowe Schoolcraft had been removed from his control of the Michigan Superintendency and the former fur trader Robert Stuart had been placed in his stead. Both the Chippewa at Grand Traverse and the Ottawa at L'Arbre Croche had played a role in removing from office the Indian agent who had tried to remove them from Michigan. They objected to his policy by petitioning the United States for permission to remain in place after their reservations expired. The Grand Traverse chief Akosa wrote to American officials that his people clung to their lands tenuously but tenaciously, like "a bird clings to a branch of a tree waving ready to fall." The Chippewa chief blamed Schoolcraft's public call for their removal for disrupting their efforts to learn European-American ways. Upon hearing of their proposed removal, Akosa wrote, many men laid "down their axes saying it is of no use if they must remove."[56] While the new agent personally opposed removal, Stuart was not in a position to offer a firm guarantee that the United States government would not resort to that extreme. Still, for Grand Traverse and L'Arbre Croche both, the change in agents brought a sigh of relief. For Andrew Blackbird, however, the change had an immediate and unpleasant effect. Stuart dismissed Blackbird's friend John Johnston as the agency farmer. Andrew must have been doing well at his job assisting the blacksmith because there was no effort to remove him from his post.

Andrew Blackbird's principal job was to act as the blacksmith's striker. This entailed wielding a heavy sledge hammer and striking it down on a piece of red hot iron to flatten or mold it to the desired shape. In time, he became accustomed to the rhythmic clang of iron hitting iron and the arc of sparks that rose with each hammer blow. It was hard, hot, heavy work rewarded with the satisfaction of being able to gradually see a new iron object take shape. Only the sweat lodge could have prepared Andrew for the searing heat of the forge and only with time and a patient master could the boy learn to use the many heavy tools that hung from the smithy's shop walls. Over the years he learned the secrets of charcoal, fire, and iron. He became, if only as an apprentice, a maker of metal, something few, if any, Ottawa had ever done.[57]

The striker usually lived either in a loft in the blacksmith's shop or in the smithy's house. Living and working in such close proximity with the blacksmith made mutual compatibility an essential feature. Charges of laziness were leveled at the first blacksmith Andrew worked with. The Indian agent, however, was impressed with Andrew's work: the "striker, a young Indian lad, seems to have been the most busy." After the Johnston brothers were removed from Mission Point, Andrew worked with John Campbell. The new blacksmith was a Scotch-Ottawa mixed blood who had a large family. Andrew became particularly close with Campbell's middle son, Samuel, and corresponded with him long after he left Grand Traverse.[58]

Andrew Blackbird spent five full years working in the smith's shop at the Grand Traverse agency. In his autobiographical history, he made only a single, oblique mention of his experience during those years. One day while he was working in the shop the Chippewa brought in a giant copper kettle. "This kettle was large enough to cook a whole deer or bear in," Blackbird recalled. The Grand Traverse people called the kettle "Mani-tou-au-kick," and they told a story of its origin.

> About two hundred and fifty years ago, We-me-gen-de-bay, one of our noted chiefs, discovered while hunting in the wilderness a great copper kettle, which was partially in the ground. The roots of trees had grown around it and over it, and when it was taken up it appeared as if it had never been used, but seemed to be just as it came from the maker, as there was yet a round bright spot in the center of the bottom of it. . . . For a long time the Indians kept it as a sacred relic. They did not keep it near their premises, but securely hidden in a

> place most unfrequented by any human being. They did not use it for anything except for great feasts. Their idea with regard to this kettle was that it was made by some deity who presided over the country where it was found, and that the copper mine must be very close to where the kettle was discovered.

Blackbird "put an iron rim and bail on it" so they might hang it over a fire. Recalling the incident more than forty years later Blackbird wrote about it with Christian and scientific detachment. For him the kettle was not the relic of a sacred mystery, rather evidence "that this country has been inhabited for many ages, but whether by descendents of the Jews or of other Eastern races, there is no way for us to determine."[59]

It is odd that Andrew Blackbird wrote no more about his five years at Little Traverse because those years could have played a role in the formation of his Christian and assimilationist outlook. At Mission Point, Blackbird was in the midst of a multiracial Christian community committed to evangelization and economic advancement. His job situation afforded him access to both Peter Dougherty the missionary and Henry Bradley, the agency teacher. In his own writing, Blackbird presents himself as a young man interested in education and Christianity. Yet all he wrote about Peter Dougherty is a brief clause in a footnote that observes that the missionary "was indeed a true Christian, and good to Indians." While Andrew was in residence at Mission Point, Dougherty organized a Presbyterian congregation that included both white and Indian members. Andrew Blackbird, however, was not listed among those "in full communion," nor among those admitted to worship or baptism. When an Indian agent visited the mission he noted that Andrew "does not appear to be very well contented at Grand Traverse. He is a Catholic, and in that respect not at home." Blackbird's supervisor in the blacksmith's shop, John Campbell, was a formal member of Dougherty's congregation. Andrew's involvement may have been limited to attendance at Dougherty's popular Sunday school, where some forty adults gathered most weeks. There is no indication that Andrew attended the mission school, which would have conflicted with his duties in the shop.[60]

Andrew Blackbird's time at Mission Point undoubtedly was formative of much of his later political activity. While he was there, the reservations created by the 1836 treaty expired. L'Arbre Croche Ottawa leaders countered by appealing to the State of Michigan and the United States Congress for the right to become citizens. Andrew's erstwhile benefactor, the Reverend Alvin Coe, his father Mackadepenessy, and his cousin Augustin Hamlin were all involved in advocating for a formal change in the status of the Indians. In 1844 the Chippewa at Mission Point joined with the Ottawa in an appeal to Congress for "a permanent location in the land of their birth, and ultimately the rights and privileges of American citizens."[61]

This vigorous indigenous response to the threat of removal did not lead to a formal policy shift by Washington. Federal officials would not release the Ottawa from the threat of removal, although they advanced no plans to initiate a forced exile to the west. Michigan officials, however, were much more flexible. They recognized the progress made by the Ottawa and in 1844 they responded to the lobbying of Augustin Hamlin and the Catholic converts and passed a resolution instructing the state's senators and representatives to "exert their influence in obtaining for the Ottawa at L'Arbre Croche the rights and privileges of American citizens." This action was evidence of the political support for the Ottawa among the business interests along the frontier and within the state government in Lansing. The attainment of citizenship rights remained elusive for another six years; nonetheless, the Ottawa had secured important political allies on the local level. In later years Andrew Blackbird, like his father and cousin before him, would be enlisted to further the cause of Indian citizenship.[62]

In the autumn of 1845 Andrew Blackbird left Mission Point and his position as striker. He appears to have been doing well at his job, but there was a renewal of Chippewa pressure to have one of their own in his position. In 1843 Peter Dougherty reported to the commissioner of Indian affairs that "the young man who has been in the smith's shop has acquired a good knowledge of the trade." Unfortunately, Dougherty also indicated, "The chiefs here are desirous of having one of their young men taken into the smith's shop, and one into the carpenter's shop, to acquire those trades, so that they may have their own mechanics, as well as become their own farmers." The next year the Chippewa chief Akosa pressed Indian agent Justin Rice on the same point. "The chief," Rice reported to Washington, "asks for a situation for his son, (who appears to be a steady, active, *ambitious,* and *ingenious* young man,) as striker in the blacksmith's shop. I asked him if he was willing to have him go [to] Mackinac? He said *not.* He was afraid he would be *too much exposed to temptation;* and asked if Jackson Muccatapenace could not be sent to Mackinac, and make a place at once for his son at home?"[63]

Rice was not inclined to disrupt Blackbird since he had earned a reputation as "a good workman," but he did wish to please the Chippewa if possible. In the spring of 1844 he proposed that Andrew consider relocating to Mackinac Island. On May 14 Andrew responded,

> As you leave it to my choice to go or stay I would say that I prefer remaining here if the wages are the same. I think I can live on the wages that I now have better here than I would at Mackinac and as I have none of my relatives living at Mackinac I would rather remain among my friends here. It is my intention to leave the Department and work on my own account this fall if I can buy my stock of iron. Mr. Stuart told me last fall that I might make tools for myself if I had spare time and found my own iron and I think I can do better here than I could at Mackinac. These are my reasons for choosing to remain here at present. I hope they will be satisfactory to you.

The letter, which may have been composed with some assistance, nonetheless reveals an ambitious young man fully capable of calculating his own advantage.[64]

In his *History of the Ottawa and Chippewa* Blackbird says only that "when I quit it was of my own accord." In the five years he spent at Mission Point, Andrew had learned a new and valuable trade that he could practice almost anywhere he went. By living and working in close proximity to educated whites, he perfected his knowledge of English and built his confidence that he could interact with the Americans. Five years before he had been intimidated by the prospect of journeying to Ohio and entering school there; now he was eager to take on that challenge. The Reverend Coe's offer, Blackbird wrote, "was never blotted out of my mind." All through his years at Mission Point the thought of attending a proper white man's school glowed in his mind like the embers in the smithy's forge. So "the very day I quit the blacksmith shop at Grand Traverse, I turned my face toward the State of Ohio, for that object alone."[65]

4

We Now Wish to Become Men

ANDREW BLACKBIRD WAS IN A HURRY. HE SWEPT INTO HIS FATHER'S village on the shores of Little Traverse Bay, and with barely a *bozhoo* for friends and family he was gone again within a few hours.[1] For the five years he was at Mission Point he had thought about going east for an education and when he finally made up his mind he was anxious to be off. Yet, in spite of his sense of urgency, his steps took him first to the sandy shores of Little Traverse. He was going to Ohio with high hopes, but was realistic enough to know that like his older brother William, he might not return. So he went to Mackadepenessy's cabin to "bid the last farewell to my folks."

There is some indication that the old chief was hesitant to let his wandering son go to Ohio. In a letter composed two years after his departure Andrew wrote, "My father is old, yet suffered to let me go." Mackadepenessy, for both personal and tribal reasons, wanted Andrew near. Ottawa relations with the United States remained uncertain. The people needed new leadership to implement the 1836 treaty. Mackadepenessy, although he was the father of more than ten children, also seems to have looked to Andrew for support in his old age. Both father and son, however, seem to have agreed, at least for a time, to put aside those concerns and embrace the opportunity to secure an American education.[2]

After a hasty exchange with his father Andrew was then off to Middle Village to catch a boat for Mackinac Island. While he waited on the wharf he encountered Paul Nawogade. Distantly related to Andrew, Nawogade was "an orphan boy," responsible to no one and anxious for an adventure. Like Andrew, Paul was acquainted with the Reverend Coe. After telling Paul of his own plans, Andrew proposed that Paul accompany him to Ohio. Although Paul lacked any financial resources, Andrew, no doubt glad to have an Ottawa travel companion, offered to pay his passage to Cleveland. "So the next day we started for Mackinac," Andrew later wrote, "not knowing what would become of us if my little means were exhausted and we should be unsuccessful in finding our old friend, Mr. Alvin Coe."[3]

Andrew and Paul took passage on a southbound steamboat. Across the blue-green expanse of Lake Huron the steady thump of the engines and the rhythmic surge of the paddlewheel through the water would have reinforced the boy's sensation that they were embarked for an alien world. The two Ottawa kept mostly to themselves, but at meals Andrew had a chance to meet some of the other passengers as they spoke of homes, destinations, and sights seen. The Detroit waterfront gave them their first real glimpse of an American city. The riverfront wharfs were the economic nerve center of Detroit and to the boys it may well have seemed that most of the city's 10,000 inhabitants worked there, hauling cargoes, hawking wares, or hollering in a score of different languages. The scene was a foreshadowing of the human wave that would break over them when they landed in Cleveland.

"Arriving there," Blackbird late wrote, "we were scared at seeing so many people coming to us who wanted us to get into their cabs to take us to some hotel which might cost us two or three dollars a day." Taking his lead from other passengers and mindful of his limited financial means, Andrew made his way with Paul to the Farmer's Hotel. The choice turned out to be extremely fortunate. "In the evening," Blackbird wrote in his history, "the landlady was somewhat curious to know where we hailed from and where we were going to. I told her we came from Michigan, but we did not yet know where we should go to. I asked her if she ever knew or heard of a minister named Alvin Coe." More than forty years after the fact, Blackbird reported a no-doubt polished version of their exchange.[4]

"What," the very much surprised landlady said. "Mr. Alvin Coe the traveling missionary?"

"Yes, the same," replied Andrew.

"Why, that is my uncle," exclaimed the landlady. "What is it about him?"

"O[h], nothing; only I would like to know where he lives and how far," said Andrew.

"You know my uncle then?" she asked.

"Yes; he is my particular friend, and I am going to look for him," said Andrew.

This stunning coincidence immediately struck Andrew Blackbird as proof that "God must be with us in our undertaking." Armed with directions from the landlady, Andrew and Paul set out on foot for Vernon, Ohio, about fifty miles away. To underscore Providence's hand in their journey, one of the travelers they had met on the boat, who had also been staying at the Farmer's Hotel, was heading out in the same direction by foot. With his help the boys navigated their way through the muddy and congested streets of Cleveland, up the steep slope of Garfield Heights, and out into verdant rolling farm country. A long day on the road brought them weary legged to the town of Twinsburg. Here their traveling companion had business.

"You had better stop with me for the night," he advised the boys, "and after supper you could visit the institution in the village and see the principal of the school here; you might possibly get a chance to attend that school, as you say that was your object in coming to this part of the country."

Blackbird was taken back by their companion's advice. During the long day spent on the road he had "not said one word" about their being an academy in Twinsburg or that Andrew and Paul should consider enrolling in it. On this occasion, however, Andrew was open to what opportunity presented itself. After taking his supper with Paul he walked over to the academy. It was a whitewashed, two-story wood frame building facing the town square. A group of boys were playing on the well-worn lawn of the village green. Andrew stood apart watching these boys, so strange in their words, games, and clothes, but otherwise so similar to the boys of L'Arbre Croche in their dash and joy. As he watched them, they were watching him.

"Are you going to attend school here?" one of the older boys finally asked.

"No, sir," said the young Ottawa, "I am going thirty miles further to attend school there."

"This is the best school that I know of anywhere about this country," the boy responded. At that Andrew requested that the boy introduce him to the proprietor of the school. Together they went into the academy and Andrew met Samuel Bissell, a man who would be a lifelong friend.

"Well, Mr. Blackbird, do you wish to attend our school?" Bissell asked.

"I do not know, sir, how that might be," said Andrew suddenly feeling the full weight of his precarious circumstances, "as I have not much means to pay my way, but I am seeking for a man who invited me to come to Ohio some five years ago, and promised that he would help me all he could for my education. His name is Alvin Coe, a traveling missionary, my father's old friend."

"We have two Indian boys here attending school, and I think you will not be very lonesome if you should conclude to stay with us," replied Bissell, who probably sensed the cloak of intimidation that had fallen over the boy.

"What are their names?" Andrew quickly asked.

"One is Francis Petoskey, and the other is Paul Ka-gwe-tosong," replied Bissell, with words that must have brought an immediate smile to Andrew's face.

"I know them both; I came from the same place they did, but I did not know they were here, I only knew they were attending school somewhere among the whites," Andrew blurted out. He must have felt deeply relived that somehow, amid the hundreds of towns and cities of the white man, he had found his way to a place where he could be received and educated.

"Can you do any kind of work?" the practical-minded Bissell asked.

"I am a blacksmith by trade, sir, and besides I can do most every kind of work," Andrew said with evident pride and growing confidence.

"If you conclude to stay," Bissell offered, "I will try to aid you in finding a place where you could work to pay for your lodging and board; and in the meantime we will cause Mr. Alvin Coe to come and see you, and if he sees fit to take you away he can do so, provided you would be willing to go with him." Andrew readily agreed to Bissell's proposal and then broached the plight of young Paul, who had no real work experience, and who evidently had been afraid to accompany Andrew on his visit to the school. "After considering a few moments," Andrew recorded in his history, "he proposed to take my little companion to his boardinghouse until a better arrangement could be made. This was the end of my conversation with this noble hearted professor and proprietor of this Institution, whose name was Rev. Samuel Bissell, of Twinsburg, Ohio."[5]

Andrew hurried back to his lodgings and reverting to the Ottawa language he excitedly told Paul of the plans he had made. Physically tired, emotionally relived, yet stimulated by the prospect before him, Andrew spent his first of many nights in Twinsburg. The next morning, after breakfast at the inn, Andrew and Paul gathered their belongings and headed to the school. Reverend Bissell, an early riser, had already made arrangements for the boys. He escorted Andrew to the village blacksmith's shop, where he would work as a striker for the young smithy. Blackbird lodged with the blacksmith and agreed to work two hours in the morning, before school, and two in the evening after class to pay for his room and board.

STUDENT DAYS

Twinsburg was a pleasant, prosperous village of white clapboard buildings well spaced along tree-lined streets that seemed to oscillate between two conditions, muddy or dusty. Bissell's school shared space on the village green with a white, spired Congregational church that betrayed the New England origin of the town's pioneers. In 1817 twin brothers, Moses and Aaron Wilcox, founded the town, and scores of Connecticut Yankees followed them.

Twinsburg was in the heart of the so-called Western Reserve, a chunk of northern Ohio originally claimed by Connecticut and the site of numerous land grants to the state's Revolutionary War veterans. By the 1840s the towns of the Western Reserve were tintypes of New England villages. Settlers came with a predilection for whitewashed homes, a commitment to Calvinism, and a respect for education.[6]

Samuel Bissell was the dynamo behind the Twinsburg Institute. He was born in 1797 in East Windsor, Connecticut, of old Pilgrim stock. Bissell's family was of modest means, although they afforded the boy an opportunity to attend Yale, where he worked his way through school as a tutor. His career as a young minister was marked by his staunch support for temperance, which was then emerging as one of nation's leading reform movements, and concern for indigent youth. In the winter of 1838 he began to teach in Twinsburg. The Institute, as the school was known, was originally intended for the youth of the Twinsburg area; however, within a few years as many as forty scholars were boarding at the school. By 1843 Bissell had the satisfaction to buy out the town tavern and convert it to a boardinghouse for his Christian academy. By the time Andrew Blackbird was admitted the Institute had a student body of more than 300 and a faculty of nineteen instructors and assistants.[7]

Bissell's kind heart and the location of Twinsburg on the road to the Reverend Coe's residence in Vernon, Ohio, made his school a magnet for Indian youth from Michigan. Coe encouraged the Ottawa and Chippewa to have their children educated in English, and after the missionary returned to Ohio for the winter, Indian boys followed after him. The first group of three came in November 1844, a year before Andrew. They included both Ottawa and Chippewa, but none of the boys spoke a word of English. Somehow they made their way to the doors of the Institute, where the European-American boys regarded them, in Bissell's words, "as objects of novelty and compassion." Fortunately, the school had a French teacher who was able to learn the goal of their travels. Initially, the Indian boys were merely offered lodging for the night. In the dark Bissell reflected on the biblical passage, "I was a Stranger, and ye took me in." That morning he adjusted the student boarding arrangements and was able to make room for the boys.[8]

In the fall of 1845, a total of nine Ottawa and Chippewa arrived at the institute, Andrew and Paul among them. They were all housed at the Institute save for Andrew. His unique skills in the blacksmith shop put him in a position to earn his board. The school day sometimes began at 7:00 A.M. This necessitated Blackbird, who was required to labor in the blacksmith shop for two hours in the morning, to rise well before 5:00 A.M. He later remembered "many times I finished my hours at sunrise." After class, while his mates could lounge about on their beds or play games on the village green, Andrew was at work once more as a striker.[9]

Sometime during that first winter in Ohio, Alvin Coe visited Andrew Blackbird in Twinsburg. The retired missionary had not seen Andrew since that day on Mackinac Island five years before. It is likely he hardly recognized the big-shouldered and rather imposing man in his early twenties that he encountered at the Institute. Years of work as a blacksmith had hardened Blackbird to labor, yet they had only quickened his desire to learn. Coe retained his desire to help Andrew and he escorted the Ottawa to his Vernon, Ohio, home. There Andrew was set up in a local school. Before leaving, however, Bissell and Coe agreed that if Andrew did not like his new school he would be allowed to return to the Twinsburg Institute. After little more than two weeks Andrew Blackbird retraced his steps to Twinsburg. "I did not like the place," Andrew noted in his history. Nor is it hard to imagine why he preferred Twinsburg. Not only did Bissell operate one of the best academies in northern Ohio, but there Andrew was surrounded by ten other *Anishnabe* boys. He returned to his job with the blacksmith and attended to his studies till the academic year ended in July 1846.[10]

That summer most of the other Ottawa and Chippewa youth returned home. Andrew did not. Rather he spent the season in the Twinsburg area working to earn the cost of his tuition and board. While he labored through the humid Ohio summer, Samuel Bissell visited northern Michigan. His goal was to see his students in their native haunts and "learn more definitely their condition." He met the parents of students from Mackinac Island and recruited several new students, bringing the total number of Indian pupils at his school to nine.[11]

Save for Andrew, who continued to stay with the blacksmith, all of the other Indian youths were boarded with the Bissell family. Aware that an educational fund had been established for the Ottawa and Chippewa as part of the Treaty of Washington, Bissell, with the support of Alvin Coe, requested federal funds for the students at Twinsburg. Senator Lewis Cass recommended that such aid be forthcoming; however, the Office of Indian Affairs argued that all educational funds flowing from the 1836 treaty had already been apportioned to the various denominations that had missionaries active in northern Michigan. As a result a single, one-time-only $200 appropriation was made to Bissell. These were funds that had been left unspent in 1836 and, the Indian department argued, were the only uncommitted educational funds available to the Ottawa and Chippewa.[12] It may have been at this time that Andrew Blackbird penned an undated personal appeal to William Medill, the commissioner of Indian affairs. In the request he stressed his desire to learn both religion and the "arts and sciences, which contribute so much to the happiness of mankind." He was, however, no more successful than Bissell in winning an annual appropriation from the Office of Indian Affairs.[13]

The burden of educating and boarding the young Indians, therefore, fell squarely on Samuel Bissell. Since he could scarcely afford the cost but was unwilling to turn away motivated students, Bissell elected to launch a public appeal for his *Anishnabe* students. In 1846 Bissell solicited funds from Christian congregations in northern Ohio. He received some cash support and a supply of clothing for his efforts. In December 1847 after classes had ended for the holidays, Reverend Bissell took Andrew Blackbird on a tour of the eastern states. Bissell did not indicate why he took Andrew and not one of the other Indian students; it is likely that Andrew's maturity and experience using English prompted the selection. On the other hand, Andrew was the only one of the Indian students with work skills and he was at the time paying for his own room and board. Their first stop was Philadelphia, which they reached via Pittsburgh in a series of stages that involved the use of canal boats, steamships, horse-drawn coaches, and finally the railroad. They checked into the Morris House Hotel located on Chestnut Street amid the bustle of what was at that point the largest city Andrew had ever seen. Tears filled his eyes as anxiety and self-doubt battled hope in his heart. "When I beheld the city," Andrew confided in a letter to a friend, "it looked so gay & so richly & vast of wealth, I began to give expression to think here is the place where the friends of the Indians dwelt & here I am alone and begging for knowledge."[14]

On Sunday Bissell and Blackbird made the rounds to the Presbyterian churches and Sabbath Schools in the city. Bissell told the story of how Indian students in search of learning had come to the door of the Twinsburg Institute and he expressed the hope that "no Christian or philanthropist would be willing that one of these youth should return to his countrymen without receiving the education which they so ardently desire." Pastors endorsed Bissell as someone who with great sacrifice had paid part of Christian America's "common indebtedness to this much injured race." Of course, Andrew also addressed the Presbyterian congregations. He was introduced as "A.J. Maccadabenasbi or Blackbird," son of an Ottawa chief. In the unfamiliar position of soliciting aid, he took on the tone of one "unworthy to go to any public assemblies." With Bissell's help Andrew cast himself as "an Indian, poor, an outcast, the prodigal son."[15]

The Philadelphia Presbyterian appeal was less than a success. "I almost got discouraged," Andrew confessed. Then on New Year's Day, 1848, Bissell and Blackbird moved on to New Jersey. They spent ten days in New Jersey, most of the time in Newark at the City Hotel. Newark was a Presbyterian stronghold and it was there that Andrew had a valuable encounter. "At last," he wrote in his history, "Dr. Brainsmade, of Newark, New Jersey, took a deep interest in my welfare and education, and he proposed to aid me and take me through the medical college." Blackbird never again mentioned Brainsmade in his history, nor does his name appear in Bissell's correspondence. Yet the Newark visit reaped significant benefits for Andrew. Because of Brainsmade's aid, he was able, upon his return to Twinsburg, to abandon work in the blacksmith shop, board with the other students at the institute, and devote himself completely to academic pursuits. The brief mention of Dr. Brainsmade also marks the first reference to Andrew's interest in a career in medicine. There is no record of his having previous contact with a trained physician. While at Old Mission he had seen the Reverend Dougherty bleeding or applying blisters to the sick, but Dougherty was not a trained physician. Still, the need among the Indians for Dougherty's untutored ministrations and perhaps Andrew's own memory of his mother's untended death following a painful burning may have influenced his avowed interest in medicine.[16]

From Newark the fund-raising tour continued to New York City and then on to New England. For a month Bissell took Andrew across the frozen countryside, visiting scores of towns in Connecticut and Massachusetts, the heartland of American Presbyterianism and Congregationalism. For Bissell this was a homecoming to the places and people of his youth, which may explain why they used New Haven as their base. In February they concluded their trip with brief visits to Baltimore and Washington, D.C.[17]

The tour of the eastern United States gave Andrew Blackbird an invaluable glimpse of the size and diversity of the American nation. It strengthened him in his goal of obtaining an education and helped to shape within in him a sense of mission, a desire to better the condition of his people. Being among whites in Twinsburg and engulfed in a sea of their faces in the cities of the east gave Blackbird a new consciousness of being an Indian. Andrew felt this racial identity and his historical relationship to the European-Americans most strongly in New Haven. Here in the city where Reverend Bissell celebrated his Pilgrim ancestors, Andrew imagined a different history.

> One morning it was very pleasant & calm. I walked down to the edge of the water where I beheld schooners & ships spreading their wings most gracefully upon the water. I could gaze upon the shades of the sails in the water, but alas! At once my eyes were filled with tears. When I thought it is the place where my

> forefathers espied something at a distance moving upon the water. What could it be baffled all conjecture. Some supposed it to be a large fish or animal; others that it was a very big house floating upon the sea in which the Manitou or Great Spirit was coming to visit them. It was a wonderful phenomenon. They were much afraid & assembled together & meat was prepared for sacrifice without knowing that the assault would be. They were all in confusion. The great dance also commenced & the idols were put in order that the Great Spirit might be pleased. And this was the cry of my heart. O where are they now, these broken remains of my race! Alas! they have mouldered & gone to decay. The plague of the White Man hath swept them away.

It was in this heartfelt passage, part of a letter to an unnamed correspondent, that Andrew Blackbird took his first step as a historian.[18]

In financial terms the trip was not a huge success. A trickle of funds from the east was sent flowing, at least temporarily, to Twinsburg. Among those who heard the appeal was the noted Congregationalist divine Henry Ward Beecher, who pledged support for Indian education. More common were small contributions collected from white Sabbath School students. Blackbird was a prime beneficiary of the trip, due to Dr. Brainsmade's patronage. In a text he prepared as his part in the appeal Andrew hinted at why they might not have been more successful. He could have made more money, he said, if they went "foolishly, as a monkey show." This seems to be a reference to appearing in some type of Indian costume and marketing himself as a "son of the forest," not as an indigent student. Bissell and Blackbird did not stoop to this convention. Yet by the 1840s it was widely expected that even educated Indians, including those who had published books or had become ordained ministers, would be obliged to appear as wild men of the forest. The Reverend Peter Jones (Chippewa), a Methodist minister, complained to his wife in 1845 that during a fund-raising trip to Great Britain he was obliged to appear in an "*odious* Indian costume." George Copway, like Jones a Canadian Chippewa, was in the midst of his own tour of the eastern United States at the same time Blackbird made his appeal. Copway embraced the dual roles of noble savage and Christian convert. He lectured on topics such as "The Religion, Poetry, and Eloquence of the Indian," but appeared on stage, to his audience's delight, in a "chief's costume" fringed with jangling little bells. In contrast evidence indicates that Andrew Blackbird dressed in a coat, pants, vest, and shoes that were typical of young white men. Whether Blackbird witnessed a stage Indian performance during his two months in the east is unclear, but he believed, or was led to believe, that giving the audience what it wanted to see as well as hear amounted to a "monkey show." He would later in life, whether due to circumstance or conviction, behave otherwise.[19]

Back at Twinsburg Andrew devoted himself to his studies. Dr. Brainsmade's support brought him fully into the Institute's residential life. The Indian contingent seems to have formed a close group. Most of them were from the L'Arbre Croche area or from the nearby Straits of Mackinac villages. The Petoskey brothers, Francis and Mitchell, along with Andrew Blackbird, Paul Nawogade, and Joseph Shirgawnabanoo, were from the Ottawa villages along Little Traverse Bay. Andrew's cousin Catherine Hamlin, and later her brother Moses, were among the group from the Mackinac area that attended the school. This included Augustus Mixinassau and his sister Tirza as well as a number of mixed-blooded children whose fathers were traders, such as Paul and Louis Martin. The Petoskey boy's cousins, Josette and J. H. Perrault, also joined the student body. Later another cousin of Andrew's, Joseph Wakazoo, came to Twinsburg. News from home came sparingly during the school year. The brief reports they sometimes received were more source of anxiety than comfort, such as the March 1848 letter announcing that an epidemic had swept through northern Michigan, killing many children.[20] Most of the Indian students attended the school only for a year or two, and most returned home during the summer. Andrew, however, remained in Ohio for four years. He spent his summers, in spite of the Brainsmade donation, working to help pay his board for the coming year.

Among the Indian students who studied with Andrew at Twinsburg was a Michigan Potawatomi, Simon Pokagon, who would later become a celebrated lecturer and the author of several fanciful books on Indian life. Simon was the son of Leopold Pokagon, the skillful leader of the Catholic Potawatomi bands. They had used their association with the Church and their interest in agricultural settlement to avoid removal from Michigan. After some initial schooling at Notre Dame Academy, at the South Bend of the St. Joseph River, Simon Pokagon made his way to Bissell's school, where he studied for two years. Blackbird made no mention of Pokagon's presence at the school in his autobiographical history. Pokagon, however, offered one brief anecdote regarding Blackbird's time at the academy. In a September 1897 letter to the editor of the *American Monthly* regarding Indian names, Pokagon recounted,

> When a young man I attended school at Winsburgh, Ohio, with a son of an Awteiva chief, "Nlack-a-de-pe-neesy" (Black Hawk). Some teacher of authority in languages, learning that ma-kaw-te as a qualifier meant "black," and that "pe-nay-shen" meant "bird" in Ottawa dialect, called him Andrew Blackbird, which to him was very humiliating.

Pokagon was indeed correct that Andrew was sensitive about the way white men translated his name as Blackbird; however, the practice did not originate with a Twinsburg teacher. Mackadepenessy had long been called Blackbird by United States authorities, and naturally his son Andrew was also referred to as Blackbird. Nonetheless, it was something bothered the young man.[21]

The basic program at the Twinsburg Institute was college preparatory. The Indian students, however, lacked the basic background for that program, so Samuel Bissell employed three remedial teachers to give them the reading and writing skills necessary for advanced class-work. For many of the *Anishnabe* youth this basic tutelage in literacy was sufficient to their purposes. Paul Nawogade, who had accompanied Andrew to Ohio, left school after the academic year. Yet even those who received only remedial education took marked pride, as one wrote to Bissell, in being able to "compose a letter in English language." Andrew, however, stood out in his desire to obtain what he referred to as "understanding." He was determined to know what the white people knew. He committed himself to the academy long enough to advance into the regular college preparatory program. Among the subjects presented to him by the faculty were mathematics and its application to bookkeeping, navigation, and surveying. All students were trained in a core program of language training in Greek, Latin, French, and German. In those classes and throughout the curriculum, great stress was placed on rhetoric, composition, and elocution. Weekly exercises allowed students to demonstrate their proficiency through formal presentations. Andrew, like the other students, participated in making presentations and there is some evidence that he excelled at them.[22]

According to the 1881 *History of Summit County, Ohio,* Blackbird was regarded as an excellent writer and that at one point in his tenure in Twinsburg he authored a three-hour comic play that was performed before a large audience of students and townspeople. This account was published while Samuel Bissell was still alive and it is likely that he was the source of the section on the history of the academy; however, it is also likely that some distortion entered the record. By 1914, when both Bissell and Blackbird were dead, an Ohio newspaper article on the history of Twinsburg described "Jackson Blackbird" as having a "marked ability in playwriting." Andrew Blackbird's letters from this period, however, reveal a student with a shaky grasp of English syntax, nor is there anything in the written record that would indicate an interest or aptitude for comic writing. In a March 1849 letter Blackbird admitted to having trouble keeping up with his white classmates, a frustration that brought tears to his eyes.[23]

Blackbird's scientific education would have included lab work in chemistry and an introduction to physiology, which may have prompted his interest in advanced medical training. Like all the students he was taught bookkeeping and cursive writing by Warren P. Spencer, nephew of the man who invented the Spenserian style of writing, distinctive for its fifty-degree slant in the script. These lessons gave Blackbird a clear, confident hand and a basic background in business that would help him in later years.

During his years in school Blackbird adopted many of the social and political ideas that he would hold throughout his life. The Western Reserve region of Ohio was animated by the reformist spirit of a socially conscious and evangelical Protestantism. While no particular denomination was advanced by Samuel Bissell, all students were required to attend some type of Sabbath worship. Bissell and the faculty were themselves models of a high-minded and optimistic engagement with social problems. They favored hospitals, poorhouses, and asylums for the unfortunate, temperance for the inebriated, freedom for the enslaved, and revivals for backsliders. Blackbird internalized their commitment to liberty, equality, and education. These values, particularly temperance and antislavery, would eventually push Blackbird into the Republican Party.

The sympathy and support that Blackbird and other *Anishnabeg* encountered at Twinsburg was a manifestation of sentiments that were broadly shared in Protestant America. Men like Bissell deeply felt a moral responsibility to act in favor of the Indians. America was guilty of abusing its native people and Bissell was sensible of the need to make amends for the misdeeds of past generations. Missionaries such as Peter Dougherty and George Nelson Smith, who worked with the *Anishnabeg* in Michigan and sent students to Bissell's academy, were likewise motivated by the need to purge the nation's guilt. This same sentiment energized the antislavery movement. In 1851 Smith wrote to Bissell that "the American people by their treatment of the Indians in past times have put themselves in a condition of fearful responsibility." In his opinion, "these responsibilities must be cancelled or a blight awaits us."

> It was doubtless one of the designs of Providence in planting the Puritans on American shores that they should be instruments for Christianizing the natives of this Continent, so some of them thought, if I remember right, but cupidity, worldly mindedness & policy have nearly paralyzed every effort & it remains for us in some measure to redeem ourselves. We must be true but let us not be faint. I still have hope but sometimes it looks as if it were against hope. I believe God still has a people even among the Aborigines of America therefore I am still encouraged to labor.

Andrew would not himself become a missionary, but his education at Twinsburg did instill in him the belief that Protestant Christianity had both the power and the duty to help Indian people.[24]

Andrew seems to have enjoyed the structure and camaraderie of life at the academy. A bell rang each day at 5:00 A.M. to rouse the boarders. A second bell an hour later signaled breakfast, which was taken at a long table, with forty or more places set. At the head sat Samuel Bissell. All stood, heads bowed, for his invocation before tearing into their food. A bell signaled the start of classes and later the end of the school day. At 10:00 P.M. every evening Bissell took the great iron key to the dormitory door and locked it for the night. Boys lingering in the night air were left to fend for themselves. Bissell was a disciplinarian who did not hesitate to use the rod on those who transgressed the school's rules. But he also seems to have understood that the young boys and girls of the school needed to have an outlet for their energy and imagination. One Halloween night some of the students hit upon the prank of hijacking Bissell's carriage and hauling it to some distant farmer's field. Bissell heard of their plan and secreted himself in the carriage. In high spirits the boys pulled the carriage as far as Tinker's Creek when Bissell suddenly emerged from the darkness. He must have given them quite a scare. Rather than punish them he merely said, "Boys, I guess you have brought me far enough, now you may draw me back," and sheepishly they did as they were told. As a former student recalled, a common prank was for the students to place a bucket of water atop a slightly open door, "so that a latecomer received an unwelcome shower bath." If, however, the noise level from any of the dormitory rooms became too loud, it was only necessary for Bissell to rap on the door "and all would be silent within."[25]

Andrew formed a lasting friendship with Samuel Bissell and long after his time at Twinsburg ended he regarded his teacher as a friend and mentor. He also seems to have bridged the cultural divide and formed friendships with some of his European-American classmates. Six months after leaving Ohio Andrew wrote to Bissell indicating he missed "my fellow students, especially Mr. Macklane my old friend. I think of him about every day." Andrew missed his home on the Lake Michigan shore but he also regretted being parted from his school friends when the academic year ended. In an 1849 letter to an unnamed patron Andrew confided his feelings.

> It is very lonely since we had vacation, our acquaintance are all scattered about, I am almost believe, this place is very bad place to live, as we have been flocking together the whole winter and belonging all the same family and treating one another as brothers and sisters. But when the spring cometh and the wind

> bloweth from the south, friends and all blows off like a feathers and some of them left behind with tears in their eyes, and I am one of them.

The boy who had been "a perfect wild rover" following the death of his mother, and who boldly had gone off to live and work among the whites when he was in his early teens, appreciated deeply the warmth that even a surrogate school family could provide.[26]

Twinsburg, however, was not home and Andrew Blackbird had the Ottawa people and their endangered Michigan homeland in the forefront of his mind while he pursued his education. He seems to have stayed in touch with events on the upper Great Lakes frontier through correspondence with his cousin Augustin Hamlin. In correspondence with white donors who helped to support Indian education at Twinsburg, Blackbird cast his pursuit of education not as a personal desire but as a quest motivated by his concern for the Ottawa. In one letter he confided that he had initially been very fearful to go among the whites for an education.

> I trusted the Great Spirit would take care of me as well as he had done at home. My father is old, yet suffered to let me go. I have been here now more than two years & many of my countrymen are now with me, that they may know the benefit of an education. I hope they will soon have understanding & be useful to our poor countrymen hereafter, if the Great Spirit spares our lives. We feel very grateful for the kindness, as far as the Christian people have shown us & hope not to disappoint their wishes for us that we may do good for our people. My friends, perhaps you will think if we get a good education, that we will not go back to our people. Not so. I am only here as self denial for love of my people. Nature still will be nature.[27]

In a similar view Blackbird wrote to another correspondent, "I did not come here with the childish mien simply to study, but I left my parents & friends at twenty years of age induced simply by the belief that there was something noble in the spirit of education & needful among my people."[28]

Blackbird believed that by 1849 the Ottawa had reached a critical "threshold" that offered "the light of civilization." His father, Mackadepenessy, had made a treaty with the Americans in 1836 with the aim of crossing that threshold. Since that time, Blackbird complained, the government had done precious little to help them attain their goal. Instead of threatening removal, he recommend "they ought to enlighten them [the Indians] and teaching them the words of God, instead of compelling them at the point of a bayonet to retire to a strange land where there is no inhabitance to welcome them, and forming perpetual hatred to the white man, in the heart of the red man." Educational funds promised in the 1836 treaty were not under Ottawa control, but dedicated by the government to Christian missionary groups for the operation of schools. Blackbird wanted those funds available in a public account for the Ottawa themselves "for the purpose of educating the young men or girls who may go among the whites." For Blackbird it was critical for the Ottawa to raise up an educated elite who could manage his people's relations with the United States. "Shall we always depend upon the Whites to transact our business," he asked one correspondent, "& feel perhaps that they are deceiving us, even if they are up right. No! I say let us have our own commissioners who will transact our business, & in whom we can repose confidence, & let us have teachers & preachers & then shall we feel at home."[29]

Blackbird believed that the key reform necessary for his people to avoid removal's "bayonet" was for them to become citizens of the United States. The Protestant missionaries Alvin Coe and Peter Dougherty had been advocates of citizenship, as had the Catholic missionary at L'Arbre Croche, François Pierz. Interest in Indian citizenship, among both whites and Indians, grew in Michigan during the late 1840s. His father, Mackadepenessy, had petitioned the United States for citizenship. Anxious to advance this cause and concerned about his elderly father's situation, Andrew Blackbird determined in March 1850 to return to Michigan for the summer. He did not know it at the time, but he was leaving the Twinsburg school for good and it would be five long years before he would see again his "dear friend" Samuel Bissell.

COUNCILOR FOR MY PEOPLE

For Andrew Blackbird, returning to northern Michigan was both stimulating and reassuring. Not only had he lived more than four years among strangers, he labored in a alien, domesticated landscape. Summer in Ohio's Western Reserve region is humid and green. Andrew grew up with blue and gold summers along the broad beaches of Lake Michigan. The sight of the Little Traverse shore was like returning to a mother's comforting embrace. Long before he saw his father and siblings, the familiar landscape, its cool, comforting billows, refreshed his soul and told Blackbird he was home.

He did not intend to long interrupt his education. Andrew left Twinsburg thinking he was only returning home for the summer, to visit his aged father and to see what he could do to win citizenship for the Ottawa people.

Stepping back into the role of Mackadepenessy's son, however, immersed Andrew in a torrent of personal and tribal business that all but swept away his hopes of further education. In October 1850 he was forced to write "in haste" to Bissell,

> I hope you will not think I have forgotten you and left the School entirely, not at all, be assured sir: [the] more I thought of my Schooling more I want to get back. But I have plenty business to attend to thus hindering me from going to School. And my people pulled me in every which way after I got here; they do not wish me to go back, and some wanted me that I should keep schools and others wished that I should go to Washington and arranged their business.

Even then Blackbird believed that he would be able to return to Twinsburg later that winter or in the spring. "I wish you to remember that I am coming and determined that I will have an education," he wrote. So certain was he that he would return he requested Bissell to continue to draw funds from Dr. Brainsmade, "for my school will be more costlier than it ever did. As I am intended to continue my course and enter in to the medical college."[30]

Blackbird had not been home long before he noticed significant changes afoot in northern Michigan. While he had been away European-American settlements, which previously had been restricted to the Straits of Mackinac and Sault Ste. Marie, had begun to expand into the heartland of the *Anishnabeg.* Agricultural settlements were still restricted to the area just north of the Grand River, but by 1850 logging enterprises were established across the breath of Ottawa and Chippewa territory. The opening of the Illinois and Michigan Canal in 1848 provided a key transportation artery between the pine forests of Michigan and the treeless prairies of Illinois. A great new demand for dimension lumber for houses, posts for fencing, and shingles for roofing was answered by entrepreneurs who valued the region's fir trees rather than its fur. Lake Michigan schooners increased in size and number, linking the lumber market in Chicago, soon to be the world's largest, with northern Michigan's pioneer mills. The Muskegon River, where Andrew had hunted as a boy with his father and brothers, was on its way to becoming an industrial waterway. Hundreds of lumberjacks were at work in camps spread out across its long valley. At its mouth a half dozen mills belched smoke and sawdust. Other mills were established at the White River, Big Sable, and Pere Marquette rivers. Even at Grand Traverse Bay the cry of the loon had been subjoined by the shrill whistle of a steam mill at Traverse City.[31]

The quickening of change in the region inevitably affected the *Anishnabeg.* Opportunities for wage labor expanded with the lumber industry. The

Chippewa with whom Andrew Blackbird had lived for five years at Mission Point took advantage of the expanding market and in 1849 signed contracts with Chicago tanneries to peel hemlock bark and transport it to the lakeshore, from whence it would be carried by ship to the city. On the negative side, greater *Anishnabeg* integration with American society meant increased exposure to alcohol and disease. Small trading vessels frequented the lakeshore, selling whiskey and driving missionaries to despair. Ships stopping to trade or refuel either at Grand Traverse or Little Traverse brought people, products, news, and, all too often, deadly microbes. In 1849 Chicago was ravaged by cholera and from that transportation hub the disease spread throughout the Lake Michigan basin. Some *Anishnabeg* who attended the annual treaty payment at Mackinac were mortally infected. That same summer smallpox was brought to the Manitou Islands by a steamboat that had sought shelter in the protected reach of Crescent Bay. Catholic missionary François Pierz immediately launched an inoculation campaign among the Ottawa to limit the danger.[32]

As the entire state of Michigan shook off the cobwebs that enmeshed it for nearly a decade after the Panic of 1837, some Indian communities found themselves overwhelmed. In the western Upper Peninsula copper and iron mining boomed. The Chippewa there had been forced to cede their lands in 1842 and in 1850 President Zachary Taylor ordered them removed to the west. The removal was postponed, but it sent shock waves throughout the state. In 1847 the Ottawa agricultural community in Allegan County founded by Ogemainini (aka Joseph Wakaso) was disrupted by the arrival of 1,500 Dutch settlers. The free-ranging livestock of the newcomers played havoc with the agricultural fields of the Ottawa, who had purchased the land around the Old Wing Mission after the 1836 treaty. The Dutch also brought smallpox to the area, which understandably set off a panic among the Ottawa. In spite of the efforts of their missionary, the Congregationalist George Smith, the Ottawa determined to sell out and return to northern Michigan, where recent land surveys made it possible for them to now buy land. In 1849 these people moved to a beautiful location on the Leelanau Peninsula, near the present town of Northport. George Smith moved with them in an attempt to keep his mission active. At the same time several non-Christian, traditional Ottawa bands also moved to the Grand Traverse region. The rapid settlement of southern Michigan was forcing more Indians to concentrate in northwest Michigan.[33]

Even Blackbird's home, the town of New L'Arbre Croche, had been touched by the changes sweeping the region. The mission and school continued as before, but were augmented by a sawmill. The acreage under cultivation outside the village had increased and a number of Ottawa men had become skilled carpenters and barrel makers, useful trades in a forested region with a thriving commercial fishing industry. Other changes were more unsettling for Andrew. There were, for example, several white merchants in the town. Originally, Catholic missionaries had pressed tribal leaders to forbid any traders from living permanently within the village. This was part of a program to keep alcohol out of the settlement. By 1850, however, the Ottawa began to resist the paternalistic control their pastor Father François Pierz attempted to exert. In frustration Pierz requested that the bishop reduce New L'Arbre Croche from a mission site to simply an affiliated station, for "so long as they remain slaves of the woods they will not listen to the voice of the priests." When two French-Canadian whiskey sellers were added to the three existing commercial establishments in town, Pierz despaired that "all the time . . . things get worse." Andrew was quick to note the change in his home: "I found my people to be very different from what they were, as they were beginning to have a free use of intoxicating liquors."[34]

The dependence and vulnerability of his people was especially brought home to Andrew when he joined them in their annual trip to Mackinac Island to receive their treaty payments. Indians began to arrive at the island in mid-September and their numbers grew as the month progressed. The government set no firm date for the payment; its agent at Detroit had to await the arrival of funds from Washington, so payments were only tentatively scheduled. In 1850 Blackbird and his family waited more than a month for the agent to arrive. What he saw in that time sickened him. The merchants of the island were more than willing to advance credit to the Ottawa who were soon to receive gold coin. Whiskey was openly hawked among the Indian lodges that dotted the lakeshore. Missionary George Smith complained to Samuel Bissell in a letter.

> Visit Mackinac during one of the payments & you might as it were get a peep into the scene. It seems as though the irreligious Whites were now with Locomotive & Electric speed . . . charged with engines of both, night & day to accomplish their object. Liquor & licentiousness are the chief instruments of destruction.

By the end of October, after two full months of waiting, the federal paymaster still had not arrived and even Ottawa and Chippewa who had resisted the proffered alcohol had accepted credit that exceeded their $8 annuity. Mackinac merchants were generous with credit because they had in the works a plan to secure another large payment of Ottawa treaty money.[35]

The treaty of 1836 had dedicated as much as $300,000 of the money the Ottawa and Chippewa received for the sale of their lands to the payment of the *Anishnabeg*'s outstanding debts to fur traders. When the all legal debts were settled $75,000 remained in the debt fund. This money was placed in public stock for the eventual use of the Ottawa and Chippewa people. A decade after, the treaty merchants began to advocate the appropriation of these funds for another round of debt relief. The money left in the debt fund was believed to have ballooned to nearly $150,000, and some Mackinac merchants loosened their credit to even the most prodigal customers in anticipation of a lucrative payday. With the merchants' aid some Ottawa and Chippewa leaders signed petitions to Washington in favor of debt relief.

When Andrew returned from Ohio the debt fund was one of two major issues before the Ottawa people. The other was an effort to eliminate the threat of removal by having the Indians made citizens. By 1850 the issues of removal, citizenship, and the debt fund were all entangled. Resolution was complicated by white "friends" of the *Anishnabeg* who were deeply interested in both issues and had enmeshed themselves in tribal councils. The traders, for example, were often blood relations accustomed to mixing their personal financial requirements with their duties as kinsmen. Missionaries were accustomed to regarding their congregations paternalistically, and all too often they acted without proper consultation.

The merchants' blend of self-interest and genuine support also was revealed in their encouragement of Ottawa citizenship during the 1840s. It was a strategy designed to keep the Indians in Michigan as future customers. When the government dragged its feet on citizenship rights the merchants supported Ottawa efforts to purchase land. They were aware that when Indians, either as individuals or as extended families, purchased parcels of the public domain, they gained a private property right that could secure themselves from removal. In 1844 the L'Arbre Croche Ottawa applied annuity money to the purchase of 1,000 acres of Little Traverse land. By 1855 they had completed the purchase of 16,000 acres of land from the General Land Office. Merchants benefited from this because their Ottawa customers now had tangible assets that could be attached if Indians incurred debts. Missionaries such as Peter Dougherty and François Pierz saw this danger and they warned their congregations of the risk of buying goods on credit. Father Pierz advocated the passage of special laws protecting Indian land from attachment by debt, but neither the Office of Indian Affairs nor the State of Michigan was inclined to act on his proposals.[36]

While Father Pierz was a strong supporter of Indian citizenship and property ownership his ingrained paternalism eventually led him to overstep the limits of his place in Ottawa society. In 1849 he acted upon his belief that the Mackinac merchants had too much influence over the Ottawa. He petitioned the federal Indian agent that the Ottawa be paid not at Mackinac, but at one of their own villages on the shore of Little Traverse Bay. His well-meaning goal was to reduce their exposure to alcohol, disease, and most especially, debt during their often long wait for the paymaster. Pierz then went beyond this well-meaning suggestion and attempted to have a Catholic merchant at Mackinac, J. A. Theodore Wendell, vested with power of attorney for all Ottawa legal matters. This was too much for even the Catholic Ottawa chiefs to tolerate. They would not allow Pierz to place a white man in charge of their legal affairs just because he had a confessional connection with them. Unfortunately for Pierz this dispute came up at the same time that the missionary had been instructed to inform the Ottawa that, in keeping with worldwide Catholic practice, the land on which all churches stood must belong to the bishop. This made the Ottawa anxious regarding all of the land that Father Pierz had helped them obtain from the government. They informed the Indian agent that Wendell and Pierz did not hold their trust and that the Ottawa, after a lengthy council, had directed Abram S. Wadsworth to act on their legal behalf. Wadsworth was a deputy federal land surveyor newly arrived from Connecticut and based with his family in a small cabin at Elk Rapids, on the shore of Grand Traverse Bay. He seems to have been selected by the Ottawa simply as a way to discredit Pierz and Wendell, and his charge was strictly limited to lobbying the federal government for payments due under the 1836 treaty. For his part Pierz believed that the reaction against him was the result of the intrigues of Protestant merchants in Mackinac. Nonetheless, he lost prestige and influence at L'Arbre Croche and he unsuccessfully petitioned the bishop to allow him to move on to a missionary position on Lake Superior. He complained that the Ottawa were "changing and influenced by the traders and the pupils from the Ohio school."[37]

Prominent among those "pupils from the Ohio school" was Andrew Blackbird. He was thrust into the debate regarding the debt fund and the fight for Ottawa citizenship. He saw that the traders had skillfully planted the notion that the debt fund money could only be used to pay merchants and it could not be used for any other purpose. The traders also tried to play the Ottawa and Chippewa against each other by threatening that if one tribe did not request debt payment all of the fund would be spent to clear the debts of the other. Andrew Blackbird refuted these distortions. In open council he translated the actual text of the 1836 treaty, which clearly stated that any extra money in the debt fund was "to apply to such other use as they [the Indians] may think proper." He characterized the remaining funds as "national money," belonging to all of the Ottawa and Chippewa people. Using such funds to pay private debts "is like stealing away the money of the innocent." Rather, Blackbird advocated, some of the money should be set aside for the purpose of educating Ottawa youth. He later told Reverend Bissell that "we had a most excellent class of Indians on our side," while the "majority who went for the traders are drunkards, lazy and debtors." When he was done speaking, Blackbird felt "the traders hated me worse than a dog because I oppose their proposition and read the articles of the treaty to the Indians." However, in the end, "The tongues of the traders were so sweet, so enticing to the ignorant we were overpowered."[38]

That winter Andrew Blackbird made one last effort to save the debt fund surplus for his people. He prepared a petition to President Millard Fillmore. "We remonstrate," Blackbird wrote, "because we, the Ottawas, are not in debt beyond our private means of paying and we are not only able but willing to pay all we owe, and we are sorry to believe that the Chippewas are in debt, therefore we do not feel willing that our share of the National Fund should be taken to pay that for which we have received nothing." Blackbird told the president of the Ottawa's "struggle between civilization and barbarism" and their desire to save all surplus funds in order to educate the rising generation, for "we desire to see the day when we can have Teachers of our own young men, and how are we to obtain that end when our money is gone." The chiefs of the three largest L'Arbre Croche coast villages signed the petition, but it availed them not. Later that year the Office of Indian Affairs yielded to the traders' lobby and the debt fund was plundered by the merchants.[39]

No sooner did the traders get their hands on the money remaining in the debt fund than they planned to raid another lode of cash outstanding from the 1836 treaty. When the Senate revised Schoolcraft's original agreement with the Ottawa and Chippewa, it limited the Indian's tenure on their reservations to five years. The revised treaty promised the *Anishnabeg* a payment of $200,000 upon the abandonment of their reservations. Some of the reservations, like the Chippewa reserves along the north shore of Lake Michigan, had never really been occupied. Other reserves, such as at Little Traverse and Grand Traverse, were the sites of extensive Indian farming communities. The treaty limited the *Anishnabeg* tenure to the reserves to a mere five years; after that they could stay on the lands only on the sufferance of the United States. This provision had been the source of Indian anxiety over removal since the five-year reserves expired in 1841. By 1850 the federal government had not acted to remove the Ottawa and Chippewa, nor had it paid the Indians the $200,000 fee for the reserves. Greedy merchants on Mackinac Island were anxious to have the $200,000 distributed to individual tribal members, so it could flow quickly into their cash drawers. For their part the Ottawa at L'Arbre Croche intended to continue to occupy their reserved lands and had no intention of accepting the cash award. Traders once more tried to influence individual *Anishnabeg* to lobby the federal government for the payment, while Andrew Blackbird and his cousin Augustin Hamlin led the effort against them.[40]

In the midst of this controversy came exciting news regarding Indian citizenship. In 1850 the state of Michigan held a constitutional convention with the purpose of expanding the direct political power of the electorate. The democratic spirit of the new document was reflected in its extension of the right to vote to male aliens who merely expressed the desire to become United States citizens and the extension of property rights (although not the ballot) to women. The convention also acted on the sentiment, expressed by the state legislature in 1844, that American Indians in Michigan should have the opportunity to be citizens. The new constitution stipulated every "male inhabitant of Indian descent, a native of the United States and not a member of a tribe," was entitled to the rights and responsibilities of citizenship.[41]

Clearly, this was an important development for the Ottawa's ongoing effort to fight removal, but the wording of the constitutional provision was ambiguous at best. Andrew Blackbird later wrote in his history that the Ottawa "were repeatedly told by our white neighbors that we could not very well be adopted as citizens of the State as long as we were receiving annuities from the general government on account of our former treaties." Initially, the leaders of L'Arbre Croche sought send an official delegation to Washington to determine the impact of the new constitution on Ottawa–United States relations. Blackbird was mentioned as one of the delegates, but then the plan was scratched due to discord among tribal leaders. This was caused by the cabal of merchants who saw the delegation as an opportunity to push the Ottawa and Chippewa into a hasty acceptance of the $200,000 for the reserved land. Blackbird bitterly condemned "the jealous eye" of the Mackinac traders, "those tyrants. . . . the whites of this place."[42]

Determined to grasp the chance for citizenship, Andrew led a smaller mission to consult with state authorities in Lansing. Joining Andrew in the delegation were "one of our young chieftains from Cross Village" and Abram Wadsworth, recently appointed as the "friend and advisor" of the Little Traverse Ottawa. All shipping on the lakes had already been suspended and so what otherwise would have been an easy steamboat passage instead necessitated an arduous and dangerous winter journey.[43]

The three men set out in February on an overland march through the wilderness of the interior of the Michigan peninsula. Hiking with snowshoes to the southeast, away from Lake Michigan, they entered the interior highlands region of the state, the coldest and bleakest part of Lower Michigan. It was a game-scarce region seldom visited even by the *Anishnabeg* bands that still conducted winter hunts. The men had no tent; rather they made their night camps in the manner of the voyageurs of northern Canada. When twilight overtook them they sought out a patch of thick trees to shelter them from the wind. Each man then made his bed of fresh-cut pine boughs and one or two woolen blankets. They crowded as close to each other and to the night fire as possible. On the coldest nights, when the winter sky cleared, Andrew shivered in his blankets, while seemingly at arm's reach above him hung an icy canopy of stars. Andrew had not lived the life of a hunter since he was a boy of seven or eight years of age. Unused to the elements, he must have found the journey both wonderful for its beauty and terrible for its hardship.[44]

After days of hard walking they reached the shores of Houghton Lake, near the head of the Muskegon River. They crossed its vast frozen surface and made camp amid the towering white pines on the far shore. That night, huddled around the fire, they ate the last of the food they had brought from home. Stiff and cold, they rose the next morning and without breakfast set off on their snowshoes. They traveled two full days without food to help fight off the biting cold. At the end of the third day, their steps slowing and their spirit flagging, they reached the Tittabawassee River. It was a welcome sight, as they knew they were nearing the haunts of the Saginaw Chippewa. They shuffled "down that stream on the ice" until "we came to an Indian camp which stood by the river side." Excitedly they shouted out their approach, with keen anticipation of a warm lodge and a hot meal. The camp, however, was deserted, although they "saw many human foot-prints on the ice." Nor did they find any food in the lodge. Dejectedly they pressed on, following the river, their haggard, hungry bodies bent into the arctic blasts. Fortunately, only a half mile further they spied a second Indian camp, and this one, blessedly, had "blue smoke coming out of it."[45]

It was a Chippewa hunting camp. The men were all out hunting, but the women and children, who were tending to the pelts, immediately set to fixing the famished travelers a much needed meal. The three men set out again the next morning and before long reached Saginaw. They had traveled more than 200 miles through the wilderness, overcoming extreme cold and hunger. Thinking back on the journey in later years, Blackbird recalled, "I have suffered very great hardships for this cause [citizenship], as I had to walk . . . almost the entire length of the southern peninsula of Michigan." From Saginaw south to Detroit, Blackbird and his companions had established, if deeply rutted, roads to follow. The hazardous part of their journey was over.[46]

The delegation's mission first took them to Detroit. They visited the office of Justice Warner Wing of the Supreme Court of Michigan. Wing was a veteran Democratic politician who, unlike many officials of his day, maintained a largely nonpartisan approach to public business. Blackbird and his companions were greeted by a handsome man known for his "genial wit and humor." Andrew requested Justice Warner's interpretation of the new Michigan constitution's Indian citizenship provision.

> We had a pleasant visit with him, and he gave us his legal opinion of this matter, that he did not think that it would debar us from being citizens of the State, because the Government owed us a little money on account of our former treaties, provided we should renounce our allegiance to our chiefs and recognize no other chief authority than the President of the United States; and that we would not be required to have any writ of naturalization as we are already naturalized by being American born.

This was exactly the interpretation that Andrew Blackbird wanted to hear. Federal treaty obligations would not be abridged by the acceptance of state citizenship.[47]

That Justice Wing emphasized the role of chief's in Indian government revealed how little Michigan authorities understood Ottawa and Chippewa life. Wing saw Indian people as having an "allegiance" to their chiefs that was similar to the oaths sworn by Europeans to their sovereign. The United States required naturalizing immigrants to abandon their allegiance to all foreign monarchs. Ottawa men, on the contrary, were bound by no formal oath to respect the authority of chiefs. The new constitution's citizenship offer placed emphasis on an Indian man being "civilized" and not a member of a "tribe." For the Ottawa of that time tribal membership was a condition of birth or adoption. Since Wing did not regard receiving annuities as a factor negating the offer of citizenship, the sole standard for determining if a male Indian might vote or otherwise act as a citizen was his status as "civilized." Most L'Arbre Croche residents, Blackbird realized, could justly claim to be "civilized." They lived in cabins and grew crops or harvested fish for the market. Many were Christian. Some even had become landowners. Under Justice Wing's minimal standards for citizenship the constitution's offer was open to nearly any Indian who wanted to accept it.

After consulting with Justice Wing, Blackbird once more took to the road. He and his companions were off to the state capital at Lansing. Detroit had served as the capital until 1847, when Lansing was chosen for its central location. As Blackbird left behind the urban comforts of Detroit for several more days of wintry travel, he and his companions must have deeply regretted the recent change of venue. If not, they surely did when they reached Lansing, a dismal, drab smear of mud and sawdust on the banks of the Grand River. When it had been named the capital of Michigan three years before, it had only two buildings, a log cabin and a sawmill. Since that time the town added several boardinghouses and a white frame capital building that looked like a boardinghouse. In the latter building Blackbird met with John S. Barry. Governor Barry was a no-nonsense Democrat who brought to the executive office the level head of a successful country merchant. He won wide respect for helping to bring state government out of the deep debts caused by an overly ambitious program of internal improvements and the disastrous Panic of 1837. When Blackbird met him he was in the middle of his unprecedented third term.

Blackbird presented the Governor with a petition that he had drafted, signed by the chiefs of the L'Arbre Croche region. It was an appeal that the Ottawa be adopted as

> Common citizens of the state of Michigan, to have all the rights and privileges of American citizenship. And that we should forever remain in this land of our fathers, such who are enlightened and civilized Indians.

Blackbird also put to Barry the same question he had earlier asked Justice Wing. Barry had been a member of the Constitution Convention and he explained to the delegation that it was not the intention of the new law to place obstacles before Indians who wanted to be citizens. Blackbird later wrote in his history,

> The Governor received us very kindly and gave us much good counsel on the subject of citizenship, giving us some instructions as to how we should live under the rule of the State if we should become the children of the same. He talked to us as though he was talking to his own son who had just come from a far country and asked his father's permission to stay in the household.

This account recalls Blackbird's earlier use of the prodigal son parable in his appeals to Presbyterian congregations in 1848. After his hazardous winter journey Andrew may well have felt like someone who "had just come from a far country." He seems to have accepted the paternalism of Governor Barry in the spirit of that more deferential age and did not intend the irony of the native Ottawa asking a white politician for "his father's permission to stay in the household."[48]

While in Lansing, Blackbird and his companions also sought out Michigan's secretary of state and "some members of the State Legislature." Again, they received assurance that it was Michigan's intent that willing Indian men should be granted the rights of citizenship, regardless of the treaty obligations of the United States government. Blackbird may have presented the state officials with a preliminary list of Ottawa men who "may be entitle[d] for voting." Blackbird lobbied the legislators about the importance of having the Office of Indian Affairs recognize the altered status of Michigan Indians. This bore fruit on April 7, 1851, when the legislature approved a formal resolution to Congress.

> Whereas the constitution of the State of Michigan gives unto all civilized persons of Indian descent equal rights and privileges with the white inhabitants of said state, and whereas by the adoption of said clause in the constitution, the people of this state have evinced a just and humane desire to see the Indians who now inhabit Michigan raised from a state of semi-barbarism to one of enlightenment and have by it removed one great barrier that has hither to prevented the consummation of this philanthropic object. And whereas the Ottawa and Chippewa Indians residing amongst us are a civil, well disposed, peaceable and orderly people, and have during the past few years made great advancement in the agricultural and mechanics arts, and a large portion of them ardently desire to remain in Michigan to become civilized and share with us in our social, political, and religious privileges. Therefore be it enacted by the Senate and House of Representatives of the State of Michigan that we do hereby request the government of the United States to make such arrangements for said Indians as they may desire for their permanent location in the northern part of this state.

Governor Barry sent this resolution not only to Michigan's congressional representatives to be placed before Congress, but to ensure that its intent was not lost on the administration, copies were also forwarded to the secretary of the interior, the commissioner of Indian affairs, and the president of the United States.[49]

In later years Andrew Blackbird would imply that the Indian citizenship provision in the 1850 constitution was the result of his lobbying. "My object of promulgating this cause was," he wrote in his history, that "I thought it would be the only salvation of my people from being sent off west of the Mississippi, where perhaps, more than one-half would have died before they could be acclimated to the country to which they had been driven." Yet citizenship had been an avowed goal of the L'Arbre Croche Ottawa since December 1835, when Augustin Hamlin, Apokisigan, and Mackadepenessy mentioned it as an alternative to removal in a petition to the United States. His father, cousin, and friend, Alvin Coe, had all played a more important role than he in advancing that effort. Blackbird's recent opponents at home, the Mackinac traders and L'Arbre Croche's Catholic missionary, François Pierz, had also fought for citizenship longer and more effectively through repeated letters and petitions. Andrew Blackbird came late to the citizenship fight, although it was an issue that was always on his mind when he was studying in Ohio.[50]

Andrew Blackbird's genuine contribution to Indian citizenship in Michigan came after the approval of the 1850 constitution. His timely consultations with Justice Wing and Governor Barry helped to provide immediate clarification of the constitutional convention's legislative intent. Many Indians believed, as the Chippewa of the Upper Peninsula expressed in a petition to the commissioner of Indians affairs, that they could not collect their federal treaty payment and still accept Michigan's offer of citizenship. "We have a hard alternative before us," they wrote, "to forgo all the benefits of the treaty of 1836, or to accept the protection of the Constitution." Blackbird's meetings with state authorities marked the first steps in a long legal journey, one that continues to this day, in which Michigan's native people have negotiated their dual status as *Anishnabeg* and as citizens. His efforts staunched the flood of misinformation that was sweeping through northern Michigan. After his trip to Lansing, Blackbird wrote, "Not many Indians believed these flying reports gotten up by our white neighbors."[51] Blackbird's intervention also yielded the important joint resolution from the Michigan legislature that enjoined the United States to treat with the Ottawa and Chippewa and arrange their "permanent location in the northern part of the state." It is possible that he actually wrote the first draft of the document and submitted to the legislature. A copy of the resolution written in Blackbird's hand was sent to Samuel Bissell, which testifies to the pride Andrew took in lobbying for its passage.

Andrew Blackbird was right to take pride in the acquisition of citizenship because it is unlikely that Indians would have secured that legal status without their direct action on their own behalf. In June 1850, when the state constitutional convention debated granting rights to Indians, the issue focused largely on the rights of mixed bloods. William Norman McLeod, a Mackinac merchant, advocated for the suffrage rights of individuals who were the result of marriages between "the French and Indian races." This implied the constitutional provision giving the vote to "every civilized male inhabitant of Indian descent, a native of the United States and not a member of any tribe," originally was intended to apply only to mixed bloods like Andrew's cousin Augustin Hamlin. Indeed McLeod was a friend and associate of Hamlin and Mackinac County, Michigan, contained a large number of men who shared Hamlin's Franco-*Anishnabe* ancestry. Ottawa and Chippewa leaders, however, took the constitution's provision literally, as their petitions to the federal government reveal. Andrew Blackbird's mission to Lansing further pressed the issue and resulted in the 1851 joint resolution by the Michigan legislature that essentially accepted the Indian interpretation of the 1850 constitution. Indian initiative in the political sector transformed what might have been simply a provision for mixed-blood voting rights into a broadly recognized opportunity for Indians to secure "equal rights and privileges with white inhabitants." What both the State of Michigan and the Indians recognized, however, was that in order for *Anishnabeg* to secure such rights, they needed the cooperation of the federal government in securing a place for them to live.[52]

In the wake of the state joint resolution, the Office of Indian Affairs dispatched a special agent, Elias Murray, to northern Michigan charged with determining if the Ottawa had indeed made progress on the path of civilization or if they should be removed. Blackbird was determined to impress Murray. The agent visited whitewashed L'Arbre Croche villages, with their streets and rows of log and frame houses, the steepled churches, and their schools. At a formal council in August 1851 Murray asked the Ottawa if they were willing to emigrate. Andrew Blackbird was called upon by the chiefs to "speak to the commissioners." He clearly stated, "We do not wish to emigrate to any place." Blackbird then went on to emphasize that the Ottawa were now property owners with a right to stay on the land. They loved the country of their birth and they lived in a place where they "trouble nobody."[53]

Afterward, Blackbird told Bissell that the "subject of emigration is left without any conclusion on their part. But on our part. . . . .we never will emigrate to the west even if they do threaten us to put an end of our existence." Fortunately, that was also the conclusion that Elias Murray reported to the commissioner of Indian affairs in Washington. By the fall of 1851, citizenship and the "civilized" look of their villages finally dissipated the dark cloud of removal that had so long hung over the shores of Little Traverse. Andrew Blackbird's successful mission to Lansing, his role as spokesman to the United States commissioners, marked him as one of the rising young leaders of the Ottawa nation and the successor to his father's leading role in the civilization program.[54]

That fall Andrew might have returned to Ohio to complete his education. However, Mackadepenessy, his now aged father, depended upon Andrew. The old man needed a new house, and building the structure became Andrew's responsibility. In November 1850 Andrew had informed Bissell, "I want to build a house for my father and after that my father is willing that I may go to school for as long as I please." That Mackadepenessy needed a new house is made clear in another letter from that time. Samuel Bissell had made overtures that he might visit Andrew in Michigan. Andrew replied, "I hope you will not come until we finish our house or till I get back again so I can come along with you. But we have no place now for to take you in, except old log house and it is not fit for the white man or clean person to go in to."[55]

By now he had readjusted to the harsh rhythms of life in northern Michigan. Andrew once more took to the lake, fishing for the "fresh Mackinac Trout" he loved to eat. He likely helped to harvest crops of corn and beans in the fall, and make maple sugar in the waning days of winter. As he did so he saw again firsthand the vulnerability of his people to the white man's poisons and the whims of nature. After the 1850 payment northern Lake Michigan was hit by a "dreadful storm." Andrew and Mackadepenessy along with their relations left the island immediately after the payment and reached their homes just before the storm broke. Many others, however, lingered and indulged in another "firewater" frolic. Some of these were caught on the open water by the November gale. Even some of those ashore were caught by the tempest. Some Ottawa "drowned on dry land," due to the "sudden rush of the water come up from the lake." The storm surge flooded much of Mackinac's business district and its wharfs were uprooted. As many as seven vessels in the area were driven ashore. Andrew's friends from school, Augustus and Tirza Mixinassau, lost their sister in the storm, while another friend lost her mother when her canoe capsized off Cheboygan.[56]

Blackbird nursed a growing resentment of the Mackinac traders and their role in the liquor trade. He attempted to tackle what he saw as an increase in alcohol abuse among the Ottawa by launching a temperance campaign. He adopted the methods he had seen used by Protestant clergy in Ohio: "Seeing them degrading themselves by the free use of intoxicating liquors, I immediately formed a constitutional pledge & got the chiefs to authorize it, so as to give effect & got them all to sign said pledge." Andrew took the pledge from L'Arbre Croche to Middle Village and Cross Village. He later wrote in his history, "I was quite successful, as almost everyone pledged themselves never again to touch intoxicating drinks."[57]

Blackbird also once more clashed with the Catholic clergy who managed the L'Arbre Croche missions. While he was in Ohio he tentatively moved his religious allegiance from the Catholic Church to Presbyterianism. Religion was not one of the formal subjects taught at Twinsburg, but each student, in the words of the school handbook, participated in "Biblical exercises, each Sabbath." Andrew's nine years living among evangelical Protestants, first at Mission Point and later in Ohio, were formative. Yet in his history he was careful to state that it was not due to the "personal persuasion" of ministers or teachers that he was converted. He studied the Bible on his own and concluded, "By terrible conviction on reading the word of God—'That there is no mediator between God and man but one, which is Christ Jesus, who was crucified for the remission of sins.'" At the heart of his conversion was a rejection of the role of the clergy as an indispensable conduit between a believer and God. This belief put him on a collision course with the missionaries and strained relations between Andrew and many of his friends, including his sister Margaret, who worked as a teacher in the Catholic mission school.[58]

At first Andrew did not make a show of his formal change of religion. It was soon noted, however, that he did not attend confession. The Church tried to woo Blackbird back into the fold. Bishop Peter Paul Lefevere personally sought out Andrew when he visited the L'Arbre Croche mission in the summer of 1851. The young Ottawa's education and family connections made him a valuable parishioner. Like all of the Ottawa mission priests, Lefevere was European born and accustomed to deference from the laity. What he unexpectedly encountered in his meeting with Blackbird was a confident young man who proceeded to draw the prelate into a debate on God's saving grace.

The bishop began by reminding Andrew of his baptism into the Catholic Church, and his responsibility to follow the "orders" of the Church, including attendance at confession. Blackbird replied that while he had in the past practiced the Catholic sacraments he had never really "converted to Christ." By this Andrew meant the rebirth that Calvinists believed came to adult Christians when God's grace entered their lives.

"Do you expect that God will do a miracle upon your heart?" the bishop challenged.

Andrew responded, as he later told Samuel Bissell in a letter, with his own challenge. "If a man professes to do [a] miracle on this earth, God will do [a] greater miracle than any earthly being?"

The bishop and Father Pierz "were all furiously mad" because Andrew called into question the Church's mediating role between man and God on earth. There followed a heated exchange about Church's role in salvation. Not surprisingly, Andrew reported, "I could not reason with them at all."

The bishop warned Andrew that unless he submitted himself to the Church, the mission would oppose Blackbird's role as spokesman and counselor of the Ottawa. Nor would they allow him to teach school at L'Arbre Croche. On the other hand, if Andrew returned to the confessional fold, the Bishop promised, "He will favor all my undertakings." It was a critical moment for the young man. Although it sometimes overreached its authority in Ottawa politics, the Roman Church was an extremely influential community institution in all the villages along Little Traverse. When Andrew stepped outside its circle he isolated himself and inaugurated a cold war with the Church.[59]

Blackbird's well-meaning temperance pledge became the first battle as the missionaries moved to erode Andrew Blackbird's position in Ottawa society. In the wake of his successful temperance pledge, Fathers François Pierz and Ignatius Mrak, in Blackbird's words,

> began to persecute, excommunicating all those who have taken my council & causing them to withdraw or blot out their names from the pledge, telling them that they had done a great wrong in listening to me, because I was evidently a Protestant. Priest Mrak told the Indians at Cross [Village] that whenever I come here they must not even look at me, nor speak to me. If I were hungry they must not give me anything to eat. If I was cold they must not let me into their house.

Blackbird was shocked by the priest's strong reaction against him. "What if I should perish at the door of my own brother," he complained to Bissell, "just because I am trying to do them good! Monstrous! What dark instruction from him who claims to be an interpreter of my God?"[60]

Pierz and Mrak were not against Blackbird's message of temperance; rather they regarded the messenger as part of the problem. They were concerned that alcohol abuse was on the rise. In the past the priests had organized the signing of abstinence pledges. They saw Protestant missionaries, federal Indian agents, and the whiskey-selling merchants of Mackinac all as threats to the Catholic Indian colony they hoped to build along the shores of Little Traverse. Pierz and Mrak were Slovene priests who spoke little English and had an ingrained distrust of the republican government of the United States. While some Ottawa had converted to Catholicism as a means of adapting to the rising American tide, the missionaries hoped to create isolated, largely self-sufficient Christian communities. For a time this appealed to Ottawa concerned with retaining their political autonomy. One of Pierz's strongest supporters among the Ottawa was Mokomanish, the aged warrior who was one of the few L'Arbre Croche chiefs unwilling to sign the 1836 treaty of cession. Although he often overreached his authority,

Pierz worked hard to keep whites from residing in the Little Traverse villages and he tried to limit Ottawa contact with Mackinac merchants.[61]

Pierz was a man of strong opinions and ramrod will. He had first come to Michigan in 1835 at the age of fifty, a time when most Slovene parish priests were settled in placid sinecures. Pierz, on the contrary, was a man of restless energy with a bent for practical problem-solving. With great difficulty he learned and then mastered the *Anishnabe* language. During his time at L'Arbre Croche he was constantly in motion, introducing new crops at Middle Village, rushing up to Cheboygan to inoculate Indians at risk for smallpox, undertaking missionary journeys to Beaver Island or as far down the lakeshore as Muskegon, everywhere advocating Catholic catechism and practicing homeopathic medicine. Ignatius Mrak was equally formidable. He had been with the Ottawa since 1845 and would eventually succeed Pierz in directing the Catholic effort among them. Mrak would be named bishop of the Marquette diocese in 1869. After serving in that capacity for a decade he retired due to rheumatism, yet he immediately returned to his work as a pastor among the *Anishnabeg.*[62]

Pierz held a special contempt for the contingent of Ottawa youth who during the 1840s and 1850s went east to Ohio for an English-language education. In his 1855 book *Die Indianer in Nord Amerika,* Pierz described the flow of students to Twinsburg as a Protestant plot to use a few well-educated returning students to highlight the failures of Catholic education.

> However, the contrary soon became evident; for the people recognized in them labor-Shirking dudes and proud vagabonds that aside from a few English phrases, they had learned nothing save the vices of the whites. They proved themselves everywhere to be liars, silly kickers and impudent mockers of religion. By their corrupt morals and seduction of girls, they also made themselves contemptible among good Christians. Their very face afforded the proof that Protestant educational institutions are not suitable for imparting a Christian training to savage Indians.

Pierz's harsh judgment, while clearly biased, had some merit.[63]

In 1850 the Congregational missionary George Smith admonished Samuel Bissell that "the young men who have been to Twinsburg" were in his opinion "much worse than they were before & the worst young men we know in the region." On the other hand, Smith believed the problem with Bissell's institution was that it allowed Catholic students to remain Catholics. He complained that Presbyterian boys like Andrew's cousin Joseph Wakazoo who attended the academy were overly influenced by the Catholic

Ottawa boys in residence. Those students returned to Michigan "stronger Catholics & less correct in their conduct."[64]

Ironically it was the Protestant ministers who may have had more trouble than the Catholics with the boys newly returned from Ohio. In the summer of 1850 Paul Nawogade, the young Ottawa who had journeyed to Twinsburg with Andrew, and his brother John Nawogade, who also was enrolled at Bissell's school for a time, attended one of Reverend Smith's Sunday school services at Northport. The boys were friends of Joseph Wakazoo, nephew of the deceased chief of the band. Smith was attempting to read the Ten Commandments in Ottawa to a room crowded with young people. The Nawogade brothers, Smith later complained, had the "boldness & impudence to say I was not correct." Smith responded he "read them as God gave them to Moses." Paul then retorted that Smith lied, and he proceeded to "prove" his point, by reading the Commandments to the class "as rendered in the Roman prayer book to the Indians, as if he were installed in my place." Later, on the Fourth of July, the Nawogade brothers disrupted Smith and Dougherty's joint mission celebration of the day by showing up in their boat and luring most of the young people away for a high-spirited trip to Little Traverse.[65]

That Ottawa boys from Twinsburg had some problems readjusting to L'Arbre Croche is understandable. They were a largely self-selected group. Those bold enough to set off on their own for Ohio were likely independent youths who would chaff at clerical authority, regardless of its confession. Besides, most of what the missionaries objected to were offenses typical of any adolescent. Moreover, unlike Andrew Blackbird, few of them had stayed in school long enough to learn more than basic literacy. They did not really return home with skills that were immediately valuable. This became another aspect of the conflict that emerged between Blackbird and the Catholic priests. Blackbird placed a high value on English literacy, while Father Pierz's mission focused more on creating a community of faith and work.

Andrew Blackbird had lived and labored among the whites. During his time at Green Bay, while at Mission Point, and, most importantly, during his four years at Twinsburg he formed friendships among them, acquired skills, and became educated. Blackbird had learned the ways of the Americans. He believed the Ottawa needed to know the language of the newcomers whose tidal waters were already washing against the beaches of Little Traverse. Pierz, on the contrary, believed that contact with American society had a negative impact on the Ottawa and should be avoided. He believed that the *Anishnabeg* were naturally "contended, peaceable and good people."

Only those with "much association with disorderly whites" came to "lead evil lives and go astray." Rather than teaching the Ottawa how to fit into American society Pierz believed it was his duty to help insulate them from it in the cocoon of a Catholic colony, outside the American mainstream. For this reason Pierz funded with his own money the building of a sawmill and a flourmill at Cross Village. Thus Indian carpenters, barrel makers, boat makers, even farmers need not depend on American merchants to practice their trade. School was important because it taught the Ottawa about their faith, but for Pierz it was also important that Indians learn trades and other skills of sedentary life. Pierz even taught the Ottawa new farming techniques, a subject on which he had written a book when he was a parish priest in Slovenia. While Blackbird experienced what Pierz called a "literary education," the Catholic mission was more vocationally oriented. Pierz's focus was always on the continuation of a Catholic Indian community. During the 1840s he supported the use of annuity money to purchase land, but he always encouraged that the land be held in common, so that whites would not settle among them. In 1851 he entreated with Bishop Peter Paul Lefevere to "do something" to prevent whites from buying land along Little Traverse. He assured the bishop, "The savages would be good citizens if kept away from the whites." For Pierz the Catholic Church should be for the Ottawa a bulwark against unwanted change. For Blackbird, Protestant Christianity was a necessary step toward an inevitable change.[66]

Inevitably Blackbird challenged the Roman Church on the educational front. Since his return to L'Arbre Croche, Andrew had been pressed by Ottawa men interested in learning English to open a school. Most Catholic schools were taught in the *Anishnabe* language by Ottawa teachers. English had only been taught off and on at the Catholic schools. Blackbird's cousin Augustin Hamlin was so employed in 1836 but he later quarreled with Pierz and was discharged. Nor was Pierz vigorous in recruiting new teachers, not when the same funds could be used to establish outlying Ottawa mission schools at Beaver Island and along Grand Traverse Bay. Andrew Blackbird charged that the Catholic hierarchy purposefully prevented English-language instruction. By 1852 he operated his own school. It was located in his home village of New L'Arbre Croche. Classes were held in the evening. Blackbird initially encountered "a great deal of difficulty for the want of books," but eventually local missionaries rallied to his aid. Pierz countered by opening his own English-language night school in direct competition with Blackbird. "However, with all their crafty mode," Andrew wrote, "I had more scholars than they & the most excellent class of young men. We also had a Lyceum once in two weeks." Blackbird's school, nonetheless, was short lived. It lacked a formal school building, classroom, and tables. He told Bissell, "When my school closed theirs did also, & so they are on their old track again."[67]

One of the reasons Blackbird may have closed his school was the successful establishment of a Presbyterian mission school on the shores of Little Traverse. This development was the result of the breakup of Peter Dougherty's Grand Traverse mission. By 1850 a significant number of both Ottawa and Chippewa determined that in lieu of a federal guarantee, the best way for them to secure a place for their families was to purchase land. The Mission Peninsula, where Dougherty's operation was based, was closed from public land sales as an Indian reservation. As a result Indian families began to leave the vicinity of Dougherty's mission and settle on land they bought on the mainland to the east and west of Grand Traverse Bay. In 1852 Dougherty moved his operation to the west shore of the bay, near the present town of Omena. It was also at this time that the Catholic Indians along Grand Traverse relocated and founded the community of Peshawbestown. However, a handful of the families who had resided with Dougherty's mission relocated farther to the northeast at Bear River, on Little Traverse Bay. This group successfully appealed to the Presbyterian Board of Foreign Missions for an English-language school. In the spring of 1852 Andrew Porter, a lay teacher who had previously worked at Mission Point, established the first Protestant school on Little Traverse Bay.[68]

What made Bear Creek a viable community was the arrival of Chief Petosega and a number of Ottawa families from Middle Village. Petosega, or as his name became more commonly spelled, Petoskey, had sent his two sons, Francis and Mitchell, to the Twinsburg Academy, much to the disgust of Father Pierz. The priest lobbied Petoskey's wife, Kewaykabawikwa, a pious member of his congregation, to have the boys withdrawn from the Protestant school. Chief Petoskey, however, resented Pierz's intrusion into his domestic arrangements. He withdrew both himself and his wife from the Catholic Church and together with several related families moved to Bear Creek when that place was just being founded.

It is likely that Andrew Blackbird participated in the founding of the Bear Creek community, what would later become the city of Petoskey, Michigan. He described Chief Petoskey as a "most excellent, enlighten[ed], promoter of education," and he had already been in contact with Andrew Porter when he needed books for his own short-lived school. Blackbird may even have been among the enthusiastic handful who gathered on the beach in June 1852 to help erect the Presbyterian schoolhouse. The schooner *Eliza Caroline* had deposited a pile of lumber. Unfortunately, it was agreed the best site for the school was on high ground a half mile away from the lakeshore. A trail had to be hacked out up the hill and then with a combination of horse power and brute manual labor the boards were hefted up to the school site.[69]

For a time the Presbyterians were also able to open a school at Middle Village. Andrew Blackbird worked as one of the teachers and as the translator. H. W. Guthrie, a newly ordained Presbyterian divine with no knowledge of the Ottawa language, split his time between Bear Creek and Middle Village. His linguistic limitations made Andrew's ability to translate all the more valuable. After two years, however, Guthrie quit the mission, and the Middle Village school had to be abandoned. In his history Blackbird described these years as consumed by "doing a little of everything, laboring, teaching, and interpreting sermons among the Protestant missions."[70]

Courtesy of the Library of Congress.

Henry Rowe Schoolcraft, Indian Agent for the Little Traverse Ottawa from 1833 to 1841. A pioneer geologist, geographer, and ethnologist, Schoolcraft tried unsuccessfully to control the Ottawa's efforts to accommodate to American political and economic power.

From Samuel Alanson Lane, *Fifty Years and Over of Akron and Summit County* (Akron: Beacon Job Department, 1892).

Reverend Samuel Bissell was the founder of the Twinsburg Institute and a strong supporter of the education of Great Lakes region Indian youths. He was a lifelong mentor and friend of Andrew Blackbird.

Courtesy of the Library of Congress.

Andrew Blackbird's allotment under the 1855 Treaty of Detroit eventually became a golf course for visiting tourists.

Courtesy of the Library of Congress.

In the late nineteenth and early twentieth centuries passenger ships offered daily service to the Little Traverse Bay towns of Petoskey and Harbor Springs. Fast vessels could provide overnight service to urban centers like Chicago.

Courtesy of the Library of Congress.

Harbor Springs as it appeared in the 1890s. Fifty years prior, Andrew Blackbird watched from this vantage point as his father departed by canoe to meet with President Andrew Jackson.

Courtesy of the Library of Congress.

Harbor Springs, Michigan from the Point.

Courtesy of the Library of Congress.

The waterfront hotels and boarding houses for elite white urbanites replaced the log and frame homes of the Odawa who founded Harbor Springs, Michigan.

COURTESY OF THE LIBRARY OF CONGRESS.

LITTLE TRAVERSE BAY, CIRCA 1890.

COURTESY OF THE LIBRARY OF CONGRESS.

THE PETOSKEY RAILROAD STATION, CIRCA 1890. THE GRAND RAPIDS AND INDIANA RAILROAD FIRST REACHED LITTLE TRAVERSE BAY IN 1873. RAILROAD CONNECTIONS TO DETROIT AND CHICAGO RADICALLY TRANSFORMED THE LITTLE TRAVERSE REGION AND BROUGHT WITH IT A FLOOD OF EUROPEAN-AMERICAN RESIDENTS.

Courtesy of the Library of Congress.

In the 1880s Odawa families still visited Mackinac Island to trade. Instead of furs they then marketed fish, finely woven baskets, or birch bark boxes for sale to tourists.

COURTESY OF THE LIBRARY OF CONGRESS.

AN ODAWA CHURCH IN PETOSKEY, MICHIGAN. CHRISTIANITY, BOTH CATHOLIC AND METHODIST, BECAME AN IMPORTANT INSTITUTION SUSTAINING ODAWA COMMUNITY AND IDENTITY.

Courtesy of Jane Cardinal.

Margaret Boyd was Andrew Blackbird's sister. She was a lifelong resident of the Harbor Springs area and she played an important role in the Odawa program of resistance through accommodation. She was educated in a Cincinnati convent school and returned to L'Arbre Croche to teach in the Catholic mission school. This photograph illustrates her devotion to Catholicism as well as to Odawa traditional culture. In the foreground is a beautiful example of the quillwork vessels that Odawa women made for sale to tourists. Margaret Boyd was a master of this work, and she played a major role in the revival of this craft tradition.

Courtesy of the Library of Congress.

The Wequetonsing Resort on Little Traverse Bay was located adjacent to Andrew Blackbird's eighty-acre federal land allotment.

Courtesy of Jane Cardinal.

Andrew Blackbird's home in Harbor Springs where he and his wife Elizabeth raised their four children. Attached to the house is the false-faced post office Blackbird built in 1877 but was never able to use because he was forced out of the position of town postmaster.

5

Citizen Blackbird

During the protracted winter of 1850–51 Andrew Blackbird spent much time with his father. The son cut timber to build a new house for the old man and in the evenings it is likely they sat by the fire while Mackadepenessy spun out stories about his own adventures in the white man's world. They may have talked of Andrew's mother and of the many winters they had spent as a family hunting on the upper Muskegon River. Counting back over the winters, they together worked out how many years had passed since Andrew had been born. Blackbird had never known for sure what his age was and it had never been regarded as important, either by him or his father. Since Andrew had returned from school in Ohio, however, he had begun to feel anxious about the passage of time. The number of winters Mackadepenessy counted since his son's birth surprised and disheartened Andrew. "I am nearly 30 years of age," he wrote Bissell in 1851, "older than I ever thought I was."

The thought that he was "nearly 30 years of age" seems to have oppressed Andrew in a way that neither his father or his sisters and brothers would have understood. Indeed, it was a measure of the degree to which Blackbird had incorporated into his worldview the European-American sense of time. Sitting with his father he had suddenly discovered he was no longer young. Just a few years before, he had been among the bright-eyed boys at the Twinsburg Academy sharing books and dreams of the future. Then between 1850 and 1855 he was back in Michigan, and time passed in the Indian way with the seasons, as he moved from job to job, fishing, cutting timber, harvesting corn, teaching occasionally, translating for whites better educated than himself. While he might have taken pride in his successful mission to Lansing and his role as a tribal spokesman, he also seems to have felt anxious and unfulfilled. In spite of having more education than any other Little Traverse Ottawa, save for his cousin Augustin Hamlin, he was prevented from taking a place in the Indian school because of his break with the Catholic Church. Frustrated, he thought of his dream of studying medicine, which seemed to be his future when he was in Ohio. Had the prospect of medical education already slipped beyond his reach? At L'Arbre Croche he did not even have access to a medical dictionary, not that he had "any leisure hours at home to study" due to the need to constantly be "employed at something." For Andrew Blackbird, life seemed to be slipping away.[1]

THE TREATY OF 1855

In the spring of 1855 Blackbird received a call to action. The commissioner of Indian affairs, George Manypenny, summoned the leaders of the Ottawa and Chippewa to meet him at Detroit to resolve the permanent status of the Indian people of northwest Michigan. A new treaty had been in the works for many years. The Ottawa had many times petitioned Washington to recognize their persistence in Michigan and move toward a set of policies that would facilitate the economic and cultural changes they had embraced. Only the winter before, a delegation of Grand River Ottawa made their way to the capital to press the government to act. For its part the United States had largely forsaken the removal policy of Andrew Jackson. The rapid movement of American citizens into the region west of the Mississippi River, which accelerated after 1848 and the successful completion of the Mexican War, doomed the fantasy of a "permanent Indian frontier." Northern Michigan lands were selling briskly, but were actually in less demand by American citizens than lands in Kansas, Missouri, and Iowa. Michigan's offer of citizenship punctuated the European-American repudiation of removal.

The prospect of citizenship for all of the Ottawa and Chippewa people in Michigan necessitated a new treaty. The 1836 agreement had only provided for the temporary persistence of the *Anishnabeg* on their old lands. The long-ago expired reservations had become an obstacle to both Indians and whites alike. The treaty had envisioned the surrender of the reservations within five years, but after that deadline arrived in 1841, no removal took place and the lands became a real estate limbo. Whites could not buy reserved lands and *Anishnabeg* could not improve them because the future status of the land remained uncertain. A considerable number of Ottawa and Chippewa abandoned their homes on the reservations in order to secure clear title to farms elsewhere. The government had to resolve the issue of where the Ottawa and Chippewa would reside in Michigan. Taking a cue from Indian property owners, Commissioner of Indian Affairs Manypenny believed that homesteads allotted to each family were the proper answer.[2]

Andrew Blackbird was selected by his people to be among the more than fifty-four Ottawa and Chippewa leaders to travel to Detroit to consult with Commissioner Manypenny. He boarded the steamboat for Detroit with a personal agenda for the coming council. Education was the cornerstone. His personal experience and his family background conditioned him to see education as the foundation of his people's future. As a child he had seen Mackadepenessy teaching the "Paw-pa-pe-po" Indian syllabary, while the lives of his brother William and sisters Margaret and Electa were shaped by their success in European-American education. At Twinsburg Ottawa students had been driven by the desire "that we may do good for our people," without the interference of agents or missionaries.[3] In 1850 he had tried and failed to convince the Ottawa that the $150,000 remnant of the 1836 debt fund should be dedicated to paying to educate *Anishnabe* youth in distant white schools. Instead men with short-term vision yield to the blandishments of the Mackinac traders, and those funds were squandered. At Detroit Andrew Blackbird wanted to secure tribal control of their educational resources and direct those resources to successful English-language educators.[4]

The composition of the L'Arbre Croche delegation revealed that a "changing of the guard" had taken place among the Ottawa leadership. Chief Apokisigan, who had played such a prominent role in encouraging the Ottawa embrace of American civilization, had died the year before. Mackadepenessy was too old and weak to any longer play a large role in political affairs. Assiginack, who had teamed with his brother in the cultural transformation of the early nineteenth century, was long gone to Upper Canada. Few of the old chiefs who had signed the 1836 treaty were included in the delegation. Elevated in status were Chief Wasson, who would assume the role of principal spokesman, and Augustin Hamlin. Although the latter was officially an interpreter, Andrew's cousin was also an esteemed and trusted Ottawa leader. Andrew Blackbird was listed among the official delegates as a "headman." He was too young to be among those playing a leading role but he was regarded as "councilor."

Blackbird arrived in Detroit with the other Ottawa men on a muggy July day. The entire council was held in oppressive heat that made the *Anishnabeg* long for the refreshing breezes of the northern lakes. Upon arrival the government gave each Ottawa a new suit of clothes, so that they would "appear decent" during the public negotiations to follow. While Andrew may have lacked the status of a leader, he was a very useful member of the Ottawa delegation. Unlike most of the tribal elders, he was familiar with travel by steamboat. He had negotiated the crowded Detroit riverfront on previous occasions, and he had a comfortable familiarity with the white men's tongue. Like his cousin Hamlin, Blackbird's knowledge of the European-American world made him an indispensable figure in dealing directly with the United States, even if some elders viewed his ideas and values as suspect. On a personal level, he must have enjoyed associating with Hamlin and his old friend from Grand Traverse days, John Johnston, who was also there as an official interpreter.[5]

The 1855 Detroit treaty was much more of a genuine negotiation than the 1836 council that Mackadepenessy had attended in Washington nineteen years before. Instead of Andrew Jackson's removal policy leveled at the Ottawa like a gun, the principal concern of the United States was to equitably close its dealings with the *Anishnabeg* and to turn them over to the State of Michigan in a prosperous condition. "We are seeking no lands—nothing from you," Commissioner Manypenny said at the start of the council, "We are here simply to settle your business already subsisting." Manypenny charged the delegates with the task of planning "for the future, that you may maintain & increase your present standard of civilization."[6]

Over the course of four days Commissioner Manypenny and the Ottawa and Chippewa chiefs marked out a bold new course in American-Indian relations. The Ottawa and Chippewa of Michigan would be among the first Indians in America to embrace what would soon become the government's new, one-size-fits-all policy for native peoples. Allotment, the private, individual ownership of land—it was believed—would transform Indians from their traditional communal cultural values and force them to become independent market-oriented agriculturalists. The idea behind the program was that if Indians were forced into the same competitive economic circumstances as their white neighbors, the market would gradually erode the cultural differences that separated a Native American from a European-American, and in so doing solve the "Indian problem." Unlike many western Indian tribes who would be forced under this policy during the decades after the Civil War, significant factions of the Ottawa and the Chippewa knowingly and willingly embraced allotment as their future.

The chief spokesman for the Ottawa's was the Little Traverse chief, Wasson. In his comments he stressed that his people were ready for allotment. "I have abandoned the woods for [my] maintenance & am now a farmer," he told the commissioner. "I no longer go into the woods & look for wild animals when I want to eat; but I kill one of the cattle I raise for myself." During the discussion of how the *Anishnabeg* were to be granted land, Wasson and other leaders demonstrated an understanding of private property ownership. A common refrain was, as Wasson said, "We desire one thing of our father and that is that patents be issued to us with our lands." Another Ottawa, Kenoshance, reinforced this point. "It is the desire of my chiefs that we have a patent to hand down to our children from generation to generation."[7]

Andrew Blackbird entered the debate by reminding the commissioner of Indian affairs that many Indians were already owners of private property and that under Michigan's laws they had "the same footing as yourself, we are citizens, your laws govern us." He went on to propose that the Ottawa and Chippewa be given land warrants, similar to those the government granted military veterans. This would have allowed the *Anishnabeg* to locate lands where and when they wanted and was in keeping with Blackbird's commitment to Ottawa self-determination. Land warrants would have freed native land selection from the Indian Affairs bureaucracy. Commissioner Manypenny responded condescendingly that he was "glad to hear the young man talk & to see how inquiring a course his mind has taken." However, federal officials were unwilling to grant Indians the broad autonomy in selecting lands that Blackbird envisioned. Manypenny wanted the Ottawa and Chippewa bands to locate lands in common areas where the government's agents could effectively deliver educational and agricultural assistance services. As it turned out, government's insistence that allotment be controlled by its agents tied the Indian's future to an inept and often corrupt system that undermined the promise of independent native landownership. While Blackbird's request for land warrants may have thrust too much responsibility on individual *Anishnabeg,* it is hard in hindsight to see how his proposal could have worked out worse than the way the Office of Indian Affairs managed allotment.[8]

While other Indian spokesmen at the treaty council did not specifically endorse Blackbird's proposal for land warrants, they all shared his commitment to self-determination through the insistence that they be free to make their own individual land selections. Kenoshance said, "We want to select our own lands as we are to cultivate them." Assagon, a leader from the Straits of Mackinac, bluntly stated, "We cannot select any lands until we see them & know whether they are good." He also challenged Commissioner Manypenny on the size of the individual allotments. Rather than accept the proposed forty- to eighty-acre parcels mentioned by Manypenny, Assagon suggested that the United States grant "to each of us men, women, & children 160 acres." After all, federal preemption laws encouraged white settlers to stakeout a quarter section of land. If 160 acres was a desirably sized farm for a white settler, why not for an Indian? When Manypenny brushed aside Assagon's suggestion the Indian leader eloquently expressed his frustration: "Father you said to me the other day I was extravagant in my demands. You seem to think me a glutton, never satisfied. Now I live only on corn soup at home & you have every luxury of life. Is it strange that I should try to get as good as you!"[9]

One of the remarkable features of the 1855 treaty record is the assertiveness and independence of the Ottawa and Chippewa leaders. They repeatedly and effectively pressed the government for a full accounting of their rights under past treaties and they boldly embraced the responsibilities of citizenship. Wawbojieg, the Chippewa leader from Sault Ste. Marie, requested Indian control of land patents by saying, "We think we are old enough to take care of our papers. We have bought lands already & we take care of our papers, that our great father gives us. We think we can take as good care of your papers as we do of his." This same self-confidence was exhibited in a debate over whether the Indians should pay taxes on their allotments. Some Indians had already lost private holdings because of a failure to pay taxes, but most leaders expressed their desire to hold land on the same terms as the white man. Wawbojieg stated, "I have already taken your path & become a citizen, only I shall never be able to change the color of my skin. My father, we have accepted the land & wish to live on it. We are able to live—not perhaps in as good a style as you do, but we are still able. We are willing to pay our way upon this land—to pay our taxes as you do. You have opened your heart to give us land; we do not think you ought to feed us & our children forever, besides. We will pay our own taxes."[10]

Behind the willingness to pay taxes and the desire to control their own land patents was a determination on the part of both the Ottawa and Chippewa to assert autonomy, to control their own fate. This desire was also expressed in terms of education. A sizable amount of the money due the tribes from the 1836 sale of their lands in Michigan had been dedicated to education. The bulk of this money went to various Christian mission organizations that operated schools as part of their proselytization programs. Chief Assagon expressed the *Anishnabeg* dissatisfaction with the results of those efforts. Pointing to some of the Ottawa children he said, "Here are boys who have not learned enough from those school masters to say in English 'give me a drink of water.'" He believed that the key to improving educational performance was for the Indians themselves to control the distribution of the educational fund. "We want to hire our own school masters & then if they do not suit us, we can send them away." Assagon's request was largely deflected by the government. During the ten years that the educational fund remained in effect, the "appointment of teachers and the management of schools" remained in the Indian agent's hands, modified only by a treaty clause stating that "the Indians shall be consulted, and their views and wishes adopted so far as they may be just and reasonable."[11]

Because of his long personal struggle for education, Andrew Blackbird was particularly interested in using the treaty negotiation to reform the use of the educational fund. He was opposed to the use of Ottawa money to operate denominational schools. Rather, he advocated that local common schools be established and funded the way white communities funded their schools, from local taxation. The $80,000 that remained in the Ottawa and Chippewa educational fund he wanted used to provide scholarships for Indian youths who sought an education, as he had done, "among the whites or in civilized communities." He also wanted scholarships offered to "Indian youths" who sought a college education. These sentiments reflected Blackbird's belief that a select number of Indian youths needed to be educated in white schools. According to the treaty journal, which is not a complete transcript of the negotiation, Blackbird said to the Commissioner: "I wish my father would set aside an amount in the treaty to send some of our boys to college. We want to send them to your big schools so they can learn." In the journal Indian agent Henry Gilbert attempted to deflect Blackbird by lamely pointing out the funds would be spent the way the Indians pleased.[12]

In his *History,* however, Blackbird recalls his proposal receiving a much more sympathetic hearing from Commissioner Manypenny.

> The Hon. Commissioner was much taken up with my remarks on the subject, I being the youngest member, and told the older members of the council that he would like to hear some of them on this subject. "The young man who has been making remarks on this matter has a very good idea with regard to your education funds; now let us hear farther remarks on this subject by some other members of the council." But not one Indian stirred. And again and again the next day, I tried to urge this matter to the Hon. Commissioner and the Indians to cooperate with me, but they would not, because my people were so ignorant and they did not know the value of education, or else they misunderstood the whole subject.

As Blackbird recalled the incident, resentment on the part of some of the older leaders toward a younger man's new ideas stymied his efforts.

> On the third day, as I was about getting up to make further remarks upon this subject, one of the older members, who was the most unworthy of all the company, as he got very drunk the day we arrived in Detroit and was locked up in jail as disorderly two or three days, arose and said to the Commissioner that I

> was not authorized by any council to get up here and make such remarks. "We did not come here to talk about education, but came here expressly to form a treaty." Then burst into a great laughter all the spectators of the council and some of the members too.

No doubt deeply mortified, Andrew Blackbird took his seat and spoke no more about the education fund.[13]

Later, Blackbird contended his censure was "a put up job to prevent any change by persons who had been handling for years this Indian education fund, as there was a number of them in the council hall." Certainly, the religious denominations that had been conducting Indian schools did not want to see their revenue stream summarily interrupted; however, it is also easy to see how Blackbird's proposal may not have seemed attractive to many native leaders. Shifting the burden of primary school education on to local property owners when most of the Indians would be becoming property owners and taxpayers for the first time, could have endangered *Anishnabe* land tenure. Further, given his own interest in attending college, it is not hard to see why some tribal elders would have regarded Blackbird's proposal as self-serving.

On July 31, as a stifling, fetid Detroit day drew to a close, fifty-four Ottawa and Chippewa leaders put their marks of assent upon the new treaty with the United States. The core of the treaty was the vision that the Ottawa would endure in Michigan as private citizens. To secure for them a place of residence a 336-square-mile block of land, in what is now Emmet and Charlevoix counties, was temporarily reserved from all other claims in order to allow each head of a family to select eighty acres, forty acres in the case of single persons. These lands were to be held as individual allotments, although the government would forbid an Ottawa freeholder to sell the land for ten years, so as to give them a chance to be securely established as property holders. An educational fund of $80,000 was established to be paid out in ten annual installments. The fund would remain in the hands of the Indian agent. The best that Andrew could achieve was the government's promise that the Ottawa would be "consulted." Technical assistance for farming and blacksmithing as well as individual annuities were also secured for ten years. Finally, the treaty stated that save for what was necessary to carry out the agreement, the United States "dissolved" the "tribal organization" of the Ottawa. This last provision was deemed necessary to meet the State of Michigan's provision that Indians "not members of a tribe" could qualify for citizenship. The Ottawa chief Paybahmesay affirmed at the end of the treaty that he understood "we should be Christians, civilized & educated & honest." In the wake of the agreement, Commissioner Manypenny predicted that most of the Ottawa were now "qualified to enter upon and discharge their duties and assume the obligations imposed upon the citizens of the State of Michigan."[14]

FELLOW CITIZENS OF MICHIGAN

Andrew Blackbird left the treaty much less encouraged than Manypenny about the prospects of the Ottawa. "When the Council was closed and the treaty signed," he wrote, "I turned my face to the South, with spirit depressed, that I might visit the favorite spot of my educational privileges in the State of Ohio." Blackbird took steamboat passage from Detroit to Cleveland so he might visit his old mentor Samuel Bissell. It was with Bissell's encouragement that Blackbird then wrote a newspaper article on the educational issues raised by the 1855 treaty council. The article was published later that summer by the *Detroit Tribune* and Bissell and Blackbird then had a pamphlet made of the piece.[15]

The pamphlet was framed as an overt appeal to evangelical Protestant church members for donations to support Indian students at the Twinsburg Academy. Bissell introduced Blackbird as a "poor Indian" who had accomplished much.

> When he came to us, he was a poor, ignorant and superstitious Catholic. He is now a thorough Protestant, helping missionaries both as interpreter and teacher. . . . laboring every way to reveal the errors of Catholicism and the wickedness of the priests, and at the same time to induce government and the philanthropists to educate among the whites more of the promising youth.

Andrew's portion of the appeal kept up the attack on the Catholic Church's management of the Ottawa education fund.

> Not one Indian youth has been educated of this class for the last twenty years, who can spell *Baker,* although it was reported by our Catholic Clergy that the Indian boys and girls are educated in the English branches, so as to be quite grammarians, geographers, etc., at the same time naming such teachers, for instance, as Kah-wa-go-ma-ah my own cousin, and who does not speak a word of English.

All the Catholic mission schools were good for was to "catechize little children in our own language."[16]

The overt anti-Catholic tone of the pamphlet flowed from Blackbird's bitter experience at Little Traverse, but it also reflected the sentiments of a large portion of Protestant America, that the Catholic Church was an insidious and dangerous institution. During the mid-1850s dozens of Catholic churches across the nation were burned by Protestant mobs. Besides religious prejudice, Catholics were seen as obstacles to liberal Protestant reforms. Foreign-born Irish and German Catholics opposed Protestant temperance laws, and Catholic clergy resisted publicly funded schools that taught the King James Bible. Through the Know-Nothing Party, anti-Catholicism and anti-immigrant sentiments were broadly circulated in the 1850s. The Bissell and Blackbird pamphlet, while relatively mild in its language, attacked an institution that was a familiar evil to Protestant congregations.[17]

Blackbird also used his pamphlet to release some of his frustration from the treaty council. He criticized the lack of interest tribal leaders showed in the education fund: "Our old men were so blind they could not see or appreciate this subject." In his opinion education was "the main business that should have occupied the attention of the Council. We must educate! We must educate!! or sink into the vortex of destruction." Nor was Blackbird impressed by Commissioner Manypenny's commitment to properly supervise the educational fund. "Yes, so they have always said; but the question is, will he be there to see to it?"[18]

At heart both the newspaper editorial and the pamphlet were an appeal to the people of Michigan for funds. Modestly he requested that whites educate annually two or three young people "in some of your Institutions in your State."

> We wish now to become men, men of knowledge and education, that we may hold an equal standing with our white brothers, since we have abandoned our laws, manners and customs having renounced our chiefdoms under the most solemn declaration to uphold and support the government of the United States as directed by the *President,* the *Head Chief* of the *Nation.*

Blackbird closed his appeal with the guilt-laden image of the "vanishing American."

> A small remnant of a nation once so powerful are here, but few in number, and still vanishing away like a snow flake before the rising sun; these few have thrown themselves under the protection of the white man, and wish to comply with the laws of civilization; but are poor because they have not the means and advantages like the whites; yet I hope there is a day coming when they shall be truly enlightened and educated, like the white people.

The best way to achieve this goal was to allow Indian youths to be educated at white institutions.[19]

The pamphlet was published by William F. Geddes, a Philadelphia printer who specialized in Christian and abolitionist tracts. Some donations of money and books were received by Bissell in answer to the appeal; however, no formal program for regularly meeting the needs of Indian students result from the effort. After preparing his appeal, Blackbird returned to northern Michigan and for the next several years he annually sent one or two young Ottawa to Bissell's Twinsburg Academy; presumably some of their educational costs were covered by the proceeds of the pamphlet.

Blackbird did not content himself with a public venting of his views. He also repeated the pamphlet's basic arguments in a petition he raised among the Ottawa and sent directly to Commissioner of Indian Affairs Manypenny. With a handful of the younger and more engaged Ottawa leaders behind him, Blackbird particularly critiqued the Office of Indian Affairs' inability to properly monitor the expenditure of the Michigan Indian education fund. They called upon Manypenny to end the "blind-dealing" that characterized the granting of funds to mission organizations and pressed for more rigorous English-language instruction.[20]

One of the arguments Andrew Blackbird made in his pamphlet was that as citizens the Ottawa and Chippewa needed to be ready to take their place in local government: "We ought to be capable of doing our own township business, and all other matters that may be required of us." Indeed, these duties were thrust upon him when he returned to Little Traverse. In 1843, the L'Arbre Croche coast area had been designated by the Michigan State Legislature as the County of Tonedagana. It was a county in name only as it was essentially unorganized. Three years later for no particularly good reason the county, almost entirely populated by Indians, lost its Native American name and was rededicated as Emmet County, in honor of the Irish patriot Robert Emmet. County government did not exist until 1853 when Mormon settlers on Beaver Island organized an administration. Their county government was essentially a Mormon government for Mormons, and they neither included nor exploited the Ottawa communities on the mainland. The Detroit treaty, however, changed this. The Ottawa were now accorded citizenship status and in recognition of this, and to undercut the Mormons, the legislature detached Beaver Island from Emmet County. Upon their return from Detroit the newly minted Ottawa citizens were called upon to participate in their first election.[21]

In November polling Andrew J. Blackbird was elected register of deeds and probate judge. Other young literate Ottawa took office as deputy sheriffs or supervisors of Little Traverse Township or of the other largely Ottawa townships of Bear Creek and La Croix (Cross Village). While the traditional power structure of his tribe had no place for Andrew or other young men, the American political system in northwest Michigan valued the few voters eligible to hold office. Overnight the Ottawa went from being simple wards of the federal government to masters, for a brief time, of their own Michigan local governments. Only gradually did the first officeholders take on actual administrative responsibilities. Nonetheless, Indian agent Henry Gilbert was impressed. He wrote to Commissioner Manypenny that the Ottawa "have an organized county and with some help manage to get along with their business." The Ottawa also became participants in statewide elections, and in 1856 they voted in their first presidential election. That election, however, taught Blackbird that there were risks as well as rewards to be encountered in pursuit of political empowerment.[22]

The Ottawa entered electoral politics while Michigan and the nation were undergoing a revolutionary change in the party system. In 1854, in reaction to the threat of slavery expanding into the western territories, the Republican Party was formed. The party held its first organized meeting in Jackson, Michigan, and it was in Michigan that the party first swept into power. Before 1854 the Democratic Party dominated Michigan politics; however, afterward for more than a century the state would be a Republican bastion. Although Republicans controlled the state government, the Democrats in 1856 still controlled the national government, most importantly the presidency. This meant that "the Great Father" was a Democrat and so was his agent. When it came to elect state legislators and to vote for president of the United States in 1856, the Democratic Party used all of its considerable influence over the new Indian voters to get them to support the "Great Father's party."[23]

As election day 1856 neared Agent Henry C. Gilbert hurried up to northern Michigan to exert his influence. The Democrats were desperate to regain their footing within the state and to beat back the surging Republican presidential candidate, John C. Fremont. Gilbert was at Grand Traverse and Northport personally "managing the Indian votes." He appointed a "young man" to represent the Democratic Party's interest at the Little Traverse polling place. He seems to have done well because Andrew Blackbird later reported that only two Republican votes were cast there that day. For most Ottawa, unfamiliar with proper procedure, following the agent's advice seemed sound. Andrew, however, had his own views on slavery and he intend to vote his conscience.

> As I deposited my ballot, this young man was so furiously enraged at me he fairly gnashed his teeth, at which I was very much surprised, and from my

> companion they tried to take away his ticket. Then they tried to make him exchange his ticket [for a Democratic ticket], but he refused. We went out quickly, as we did not wish to stay in this excitement.

The vote and the furor of casting it greatly upset Andrew. The election occurred shortly after another jarring incident. He was persuaded by a friend to attend a Catholic mass in Middle Village, yet when the priest saw him in the congregation, "He came and forcibly ejected me out of the room." Now, any pleasure in exercising citizenship had been compromised by the animosities aroused by the process and the realization that in politics as in religion he held views at variance with most of the Ottawa. "At that time," he later wrote, "I felt almost sorry for my people, the Indians, for ever being citizens of the State, as I thought they were much happier without these elections." Not for the last time Blackbird realized that holding a legal right was not the same thing as being able to exercise it.[24]

A LAST CHANCE FOR HIGHER EDUCATION

For defying the agent, Andrew Blackbird was soon penalized. He had long desired to continue his education. His duty to his father and his responsibilities with the Ottawa, first in treaty negotiations and later in local government, had kept him home long after he had hoped to be away to college. In November 1856, shortly after narrowly losing a race for Emmet County clerk, Andrew acted impulsively on his long-suppressed desire. Agent Henry Gilbert had just concluded the 1856 annuity payment and had embarked for Mackinac on a schooner. Andrew stood on the beach at Little Traverse, the gold coin of the annuity in his pocket, and he reflected that the ship was likely the last vessel of the season. Soon the long northern Michigan winter would descend and another year in his life would have passed.

> As I looked toward the vessel I wept, for I felt terribly downcast. As they were going very slowly toward the harbor point, I asked one of the Indian youngsters to take me and my trunk in a canoe to the vessel out there. I had now determined to go, in defiance of every opposition, to seek my education. I hurried to our house with the boy, to get my trunk and bid good bye to my aged father, and told him I was going again to some school outside, and if God permitted I hoped to return again to Little Traverse. All my father said was, "Well, my son, if you think it best, go."

After a hard paddle Andrew caught up with the schooner, her sails still slack in the still evening air.[25]

No sooner did Andrew put his feet on the deck of the ship than he was confronted by Agent Gilbert. Earlier that day Andrew had approached Gilbert about his desire to continue his education. He indicated that he wished to attend college and perhaps to eventually receive a medical degree. Andrew asked the agent's help to tap the treaty educational fund to pay some of the cost of tuition. "He bluffed me off," Andrew later recalled, "by saying he was sorry I had voted the 'black republican ticket.'" Now, in spite of that rebuff, Andrew was following through on his dream.

Gilbert's "face turned red" when he saw Andrew. "Are you going?" he tersely asked the young Ottawa. "Yes sir, I am going," and with that Gilbert turned his back.[26]

During the slow voyage to Mackinac, Andrew Blackbird had plenty of time to observe and judge Agent Gilbert. Throughout the night Gilbert sat up with the captain playing cards, "by which the agent lost considerable money"; nor was that the only moral failing Blackbird saw in his agent. At annuity payments Gilbert was known to leave the boring duty of dolling out coins to his interpreter while he caroused at parties or dances. At night he was said to seduce young Indian women to his tent with offers of "plenty of things." Perhaps Blackbird had hoped that as a Presbyterian Gilbert might have been inclined to help Andrew, who after all was among the few Protestant Ottawa. What Andrew did not know was that Gilbert had been excommunicated from the Church the year before and that he had become a committed Spiritualist. He was in fact a regular participant in séances. It gave Andrew no comfort that this was the man who lorded over Michigan's native people.[27]

For Blackbird, however, Gilbert was a bad man to have as an enemy. As agent he had great latitude in controlling Indian Office resources in Michigan. By voting Republican Andrew had crossed a man whose principal purpose in carrying out his duties as agent was to strengthen the Democratic Party in Michigan. Gilbert was a Coldwater, Michigan, attorney whose work for the party led to his being named a delegate to the 1852 National Convention and eventually to appointment in 1853 as Indian agent. Gilbert had done a good job pushing the government to settle its long-unsettled affairs with the Ottawa and Chippewa. In executing the treaty, however, Gilbert revealed the seamy side of his character. He was sloppy as well as tardy in helping the Indians make their allotment selections. Worse, he studied ways he could defraud tribal members of their annuities and set in motion schemes to profit from their land allotments. At the very time

Andrew shared a lake passage with Gilbert, charges against the agent were beginning to pile up in Washington, D.C. In May 1857, even the inefficient administration of President James Buchanan could wait no longer. After the commissioner of Indian affairs had been sent fourteen pages of charges, Gilbert left the service. Of course, as a loyal Democrat, he faced no criminal charges and he was allowed to officially "retire." That, however, was still in the future on the cold November morning when Blackbird and Gilbert arrived at Mackinac.[28]

With nothing to lose Blackbird made one final attempt to win Gilbert's support. Gilbert smugly reminded the Ottawa of his Republican ballot.

> Then as I was beginning to feel out of humor, and I spoke rather abruptly to him, saying, "Well, sir, I now see clearly that you don't care about doing anything for my welfare because I voted for the republican party. But politics have nothing to do with my education; for the Government of the United States owes us that amount of money, not politics. I was one of the councilors when the treaty was made, and I will see some other men about this matter, sir."

Blackbird recalled that while he spoke Gilbert's face "turned all purple." Yet, as Andrew started to leave, Gilbert composed himself enough to ask:

> "Mr. Blackbird, how far do you intend to go to get your education?" I said, "I intend to go to Ann Arbor University, sir." "Well, I will do this much for you: I will pay your fare to Detroit. I am going by way of Chicago, but you can go down by the next boat, which will be here soon from Chicago." I thanked him, and he handed me money enough to pay my fare to Detroit.

It was likely that it was Blackbird's veiled threat to take his appeal to "other men" that prompted Gilbert to part with a few dollars; even so the agent did little to help with the young man's educational ambitions.[29]

Upon arrival in Detroit Andrew made good his threat. He went to the home of the most important person he could think of, Lewis Cass. The former governor of the Michigan Territory, former secretary of war, and former presidential nominee, and soon to be former United States senator, was by far the leading Democratic politician in the state. Although always an American nationalist who negotiated many native land cessions, Cass also considered himself a friend to the Indian people of Michigan. He was old enough to remember a time in the state when the Indians held the military upper hand, and he knew how much they had lost in the years since. At the 1855 treaty council Cass made an appearance to counsel the tribes to accept allotments. Andrew may have recalled that the *Anishnabe* spokesman Assagon complemented Cass on "how kind you have always been to the Indian, when he came to you for advice & assistance." So it was to Cass's door that Blackbird went.[30]

Blackbird may have been surprised that when he knocked at that door and the great man himself came to answer it. Andrew thrust out his hand and as Cass shook it Andrew said he was there on business. Cass invited him in. The old man was still reeling from the beating the Michigan Democrats had just suffered at Republican hands. He understood the new legislature would soon vote to end his service in the Senate. Had the Democrats won the election Cass's front porch would have likely been swamped with office seekers; few people, however, were knocking on his door now that his political career seemed at its end. "Well my friend," Andrew said, "I come from Arbor Croche." He went on to say the he was the nephew of Chief Wing. Cass immediately recalled the old warrior who supported the United States in the dark days of the War of 1812. He then went on to request that Cass intercede and help Blackbird obtain government funding for his education. Cass seemed surprised when Andrew told him that he had been twice refused assistance by Agent Gilbert. "Why, why!" Cass said, "it seems to me there is ample provision for your people for that object, and has been for the last twenty years. What is the matter with him?"[31] Cass was bound for Washington in a few days and he promised to take the matter up personally with the commissioner of Indian affairs. "I know they can do something toward defraying your expenses."

While Cass supported Blackbird's educational aspirations, he discouraged Andrew from going to Ann Arbor and the University of Michigan. "Is it possible, are you prepared to enter such a college?" the old man asked. The question triggered doubts Blackbird had nursed for the past few years. Since leaving the Twinsburg Academy in 1850 he had seldom been able to read more than the Bible. He feared not only the shortcomings of his few years of education, he doubted his ability to recall all that he had learned six years ago. "Well, sir, I think you had better go to Ypsilanti State Normal School instead of Ann Arbor: it is one of the best colleges in the State." Cass promised to write to Andrew in Ypsilanti as soon as he conferred with the commissioner of Indian affairs.[32]

Blackbird had never even heard of a school in Ypsilanti, yet the next morning, in spite of a "terrible snow storm," he set off on foot for the teacher's college located thirty miles west of Detroit. He arrived there late in the day and used some of his rapidly dwindling coins to get a room at a hotel. Andrew made his way to the school's Main Building first thing in the morning. The semester had already begun and he saw the students and faculty head toward the three-story brick structure. Built only five years before, the Main Building was all there really was of the Normal School campus. On the first floor were the library and science labs, while the upper floors were taken up with offices and classrooms. Andrew met a number of the faculty and inquired about the cost of tuition, room, and board. Since he had no means to attend school immediately he also inquired about a job and by days end he was situated as a hired hand on a farm three miles outside town. He worked there for three weeks, torn between "doubt and hope" that Cass would make good his pledge to secure government aid for his schooling. Then one day the old farmer for whom he worked returned from a trip to the post office with a bundle of letters for Andrew. Included were correspondence from Cass and the Office of Indian Affairs. Andrew's hands "fairly trembled" as he opened Cass's letter, but upon reading its contents, he later wrote, "My fears were changed into gladness, and quickly as possible I settled with the farmer, and away I went towards the city, singing as I went along."[33]

Andrew's song of joy was triggered by Cass's report that he convinced the Office of Indian Affairs to pay for all of Blackbird's educational costs, tuition, room, board, even a clothing allowance. Yet as he hiked back to Detroit the singing stopped when he reflected on the contents of the letter from the Office of Indian Affairs. He was instructed to report to Agent Gilbert, who would personally make all of the arrangements. A more confident or aggressive individual than Andrew may well have relished the chance to savor his triumph over the agent's obstructions, but Blackbird disliked confrontations and was deeply suspicious of Gilbert. "O, how I did hate to have to meet the Indian Agent again on this subject; to stand before him, and to have him think that I had overcome him, and succeeded in spite of his opposition to my desire," Blackbird recalled. "O, how I wished this matter could have been arranged without his assistance."[34]

Nonetheless, within a day of receiving these letters Andrew Blackbird stood outside Agent Gilbert's office. Located on the Detroit waterfront, the Mackinac Indian Agency was an unimpressive and ill-kept single-story wood frame building. Stiffening his resolve, Andrew entered the reception room, an uninviting enclosure decorated with a threadbare carpet and soiled furniture, with, as one visitor noted, "the dust of ages hanging over it." Henry Gilbert was in the adjacent office, working at one of two old desks. Without offering Andrew so much as a "How do you do?" Gilbert barked out: "Well, sir how much do you think that it will cost for your schooling at Ypsilanti?" Blackbird was intimidated and cautious. He answered, "I don't know, sir."

> "Well, who knows? I think you ought to know, as you have been there," he said in a gruff voice. "I have not been to school at all, sir." I said, "but have been working on a farm up to this morning." "Working on a farm, eh? I thought you came here on purpose to attend school?" "I did, sir; but you know I was very short of means, so I had to do something to keep me alive." "Can't you tell me the cost of your board per week?" "The private board is from $3.50 to $4 per week, sir, as according to accommodation." "How much for books and clothing?" "I don't know, sir but I think I have enough clothing for at least one year."

Andrew's persistence had won him the government assistance to which he was entitled, but faced with the anger of a petty and officious agent, he responded timidly. While Blackbird in his 1887 *History of the Ottawa and Chippewa* reported his exchanges with Gilbert in precise grammar, it is likely that at that time he did not have the confidence to banter with the agent. As late as 1858, after two years of school, he confided to a friend that he spoke English "indistinctly, ungrammatically." What ever the reason, Blackbird's failure to challenge Gilbert cost him dearly. Gilbert followed through with the letter of his instructions. He arranged for Blackbird's tuition, but provided scanty support for the Ottawa's living expenses. Andrew accepted this, perhaps because he wanted no further conflict with Gilbert. Later, however, he felt it severely compromised his chance for academic success.[35]

The next day Blackbird was back at the campus of the institution that was officially known as the Michigan State Normal School. The school had opened in 1853 and was the first teacher training school west of the Allegheny Mountains. The faculty helped Andrew find a room at a nearby boardinghouse, as there were no official dormitories for students. He was one of about 120 students enrolled. Some were as young as fourteen, while Andrew in his thirties was among the more mature students. They were of varied academic background. For some the normal school functioned as a high school; for others it was a college. A student like Blackbird who did not have a high school diploma would have had to pass an entrance examination. Upon acceptance he had to choose between two courses of study. The so-called "English Course" was a two-year program designed to give students the broad training they would need to become primary school teachers. The "Classical Course" was a three-year program designed to train high school teachers or prepare students for advanced study at a university. It is not clear which program Blackbird entered. He had expressed an interest in teaching on several occasions and he had some experience doing so; on the other hand he also desired to become a medical doctor, which would have required the "Classical Course."[36]

Little is known of Blackbird's two and a half years enrolled at the Normal School. The slender evidence of his academic progress includes a brief notation in an unmarked record book. That note reads: "Andrew J. Blackbird of Little Traverse, for Term 12 [October 1858 to March 1859] has passed most studies to date." He was listed as having completed what was known as "Class D," the equivalent of the sophomore year of studies. There is some reason to believe that he at least had an exposure to Latin because he wrote in the summer of 1858 that he had begun an Indian grammar based "upon the same plan in which our first books in Latin and Greek are written." Andrew must have been a bit of a celebrity on campus. His presence as a student was notable enough to merit a front-page, if inaccurate, newspaper notice. It read: "A member of the Chippewa tribe is at present a student at our State Normal School. He has the euphonious name of A.J. Blackbird." As time went on, however, Andrew was not pleased with the progress of his studies. He confided to his old teacher Samuel Bissell that he was "getting some what discouraged" about his ability to master English. "I have begun rather too late," he worried, and feared he was too "deeply rooted or stained with my own language."[37]

Outside the classroom Andrew's experience at the Normal School was grim. Thanks to Agent Gilbert, he had a total allowance of $37 per academic term. This forced him into poverty. Appeals to Lewis Cass in Washington were successful at keeping the commissioner of Indian affairs from following through on threats to cut the allowance altogether, but no letters from Blackbird could win an increase in funds. When summer vacation came he was unable to return north to visit his father; instead he tramped down the roads leading into the countryside, looking for a farm job that would pay room and board. While most students took their meals at their boardinghouses, Andrew lacked the funds. He provided his own food based on how much money he had left each week. According to the account in is *History of the Ottawa and Chippewa,* by the time he entered his third year of study he was reduced to a diet of bread and water. Only rarely did he have enough money for firewood to heat his room. Cold and hunger eroded his spirit. "I was very much reduced in flesh, and on the least exertion I would be trembling, and I began to be discouraged in the prosecution of my studies." After three months he felt he "could not stand it any longer," and he gave up his hope of graduating and left the State Normal School.[38]

While he did not obtain his educational goals, the years he lived in Ypsilanti were highly influential in shaping his future life. He seems to have made a number of friends in the community. Later in life he turned to Ypsilanti for financial and editorial assistance in publishing his history, and it is likely that when he did so he was drawing upon associations established during the time he was a student at the Normal School. While he was at school he also again changed Christian denomination, from Presbyterian to Episcopal. Why he made this change he never said. Certainly in the Episcopalians were closer in ritual to the Christianity he had known as a child in Catholic L'Arbre Croche. It was an unlikely change, however, because unlike the Presbyterians or even the Catholics, the Episcopalians did not have missions to the Ottawa and Chippewa. It is possible that it was personal associations that drew him to the Episcopalians, for sometime during his residence at the Normal School, Andrew met a young English woman, Elizabeth Martha Fisk.[39]

The most important result of Blackbird's two and a half years in Ypsilanti was his courtship of, and marriage to, Elizabeth Fisk. They seem to have met in Ypsilanti and they were wed in Toledo, Ohio. There is no record of her as a student at the Normal School, although she may well have been. She was likely in her early twenties at the time of their marriage and described by those who knew her as "a very beautiful young English woman." She had very striking light blond hair matched by a very pale complexion. In later years people told stories to explain how she came to marry Andrew Blackbird. One had Blackbird traveling to England for his education and Elizabeth marrying him because he was a chief, expecting that upon his return home, "she would be in America a member of the nobility." Such stories reflected the improbable if not somewhat scandalous nature of the cross-racial relationship between Andrew and Elizabeth. Andrew himself was painfully aware the way their love might be viewed, even by his friends. When he first informed his old mentor Samuel Bissell that he had wed, he said nothing about whom he had married. Rather he merely described Elizabeth as "a well educated woman who is willing to take all to a good heart whatever adversities we may meet during our lives, and willing to take hold in trying to enlighten my nation, but she is as poor as I am." Later when he informed Bissell that she was an "Englishwoman" he stressed, "She is a truly noble hearted woman."[40]

From September 1858 through March 1859 Andrew and Elizabeth struggled with studies as well as the need to obtain heat and nourishment. It may well have been his inability to provide for his wife that was the figurative final straw that prompted Blackbird to quit school. Leaving school, however, did not solve their financial problems. Indeed, they even lacked the means to purchase boat passage back to northern Michigan. Andrew therefore took a number of temporary jobs. He also undertook a number of lectures that were his first public presentations of the Ottawa traditions that later became part of his book. One of his lectures was given in May 1859 at the Young Men's Christian Association (YMCA) Hall in Detroit. The announcement promised, "Mr. B. will appear in full Indian costume and recite an original Indian Lament, speak of the history of the Michigan Indians and their origin." The program made clear the paid attendance "will benefit a worthy man, who was lately a student at the State Normal School at Ypsilanti." Similar lectures were offered at various venues in southern Michigan and northern Indiana. Finally, in the summer of 1859 Andrew and Elizabeth Blackbird made their way to the Detroit waterfront to board a steamboat. Behind them was a frustrated dream of higher education and a career as a doctor, before the young couple lay a new life on a rapidly changing frontier.[41]

As Detroit slowly receded in the steamboat's wake, Blackbird may have looked forward to seeing his aged father. It is also likely that he thought of his angry encounters with Agent Henry Gilbert that in the end helped to frustrate his educational plans. Andrew's frame of mind might well be glimpsed in the last lines of the "lament" he performed so many times that summer. That program concluded with the defiant words,

> When the white man took every foot of my inheritance, he thought to him[self] I should be a slave. Ah, never, never! I would sooner plunge the dagger into my beating heart, and follow the footsteps of my forefathers, than be a slave to the white man.[42]

Andrew returned to the Little Traverse Ottawa homeland with a heightened sense of his Ottawa identity and a very American determination to live his life as he saw fit.

6

Doing Good amongst My People

As his ship edged into Little Traverse Bay Andrew Blackbird had not seen its familiar waters for nearly three years. Many times over those years he had returned in his mind's eye to its shores. He had an abiding attachment to the waters and woods of L'Arbre Croche. In his writings he mentioned that "the dearest spot to me in this wide world" was a glade of basswood trees where as a boy he listened to the song of his special "messenger," a brown thrush. Now he would share that place and all of his beloved, beautiful home with the new wife who stood at his side.[1]

For Andrew, the thrill of returning to his home waters no doubt was mixed with anxiety, perhaps about the reception his white wife would meet, but certainly over news of his father. For three years he had heard little from home and he suspected the venerable Mackadepenessy was in poor health. Andrew had worried that his father would pass away before he could again see him, so he was no doubt relieved to find him alive living in a cabin at Bear River, even though he was "old and feeble." Shortly after Andrew's return, however, he took a turn for the worse and the old chief's family began to gather for his last hours.

Mackadepenessy had ten children by Andrew's mother, and an unknown number of children by his second wife. In his younger days he had traveled the continent, from the subarctic far northwest to the marble-lined corridors of Washington, D.C. He had been a trader, trapper, warrior, teacher, and peace chief. He had known the mysteries of the *Gitchi Manitou* and he had helped introduce the seven sacraments of the Christian religion to his people. Perhaps most important for Mackadepenessy, as he saw the children and grandchildren around him, was that they were together in the land of his fathers. Unlike most of the Potawatomi, the Ottawas of the

Maumee, the Shawnee, and so many others who had once been his allies in war, Mackadepenessy's people had persisted in their homeland and avoided removal. "Soon after I came to my country," Blackbird wrote in his *History*, "my father died at a great age."[2]

PERIOD OF ADJUSTMENT

Grief over his father's passing mixed with hard times for Andrew and his new wife during their first year together in northern Michigan. Work was hard to find, although Andrew was able to make some money working as a blacksmith. Andrew and Elizabeth both had hoped to be able to use their education to earn a living as well as to help the Ottawa. "I wish to teach my people the English Language," Andrew wrote to his old friend Bissell, "so as to be able to understand it and by means of which they might be brought to the light of civilization, education, & religion." While he was at the Normal School he had solicited books and school supplies from church groups for the Ottawa, including "Spelling books, Small reading books, Arithmetics, and a Testament & Paper, etc." Unfortunately, Andrew's religious and political views still made him an outsider in his hometown. There was no place for him in the Catholic-run school, nor would there be any preference for him in the Democratic Party–dominated Indian agency. He did have, however, a small piece of land and a cabin so at least they had a place to live. Nonetheless, as Blackbird noted in his *History*, "We struggled quite hard to get along."[3]

It galled Blackbird that in spite of all he had done to improve himself and his aspirations to help the Ottawa, he was frozen out of any useful post. He wrote Bissell, "If I was a good Politician, I might then somewhat [have] realized what I have desired." Every time he approached authorities with a proposal "to be useful amongst my people," he would hear "that fatal word 'If.'" He lamented, "I have done everything that could be done, to have the Indian Agent consent, but I could not succeed because the Indian Agent was a big Democrat and I, being a Republican, though I might shed many tears before him, yet I could not avail in anything." His outsider status was particularly irritating because the Indians complained about the Little Traverse schoolteacher, an Irish immigrant and strong Democrat whose brogue was so thick the Ottawa could not understand him. Andrew himself admitted, "I cannot hardly distinguish his speech!" Blackbird was even unsuccessful in his attempt to win election to his old position as register of deeds. Perhaps he felt as if he were a stranger in his own land.[4]

It is possible that Blackbird's white wife contributed to his problems reintegrating into the Little Traverse community. There is no direct evidence of how Andrew's large number of brothers and sister reacted to his marriage. It certainly must have been a shock when he unexpectedly disembarked with a blonde-haired English bride. On the other hand, racially mixed marriages were not all that uncommon in northern Michigan. Many of the most prominent merchants on Mackinac Island had Ottawa wives, although that fur trade era social pattern was clearly on the wane. Andrew's sister Margaret married Joseph Boyd, the illegitimate mixed-blood son of George Boyd. While Margaret's husband was born out of wedlock, his father was a former Indian agent and his family was related by marriage to President John Quincy Adams. His sister Electa had married a Scotsman named Gibson.[5]

Yet interracial marriages in the Great Lakes region were much more commonly between Indian women and European-American men. Mary A. Henderson, a contemporary of Blackbird's, was a rare example of a white woman who married an Indian man. She was a Massachusetts-born woman who in 1863 married Joseph Cabay, a Chippewa man preparing to enter Harvard University Divinity School. Her father so disapproved the match he did not attend the wedding. To make matters worse, shortly after the couple arrived at an Indian town on Saginaw Bay, Joseph Cabay died. Mary faced grief as well as a new family.

> I was so lonely, so desolate, so far from home. No white people lived within miles of the place, nor did I understand one sentence of their language. My feelings were indescribable.

Henderson's commitment to being a missionary and an adoption ceremony administered by her dying husband's father helped her to adjust. In the ceremony her husband's father, Chief Elliot Cabay, grasped her hand and said he would take her as a daughter.

> He then raised his eyes heavenward and asked God to bless his white daughter and help her to love her Indian brothers and sisters and do them much good. He then gave me an Indian name, Wah Sash Kah Moqua, which means "There was darkness but your coming brings light."

It is not known if Elizabeth Martha Blackbird went through a similar adoption ceremony, although she was given an Indian name, Ogechegumequay, Ocean Woman. She seems to have been known by that name for more than a decade, although as more European-Americans moved into the area, the use of it ended.[6]

There is some evidence, however, that Elizabeth was not broadly accepted into the Little Traverse Ottawa community. A rather ugly story that circulated through Little Traverse in the early twentieth century revealed animosity between some Ottawa women and Elizabeth. One of Elizabeth's striking features was her very light, blond hair. Perhaps in an effort to stand out less, the story goes, she accepted a bottle of hair tonic several of the Indian women assured her would make her "hair darker and more glossy." Elizabeth tried the tonic and within a few days her long hair began to fall out. Soon she was completely bald. According to the story:

> No treatments ever brought back her hair, and for the rest of her life she kept her head covered with white cloths. While the tale seems more like legend than truth, Elizabeth *was* bald, and residents of Little Traverse accepted this explanation for her baldness.

The source for this incident is Grace Walz, who in 1964 published a fine master's thesis on Andrew Blackbird. Walz, who grew up in the Little Traverse Bay area, heard the story from her mother. "Elizabeth told the story of her humiliation to my mother as she cared for Blackbird's widow in the last years of her life," Walz wrote."[7]

Walz's documentation makes the disturbing story seem creditable, coming as it does from her mother, who received it directly from Elizabeth Blackbird. On the other hand, Walz's mother knew Elizabeth Blackbird long after her arrival in northern Michigan and in that women's declining years. There was much popular lore about the Blackbird's that floated around Little Traverse in later years that was patently false. One rumor had it that Elizabeth was the daughter of an English ship captain who sailed the Great Lakes and that Andrew met her when their schooner came to port. Another tale had the couple meeting in Great Britain. It must also be remembered that the late nineteenth century was the heyday of medical nostrums. There were hundreds of different types of hair coloring and hair restoration "patent medicines." Some of these were literally made of snake oil; others claimed to be made from secret "Indian medicine." Some of the patent medicine shows featured actual Native Americans as part of their entertainment. Memories of such shows could have been the tissue out of which was spun the story of Elizabeth Blackbird's baldness.[8]

U. P. Hedrick, a University of Michigan professor who grew up in the Little Traverse area in the 1870s, remembered Elizabeth Blackbird as an unhealthy woman, but not as bald. He wrote:

> Chief Blackbird's white wife seemed never in her proper element and had the look in eye and color of a women suffering from a strange disease. She was so blond as to be almost an albino; because of her color, the Indians regarded her as more foreign that the general run of whites.

It may have been ill health, or bad medicine that later caused the woman's hair loss. Elizabeth's daughter writing in the mid-twentieth century also did not mention anything about baldness; instead she commented on her mother's beauty. Such memories, of course, are no sounder than those cited by Walz. One point, however, all sources agree on: for whatever reason, Elizabeth Blackbird held herself aloof from most of her Ottawa neighbors. Whether her reason for doing so came from bitter personal experience, we will never know.[9]

Andrew Blackbird had to contend with his own disputes those first years back home. Once again the cause of difficulty was his maverick Republicanism. He would not compromise his principles in order to curry favor. In 1860 Catholics and Democrats in the Mackinac area rallied behind the candidacy of George J. Wendell for the Michigan House of Representatives. Wendell was the well-endowed son of an influential Mackinac Island commercial family. Eleven years before Blackbird and his father, Mackadepenessy had blocked the attempt of Father Pierz to have Wendell's father, Theodore Wendell, granted power-of-attorney for all Ottawa business affairs. Even though they thwarted Wendell at that time, the merchant continued to have considerable influence in Little Traverse. When Andrew guided the Ottawa chiefs to Detroit for the treaty conference in 1855 George Wendell came along as a "witness." Near the conclusion of the negotiation Wendell clashed with Blackbird when the former pressed his claim that a share of any treaty payments should go directly to Mackinac merchants such as himself who claimed to hold thousands of dollars worth of individual Indian debts. George Wendell was the favorite of Democratic Party bosses and he was rewarded with the patronage plumb of census taker for 1860. In northern Michigan he acted in the place of the usually distant agent and it was known he controlled all Indian Office appointments in the area. A seat in the legislature was to be his next step. When the 1860 canvass was held, Andrew Blackbird once more cast a very public ballot for the Republicans and against Wendell.[10]

Indian agent Andrew M. Fitch tried to use his authority to the advantage of the Democratic Party. Fitch actually sent out a letter to all employees of the agency in Michigan.

> Make it your business to have the entire vote cast for the Democratic candidate for governor. There may be apathy among the Indians or many of them will be away. Make your arrangements to see that they are in and vote. . . . I have been blamed by some that at the last election but little was done by the government employees in influencing the Indians to the polls; let it not be said so this year. *Don't* show this letter to all.

Among those who pushed Fitch to greater activity was Wendell, who actually had complained to the secretary of the interior that the Indian agency was not partisan enough.[11]

The Republican political landslide that swept over the rest of the state of Michigan isolated Wendell and the Mackinac Island Democrats who were used to dominating the local political scene. Abraham Lincoln's election brought the federal government for the first time into the hands of the Republican Party. In spite of this turn of events the bitter Wendell blustered and threatened. Blackbird understood the new opportunities that now were open to him and immediately applied to be named the United States interpreter for Little Traverse and for his wife to be named teacher at the Indian school. Yet Blackbird was worried he would be undercut somehow by Wendell. Blackbird confided to a friend that Wendell "is bragging to me, that he is going to work against me, if I should ask any favor from the Republicans." Fortunately for Andrew, however, the political spoils system for once worked in his favor. The new administration at least partially granted his wish and he was named to the interpreter post.[12]

Andrew Blackbird was appointed United States interpreter at Little Traverse by DeWitt Clinton Leach, the new Indian agent for Michigan. Leach was a Lansing, Michigan, man who had served a single term in Congress. He brought no special background to the job of Indian agent other than being a founding member of the Republican Party in Michigan. In 1850, as a convention delegate, he had played a small role in helping to get the Indian citizenship provision included in the state constitution. That initiative revealed his broad commitment to social and political liberalism. As agent Leach proved to be a thin cut above the usual dismal standard of Indian Office appointees. Leach brushed aside Wendell's attempt to disparage Blackbird and gave him the appointment based on the latter's education and Republicanism.[13]

The interpreter's position brought with it a salary of $400 annually, which quickly moved Andrew and Elizabeth from poverty to modest prosperity. More importantly, the position was one that carried with it considerable influence and responsibility. Interpreters did much more than translate for the Indian agent or other visiting government officials. The agent was based in Detroit and had charge of close to 10,000 Indians spread out over a larger territory than any other federal Indian agency. With railroads largely restricted to southern Michigan, and most Indians in the northern and central parts of the state, a great deal of time and distance separated the agent from his responsibilities. Water transportation was the only effective way for the agent to visit the Ottawa or the Chippewa and that was impossible during the long winter months. Typically the agent would visit the Ottawa only on an annual basis, in order to make the annuity payments due under treaty. The interpreter, therefore, was the official on-site representative of the United States. The agent relied upon the interpreter for information about what was actually happening among the Indians and to carry out the basic reportorial requirements of the Office of Indian Affairs. As the U.S. interpreter Andrew Blackbird became a vital cog in the undersized federal bureaucracy.

As important as he was to the Indian agency in Michigan, he also now became a key member of the local Republican Party organization. Now that they were in control of the machinery of government the Republicans were intent on using every advantage the Democrats had formally employed against them. Before every election, Andrew, as the federal interpreter, would receive a packet of premarked sample ballots that he was instructed to distribute among the Ottawa. While there is no evidence he employed the strong-arm tactics that had been used against him, Blackbird by necessity became a partisan player for as long as he worked for the United States government.[14]

The Ottawa had expectations of the interpreter as well. Because the agent was a distant figure, they too regarded the interpreter as the day-to-day face of the government. Andrew's appointment came at the expense of his older cousin, Augustin Hamlin, who had held the post for many years. As a mixed-blood tribal member, Hamlin used the position to mediate between the government and the Ottawa as well as to bolster his own leadership position within the tribe. Hamlin functioned as an influential counselor. Policy and decision making were still made by traditionally appointed chiefs, but Hamlin was intimately involved in shaping the direction of all relations with the Anglo-American world. Hamlin enhanced his position by maintaining the mutual trust of traditional L'Arbre Croche leaders as well as that of the Indian agent. Hamlin mastered this tricky balancing act until the 1860 election cost the Democratic Party its hold on the national government. Indian agent Andrew Fitch described Hamlin as "a good Democrat, [who] has acted with the party, and to my certain knowledge interested himself and labored in the last canvass to secure success of the Democratic cause." A Republican victory meant Hamlin had to go. Sadly, Hamlin became ill shortly after leaving his post and following a "lingering illness" died in July 1862. His passing severed another link between Blackbird and the generation that had begun the Ottawa program of cultural and political accommodation with the United States. Fortunately, as the new interpreter, Blackbird had the example of Hamlin to follow as he took up his new duties.[15]

SUBDIVIDING THE LAND

The bulk of Andrew Blackbird's public career, as an official interpreter and as an unofficial spokesman of the Little Traverse Ottawa, was devoted to dealing with issues of landownership. The 1855 treaty had officially dissolved the Ottawa as a tribal organization, save for those dealings that were necessary to carry out the requirements of the treaty. The key terms of that treaty were the creation of individual allotments of land for tribal members. Although nearly one hundred separate members of the Little Traverse bands had already purchased land as private citizens before Andrew ever took office, the majority of the Ottawa were counting on the allotment process to secure them a guaranteed place of residence. The absolute failure of the United States government to effectively administer the allotment process undermined the dream of turning the Ottawa into American-style homesteaders. By the time Andrew became involved in the allotment process it was already badly compromised and drifting toward chaos.[16]

In accordance with the terms of the 1855 agreement, the selection of allotments was to take place immediately following the official proclamation of the treaty. The agent at the time, Henry Gilbert, did begin the process, and some Little Traverse Ottawa did make their selections of forty- or eighty-acre tracts. When Agent Andrew M. Fitch took over, the process was not yet completed, and he complicated matters by allowing some Ottawa to change their selections. As he recorded the new selections he found numerous errors in Gilbert's previous list. Both Gilbert and Fitch further muddied the water by placing white men and mixed bloods, some operating under assumed Indian names, on the allotment rolls. Complaints of criminal misconduct in this regard were received in Washington, so that in 1861, when D. C. Leach took over as agent, he was charged to "carefully review said lists." The incompetence, if not criminality, of his predecessors, therefore ensured that Leach would have a more difficult task than simply starting over.[17]

Six years after allotment was supposed to have been executed, Agent Leach and interpreter Blackbird had to sort through the inadequate records in an effort "to do justice in the matter." During a June 1861 trip to Little Traverse, Leach and Blackbird worked out who did not deserve an allotment and which tribal members who did still needed to make a selection. Within the year Leach recorded the legal land description (township, range, section, quarter section) of each tract of land chosen from the Ottawa's vast 336-square-mile reserve. It is not known if Leach had a General Land Office map at hand that would have allowed allotees to point out their selections on the map. Later confusion would result over which lands actually had been allotted to whom. Certainly those Ottawa who selected land did so only after inspecting its location and resources. Many put a priority on selecting excellent maple sugar groves because the production of that native sweet was a major source of cash income. By January 1863 Leach was able to report to Washington that he had recorded all of the Little Traverse Ottawa selections and that in Michigan there only remained "a few small bands situated remotely who have not as yet furnished him the necessary selections." Gilbert's list included 1,344 individual selections made from various band reserves scattered across central and northern Michigan. In May 1864 the Office of Indian Affairs issued certificates of ownership to most Ottawa who had made selections. The certificates were statements of landownership, but unlike land patents, they could not be sold, nor was land held by certificate subject to taxation. According to the 1855 treaty, these certificates were to be held by the Ottawa for ten years, a period in which the United States would act as a trustee before full free patents were to be issued. The certificates both protected and hamstrung Ottawa landowners, and Leach reported that the "more intelligent among them" understood they did not have full title and requested patents. Leach, however, did not think this was "prudent" and he refused to issue patents.[18]

Acting with dispatch Leach was able to quickly get the land allotment process on track, or so it seemed. Unfortunately, few things were as they seemed when it came to awarding government land. At some point the Office of Indian Affairs in Washington, D.C., lost the list of who had been issued certificates. The result of this was the government did not know who had justly been allotted land and who had not. To make matters worse the General Land Office reported that there were conflicts between tracts issued to Indians and lands that had previously been awarded to private corporations or to the State of Michigan. Rather than focus on these issues, Leach turned his attention to making a fundamental shift in Michigan Indian policy, one that would of necessity lead to a restructure of the allotment process.[19]

After a year in office Agent Leach came to share Andrew Blackbird's bleak view of the treaty-funded Indian education system in Michigan. The program was well-financed and extensive with thirty day schools scattered across the state's reservations. In fact, during the 1860s better than 80 percent of all federal Indian schools were located in Michigan. The schools were spartan one-room affairs but they were generally staffed with well-paid and competent teachers. The problem that Leach had with the schools is that they were not well attended. "Everywhere it is found difficult to keep the Indian children in school," he informed the Office of Indian Affairs. It did not help that the teachers were almost entirely English speakers with no background in the Ottawa or Chippewa language. Like Blackbird, Leach advocated the development of bilingual textbooks that could help *Anishnabe* children make the step from native homes to English-speaking classrooms.[20]

The challenge of educating children had been exacerbated, Leach believed, by the allotment process. Numerous large reservations from which individual Indians could choose their allotments had the effect of scattering native people broadly over the landscape. At the same time many Ottawa and Chippewa still pursued, at least in part, a seasonal hunting-gathering cycle, making day schools in fixed locations less than ideal. An inspector from the Washington office, H. C. Alvord, reported that the day schools were "almost an entire failure." Leach and Alvord came to believe, as Blackbird had advocated at the 1855 treaty discussions, "The only true and successful method of educating Indian children is to remove them from their home influences, by placing them in boarding schools upon the manual labor plan."[21]

Leach came to believe that the way to solve the education problem and to improve the delivery of other services to the Indians, such as agricultural assistance, was through the consolidation of reservations. While Blackbird likely agreed with Agent Leach about the Indian schools, it is not clear from the record how he felt about Leach's advocacy for moving all of the Ottawa and Chippewa in lower Michigan onto one or two large reservations. What is clear, however, is that Leach began to focus his attention on achieving a "gradual concentration of Indians," rather than resolving allotment issues at the numerous existing smaller reservations. The places Leach believed to be best suited for the concentration of native peoples were Blackbird's Little Traverse Reserve and the Saginaw Chippewa Reserve in Isabella County, Michigan. Writing about Little Traverse Leach noted:

> Some of the most temperate, intelligent, industrious and thriving Indians in the State are located here. This reservation contains a large amount of good farm

> land yet unoccupied, and on it might be concentrated several bands of Indians from the smaller reservations, without detriment to the present occupants, and with fair prospects of great good for those transferred.

The commissioner of Indian affairs, William P. Dole, supported Leach's view and he gave the agent approval to negotiate new treaties with the *Anishnabeg* to achieve the consolidation.[22]

In the fall of 1864 Leach succeeded in securing a new treaty with the Saginaw Chippewa in which those Chippewa who lived on the Lake Huron shore agreed to surrender their 150-square-mile reservation and accept allotments within the Isabella County reserve. The carrot Leach held out to effect the consolidation was the offer of new allotments to next generation of *Anishnabeg.* Leach proposed an even better deal for those bands he wished to consolidate at Little Traverse. He called for enlarging the 330–square-mile reserve by adding several townships. Leach also stated,

> I would guarantee the whole of said reservation to the Indians; that is, instead of bringing the balance of the reservation into market [open it to white purchase], after the Indians entitled to land have made their selections, I would hold it in trust for them, and permit every young man among them, when he arrived at the age of twenty-one years, to select forty or eighty acres, and receive a certificate for the same.

Leach believed that in time the prospect of free land would lead most young people from the other bands in northern Michigan to act on their own and seek homes within the enlarged Little Traverse Reserve, making it a multiband Indian homeland. In April 1864 President Abraham Lincoln, based on Leach's recommendation, ordered that six additional townships be added to the reserve. Unfortunately, by the time the Saginaw Chippewa consolidation treaty was effected, it was deemed too late in the year to gather the leaders of the bands Leach wanted to concentrate at Little Traverse. A treaty council was put off for the winter. Later it was tabled altogether after Leach and Dole both left office.[23]

There is no clear reason why Leach did not proceed with the expansion of the Little Traverse Reserve. A large block of new land had already been put aside and would remain in reserve status until 1872 when President U. S. Grant finally opened it to normal settlement. It is hard to see why the Ottawa would not have welcomed the new treaty, since it opened to men of Blackbird's generation the chance to secure allotments for their children. On the other hand, Ottawa living around Mackinac might have been cool to the idea of leaving the familiar haunts of the Straits region.

Grand Traverse Chippewa bands had already relocated to Omena, Michigan, where they formed a community around Blackbird's old acquaintance, the Presbyterian missionary Peter Dougherty, and there was an Ottawa town established at what is now Northport, Michigan, with missionary George Smith. Opposition from Indian farmers unwilling to give up a decade of improvements and missionaries unwilling to uproot thriving congregations may have doomed Leach's initiative. The Saginaw Chippewa consolidation was not without opposition from some bands, but as will be shown, Civil War era politics may have persuaded Leach to override minority opinion in that case. One thing is sure, the failure of *Anishnabeg* consolidation around Little Traverse left the Ottawa and Chippewa bands isolated and vulnerable to being overwhelmed by the tide of European-American settlement that would wash over northern Michigan after the Civil War.

For the rest of his life Andrew Blackbird had to contend with the consequences of Leach's stalled consolidation plan. A brief moment of opportunity opened with the coming of the first Republican administration of Indian affairs, but it closed quickly. The educational programs Blackbird advocated would not be tried for decades. The land tenure of the Ottawa remained in a confused and compromised state. Never again would the government propose to guarantee land for future generations of Ottawa. A national government locked in the turmoil of a Civil War, national reconstruction, and territorial expansion paid only fleeting attention to the Ottawa of Michigan.

CIVIL WAR

Blackbird's initial tenure in the Office of Indian Affairs coincided with the outbreak of the American Civil War. As a longtime and loyal Republican, Blackbird was an enthusiastic supporter of Abraham Lincoln's efforts to put down the slaveholder's rebellion. In later years Blackbird frequently made reference to his service during the crisis. In his *History of the Ottawa and Chippewa,* he wrote:

> During the Rebellion I was loyal to the Government, and opposed bad white men who were then living in the Indian country, who tried to mislead my people as to the question of the war, to cause them to be disloyal.

A group of leading local citizens in a testimonial that served as an introduction to the volume went further. They wrote, "He broke up one or two rebellious councils amongst his people during the progress of the rebellion." Such statements reflect the inflated political rhetoric of the Civil War home front as well as genuine fears of Indian loyalty during the conflict.[24]

Early in the Civil War the Lincoln administration was concerned about the status of its lightly defended northern border and the Indian tribes that lived in that region. The new commissioner of Indian affairs, William Dole, was an old friend of Lincoln's from the president's days as a circuit-riding lawyer. Dole did not have great experience in Indian policy, but he acted prudently when it was "represented to the Department at Washington that an 'uneasy feeling' exists among the Indians in Michigan, Wisconsin, and Minnesota bordering on the Canadian frontier." Thomas Slaughter, a special agent in the Office of Indian Affairs, was sent to northern Michigan to investigate the situation there. He traveled by steamboat to Sault Ste. Marie and Mackinac. He found many rumors roiling Indian country, but little genuine discontent. In Slaughter's opinion "unprincipled and disloyal men" were responsible for misrepresenting "the designs of the government." Indians had been told they would not be paid their annuities and that they would be drafted to fight in the army. Slaughter did his best to dispel these concerns, although before the war was over both would resurface as genuine issues. In his final report to Dole, Slaughter stated, "I was entirely satisfied of the loyalty of the Indians residing near Mackinac and those south & west of them in the State of Michigan."[25]

When Indian trouble came in the Upper Midwest, it was not from Michigan, but Minnesota. The 1862 Dakota War briefly brought the question of Indian affairs to the forefront of policy. The sudden turn of the Dakota in the Minnesota River valley from peaceful farmers to vengeful warriors shocked the nation. The outbreak should have prompted an examination of an Indian agency system that was rife with corruption and inefficiency. Instead the result was a military campaign that spilled out of Minnesota and out on to the High Plains. The death of nearly 500 white settlers and soldiers sent a shudder across the entire Great Lakes region. Although attacks on white settlers were limited to Minnesota, there was initially considerable fear that the more numerous Chippewa in Minnesota, Wisconsin, as well as Michigan, might seize the occasion to drive the Americans from the region. A petition signed by 127 citizens of Juneau County, Wisconsin, hysterically and erroneously complained to Washington that "from one to two thousand Indians in this county and vicinity" were "murdering and constantly committing serious depredations upon our people."[26] In northern Michigan neither the Ottawa nor the Chippewa displayed any desire to join the Dakota, their long-held enemies, in an ill-conceived revolt.

The most obvious impact of the Civil War on the Ottawa came when Agent Leach sought to pay the annuities, not in the usual gold coin, but with "green back" dollars issued by the cash-strapped Union treasury. As interpreter it was Andrew Blackbird's job to convince the Ottawa, who well knew the premium frontier merchants placed on specie, to accept the paper money. Blackbird was assured by Leach that once the crisis of the union had passed, the government would make up the difference in value in gold. With this promise in mind, the shortfall in market value between coin and paper was absorbed by the Ottawa, which became an escalating burden in 1863 when inflation swept the country and the price of the supplies they needed rose precipitously. Little did they realize that the government would not fulfill its promise of making up the shortfall until the middle of the twentieth century. To at least buffer complaints against the government's willingness to execute its commitments to the Ottawa, Blackbird and Leach begged Washington to release the long-promised allotment certificates. When those certificates were issued in the spring of 1864, the agent at least had some tangible sign of good faith. The annuity shortfall was easier to absorb because the war also brought an increased demand for the products marketed by the Indians. Maple sugar prices rose, and Ottawa trappers enjoyed what Leach regarded as "fabulous prices for furs." Across the Great Lakes region logging operations were desperate to find the labor to meet the wartime economy's need for lumber, and many Ottawa for the first time went into the woods as lumberjacks.[27]

As the Lincoln administration struggled with mixed success to defeat the rebel Confederate states, disaffection grew among the Democrats and other Republican opponents. In the 1862 elections in Michigan the Democrats were able to significantly reduce the size of the Republican majority, and as the 1864 election cycle neared, competition between the two major parties in the state was keen. The favor of Indian voters was desperately solicited. The Emancipation Proclamation and the suspension of the right of habeas corpus by Lincoln convinced some Democrats that acceptance of Confederate independence was preferable to more war and the further erosion of traditional rights. For most Republicans a willingness to sacrifice the union was akin to outright treason and they labeled such Democrats as "copperheads," after the snake that hid in the grass. Rhetorical attacks escalated ever more shrilly as the election neared. When Indians complained about being paid annuities with paper money, Agent Leach attributed it not to *Anishnabeg* resentment over broken promises but to the "gross falsehoods told them by disloyal white men." Leach accused the Democrats of trying to "poison the minds of these ignorant Indians and prejudice them against the government that, with fatherly kindness protects and cares for them."

When Andrew Blackbird later in life wrote of his opposing "bad white men" during the Civil War, he was employing the heightened rhetoric of wartime politics. What he really was doing was defending the Lincoln administration from attack by its Democratic opponents.[28]

Agent Leach's eagerness in 1864 to engage the Ottawas and the Saginaw Chippewas in a new round of treaty making was in part derived from his desire to bind them to the Republican ticket in what appeared to be a desperately close election for national and state office. A month before that crucial canvas he wrote to Commissioner Dole:

> We hope to make the proposed changes in the Treaty of some political use to us. Our Indians, as you are aware, are voters and their votes (particularly those of the Chippewas of Saginaw) may be of great importance to us at the approaching election. They reside in the closest Congressional District in the State, & hence, any thing fair and honorable that we can do to put them in good humor, & to favorably dispose them towards the Government we wish to do.

Missionaries working among the Saginaws also made an effective partisan pitch for their congregations to receive a new treaty. One minister wrote to Washington that the Saginaws were being enraged by the actions of lumbermen whom he dubbed "Pine land Sharks." These individuals were "all good Democrats & savor very much of 'Copper.'" The minister warned that only a new treaty would "save us from similar scenes that were enacted in Minnesota." In the end it may have been this veiled threat of violence together with the fact that the Saginaws voted in a tightly contested district that determined why they and not the Ottawa were given a new treaty.[29]

When the Civil War broke out few Ottawa felt the conflict would have a direct impact on their lives. In 1861–62 there was no effort made to recruit Indians to serve in the armed services. George Copway, a Canadian Chippewa who had lived and lectured in the United States, was rebuffed by the Michigan legislature when he proposed to raise an *Anishnabeg* regiment. One of the few Ottawa to see early service in the conflict was Andrew Blackbird's cousin, Joseph Wakazoo. Joseph had joined Andrew at the Twinsburg Academy in the late 1840s. Joseph's father, Peter Wakazoo, was Andrew's uncle and the chief of the Ottawa-Congregational mission colony at Northport, Michigan. In the fall of 1861 young Joseph journeyed to Virginia and enlisted in the Sixteenth Michigan Infantry. The next spring that unit advanced on Richmond and Wakazoo was slightly wounded in the desperate Seven Days Battle, at the conclusion of which he deserted the regiment and returned to northern Michigan. His graphic description of the fierce combat at the Battle of Fair Oakes should have been enough to satisfy any young Ottawa who wondered what war was like. Andrew Blackbird wrote to a friend, "I would have gone to the front as a soldier at the outbreak of the rebellion, but the Government could not spare me as U.S. Interpreter." Most likely his recent marriage and the fact that he had finally attained a position of influence among the Ottawa shaped his actions. Other young Ottawa men, however, grew restless as the conflict dragged on.[30]

The opportunity for active participation in the war came in the summer of 1863. A new regiment was being raised, the First Michigan Sharpshooters. The goal was to recruit a group of fine marksmen and arm them with the new Sharps NM 1859 breech-loading rifle, a weapon capable of firing ten shots per minute. The head of the recruitment effort was Captain Edwin V. Andress. He was a Saginaw County resident reputed to be a fluent Chippewa speaker. The first *Anishnabeg* enlisted into the regiment were Chippewa from the Isabella Reserve. Among the Ottawa to enroll in the regiment were Garret A. Gravereat and Henry G. Gravereat. The later was better known by his Ottawa name, Mankewenan. He was a band leader at Bear River, the Methodist Indian settlement on the south shore of Little Traverse Bay. Of mixed French Canadian–Ottawa ancestry, he had been a merchant at Mackinac Island during the 1840s and 1850s, although by the time of the war he was listed in the census as a laborer, which may have been the result of a drinking problem. He was at least in his late fifties, but he enrolled in the Sharpshooters in Dearborn, Michigan, in order to serve with his son, Garret.[31]

Garret Gravereat was a man in his early twenties who was regarded as a rising figure in the L'Arbre Croche community. Like Andrew, he had been educated in the white man's world and returned to help his people. He was employed by the government as the teacher at the Bear River school, where he impressed all who knew him with his skill as a musician and as a painter of landscapes and portraits. Garret was offered a lieutenancy in the regiment and was given the commission of filling out Company K with Ottawa and Chippewa volunteers. Garret's father was enrolled with the rank of first sergeant, and an additional thirty men answered his call to the ranks. Ottawa men were drawn to the ranks for many of the same reasons white Michiganders enlisted: patriotism, a desire for adventure, and the not inconsiderable influence of government cash bonuses. Ottawa volunteers were able to claim a $50 state bounty, a $25 federal bounty, as well as the regular $13 a month enlisted men were paid. Undoubtedly, these Ottawa volunteers were also proud to do their part as free citizens of the state and to fulfill the traditional *Anishnabeg* role of warrior.[32]

The rationale behind a regiment of sharpshooters was to use such select troops to break up enemy movements with accurate fire from concealed positions or to serve as snipers during static or siege operations. In spite of numerous proofs of the effectiveness of Company K marksmen, the entire First Michigan Sharpshooters had the misfortune of being deployed as an ordinary infantry unit. They were sent to the Army of the Potomac just as that force was set to embark on the bloody "Overland" campaign, fifty-one days of conflict, broken into twelve major battles, costing the army 55,000 casualties. The *Anishnabeg* warriors participated in nearly every one of those battles. Under a unique battle standard—a "large live Eagle" perched on a six-foot pole—they suffered fearful losses. Henry G. Gravereat, Chief Mankewenan, was killed at the Battle of Spotsylvania when a bullet shattered his skull. His son fell a few weeks later at the Second Battle of Petersburg. In that engagement Lieutenant Gravereat was severely wounded in the arm, and twelve of the Indian soldiers were captured. The Ottawa and Chippewa men were eventually sent to the infamous Andersonville prison, were seven of them died. Garret Gravereat had his arm amputated, but an infection set in and he died in a Washington hospital. In a last letter dictated after his operation, he asked his mother not to be "discouraged about me. . . . This fighten for my Country is all right."[33]

As the United States interpreter, Andrew Blackbird helped with the recruiting of Company K, First Michigan Sharpshooters and he most likely helped family members stay abreast of the fate of the men once they went into combat. After the war Blackbird served as a pension prosecutor for Emmet County veterans, Ottawa as well as European-American, and their families. The work was unofficial and in large cities such as Chicago was lucrative enough to have law firms specialize in the work. In Blackbird's case, however, work was something of an outgrowth of his duties as a U.S. interpreter. Blackbird obtained from the Bureau of Pensions the required applications and helped the veteran or his dependent gather and present the necessary documents. In the case of a widow's pension, a marriage certificate was required. In the case of a disability pension, a report from a medical examination had to be provided. All these documents had to be witnessed and notarized. The whole process could be intimidating to an individual with limited literacy, which was still common among the Ottawa. For this work the pension prosecutor usually received a few dollars as a service charge.[34]

Initially pension payments to the disabled or widowed were not especially generous, although over time the formidable block of Union war veterans was able to organize politically and loosen the government's purse strings considerably. Eligibility for a pension expanded over time, keeping Blackbird engaged with pension applications for many years. One of the first war pensions in the region went to Sophia Gravereat. For the loss of Lt. Garret Gravereat, her promising son, and her husband the government awarded her a paltry $15 a month.[35]

Only Ottawa volunteers served in the war. If that war had continued longer, however, there is every indication that Indian men in Michigan would have been subjected to the draft due to their eligibility for citizenship. In February and March 1865, when local communities were confronted with the demands of a large new draft from the Lincoln administration, there was a strong temptation to exploit untapped reservoirs of potential recruits. A number of cases of Indian men being drafted were brought to the attention of Indian agent Leach. The Office of Indian Affairs argued that Indians were not eligible for the draft, but some provost marshals, who were charged with overseeing recruitment, argued that if Indians were citizens and voted in elections, then they had given up their tribal status and were eligible for military conscription. Fortunately, Union forces broke the back of the rebellion that spring and the war ended before the draft net was thrown around Emmet County.[36]

Like the rest of the nation, Little Traverse was rocked by the news of the Lincoln assassination. "O wicked world!" Blackbird complained in a letter, "treason has done its worst; but when the heart and brain recover from the stunning effects of this terrible blow all Rebeldom may look for a stern retribution. This foul murder will be avenged. The Northern heart is fired. Every loyal man is a 'Lincoln Avenger.'" Blackbird reserved special invective for the rebel's "Northern aiders and abettors," whom he regarded as "treacherous in everything and [to] be trusted in nothing." In contrast the government's agents praised the Ottawa's response to the Civil War. "From the very first outbreak they manifested . . . an earnest desire that the government should in the end triumph" and on "many a battlefield they have proved their valor, and in many instances . . . gave their lives for their country." With the union restored, Ottawas looked with confidence to the government. Families that had sacrificed a loved one for their country had earned pensions; for the rest of the Ottawa there remained the promise of land. Before the Civil War if Andrew Blackbird used the phrase "my country" he inevitably was referring to the Ottawa homeland around L'Arbre Croche. Through their participation in the war against slavery the Ottawa for the first time began to think of the United States as "their country." Although they were not a numerous people and they lived in what Blackbird called "this Wilderness," they felt, in their agent's words, they "deserve[d] none the less of that country because of the tawny color of their skins."[37]

THE RECONSTRUCTION OF L'ARBRE CROCHE

Ottawa veterans who returned from the Civil War found homes little changed in their absence. As they had done for centuries the Ottawa continued to thrive pursuing a mixed economy based on garden farming, furs, fish, and maple sugar production. Small schooners brought their products to the market at Mackinac, and they traded for the cloth and manufactured items brought to the region from the outside. The major Ottawa bands were grouped together around the four main villages that marked the L'Arbre Croche coast from north to south, Cross Village, Good Hart (Middle Village), Little Traverse, and Bear River. The town that Mackadepenessy had helped to found in 1829 as New L'Arbre Croche was now commonly known as Little Traverse. In 1865 Andrew Blackbird's hometown still boasted only a single commercial building, a waterfront combination warehouse-store, and had only a single dock. A post office was opened in 1862, but the arrival of letters remained a rarity. Little Traverse was an Indian town made up of small whitewashed wooden houses laid out neatly along Main Street, the sandy track that ran parallel to the shore of the bay. The handful of European-American residents were teachers, fishermen, and traders. The little clapboard schoolhouse built by Father DeJean in 1829 and where Andrew first attended classes was still in use. A generation after their fathers had signed a treaty that threatened removal from Michigan the Ottawa persisted on the shores of Little Traverse Bay. On a warm summer afternoon only the bleat of an occasional free-ranging goat or the cry of a high-spirited child diving into cold pure waters disturbed the natural silence. But beyond Little Traverse's beach the thunderbirds flocked in a darkening sky. For the Ottawa the 1860s were the lull before the storm that would send a great white wave breaking over the peaceful village.[38]

The rest of Michigan was in the midst of a remarkable change when the Civil War ended. During the course of the conflict its crops, its copper, its iron, and most of all its pine had all found new national markets. Railroads, the great transforming force of the age, had begun to spread their iron tentacles toward the north. In the Upper Peninsula a railroad connected Lake Michigan with Lake Superior, while in lower Michigan the first road was built to the interior, north from Jackson. Most commerce, however, continued to move on the Great Lakes, and the lumber industry, Michigan's biggest postwar business, relied upon shipping to send its vast harvest of white pine to the nation. First, at Saginaw Bay and Muskegon, and later further north at Manistee and Traverse City, the lumber industry transformed old-growth forests from a majestic landscape to a liquidated asset. Less than fifteen years after the Civil War Michigan surged ahead of all competing states and alone provided a fourth of the nation's lumber. A rush was on for access to the state's "green gold."[39]

Blackbird and other Ottawa leaders were aware of the changes that were sweeping the state. Returning veterans and newspaper stories paid witness to the changes afoot in the land. The Ottawa also had the example of the Saginaw Chippewa in central Michigan. Adjacent to the literal cockpit of the rough-and-tumble lumber industry on Saginaw Bay, the Chippewa had seen their reserved lands overrun with white lumbermen and timberland speculators. The federal government had not yet issued land patents to the Chippewa. They only had certificates of claim, which technically could not be sold. Nonetheless, Saginaw Chippewa certificates holders were beset by the pine sharks with bottles of whisky and offers of loans designed to push the *Anishnabe* allotment holder to sell the standing timber on their claim. Fortunately, in 1864 the United States granted the Saginaw Chippewa a new treaty that allowed future generations to claim allotments within the original reserve. In the face of heavy pressure by the lumber interests, the Saginaw at least had the prospect of future allotments to fall back upon. The Ottawa along the shore of Little Traverse had no such recompense. They had been put on the back burner by the government in 1864 because they were in a less politically sensitive district. In the wake of the Civil War, Andrew Blackbird and the Ottawa focused on trying to make a new treaty with the United States that would secure for future generations the ability to thrive in northwest Michigan.

Between 1866 and 1869 Andrew Blackbird was involved in a series of councils that brought together not only the L'Arbre Croche bands but the Ottawa and Chippewa in the Grand Traverse region and the former Grand River bands, now settled in Oceana County. The purpose of these councils was to petition the government for permission to go to Washington, D.C., and negotiate a new treaty. The *Anishnabeg* of northwestern Michigan shared two concerns. The first and most important was to secure a right to land for their children. The second was to arrange for the disposition of their remaining annuities under the 1855 treaty.[40]

Eleven years after Indian leaders had agreed to dissolve their tribal status and accept individual parcels of land, the United States had still not fully carried out the land distribution among the Ottawa and Chippewa. Many of the L'Arbre Croche Ottawa had received certificates for their allotments; unfortunately due to negligent record-keeping the Office of Indian Affairs and the General Land Office did not know where the selected lands were located. This meant that *Anishnabe* land title in northwest Michigan was insecure. It is understandable that with European-American penetration of their region on the increase, the Ottawa and Chippewa wanted to resolve the issue. Indian leaders were also being pressed by their young men for more land. In the more than a decade since the allotment process began a large number of young Indians had come of age. According to the treaty only individuals twenty-one years of age in 1855 were entitled to land, yet with more than 300 square miles reserved for allotments could not those who came of age in recent years claim an allotment? These were the land issues that concerned the *Anishnabeg.*[41]

Blackbird was also aware of series of financial issues that the Ottawa and Chippewa wished to resolve with Washington. The 1855 treaty promised that for ten years the government would provide schools, agricultural implements, and blacksmith shops for the Indians. These services were designed to help the Indians establish successful agricultural communities on their allotted lands. Unfortunately, allotment did not take place in 1856 as the treaty envisioned. The Indians had only recently received their certificates, and due to incompetent agents even those allotments were in question. Just when the Indians could most use the promised services they were due to expire.[42]

Finally, the government still held $206,000 in trust. These funds were due for per capita distribution over the next four years. While the influx of such funds would be welcome in many a household, most *Anishnabe* leaders did not want this last payment remaining from the cession of their lands to be squandered. Rather they saw the money as a patrimony to be held in trust for future generations. At the 1855 treaty, Wasson, one of the leading Little Traverse chiefs, tried to make this point to Commissioner Manypenny. He told the commissioner that the Ottawa wanted the funds locked up in the federal government's "bread box." When Manypenny did not seem to understand Wasson's reasoning the chief told him a parable.

> I do not wish to do with our money, as I heard a man once did with a little swan. The little swan when he went out used to pick up shillings in his bill & bring them back to his master. At last his master got to think that the swan was all money & cut him open & found no money. So he lost his little swan. Now I do not want to cut our little swan open. We wish to let him live, that our father may feed him & he may grow & continue to bring us shillings in his bill.

At the treaty Manypenny brushed aside Wasson's request. Now that the funds were to be disbursed Andrew Blackbird and the Ottawa chiefs renewed their request that the money "remain in the hands of the Government to be a perpetual Indian fund from which Indians shall draw Interest."[43]

In spite of repeated petitions, the *Anishnabeg* request for a Washington treaty council met with a stony silence. With an Indian war under way on both the northern and southern plains, as well as a divisive conflict between the executive and legislative branch over Southern Reconstruction policy, the needs of 5,000 Ottawa and Chippewa in Michigan must have seemed of small import. Blackbird's inability to deliver a new treaty was a blow to any aspiration of greater leadership influence. He was, however, hindered by the character of the Indian agent with whom he was bound to work. In 1865 DeWitt Leach, whom Blackbird had assisted for four years, was replaced by the Reverend Richard M. Smith. The change of administration was smoothly handled. Smith, a Methodist preacher, had served as Leach's clerk for several years. He thoroughly knew the treaties and annual business of the Michigan Indians. Leach had a high opinion of Smith's clerical ability. He told the commissioner of Indian affairs that Smith was "one of the most *laborious, faithful,* and *accurate* Clerks to be found in the Country." Unfortunately, Smith seems to have been so comfortable with the ordinary business of the agency that he was incapable of any type of initiative that would deviate from the norm. He was knowledgeable, well-meaning, but in the end ineffective. Whereas Leach had been a founder of the Michigan Republican Party and a former congressman, Smith had little political influence or personality. He was at heart a clerk. Leach had confidently planned to consolidate Michigan Indians on expanded reserves and he had the clout, even in the midst of Civil War, to start the process with the 1864 Saginaw treaty. Smith merely forwarded Indian petitions to Washington and blandly asked the *Anishnabeg,* year after year, to be patient while their tribal reconstruction program languished.[44]

Misfortune and downright farce combined with official lethargy to frustrate Blackbird's attempts to obtain a new treaty. In 1868 the commissioner of Indian affairs finally appointed a special treaty commissioner to negotiate with the Ottawa. Unfortunately, Agent Smith did not receive notice of this development until after he departed on his long annual trip to pay annuities. The treaty commissioner expected to accompany Smith but he arrived in Detroit after the agent had sailed. Another year went by without a treaty conference. The next year the Office of Indian Affairs changed its position. The secretary of the interior was informed that a treaty would be too expensive for the department and that if the Ottawa wanted to obtain land for their children, it would be better "accomplished by Congressional enactment than by treating with the numerous bands of these Indians, and certainly with far less expense to the government." The government's turn away from a new Ottawa treaty was part of a significant shift in Indian policy that was in the making.[45]

In 1869 after the election of former general Ulysses S. Grant as president of the United States, there was a major change in the Office of Indian Affairs. For the first time an American Indian was appointed as commissioner. Ely S. Parker was a college-educated engineer of the Seneca tribe. During the Civil War, he served as Grant's aide and rose to the rank of brigadier general. Parker was one of several close Grant confidants named to important administrative posts. Unfortunately Parker and the others shared not only Grant's outlook, but also his political inexperience. The Seneca would have a brief but rocky tenure in office. Parker came to Indian Affairs determined to do justice to the Indians and to speed their assimilation into American society. Early on he tangled with eastern reformers when he tried to have his department transferred to the War Department. Parker respected the integrity of his fellow officers and saw this as a way to rid the department of corruption, but he angered eastern reformers who saw such a move as an endorsement of a "military solution" to the Indian problem. Parker had to back off that plan, although he did appoint a military man to head the Michigan Indian agency. Important for Blackbird and the Ottawa's was Parker's belief that the government should cease the policy of negotiating treaties with Indian groups. After 1871 it became official United States policy to end the treaty system, so the Ottawa never were again given an opportunity to renegotiate with the United States.

Parker's appointment to Michigan was twenty-nine-year-old Major James W. Long. A combat veteran severely wounded in the Seven Days Battle, Long brought several years experience in military administration to the job. The appointment broke with precedent. For twenty years all agents, save for DeWitt C. Leach, had been handpicked by the Michigan Conference of the Methodist Episcopal Church. The result of that dubious arrangement was either incompetence or corruption, and sometimes both. Long, in contrast, was an extremely able man who shared Parker's commitment to Indian assimilation. Unfortunately, Long had no previous experience working with Indians and he never fully appreciated the difficult social and economic transformation that was under way among Michigan's Indians.[46]

Blackbird held his appointment as U.S. interpreter at Major Long's discretion. The two met for the first time when Long arrived in Little Traverse to make the 1869 annuity payment. The agent was shocked by the level of dissatisfaction he found among the Ottawa. Blackbird explained to him that fourteen years of an incomplete and inconclusive land allotment program had left many Ottawa angry and distrustful. The previous agent, Richard Smith, had promised that their problems were "being looked into," so no one was anxious to give Long more time to get action. After consulting with

Blackbird and the other interpreters, Long and Commissioner Parker tried to piece together a picture of what needed to be done to right the dismal state of Indian affairs in Michigan. Long advised Parker that the average Ottawa he met had "been wronged, and he feels it." They went back to the 1855 treaty and made a plan to quickly execute the terms of that agreement to the letter.[47]

Although Long believed that the Ottawa were "deserving the special good will and consideration of the government," he did not look deeply into their situation. He turned a deaf ear to all considerations that did not relate to the execution of the 1855 treaty. According to that agreement all allotment issues and annuity payments were to end in 1871 and for him that date became a deadline for concluding all their business.[48]

Agent Long was nothing if he was not efficient. In spite of the obstruction of officials at the Traverse City Land Office, who tried to keep Long from seeing their plat books, he forced access to these maps to make allotments. Unlike his predecessors who simply wrote down the legal descriptions of allotments, Long also recorded each one on a base map so that any overlapping or conflicting claims could be quickly identified and resolved. To further clear the government of treaty obligations Long identified most Ottawa allotees as "competent," which meant they would be given free patents to their selections. After only one year in office Long resolved the uncertain status of Ottawa land selections and he applied to Washington to have the patents issued to the Indians.[49]

Nothing, however, in the Office of Indian Affairs went easy. After only two years in the department, Agent Long resigned for the more independent and lucrative enterprises of Michigan's burgeoning Gilded Age economy. The conscientious and administratively constipated Reverend Richard Smith was brought back to head the agency, and the Ottawa land patents remained stacked on a Washington, D.C., desk. Smith, as a matter of principle, opposed the issuing of free simple patents to the Ottawa. Although the government was bound by the 1855 treaty to issue such patents within ten years of that agreement, Smith believed that to do so would trigger a major and immediate loss of Indian land to white speculators. Smith condescendingly noted that while the Ottawa and other Michigan tribes had made considerable progress and largely "ceased to be blanket Indians,"

> but few of them were as yet competent to take charge of their own affairs, as against the scheming, grasping white man, without further government assistance; and therefore and for that reason; they ought not be trusted with the absolute title to home lands, except, perhaps, in a few well known instances.

History would prove Smith correct, but legally the government, barring another treaty with the Ottawa, had to distribute the patents. In the fall of 1871 Smith's objections were removed when the agent, his wife, many of his allotment papers, and the ship they were on sank beneath Lake Huron's green waters. The Ottawa were put off one more time. Finally, in August 1872, they finally received their patents from the 1855 treaty.[50]

While Andrew Blackbird technically served as an assistant to the Michigan Indian agent, and he was bound by the agent's policy decisions, yet as an Ottawa spokesman he was also expected to represent the best interests of his people. During the 1860s and early 1870s Blackbird tried to carefully negotiate the limitations, opportunities, and ambiguities of his position. During the frustrating four years he served under Richard Smith, Blackbird opened a correspondence with Thomas Ferry, an ambitious young congressman from Grand Rapids. Ferry was the son of Protestant missionaries who from 1823 to 1834 had run an Indian school at Mackinac Island. Andrew's older brother William had been educated there before going on to study in Rome. Thomas Ferry had spent his early years in proximity of the Ottawa and Chippewa at Mackinac before moving to Grand Haven, Michigan. Blackbird may have hoped that the young politician had inherited some of his parents' commitment to the welfare of the Indian. In view of Agent Smith's inability address the Ottawa's grievances, Blackbird hoped that Ferry, based in the nation's capital, might be a more useful contact. Certainly Ferry proved to be both willing and able to move policy, but he was a dangerous card to play, because he also represented many of the powerful lumbermen of the Grand River valley. Mixing "pine with politics" was a favorite cocktail in Michigan and Ferry drank deeply from the cup of his well-heeled constituents. The politician was well aware they were looking to expand their logging operations northward into what had been Indian country.

In 1871 Ferry was elected to the United States Senate, and he was in an excellent position to influence Indian affairs in Michigan. The following year he sponsored a bill designed to meet the needs of the lumbermen as well as, he promised, see to the Ottawa's outstanding business with the government. With the treaty-making era over, such bills were the only way for the Ottawa to amend the government's legal obligations to the tribe. Blackbird was not the only Ottawa to work with Senator Ferry to achieve legislative relief. The Reverend John Rix Robinson, a Ottawa-American mixed blood with a large Methodist following among the *Anishnabeg* of central Michigan, was also strongly involved in pushing legislation along. In June 1872 Congress acted. In the provision that was most calculated to appease the Indians, the bill ordered patents to be awarded to all Ottawa and Chippewa who claimed allotments under the 1855 treaty. For any tribal members who came of age since the treaty, the bill granted them six months to claim 160-acre tracts within their reserves to be held under the terms of the 1862 Homestead Act. That last provision addressed the Ottawa's desire to secure land for the post-treaty generation. The rest of the 1872 act, however, focused on the needs of Senator Ferry's white constituents. Once the *Anishnabeg* made their Homestead selections, the remaining land on their large reservations in Oceana County, near Grand Traverse, and Little Traverse were to be thrown open to white lumbermen and settlers. The bill had the effect of opening the floodgates, and a stream of land speculators flowed into the formerly reserved lands.[51]

Blackbird's advocacy for the general granting of land patents helped to pave the way for white lumbermen to gain control over a large number of the Indian allotments. In retrospect, it is easy to see that the best interests of the Ottawa would have been served by the government keeping the patents and thereby shielding the Indians from local taxes and the loss of the land. At the time, however, the benefit of such a course was less than clear. The 1855 treaty had called for the Ottawa to receive their patents within ten years, and by the early 1870s many Indians were worried the government might not follow through with its promises. Patents in hand were proof of obligations fulfilled. So many allotment rolls had been made in the wake of the 1855 treaty, each one like a promise made followed by a promise broken, that in frustration a Chippewa spokesman challenged the government, "Is there one honest man in Washington?" Understandably, by the 1870s many Ottawa felt only patents in hand could secure their land tenure.[52]

Prior to 1872 most Ottawa lived near their traditional villages or on land purchased prior to 1855. Once patents for their allotments were finally in hand, the Ottawa farmers faced a dilemma. To settle the land, they needed money; to get money they had to sell land. Forests covered most of the land the government allotted from the reserve. In order for Ottawa families to successfully establish a subsistence farm on such land, they needed capital for livestock, seed, and equipment for both farming and for tree stump removal. A historian of Michigan's settlement history estimated that forested lands were the most expensive lands to settle. A contemporary estimated the cost at about $15 per acre. Government agricultural assistance promised in the 1855 treaty expired before the Ottawa received their patents. If the Ottawa were going to settle successfully on their allotments, they would need to access capital. This they could secure by either selling the timber rights to their land or by selling title to a portion of their acreage. The very act of settling an allotment very often necessitated liquidating at least a portion of its value.[53]

Blackbird was aware the Ottawa needed resources to make a home on the allotments, which is why he wanted to negotiate a new treaty with the United States. He had hoped to extend agricultural and educational assistance with new resources from Washington, D.C. At the very least, however, Blackbird and other Little Traverse leaders wanted to endow a permanent fund, held in trust by the federal government, with the last of their treaty money. In this regard Senator Ferry's land bill gave the Ottawa far less than they hoped to negotiate for, and it left the *Anishnabeg* vulnerable to every smooth-talking speculator taking a carpetbag north.

THE GREAT TIDE

On a bright summer morning in 1874, Andrew Blackbird stood on a Little Traverse wharf watching the steamer *Menominee* rise and fall across white-capped waves, a column of gray smoke rising from her single steam engine. A black top hat was set firmly forward on his head and his formal frock coat was fully buttoned to resist the cold lake breeze. He patiently waited for the vessel to make her way across the bay and tie up at the dock. The arrival of a ship was always an event of note for the isolated towns along the Great Lakes shore. The prow of a steamer or schooner was like a knife cutting through the isolation of the forested wilderness. Each landing brought supplies, mail, sometimes the return of old friends, but increasingly in the 1870s the vessels brought newcomers. Down the *Menominee*'s gangplank on this day came a family of five, lately residents of the Iowa prairie, determined to make a new start in Little Traverse. Looking at the dark rim of trees that overshadowed the little town, a young boy holding tight to his mother's dress asked: "Are there Indians in those woods?" For Andrew Blackbird, who came forward to greet the new arrivals, the questions was not whether there were Indians in the woods, but for how much longer.[54]

In 1874 the bulk of the Ottawa and Chippewa reserves created by the 1855 treaty were thrown open to white settlement. In the course of a few short years, the face of the region was transformed. The *Anishnabeg* had long been a minority within the state of Michigan, but in the band homelands in the northern part of the state they were the dominant presence. As late as 1870 the Ottawa made up better than 95 percent of Emmet County's 1,211 residents. The overwhelming majority were members of families with deep roots in the region. To the people of Little Traverse, one resident noted, "the world beyond was 'outside'; its people, 'outsiders.'" This was challenged after 1874, when the outsiders rushed in and became the majority. By the 1880 census there were 5,500 more whites than Indians in the county.[55]

With each ship arrival the "outsiders" crowded the wharf with their trunks and children. The Ottawa residents, who gathered to see what the ships brought, saw a mixed bag of prospective lumbermen, commercial fishermen, fur and game hunters, and, most common of all, farmers. The later were conspicuous for the menagerie that followed in their wake, cages of chickens clutched close due to snarling Indian dogs, followed by swine, and milk cows. Most of these European-Americans were from the eastern states, although close to 20 percent hailed from across the ocean. As the numbers of permanent settlers grew, the ships also disgorged a stream of sharply dressed "drummers" hawking the luxuries of the big city to the settlers of the Lake Michigan frontier. "How much the appearance of the village has changed," a visiting priest exclaimed. "It is rapidly becoming Americanized."[56]

The Ottawa and the "outsiders" mixed like oil and water. Ulysses P. Hedrick, the little boy Andrew Blackbird met at the lakeside dock in 1874, left a graphic account of Little Traverse's transition from an Indian to a white town. He remembered that "exploring the village was difficult during the first weeks in our new home, for as soon as my brother and I stuck our noses out of doors we were pounced upon by youthful red devils who made us fight for our lives." In summer the boys battled with sticks and stones, in winter with "hard-packed snowballs." At first the hardy Indian boys had the upper hand, but as Hedrick remembered it, "Our time came the next spring when the Indian youngsters were half starved and weak from cold and winter ailments. . . . We quickly learned that an Indian could not 'take-it' on the nose or chin, and my brother and I were soon handy with our fists." In return, the Ottawa boys gave Hedrick a nickname, *Tite Cochon*, loosely translated as the "plump little swine."[57]

In Hedrick's memory the adults interacted in business, but not socially. In describing his mother he noted, "She numbered as her friends all who had white faces and Christian names; Indians, in Iowa and Michigan, regardless of age or sex, were to her of Satan's brood." In return few Ottawa tried to bridge the social divide. Hedrick recalled visiting the home of only one French-Ottawa mixed-blood family and blandly confessed, "I never broke bread in an Indian home." The favorite place for the white men of Little Traverse to gather was W. E. Parker's false-fronted general store. Jammed with everything from foodstuffs to farm equipment, candy to tobacco, the store was heated with a "great rectangular stove" around which white folks gathered to exchange news and "yarns." Indians sometimes worked at Parker's and occasionally shopped there, although Hedrick noted, "No one was welcome in Parker's unless he had money or credit—few Indians had either."[58]

Andrew Blackbird was a familiar figure to all of the "outsiders." Blackbird had advised Hedrick's father in 1873 when the latter scouted Little Traverse as a place to settle. As the U.S. interpreter and as a township and county official, Blackbird had official status. Hedrick described his English as "fluent" and his appearance as formal.

> Blackbird was a small man with hands and feet no larger than those of a woman, body straight and trim. He wore a high, stovepipe hat and a voluminous Prince Albert coat. Always on weekdays he was shod in soft deerskin moccasins, but on Sundays he wore stringless shoes with elastic sides.

Hedrick remembered that "at the time of our arrival in the village, Chief Blackbird was walking in full splendor as the great man of L'Arbre Croche." That status, however, would not be long lived.[59]

Blackbird clashed early with the "outsiders" who sought land and profit in his homeland. From 1866 until 1871 he sparred with Dennis T. Downing over his trading activities and real estate speculations. According to the 1870 federal census, Downing was a forty-six-year-old Irish immigrant who settled in Little Traverse with his wife and two children. He initially came as a teacher in the government school but quickly moved on from doing good to doing well. He thrived in business and was one of the wealthiest members of the small community, with family assets in excess of $7,000. The core of his enterprises was a general store he operated near the wharf, although he also was a "dealer in wood." Unlike the bulk of the lands in the interior of Emmet County, which until 1874 were reserved exclusively for Indian use, the town of Little Traverse was open to public land sales. In 1855 Andrew Blackbird had surveyed the first plat of the town. Within a few years more than forty lots had been sold, one of them to Dennis Downing. The latter seems to have sold liquor at his store. This was not necessarily illegal. If, however, Downing sold liquor to the Ottawa, he was in violation of state law. Blackbird could complain about this to the Indian agent, but it was not a federal violation, because Little Traverse was not technically "Indian country."

What Blackbird could do was keep a sharp eye on Downing's wood business. Taking timber off land held by the United States in trust for the Ottawa was a clear federal violation. After warning Downing, Blackbird gathered evidence against him and forwarded proof of his trespass to Indian agent Richard Smith. Initially the agent only issued a statement of pious indignation: "Mr. Downing must stop the kind of dealing with the Indians you mention." When the violations continued, however, charges against the Irishman were filed with the U.S. attorney in Grand Rapids. Downing tried to justify himself by representing that individual Ottawa had sold or exchanged the right to cut wood on their allotments. While Indian agent Smith and even Secretary of the Interior Columbus Delano regarded what Downing did as illegal, it seems the United States attorney's office declined to prosecute either Downing or the hundreds of other lumbermen who were making similar such deals on all the Michigan Indian reserves.[60]

For his interference in Downing's profitable trade Blackbird made a dangerous enemy. The merchant vowed to pull Blackbird "down to the dust." In addition to being one of the leaders of Little Traverse's growing white community, Downing was a local political operative. He was the postmaster of the town, and he tried to use his position in the patronage hierarchy to discredit Blackbird. In 1869, in the twilight days of the Andrew Johnson administration, Downing wrote to the commissioner of Indian affairs to have Agent Smith and interpreter Blackbird relieved of their federal appointments because they were "radicals" like those who had tried to have Johnson impeached. Downing complained that Blackbird said, "Our Beloved President is nothing but a Copper-head, a Rebel Sympathizer, and a Secessionist." Fortunately for Blackbird, U. S. Grant's "radical" Republican ticket won the election and he was retained as interpreter.[61]

Downing, however, did not give up. He quickly moved to ingratiate himself with the new Indian agent, Major James Long, and to Blackbird's shocked indignation when Long conducted the 1870 annuity payment, Dennis Downing sat next to him at the "pay table." Andrew later wrote, "My very blood in my veins was boiling at the time to see that personage who never trusted a dollar's worth to an Indian" dolling out annuities. Blackbird lost face among the Ottawa because the man he had denounced as a "big rascal' had usurped his place at Major Long's side. Andrew tried to explain to Long that Downing was a "disloyal" Democrat during the Civil War and not a true Republican. The interpreter then made the mistake of contacting Congressman Thomas Ferry with the hope that he would pressure Long to break with Downing. Long, however, was too independent to brook any interference, and he threatened to fire Blackbird for going behind his back with agency business. Indeed the fracas may well have cost Blackbird his position had not Long himself shortly afterward resigned. In his last communication with Long, Blackbird explained, "I was not fighting you but I was fighting my biggest enemy in the world."[62]

No sooner was Major Long gone from the agency than Downing attempted to influence his replacement, Richard Smith, against Blackbird.

It is likely Downing was behind Andrew Keewakendo's effort to supplant Blackbird as the U.S. interpreter. Keewakendo claimed that he had the Little Traverse band leaders behind his application for the job, although he declined to produce a petition to that effect until he had Smith's support. Blackbird successfully warded off the maneuver by assuring the Indian agent that "politics" was behind the move, and that he had the support of all the Ottawa, save for those at Bear River.[63]

Downing and Blackbird also clashed head to head for elected office. In 1868 Andrew Blackbird buried Downing in the race for the office of register of deeds, 125 to 47 votes. A year later Blackbird again counted a political coup on Downing when he replaced the Irishman as United States postmaster for Little Traverse. Several years later as chairman of the Emmet County Board of Supervisors, Blackbird oversaw Downing's work as the acting county treasurer and had the satisfaction of seeing the board reject several of Downing's bills as too high. Fortunately for Andrew, Downing died in 1871, ending their bitter rivalry.[64]

From 1855 to 1874 Andrew Blackbird served in a number of local elected offices, including register of deeds, county treasurer, county board, township supervisor, circuit court commissioner, and deputy sheriff. Other literate Ottawa joined him in running Emmet County. These included Michel Kew, Louis Petoskey, Joseph Petoskey, Louis Wasson, and Paul Wasson. After 1875, however, Ottawa participation in Emmet County's political leadership fell off dramatically. A new white majority took hold of the institutions of local government, and Blackbird never again held elected office. At the same time his local political career ended, Blackbird also lost his position with the Office of Indian Affairs. The commissioner of Indian affairs acted on the understanding that in 1855 the Ottawa had been dissolved as a tribe, and that with the award of patents the United States had no further responsibilities toward them. In 1872 the position of U.S. interpreter at Little Traverse was abolished and Blackbird temporarily lost his formal position as intermediary between his people and the government.[65]

In time even Blackbird's sole remaining official function, postmaster of Little Traverse, came under fire. Initially the position of postmaster only paid a salary of $9 per year, but as the town grew, the position became more important and the salary grew rapidly. In 1873 a petition of complaint was sent to the Postmaster General's Office about Blackbird's handling of the mail. As more European-Americans came into the town they objected to having to collect their mail at Blackbird's house. Officials in Washington advised Blackbird to "please the public as well as he could." The criticism stung Blackbird, coming as it did with the rapid social changes to his hometown.

He marshaled his savings and responded by building a "comfortable office." Yet in spite of this move, in June 1877 Blackbird received word he was "removed for cause" from the job as postmaster. He protested that never had anyone complain "of having lost his money or letter through this office during my administration." Blackbird never received an explanation, although he likely realized that the postmaster position was a patronage plumb, and in March 1877 a new moderate Republican administration took power in the capital. His old political godfather, Senator Thomas Ferry, temporarily lost his position as chairman of the Committee on the Post Office, and Andrew suffered the consequence. The loss of the position was more galling when Blackbird heard white newcomers mutter, "We don't want any more Indian P.M.s." Andrew's splendid new false-fronted, white clapboard, post office building was now redundant. Since the new office was attached to his home, it was not amenable to sale or rental and it remained largely unoccupied and unused for over thirty-two years.[66]

The loss of the postal sinecure was a blow to Blackbird. It cost him his government salary just as he had invested his savings in a new office. "This left me penniless in this cold world," he later complained, "to battle on and to struggle for my existence." As important, it was a blow to his pride. For sixteen years he had been an official of the United States government, which for all its headaches had been a source of community status and a regular salary. While employed by the government, Blackbird could feel he was using his education to do "good amongst my people." Now he was thrown among the majority of Ottawa who had to scramble to make a living off the land, in a community controlled by "outsiders."[67]

THE TROUBLES

The late 1870s were hard years for the Ottawa. They struggled to adjust to the wave of white settlers who swamped their quiet communities. Many young people spent these years on isolated interior tracts trying to carve a homestead out of the forest. Confounding their effort was a weak national economy. The Panic of 1873 staggered the whole country with massive unemployment that would not improve for six long, lean years. On top of this northern Michigan was hit by successive crop failures in 1874 and 1875. Appeals for assistance flowed into the federal Indian agent snugly secured in southern Michigan. The agent reported to Washington, "These poor people in Traverse, Emmet, and Leelanau Co.s on Homesteads both

White and Indian are appealing to the sympathy of the people." Eventually "a small amount of flour" was distributed "among the Ottawas in Emmet Co." Blackbird was not impressed with the government's generosity. That summer he wrote the agent as a private citizen. With one eye on the U.S. Army's massive 1876 campaign against the Plains Indians he bitterly observed, "The United States can kill off these Indians residing in the State of Michigan or any part of the Union."[68]

Blackbird spent these years scrambling to make ends meet. In 1876 he maneuvered unsuccessfully for the position of schoolteacher for his old home of Middle Village. Although he was supported by the Ottawa residents, he was denied the place, which may have gone instead to a nineteen-year-old white girl. In spite of this frustration Blackbird did not, like most Ottawa, become a subsistence farmer or a fisherman. To a limited extent he joined the rush to exploit the area's forest resources by organizing an effort to cut cordwood and sell it to steamboats at the Little Traverse dock. Elizabeth and he continued to live in town. They owned several lots from which they may have received rent. Nearby was Blackbird's allotment. The fifteen improved acres provided enough potatoes to keep them in hash throughout the year, and the pasturage supported a couple of milk cows and swine. Unlike almost all of his Ottawa neighbors, Blackbird did not produce maple sugar for the market. Also, unlike most Ottawa he and Elizabeth speculated in real estate. In 1878 and again in 1879 he acquired Little Traverse town lots lost for delinquent taxes during the last years of the "Long Depression." Although he seems to have acquired only three lots at tax sales, such acquisitions strictly speaking did come at the expense of fellow tribesmen.[69]

Indian land loss became epidemic in the late 1870s and early 1880s. The most vulnerable lands were those claimed by the Ottawa under Senator Ferry's 1872 act. That law opened the Ottawa reserve to whites, while also attempting to recompense the Ottawa by giving them a chance to first file 80- or 160-acre land claims in the area. Many Ottawa took advantage of this last chance for land and filed claims. The problem with the law was that it did not award the Indians free patents; instead their claims were subject to the provisions of the 1862 Homestead Act. That centerpiece of Republican Party ideology offered all Americans the opportunity to file a claim on up to 160 acres of public domain. The land could be theirs if they lived on the claim for five years and improved the property by planting crops and constructing a dwelling at least twelve feet by fourteen feet. A homestead claim was invalidated if it was abandoned or if a claimant did not make the required improvements. In that case the local land office could then allow another claim to be made on the land. During the late 1870s hundreds of European-Americans filed claims on *Anishnabeg* homesteads and took the land for their own.[70]

Although he no longer was officially connected to the Office of Indian Affairs, Andrew Blackbird became deluged with the complaints of Ottawa homesteaders defrauded of their claims. For the next decade he sent a steady stream of letters to Washington. The greatest abuse centered on the Traverse City Land Office. The understaffed facility literally did "a land office business," and its employees had little means to investigate what was actually happening on the ground, so they tended to rely upon sworn affidavits. Between dishonest clerks and fraudulent affidavits, it was not hard to separate an Indian from his land. When Blackbird first complained to the Department of the Interior, he was informed they were familiar with the problem and that "proper steps will soon be taken." Instead, the cases continued to multiply, and little wonder, for in hard economic times, it was an easy way to obtain improved land. A "land shark" simply had to go to the Traverse City office and swear that a claim was abandoned. The office then had a notice of a public hearing printed in the *Grand Traverse Herald.* If an Ottawa claimant was tending to his forest farm and failed to see the notice, he could lose his home without ever knowing it was in danger. General Land Office regulations required hearing notices be "personally served" when "practicable." A well-placed bribe often determined what was "practicable."[71]

Among the more egregious thefts were those directed against the claims of John Shomin and his brother Louis Shomin of Cross Village. Both men had endured hard service in the Civil War as part of the First Michigan Sharpshooters. They had operated sugar camps on the land since they had returned from the war. They believed they had inhabited their homesteads long enough to have "proved" their claims, although they had not formally applied for their final papers. When notices of abandonment were published, the brothers lacked the funds to travel to Traverse City to contest the case. Blackbird was also involved in the case of Lucy Penaseway on and off for several years. She was an Ottawa widow with four young children. Penaseway had a comfortable dwelling on her claim, a garden, and the beginnings of an orchard. White land sharks filed on her land as abandoned when she left the farm for several weeks to pick berries. When she returned, they had a white family occupying her house and using her furniture. Blackbird and Indian agent George Lee appealed for federal intervention while the speculators had the tract stripped of its merchantable timber. Lee described Penaseway's shabby treatment as "bad as the most heartless treatment of ex-slaves of the South." The cases revealed both government impotence and the value to unscrupulous lumbermen of even temporarily occupying an Indian homestead.[72]

Intimidation played a major role in separating the Indian from his land. Blackbird reported that homesteads targeted by land sharks would often experience sniping at their cows and horses, even theft of the same. Another gambit was for a land shark to hire another white man to show up at an Indian homestead with papers purporting to prove that the Indian was on the wrong claim and then convince the Indian to leave under threat of violence or charge of trespass. If Indians did try to contest the abandonment proceeding, they faced the cost of going to Traverse City and the cost of bringing witnesses to support their claim. Before the hearing they faced a gauntlet of threats, physical intimidation, and cash settlement offers. Inside the chambers they were confronted by professional attorneys, a bewildering array of legal terms, and topped off with the threat of perjury proceedings. Blackbird attended some of the hearings to help translate or explain, but he was no lawyer.[73]

Andrew's sister, Margaret Boyd, also was deeply involved in trying to ward off the assault on Ottawa land tenure. Since her teenage years in a Cincinnati convent school, she had worked off and on as a teacher before establishing a farm with her husband, the mixed blood Joseph Boyd. In the fall of 1876 she determined to make a direct appeal to President U. S. Grant. It seems she traveled alone, paying her expenses by selling traditionally made birch bark or woven baskets. When she sold all that she brought, Margaret raised funds by taking orders for more. It was in her words "a long and bitter journey," during which she ran out of funds on several occasions and had to beg railroad conductors to let her ride for less than full fare. Her visit was not approved by the Office of Indian Affairs, but she nonetheless met with the commissioner of Indian affairs, and through great persistence she somehow she managed to obtain a meeting with the President. At the time Grant was a political lame duck and the capital was aflame with controversy over who was elected to replace him. Margaret was escorted in to see Grant, but she was barely given time to state the reason for her visit when she was led from the room. She wanted to request that the Ottawa be given patents for their homestead claims and to complain about white harassment. According to later accounts the president passed her off to first lady Julia Dent Grant and excused himself. The president's aide later gave Margaret a return train ticket and money for a pair of shoes. "I do not see why a Father does not wish to see his poor child," Margaret afterward complained, "coming to him from a long way, and not let her see him only a half a minute. Oh, tears, tears, all the way home."[74]

Margaret's mission and Andrew's letters did, at least, spark federal authorities to investigate what was happening in northern Michigan. In 1877 George Lee, one of the more contentious Indian agents to serve in Michigan, and Edwin J. Brooks of the General Land Office, heard Indian complaints and visited the Traverse City Land Office. Brooks investigated fifty-two cases of fraud perpetrated on Indian homesteaders and found that in the overwhelming the majority of these the Ottawa and Chippewa had been grossly imposed upon by speculators and General Land Office officials. Underlining these actions, Brooks found, was the general sentiment among whites in northwest Michigan that the *Anishnabeg* were at best semicivilized and that they could never be competent members of a progressive community. Many people felt that in order to achieve the "permanent and desirable development of the country," it was justifiable for whites to use "every possible means" to "dispose them of their lands." The "means" whites employed were as varied as they were unethical. Indians were tricked into signing quitclaim deeds, lured into debt by smooth-talking drummers hawking everything from sewing machines to parlor organs, and hoodwinked by the fine print on contracts they could not read. Inspector Brooks was shocked at the open manner in which white citizens threatened Indian property owners with violence, even in the presence of a federal official. One speculator unwilling to use violence baldly told Brooks that the Indian he targeted "will be hard up next winter then I can buy his land at my own figures."[75]

In the face of this, the Office on Indian Affairs was prompted to act. Andrew Blackbird was brought back as a special interpreter to at least give the Ottawa a local official through which they could communicate. Edwin Brooks recommended that the Ottawa be granted patents to their homesteads, which would have ended the scam of the abandonment hearings. Secretary of the Interior Carl Schurz embraced this report and had a draft bill sent to Congress where, unfortunately, it was received with indifference. Further recommendations designed to protect Indian patent holders received even less support, even though Brooks estimated that in less than five years one-quarter of all allotees had lost their land. In Washington, D.C., the Board of Indian Commissioners, men who fancied themselves "friends" of the Indian, officially advised against any direct intervention, callously stating, "This Anglo-Saxon race will not allow the car of civilization to stop long at any line. If the Indian plants himself on the track, he must inevitably be crushed by it."[76]

The assault on Ottawa land did not diminish. Local government, once under the direct control of Ottawa voters, now was turned into a tool for land seizures. "These whites who are here with us," Margaret Boyd wrote to

President Grant, "they Tax us so high, so we cannot no way get money to pay . . . and then they buy our Lands for tax, this [is] why they do it to take our Lands away from us poor Indians." Inspector Brooks entirely agreed with Margaret's assessment. He reported, "At Little Traverse the threat was openly made by a number of parties that if they could not relieve themselves of the presence of Indians in any other manner they would 'tax them out of the country.'" According to Boyd, a tax of $32.85 was levied on every eighty-acre tract of unimproved Indian land. Andrew, who also owned town lots, faced a tax bill in excess of $100. In the 1850s and 1860s when Ottawa officials controlled the machinery of government, taxes on eighty-acre tracts were little over $1. Of course, as Emmet County developed it needed more funds for roads and other improvements. Prior to 1872, treaty money funded schools. In 1877, after local government took up the burden for public education, a new schoolhouse was built and a "heavy" new tax was instituted. Inspector Brooks described the new structure as "a large and fine schoolhouse one much larger and far more costly than their number required or their ability would warrant." Brooks believed that the white officials purposely built the grand new building to place a crippling burden on cash-strapped Indian property holders. The high tax assessments worked hand and glove with the abandonment hearings. Indians needed cash to pay taxes. To raise cash an Indian farmer had to leave the farm to take wage labor. While he was away working, a homestead claim could be declared abandoned.[77]

The malice of the new white majority was deeply discouraging for Andrew Blackbird. He had devoted much of his life to learning the ways of the European-Americans. He had worked with his father to encourage the Ottawa to change their ancient culture, to become citizens, only to be subjected to abuse from a people whose avarice made a mockery of Christianity. At middle age he butted uncomfortably against the limits white America would allow. He vented his emotion in a letter to Indian agent George Lee.

> The Sprit is apparent. These whites have determined to send the Indians out of the Country. Although we are citizens of the State of Mich. And we are told that we have an equal footing with white citizens, but I see that there is a great antipathy and prejudice existing between these two races as we hear frequently damning remarks made by the whites towards the Indian race . . . which makes us feel we have no country now which we might call our own like [in] the older times.

Andrew, however, did not give up his dream of an Ottawa people free and equal in Michigan. He remained convinced that educating Indians would eventually lead to Indian officials "in the halls of [the] Legislature and in the halls of Congress to protect the rights of their beguiled race."[78]

Andrew Blackbird and his family suffered the same fraud and harassment that the "newcomers" inflicted on the rest of the Ottawa. His nephew Jeremiah Blackbird three times successfully defended his homestead from the land sharks. The legal cost of the last defense required he sell his only yoke of oxen. Seeing he was destitute, the sharks came after him again, and he lost the farm when he could not contest their claims. Andrew's half-brother John, Mackadepenessy's son from his second marriage, also was enmeshed in a long and bitter battle to save his land. He had a fine tract near the growing town of Petoskey. His farm was declared abandoned even though he had a large corn crop in the field ready for harvest. After three years of fruitless legal wrangling, he simply gave up the claim. Andrew devoted considerable time going to these hearings and writing fruitless appeals to Washington. In the end all he could do is to shout into the void of officialdom, "John's case is one of complete robbery!"[79]

In 1879 it was Margaret Boyd's turn to be defrauded. Andrew's sister lived with her husband Joseph Boyd on track of land near Little Traverse. They grew a small amount of grain, potatoes, and raised livestock. As was common in scores of Michigan towns, pigs, goats, and cows tended to range free, while agricultural fields were fenced. One day Henry Comstock, one of the white newcomers to the village, claimed he was gored by a three-year-old bull belonging to Joseph Boyd. He complained to the sheriff, who had all the bulls in Little Traverse assembled so Comstock could identify the offender. He did not point out any of the assembled bulls, nor could he produce a witness to the attack. Nonetheless, Comstock filed suit against Boyd, even though the latter protested he did not own a bull, only a yoke of oxen and a calf. Comstock, a thirty-five-year-old farmer from New Jersey, was according to Blackbird a notorious thief and liar who had previously tried to steal one of Boyd's oxen. At the trial he produced witnesses who swore the Boyd's did keep a bull, and that was enough to win the suit. Boyd's testimony that he did not own a bull and that of other Indians to that effect failed to sway the judge. The Boyd's were levied with a $375 judgment plus all of Comstock's court costs. It was a crippling blow to an elderly couple with little more than $1,200 in total assets. They were required to heavily mortgage their allotment. Later reflecting on this incident in his *History*, Blackbird mused, "The Indian's oath and evidence are not regarded in this country, and he stands a very poor chance before the law."[80]

Andrew had his own difficulties during these years of fraud. In 1876 he made the hundred-mile trip to the Traverse City Land Office to file a homestead claim for himself. There was a very attractive tract of land within a mile of Petoskey that had been overlooked by speculators. Blackbird knew it had been incorrectly marked as "located," and after pointing this out to the land office clerk, he attempted to file a claim on the land. The clerk immediately realized the tract was very valuable and refused to accept his claim under the guise that the official register was not present, but that as soon as he reviewed the application "he should hear from them." Of course, Blackbird never heard from them and the land was quickly in the hands of a speculator with some of the profit no doubt spilling into the pockets of the land office staff. Agent George Lee complained that the incident was only one of many "cases of like rascality."[81]

Andrew Blackbird was particularly hard hit by the escalation in property taxes that followed the emergence of a white political majority. He regarded the assessments as "outrageous," but was powerless in the face of the town's new leaders. Unlike most Ottawa who were hard pressed to find jobs that paid cash, Andrew had his government salary as an interpreter. That pay, however, came irregularly and in 1879 Andrew was unable to pay his entire assessment. He nearly lost some of his town lots. Fortunately, his salary arrived just a matter of days before the tax sale, and he was able to redeem the property.[82]

It was at this time that Blackbird's wife stopped using her Ottawa name Ogechegumequay and instead began to purchase property under the name Elizabeth M. Blackbird. Within a few years Elizabeth had a small stream of revenue independent of her husband. In 1881 Blackbird referred to paying some of his government expenses with money that "belongs to my wife which I have borrowed from her." This may have simply been a case, not unknown in successful marriages, of the spouse with the better head for business taking over family finances. Yet the change also had the legal effect of putting the white and English-born Elizabeth as the legal owner of most of the family's property at a time when Blackbird believed there was little chance for an Indian to receive a just hearing in a court of law.[83]

There was no effective government intervention to help the Ottawa. At this same time the Saginaw Chippewa in Isabella County, the Grand River bands in Mason County, and the Grand Traverse Chippewa were also being systematically stripped of their allotments and homesteads. Blackbird did what he could to document what was happening and Agent George Lee dutifully conveyed the details to Washington. Lee warned his superiors that the Michigan land sharks were pursuing the Ottawa "with the fierceness and persistence of their marine namesakes." Another time he wrote in frustration:

> The loss of an Indian homestead may seem to you an unimportant matter, yet when the most humble individual loses his or her *all*, the loss is as severe as if the same calamity befell an Astor or Vanderbilt.

What was needed was the immediate dispatch of United States marshals to protect Ottawa homesteaders. Yet as African-American freedmen in the South discovered when they were set upon by a post-Reconstruction white backlash, the United States government lacked the will to enforce its laws when they were violated by citizens with the support of local government.[84]

The plunder of Ottawa property was carried out by the leading white citizens of Emmet County. W. E. Parker, the genial storekeeper whose emporium was the favorite gathering place for Little Traverse whites, exploited needy Ottawa families. One of those whom he "donned out of her rights" was Mary Kewag, a Northport war widow whom he scared into signing over her homestead claim for a mere $10. Parker also played a key role in plundering Lucy Penaseway's homestead. Andrew Deuel, an attorney and future county judge, passed off fraudulent conveyances in order to obtain Ottawa allotments and swept up scores of properties as tax foreclosures. Carlos D. Hampton, the first physician in Little Traverse and the first president of the town, helped to lead a petition drive to keep the federal government from interfering with the seizure of Ottawa homesteads. Joining in that effort were shipowners Philo Chrysler and E. E. Hartwell. They were interested in securing the revenue that would come from shipping pine cut from Ottawa lands. L. A. Clark, who built the one of the first sawmills on Little Traverse Bay, was also involved in homestead frauds and in keeping government investigators at bay. Inevitably there were Ottawa who were complicit in the fraud. Stanislaus Skibegosh was in the pay of Parker. The Middle Village resident trolled the backcountry of northwest Michigan trying to hook the needy and the ignorant with the bait of a few dollars ready cash in exchange for a mortgage on their patrimony.[85]

Andrew Blackbird knew all of these men. Their children ran with his children through the sandy streets of the town. Skibegosh, like Blackbird, also worked occasionally for the Office of Indian Affairs, and they cooperated on filling out reports for Washington. In 1879 Blackbird also took advantage of a tax foreclosure sale to buy another town lot. During the 1870s the business of the town was land and lumber and he tried to compete. He cut lumber with indifferent results, and he bought land on a small scale, but he never stopped helping his people deal with the rising American tide. Blackbird felt the pain of the newcomer's disparaging remarks and the callousness of their hard dealing. He had been pushed out of his postal job, and he made enemies while trying to represent the Ottawa, yet Andrew was also becoming part of a European-American-dominated community.[86]

It took only a few short years of whites and *Anishnabeg* living side by side, to reveal the hollow heart of Indian citizenship in Michigan. On paper the Ottawa had secured both land and civil rights. Their right to self-determination was recognized by both the United States government and state authorities in Lansing. Yet legal rights proved illusory in the absence of the political will necessary to enforce the spirit of the law. In the land offices and courts of northern Michigan the citizenship of Ottawa men and women was mocked by a callous competitive spirit that endorsed all means necessary to secure an economic advantage. Local government institutions that in the 1850s and 1860s had been established and managed by the Ottawa were captured and then twisted by the newcomers to disinherit and defraud. In spite of the new powers the Civil War constitutional amendments gave to the federal government, Blackbird could not goad the Department of the Interior or the federal justice system to intervene in northern Michigan. The promise of Ottawa citizenship was left frozen on the north country's wintery ground.

In 1873 the first engine of the Grand Rapids and Indiana Railroad chugged into Petoskey, Michigan. The town had formerly been known as Bear River, but now sported a new name in honor of Petasoga, the Ottawa who had first settled there. Farther up the bay Little Traverse faced the prospect of fading before Petoskey's more rapid economic growth. To keep their town viable citizens actually contributed money and labor to extend the railroad, and in 1881 they finally succeeded. With the coming of the railroad the white leaders of the community determined to change the name of the town. Tourists from the cities to the south were beginning to find their way north, and the town elders wanted a name that would help attract a share of this lucrative new market. Blackbird's hometown was renamed Harbor Springs. The name Little Traverse, like that of L'Arbre Croche before it, faded into history.

7

Light and Shadows

On a late summer afternoon in 1895 a high-spirited group of tourists from Detroit ambled down Main Street, Harbor Springs. They made their way to a small frame house where they were met at the door by Elizabeth Blackbird. The visitors thought her "very handsome in spite her poverty and surroundings." To them she was the exotic "white squaw." When asked how she came to marry an Indian she answered readily.

> I don't know, he was smart and I felt sorry for him, and I was a romantic girl. You see how I live, yet I was brought up in an English boarding school and had every advantage.

The "object" of their visit, however, was to meet the man reputed to be "the picturesque relic of the Ottawa tribe." They found him, fittingly enough, sitting on a kitchen chair making a bow and arrow. A journalist in the group was surprised by his appearance,

> Sitting there "straight as an Indian" no seams or wrinkles to speak of in his copper visage, only a few grey hairs, the light in his "eagle eye" undiminished—this the chief who is said to number one hundred years who is so old that none of his people live to keep him company.

Andrew Blackbird told them a few stories of the Indian past and then rendered a dramatic recitation of his own composition, "The Lamentation of the Overflowing Heart of the Red Man of the Forest." The outing was complete when Blackbird donned his "best apology for an Indian costume" and accompanied the tourists to the photographer's studio, where he posed for pictures. The outing had been arranged by a "friend" of Blackbird's, and it no doubt ended with the old man receiving some type of monetary reward.[1]

This was Andrew Blackbird at twilight. He was a man in his eighties, short of income, long on patience, pragmatic by nature, and somewhat disappointed by experience. He had tried to bring education to his people, but had largely failed. He had tried to protect his people from those who would steal their land, but the citizenship rights he fought for proved a poor shield against white avarice and government indifference. He had sought an equal place in the American future, yet found himself exoticized as a colorful "relic" of the past. Out of the bitter experience of failure, Blackbird would, nonetheless, improvise a valuable legacy. His *History of the Ottawa and Chippewa* was born of equal parts, a need to make money by playing the Indian chief, a genuine pride in his Ottawa heritage, and a desire for personal vindication. This hybrid of need and devotion ensured that the Ottawa struggle to persist on the shores of Lake Michigan would be remembered.

TO SCRATCH THE GROUND TO SUSTAIN MYSELF

In July 1883 Andrew Blackbird's service as U.S. interpreter in the Office of Indian Affairs ended. His second stint as the government's official representative at Little Traverse had lasted for four years. He owed the renewed appointment to the flood of complaints that had arisen from Ottawa homesteaders. Blackbird played a key role bringing abuse to light, but in the end the government did not want to undertake any meaningful intervention. By ending Blackbird's service, the government saved money and reduced the number of complaints. The termination marked a big change in Blackbird's life. He had been either a student or an employee of the United States government for most of the years since 1840, when he began work as a blacksmith's assistant at Grand Traverse. The government appointments gave him status and more importantly a salary. It is, therefore, understandable that for the ten years that followed, Blackbird sought to be reinstated to an official position.[2]

Blackbird's efforts to regain a federal appointment were hindered by the election of a Democrat to the White House in 1884. Always involved in partisan politics, he was so strongly identified as a Republican that he actually came to blows with Cross Village Democrats at this time. When the Republicans regained power with the election of Benjamin Harrison in 1888, Blackbird was ready to press his case. Rather than content himself with an assistant's position, however, he orchestrated a movement to be appointed as the Indian agent. His application was supported by DeWitt Leach, the former agent who first appointed Blackbird, and by a number of leading Republican legislators. A newspaper article from the time mentions that "Michigan members of congress" and "influential people in the state" backed Blackbird with "earnestness and sympathy." A petition was put forward from the Ottawa of Little Traverse, and he had the support of at least one local chapter of the Women's National Indian Association.[3]

Blackbird's main rival appeared to be another *Anishnabe,* the mixed blood John Rix Robinson. This son of a former American Fur Company trader and an Ottawa mother, Robinson had the benefit of a Mackinac Island mission education and the support of his wealthy father. Young Robinson was involved in several questionable real estate deals relating to Grand River Ottawa lands before being born again in 1869 and taking up the cloth as Methodist preacher. His work among the Saginaw Chippewa in Isabella County made him one of the most admired *Anishnabe* clergy in the state, and his support by the Methodist Church made him a formidable rival for the position as Indian agent. Blackbird's backers pointed out to Michigan legislators Robinson's past involvement with "speculators and crooked transactors."[4]

According to a press account the nomination of two Indians for the post of agent in Michigan "caused quite a flutter in the heart of our United States Indian policy." At the time the federal government was forcing the policy that had failed in Michigan, allotment and detribalization, on the Indians of the American West. Having an Indian agent determined to right the wrongs of allotment in the nation's largest Indian agency might have proved embarrassing. On the other hand, Blackbird was a strong supporter of educating Indian children in English at boarding schools—an important part of the government's war on Indian culture. In the end, he never had the chance to lead the agency. Instead, in the last hours of the Fiftieth Congress, legislators removed funding for the position of a Michigan Indian agent. The elimination of the agency was not requested or anticipated by the commissioner of Indian affairs. Instead, the move was no doubt a victory for the influential lumbermen and land speculators who objected to federal interference with their efforts to obtain Indian lands by whatever means were necessary. This was a group with tremendous influence and they had good ideological cover. In their opinion, Michigan Indians had been citizens since 1855, and they deserved no special protection as wards of the state. This proved a powerful argument at a time when the government was pushing the same policy across the country. Michigan's congressional delegation was caught between the demands of the "friends" of the Indian and their exploiters. Closing the agency altogether, a newspaper observed, "relieved the Michigan delegation from a great pressure." So instead of Blackbird or Robinson receiving the agent position, the agency was instead closed.[5]

Upon receipt of the Congress's punitive move, Blackbird wrote an open letter that appeared in several Michigan newspapers. "I was not at all disappointed nor surprised," he wrote, "as I did not expect anything else, for I knew long ago that our government was always against the enlightenment and education [of] our Indian races in this domain." In addition to restating his often voiced complaints about the way Indian children were poorly educated in treaty-funded schools, he indicated what he hoped to accomplish as agent.

> I intended to have a good shaking to those robbers of this region who are continually removing the land-marks of the poor Indians—not excepting of the poor widows and orphans, to which it ought to have been the business and duty of former agents to attend.

Blackbird invited officials who did not think Michigan needed an Indian agent to "come to my humble dwelling and see piles of letters" from Indians and federal officials alike who requested his intervention. Bitterly he concluded that had not the names of Indians been put forward for the agency, the position would have been filled in the usual manner.[6]

The closing of the agency not only denied Blackbird the position of agent, it foreclosed his hope to be reinstated as an interpreter. In 1892 he made his last serious effort to regain federal employment. The year before, Congress had authorized the establishment of an Indian industrial school at Mt. Pleasant, Michigan. It was the government's first effort to educate Indian youth in Michigan on the model Blackbird had advocated since 1855. Naturally he was excited by this development and wanted to be part of the experiment. He immediately wrote to the school's superintendent as well as to the commissioner of Indian affairs. "I have for some time been looking for a position whereof I could be [of] any service towards the enlightenment of my people," he explained. Blackbird proposed, "I think I can do much good lecturing and teaching and otherwise." In a later application he requested an appointment as an assistant superintendent. Unfortunately, his missives seem to have garnered no interest. Besides, he was close to seventy years old, hard of hearing, and prone to illness. The creation of the school came too late for Blackbird.[7]

Blackbird reluctantly went back to scratching out a living from his allotment. He was no farmer, but he had a good piece of land. It was a partially forested tract about a mile and a half east of Harbor Springs. The views were magnificent from his garden and pasture looking out from an elevated terrace over the blue Little Traverse horizon. He also had a boat, and as when he was a boy, he would sometimes set hooks for lake trout and whitefish. Frequently a row on the lake would yield a fish for the dinner table to supplement the eggs, potatoes, and milk produced on the allotment. The land also produced some hay and oats that largely went to feed Andrew's swine and horse.

Blackbird took particular delight in his horse. The men of Emmet County took much more pride in their horses and their ability to manage them than later automobile-based generations can imagine. The horses required constant and personal care to be properly maintained. To master the grooming and handling of horses was a generally recognized badge of manhood. In the post–Civil War period most of the horses of northern Michigan were still the short, tough, long-mane equines of the *Anishnabeg* and Canadians. According to U. P. Hedrick, who grew up in Harbor Springs, the town would host a racing derby just as winter days began to warm, but before the snow melted. He recalled that Andrew Blackbird was among the most passionate racers. He would harness his favorite horse, Buckskin, his long tail carefully braided, to a small colorfully painted sledge and take on all comers. According to Hedrick, when Blackbird or one of the other drivers would pass a rival, they would "give voice to the war whoops of their tribes." People, Indian and white, from neighboring towns would crowd into the village sporting the colors of their favorite race team. There was much betting, laughing, and shouting along with some drinking as the entire community celebrated the end of winter.[8]

In the 1870s and 1880s, when Blackbird was particularly busy with Indian Office business, he had the benefit of help on the farm from his four children. Andrew and Elizabeth's first child came in 1867, eight years after they were wed. The boy was named William, a testament to the powerful influence that Andrew's tragically departed brother played in his life. Another boy, Fred, followed in 1870; a daughter, Janette or Nettie, in 1872; and finally Bert, the youngest, in 1877. Although the evidence is slight, Blackbird appears to have been an indulgent parent. U. P. Hedrick, who as a boy was burdened with chores by his mother and father, weighed in rather officiously about the Blackbird children, who had been both combatants and playmates. "Never have I known children so badly spoiled by their parents, nor human beings with less care beyond the day, as if poor things, they knew they had no future."[9]

It is perhaps surprising that while Blackbird was a champion of educating

Indian youth in boarding schools, he never sent his children to such an institution. At the time a select number of Little Traverse Ottawa youth attended Carlisle Indian School. All the Blackbird children attended the Harbor Springs grade school, located in a fine building on the bluff overlooking the town. Will Hampton, son of the town doctor, went to school with the Blackbird children and recalled many afternoons of fun. Unlike Hedrick, who recalled frequent fisticuffs, Hampton's memoir described summer days on the bay in a large pine dugout the boys dubbed their "war canoe." In winters they sped down the snowy hills on barrel staves, fashioned into a broad single ski, or they skated across the ice in long, strong strides. Janette Blackbird, five years younger than brother William, remembered her youth somewhat differently. "I do not recall knowing any Indians very well when I lived in Harbor Springs," she wrote years later. "My mother's friends were all white, and her friends and their children were my friends and playmates."[10]

For all his advocacy for Indian education, Blackbird's three boys appear to have been indifferent students who never advanced beyond the local public school. The family interest in education that Andrew inherited from his father, uncle, and older brother ended with him. In what must have been an agonizing moment for Elizabeth and Andrew in their old age, their youngest son, Bert, in 1906 served a year at hard labor at the Michigan Reformatory for disorderly conduct. Janette did better in school and appears to have had a gift for music, which her parents helped her cultivate.[11]

While Blackbird remained a ready resource for Ottawa families with legal or land problems, he may have become somewhat estranged from the life of the Indian community during his declining years. He resided in Harbor Springs at a time when most Ottawa lived in rural areas or in the *Anishnabeg*-dominated towns of Middle Village or Cross Village. There is no record of him participating in maple sugaring in the spring or a spirit feast in the fall. Elizabeth Blackbird's social circle seems to have been largely European-American. Andrew himself admitted that none of his four children could speak the Ottawa language. Susan Shagonaby, a twentieth-century Little Traverse Bay band member, recalled being told that Blackbird had the reputation among the Indians of being somewhat vain, and that this sometimes caused them to act coolly toward him. Another band member, Joe Kishigo, believed that the poor upbringing of his children caused Blackbird to lose Ottawa respect. Elizabeth Blackbird fared even worse in the inevitable gossip of the small town. The usually genial Will Hampton remembered her as a "sour puss," and that she sorely henpecked Andrew.[12]

Blackbird's religious affiliation further estranged him from the Ottawa community. Christianity, which the Ottawa embraced, in part, as a way to ward off removal, over time became a vehicle for enhancing *Anishnabeg* identity. Christian worship brought Ottawa families together with other Ottawa. Most Little Traverse Ottawa were Catholic and at the center of their practice was Holy Childhood of Jesus Church and school. An exclusively Ottawa neighborhood in Harbor Springs was located behind the church. While the parish dated to the 1829, the school was founded in 1885 by the Franciscans and staffed by the Sisters of Notre Dame. Holy Childhood was devoted to the maintenance of the *Anishnabeg* Catholic identity. Although some local European-American students attended the school, the bulk of the student population was Ottawa, with a small number of Chippewa also enrolled. Harbor Springs area Ottawa attended as day students, but most children were boarders. Parents who could not afford tuition donated produce, lumber, or labor. Neither Blackbird nor his children were part of the web of relationships that were created by the institution and which served to reinforce Indian identity through Ottawa hymns and the incorporation some pre-Christian forms. The Catholic liturgical calendar also brought a large part of the Ottawa population together for public celebrations on Christmas, the Epiphany, Corpus Christi, Easter, and All Saints Day. Corpus Christi, which honored the Eucharist, blended Old World Catholicism with *Anishnabeg* practice. Families joined together in a long and elaborate procession that snaked through Harbor Springs with frequent stops at improvised shrines or tall decorated poles, not unlike the painted poles of pre-Christian practice, placed along the way by parishioners.[13]

Historians of ethnic America cite the Catholic parish as a key vehicle of assimilation for European immigrants to America. It provided a communal environment of shared values in which the family, not the individual, was seen as the key social unit. Blackbird, in part, rejected Catholic Christianity because he thought it isolated the Ottawa too much from American society. In his evangelical zeal he did not see that Catholic social institutions could also serve to insulate core Ottawa values in a time of turmoil.[14]

Most Christian Ottawa who did not espouse Catholicism joined the Methodist Church. Near Charlevoix, Michigan, Peter Greensky, an Ottawa preacher, established an Indian congregation. While the Greensky Hill Church was a bit difficult to reach for many Ottawa seeking Sunday service, the camp meetings held each summer were immensely popular. Like Catholic parish life these evangelical gatherings served an important communal social function. Camp meetings brought disparate Ottawa families together for a week at a time. In addition to the ever popular hymn singing, the meetings united families and provided both men and women with avenues for leadership as camp officers or speakers.[15]

Blackbird had been baptized a Catholic and had explored Presbyterianism and Methodism before committing to the Episcopal Church. His practice of religion, while a key component in his life, was in many ways very American in its individualism. Blackbird studied Christian principles deeply and independently. He frequently borrowed religious books from fellow townsmen. One story told about Blackbird has his wife Elizabeth so frustrated with his focus on reading that she began to throw books at him, just to get him out of his chair. In spite of such a reaction he relished religious conversation and correspondence with whites and Indians alike. He kept up ongoing debates with Peter Greensky and with local Mormons regarding biblical prophecy. Sometimes his interest in other faith traditions was confused by his correspondents as a desire for conversion; he nonetheless remained attached to the Episcopal Church. Unlike the Catholics or Methodists, Episcopal worship in Harbor Springs lacked the strong community ties, either *Anishnabeg* or white, of Catholicism and Methodism. St. John's Episcopal Church was built by and largely for elite summer resort visitors. While the Catholics arrived by canoe and the "Presbyterian ministers did not come until the trains could bring them," a local historian quipped, "the Episcopalians awaited the Pullman Palace cars." Blackbird was a well-known, if atypical, member of St. John's Episcopal Church. As he grew older and poorer, he sometimes was ashamed to attend services amid the well-to-do congregation because of his shabby appearance. However, he greatly valued his long personal talks with the Reverend Daniel Tuttle, the presiding bishop of the American church, who had a summer home near by and who acted for many years as the summer pastor.[16]

SUMMER VISITORS

The development of the Little Traverse area as a summer resort center had a major influence on Andrew Blackbird and the Ottawa. While many European-American lumbermen and farmers viewed the Ottawa as obstacles to their personal and community development, vacationing urbanites saw the Indians in more romantic terms. To tourists the Indians were a curious, ancient, and vanishing people who lent an air of history and mystery to the woods and waters of the Great Lakes. From this sympathetic, if unrealistic, view of the Indian, the Ottawa spun a livelihood selling crafts and lore.

The tourist boom in the north owed its origin to the conjunction of railroads and hay fever. In the wake of the Civil War, a tremendous surge in railroad construction swept the nation. The iron horse was seen as the key to economic progress. Michigan like many states offered generous land grants to companies promising to punch a track of steel rails into an undeveloped corner of the state. The largest land grant for any road built in the Lower Peninsula went to the Grand Rapids and Indiana Railroad that eventually made its way to Mackinac via the Little Traverse Bay towns of Petoskey and Harbor Springs. Once the line was built, its owners were desperate to attract freight and riders. In time, they assisted in the construction of a series of hotels at attractive spots and worked to publicize the scenic wonders of the northern Great Lakes landscape.[17]

A sizable portion of the Midwest population, however, did not require much of a hard sell to attract them north. These were the people who suffered from hay fever and asthma. The fertile lands of Ohio, Indiana, Illinois, and Iowa produced a wide variety of pollens that made the summer a time of trial for the allergy sufferer. For those with financial means, the new railroads held out the hope of the cool, clean, lake breezes of Little Traverse Bay. Shortly after the first railroad reached Petoskey in 1873, informal "Achoo Clubs" were formed by groups of wet-eyed, running-nosed refugees. Sometimes they camped on the broad beaches; others crowded into rambling clapboard boardinghouses. Soon they looked for a more "pleasant, healthful and inexpensive place to spend the summer months." The Methodists got together and organized the Bay View Association near Petoskey, while the Presbyterians set up the Wequetonsing Association on eighty acres adjacent to Harbor Springs. A group of Lansing, Michigan, businessmen and professionals came together as the Harbor Point Association and purchased fifty-two picturesque acres jutting into the bay. Each of these associations built a hotel, laid out streets, and subdivided lots for individual summer homes. By the mid-1880s they were the backbone of a successful and elite resort industry on Little Traverse Bay.[18]

The resorts came to Michigan at a time when Americans had largely ceased to view Indians as a savage threat and instead embraced the opposite stereotype, the noble savage. Indians bereft of autonomy and land could be safely viewed romantically. Their culture, particularly their lore and crafts, was of heightened interest because it was seen as vanishing, doomed to be washed away by the rising tide of assimilation.

At least since the 1850s Ottawa women had manufactured birch bark boxes and baskets for sale to travelers passing through Mackinac Island. When resorts brought an even larger stream of tourists right to Little Traverse, they quickly perceived an opportunity to earn much-needed cash income. At train stations and steamship docks they laid their wares out on blankets. They sold rush mats, rattles, moccasins, and wooden utensils. Beautiful porcupine quill vessels, which in later years would be worth hundreds of dollars, were sold for twenty-five cents. Even in the 1880s, however, the work of master craftswomen such as Margaret Boyd commanded a higher price, certainly over $5. The best basket-makers could earn up to $400 a year at their trade. By the 1890s the business was well established, and Basil Petoskey opened the first Indian craft shop in the town named after his family. In 1903, Joseph Ettawageshik opened a second shop right at the foot of the Harbor Springs pier. Margaret Boyd, who had long known that there was a growing market for Indian crafts, worked assiduously in her old age making baskets and boxes for sale. The tourist trade helped to preserve many traditional crafts, just as they were in danger of being lost. More importantly, the trade provided revenue in the wake of Ottawa land loss.[19]

Ottawa men also found a new economic niche in the tourist industry. Some were sought after as hunting and fishing guides, while other found work at the resorts as caretakers, handymen, even cooks. The resorts also were a ready market for Ottawa produce, fish, and maple syrup. Summer employment at the resorts dovetailed nicely with wage labor as lumberjacks, as logging activity was most busy during the winter season when snow made it easier to move logs out of the forest. This left summers free for resort work.

As the Indian most identifiable by the white community, Andrew Blackbird played a role in the marketing of Ottawa heritage. In 1859 he had appeared in Indian dress on the stage in a number of Midwestern cities. The core of those presentations appears to have been Ottawa lore and Blackbird's original "The Lamentation of the Overflowing Heart of the Red Man of the Forest." As resorters demonstrated an interest in Ottawa culture, Blackbird returned to giving costumed recitations. The "Lamentation" was a maudlin meditation on the then popular theme of the "vanishing red man," with required mention of the deeds "of Pocahontas, of Massasoit, of Logan, and hosts of others who have met and welcomed the white man." And while the text overflows with melodramatic exclamations such as "O, my father, our happiest days are o'er," there are also passages that reflect Blackbird's genuine attachment to the L'Arbre Croche region. In particular he mentions a basswood tree he had known from his infancy: "The tree that my good spirit had planted for me, where once the pretty brown thrush daily sat with her musical voice, is cut down by the ruthless hands of the white man."[20]

Blackbird the showman was a blend of sincerity and abject surrender to convention. As a prop for these performances Blackbird, who had never been a hunter, had a bow he could hold aloft when he said, "The bow and quiver with which I have shot many thousands of game is useless to me now, for the game is destroyed." There were, however, limits to how firmly he would embrace the cliché image. One group of vacationers who heard Blackbird wanted him to conclude the presentation with a "war-whoop," and they joked about the danger of arousing a "scalping-bee." Blackbird left out the requested "war-whoop" and pressed on to his own unexpectedly fierce conclusion: "I would sooner plunge the dagger into my beating heart, and follow the footsteps of my forefathers, than be a slave to the white man." A reporter who heard the "Lamentation" described Andrew at its end as in "an exalted state," and he admitted that the audience had been "over come" with emotion.[21]

Part of Blackbird's costume for these performances was his assumption of the title of "chief." The term had in part been a white man's invention. Mackadepenessy had been an *ogima*, a respected elder and the head of an extended family. Chiefs emerged from trade and diplomatic ties with Europeans, and the title was one that became hereditary, although it did not pass directly from father to eldest son in the European tradition. A brother or other family member might eventually take on the job of dealing with the whites as a chief. Blackbird was never recognized by the United States as a chief, and he did not ever portray himself as one to the government. Nor is there any evidence that other Ottawa regarded him as a chief. The influence Blackbird had among his people came from his education and his long formal association with the government. The term "chief" was simply not relevant to Blackbird's life until vacationing urbanites began to arrive and project their James Fenimore Cooper–inspired images. Andrew willingly played along in return for their coins. In the neighboring town of Petoskey, the sons of Ignatius Petoskey also were commonly called "chief," and his granddaughter Ella was known as a "princess."[22]

Condescension and curiosity blended in the way the visitors and white townspeople interacted with Andrew Blackbird. One memoirist described him in the most fanciful, if patronizing, terms,

> There were two left-overs of Indian royalty in our little village, Chief Blackbird and his sister, Queen Margaret. They were children of a family that once had reigned in the kingdom of the Ottawa, a family now reduced in royal functions to helping the descendents of former subjects bear as best they could the miseries of the new regime.

Sometimes billed as "the last chief" of the Ottawa, Blackbird earned money posing for portraits and postcards with a feathered headdress, a bow and arrow or gun—memories of Michigan's vanishing frontier. Guidebooks like the 1898 *Northern Michigan Handbook for Travelers* included pictures of Andrew, "Chief Petoskey," and scenes of Indian homes.[23]

In 1903 Blackbird took his show on the road. He joined a group of 200 Great Lakes Indians who were gathered by the Chicago leaders to help celebrate the centennial of the founding of the "Windy City." T. R. Roddy, an assiduous collector of Indian artifacts who claimed he was elected a Winnebago chief and given the name "White Buffalo," organized the event. In Lincoln Park, on the city's lakeshore, they erected a village next to a reconstructed blockhouse meant to symbolize Fort Dearborn. Most of the Indians set up teepees, and only a handful of Chippewa erected the bark or brush mat lodges that were authentic to the region. The Potawatomi delegation was led by Charles Pokagon, the son of Simon Pokagon, one of Blackbird's classmates from his days a Twinsburg Academy. Blackbird may well have been the oldest of the Indians gathered for the reenactment of the centennial, and he further enhanced his celebrity status by claiming that he was born in 1803, and therefore was as old as city itself. After that story went over so well, he claimed that he was the last living witness to the 1812 "Fort Dearborn Massacre." To another reporter, he claimed to recall the "receipt of the news by members of his tribe of this victory of the Indian over the white man and the ardent hope that it excited in the breast of the braves that the day was not yet past when it might be possible for the aboriginal owners of the soil to check the encroachments of the alien invaders." This was, of course, nonsense, although it was also giving the Chicagoans what they wanted.[24]

By fabricating his past Blackbird was reacting to the Chicago press's insistence on treating him and the other Indians as stock characters frozen in time. He was a published author, a citizen, a former elected official and representative of the United States government. Among the other Indians were Carlisle Institute graduates who had played on football teams against some of the best American colleges. Yet the press portrayed them as uncomfortable in a white man's house and claimed that the Indian preferred teepees in which he might "live as his ancestors in the years before Chicago was born." Inevitably, Indians were also portrayed as shocked by automobiles, which they allegedly dubbed "wind cars." Such unwillingness to change made the Indian exotic and doomed. "Sadly enough, when Chicago comes to celebrate its second centennial there probably will be left no recognizable remnant of these five assembled tribes." Ironically, among the Indian activities that were demonstrated each day during the weeklong encampment were "Gambling games."[25]

Blackbird was hardly alone in exploiting white America's erroneous and romantic view of the Indian. In time, the Little Traverse Ottawa made a regular business of satisfying the resorters' desire for faux Indians. From 1901 to 1918 Little Traverse Ottawa performed as cast members in an elaborate production of Henry Wadsworth Longfellow's 1855 epic poem, *The Song of Hiawatha.* Longfellow's poem had been inspired by the *Anishnabeg* legends recorded by Indian agent Henry Rowe Schoolcraft, although the poet adapted them with considerable literary license, not the least of which was substituting the name of the Iroquois hero Hiawatha for that of the *Anishnabeg* culture hero Nanabojo. The play was performed on the shores of Round Lake, just east of Harbor Springs, in an open-air amphitheater with the real lake and forest substituting for artificial scenery. The use of the Indian cast and natural setting was trumpeted as part of the production's authenticity. The audience of urbanites were encouraged to believe that for the Ottawa cast, Longfellow's *Hiawatha* was "life, real life." Never mind that the story was a mishmash of Iroquois and Chippewa lore, performed by Ottawa actors dressed in Plains Indian costumes. The Round Lake Hiawatha show was just one of several such pageants that were staged in the Great Lakes region in the early twentieth century. The production's popularity was evidence of the way Indian images were used by white America to create a common mythic past for the increasingly polyglot nation of immigrants.[26]

BLACKBIRD THE AUTHOR

It is not clear when Blackbird began work on his *History of the Ottawa and Chippewa.* Certainly elements of it had been in the works for quite some time. As early as 1858, while a student at the State Normal School, he began work on an Ottawa-language grammar. Within a year he penned the text of his "Lamentation of the Overflowing Heart of the Red Man of the Forest," which was later a chapter in his *History,* and he presented Ottawa legends from the stage. It is, therefore, likely that Blackbird had over time taken pen to paper to record Ottawa legends and lore. The decision to pull these writings together and include an autobiographical portrait grew out of the economic crisis caused by the end of his federal employment and the rising interest in things Ottawa Blackbird saw among the growing resort population of the Little Traverse region. In an 1884 letter to his old friend Samuel Bissell, Blackbird mentioned that he had "partially written some kind of book which contain[s] the early history of my people."[27]

Much easier to answer than the question when he wrote *History* is the question why. For Blackbird it was a preservation project. It was designed to save stories and traditions he believed were gravely threatened by the future. In addition he hoped to raise enough income to preserve his own precarious financial status. It was also, however, the product of ambition. Blackbird had been largely frustrated in his intentions to help the Ottawa through education. In the 1884 letter to Bissell, Blackbird wrote that he was terribly "despondent and dissatisfied with myself" because he had done "nothing compared with other men for the advancement of our fellow beings—particularly to my people the Indians." Faced with enemies who would just as soon "see my people go down into nothingness," Blackbird wrote to preserve a record of Ottawa character and accomplishments.[28]

Blackbird was not the first Ottawa to record the lore of his people. Francis Assiginack published three brief papers in 1858 in the *Canadian Journal of Industry, Science, and Art.* Assiginack was Andrew's cousin, the son of Jean-Baptist Assiginack, Mackadepenessy's brother. Assiginack returned to British territory and he eventually sent his son to college in Toronto. Francis later worked in the British Indian Department, although like Andrew he harbored a personal ambition to study medicine. His papers dealt with Ottawa legends, traditional practices, and linguistics. Assigniack's approach to Ottawa lore is similar to Blackbird's. Both men sought to present Ottawa ideas in an unembroidered style and to reconcile them where possible with Christian belief. It is fascinating to speculate that Andrew may have been spurred to begin writing by his cousin's publications; however, there is no evidence that Blackbird ever read Assiginack's papers, or for that matter even knew his cousin as an adult.[29]

Among the *Anishnabeg* there were several historical efforts that preceded Blackbird. Peter Jones, also known as Kahkewaquonaby (1802–1856), a Mississauga Chippewa and Methodist minister in Canada, wrote *History of the Ojebway Indians; with special reference to the conversion to Christianity,* although it was published posthumously in 1861. Jones also penned an autobiographical account. Another Canadian Chippewa, George Copway, aka Kahgegagahbowh, was probably the most publicly acclaimed Indian writer in pre–Civil War America. His 1847 volume *Life, History, and Travels of Kah-ge-ga-gah-bowh* went through several editions and won the admiration of leading American literati such as Henry Wadsworth Longfellow. Three years later he published *Traditional History and Characteristic Sketches of the Ojibwa Nation.* Ethnographic in its organization, the book was based largely upon orally transmitted traditions. While Copway's literary career declined thereafter, he remained active in the United States for another ten years as an advocate for a far northwestern Indian territory that would be a homeland for all the *Anishnabeg* as well as other tribes and would rival the Oklahoma Indian Territory in size. Copway never asked the Ottawa if they wanted to migrate west of Minnesota, and many dismissed the plan as his way to create a lucrative government post for himself.[30]

The most important of the *Anishnabe* historians was William W. Warren. He was of Chippewa and Anglo-American mixed ancestry and grew up at La Pointe in northern Wisconsin. In 1853 he completed his manuscript of *History of the Ojibways,* although it was not fully published as a book until 1885 because of the author's unexpected death at the age of twenty-eight. It well may be that the emergence of Warren's volume prompted Blackbird to publish his volume. Warren's book is a self-conscious record of traditions and oral history, synthesized and arranged chronologically by the author. The purpose is purely historical, with little of the ethnographic detail that occupied so much of Jones's or Copway's attention. Warren's story ranges back several hundred years, although the bulk of the text deals with the expansion of the Chippewa into Minnesota and their long bloody war with the Dakota (Sioux). Warren did not use European or American sources; rather he took pride in getting his facts "from the lips of their old men and chiefs." Nonetheless, "the work," a contemporary commentator noted, "does claim to be one of truth, and the first work written purely from Indian sources, which has probably ever been presented to the public."[31]

Blackbird's narrative is less ambitious than that offered by Warren. Including the Ottawa grammar, the text is a mere 128 pages. Blackbird's approach is similar to Jones and Copway in that part of Blackbird's purpose is autobiographical. Yet he shares with Warren a deep respect for tribal tradition and his main purpose is historical. Blackbird tells his readers that his reason for writing is so "that the history of my people should not be lost, like that of other tribes who previously existed in this country, and who have left no record of their ancient legends and their traditions."[32]

A subtext of his history is the superiority of Ottawa sources to the accounts of European-American historians. He begins his narrative by complaining that although there has been much published on the history of upper Great Lakes Indians, he has seen "no very correct account of the Ottawa and Chippewa tribes of Indians, according to our knowledge of ourselves, past and present." Although he singles out no historian by name, it seems likely that Blackbird is directing his barbs at Francis Parkman, the most popular historian of his day. Parkman was the author of *The Conspiracy of Pontiac* and Blackbird devotes his first chapter to correcting a number of points about Pontiac and the relations between the Ottawa and British. Parkman's 1871 edition of his Pontiac book included evidence that General

Jeffrey Amherst ordered the distribution to the Indians of blankets from a smallpox ward. Blackbird makes no mention of Parkman's account. Instead he relates the Ottawa tradition of the mysterious gift of the small boxes, nestled one in the next. The final box held a small scrap of infected cloth and a deadly epidemic spread in its wake. Parkman's story is supported by quotes from actual British military correspondence. Blackbird's Ottawa tradition is allegorical not literal, but in the end better illustrates Indian understanding of British duplicity and the insidious nature of germ warfare. Each account is historical in a different way. Yet while Blackbird believed in the need to incorporate Ottawa oral tradition in history, he clearly made a distinction between stories about the past and fantastic or fictitious lore.[33]

Blackbird neatly demonstrates this difference in his analysis of the name Mackinac, or Michilimackinac. He criticizes most European-American writers for claiming that Michilimackinac takes its name from the *Anishnabeg* word "large turtle." This makes sense to any tourist arriving on the island, because from the water the island does resemble a great turtle. Blackbird tells a different tale, in which the name refers to the "Mi-shi-nemacki-naw-go," a band of Indians allied to the Ottawa, all but two of whom were slaughtered by the Iroquois. While Blackbird relates this tradition as history, he also goes on to discuss the fate of the two survivors who became supernatural beings and were believed "by every Ottawa and Chippewa" to haunt the "wildest parts of the country." Although this story, Blackbird tells his readers, is "related in our traditions," it may "be considered at this age, as a fictitious story." Similarly, he relates as history the story of the Ottawa displacing the Mascoutens as masters of the Little Traverse region, while the stories of *Anishnabeg* culture hero Nanabojo are simply presented as "peculiar legends." In this way Blackbird attempts to put Ottawa tradition to the service of both history and folklore. His book strives to record the past as well as accurately represents the worldview of his people.[34]

Throughout his book Blackbird rather successfully fuses his autobiographical and his historical purposes. The wrongs committed by the whites on the Ottawa are made intimate through the stories he tells of his father, brother, sister, as well as himself. His father is left to starve in the wilderness, his brother is alleged to have been murdered by jealous seminarians, his sister's land is stolen, and he battles against corrupt agents to secure an education. The autobiographical and historical also come together in his account of the coming of Christianity to the Ottawa. His account does not go back to the seventeenth-century Jesuit missionaries, but instead it begins with the arrival in 1824 of the Christian Ottawa, Andowish and Assiginack, "although everybody supposes that some white people or missionary societies brought the Christian religion among the Ottawa tribes of Indians at Arbor Croche." Blackbird is careful to credit the work of his uncle Assiginack as a lay missionary, and his father as one of the founders of the Catholic Ottawa settlement that would become Harbor Springs. In his account the Ottawa are the prime movers of their history; they are actors, not merely those who are acted upon.[35]

Blackbird wrote from the perspective of an unabashed Christian. He saw as his audience "all philanthropic people, and those who are endeavoring to enlighten and Christianize the Indians." His personal journey to Christ occupies an important place in the text's autobiographical chapters. In selecting *Anishnabeg* legends for his book, Blackbird carefully told stories that conformed to Judeo-Christian traditions, such as the story of the flood and of a man being swallowed alive by a fish. Yet unlike other educated Indians of his era, such as Carlos Montezuma, Blackbird saw that there was much that was good in pre-Christian Ottawa beliefs.[36]

The theme that flows like a river through his *History* is the inherit goodness of traditional Ottawa culture. He does not present a whitewashed picture of his people. He clearly states they took possession of the Little Traverse region after wiping out the peaceful original inhabitants, whose only offense was to insult the Ottawa. On balance, however, Blackbird's Ottawa are a people who did not require "saving" by missionaries. In his picture of Ottawa precontact history, murders "were exceedingly few," there "were no illegitimate children reported in our old traditions," people's behavior was "honest and upright," intoxication was unknown, and each night a peaceful quiet settled on the village without a single locked door. Such an idyllic lifestyle came not from the discipline of priests or ministers but because "every child of the forest was observing and living under the precepts which their forefathers taught them." According to Blackbird these "precepts" were "almost the same as the ten commandments which God Almighty himself delivered to Moses on Mount Sinai on tables of stone."[37]

For Blackbird the Ottawa had been natural Christians in their ethics and values, lacking only the revelation of the gospel. Like the Mashpee historian William Apess, Blackbird delighted in holding the mirror of Christian morality up to the white man. For it is with the arrival of the European-Americans that the Ottawa fell from grace.

> But now, our living is altogether different, as we are continually being robbed and cheated in various ways. Our houses have been forcibly entered for thieving purposes and murder; people have been knocked down and robbed; great safes have been blown open with powder in our little town and their contents

> carried away, even children of the Caucasian race are heard cursing and blaspheming the name of their Great Creator, upon whose pleasure we depend for our existence.

Naturally, nostalgia tinged Blackbird's account of the precontact Ottawa, "when they were all by themselves and possessed a wide spread of land, and no one to quarrel with them as to where they should make their gardens, or take timber, or make sugar." His book, however, reflects the outlook of a dedicated assimilationist.[38]

Andrew Blackbird saw value in traditional Ottawa culture, but he did not see a future for a traditional way of life. His children never learned the Ottawa language. He saw his book as a means to preserve a small but meaningful part of a way of life that had all but disappeared. He believed that in the dialogue between recorded history and oral tradition, history would inevitably win. Mackadepenessy and Blackbird had both dedicated themselves to bringing to the Ottawa what Andrew believed were "the benefits of civilization, education, and Christianity." Adopting European-American civilization was more than a tactic for them. It was in Andrew's words, "the only salvation of my people." For Blackbird it was the way to be both Ottawa and American.[39]

Writing his *History* was for Blackbird a creative and a performative act. In the text he assumed several of the "roles" that European-Americans expected of an Indian "chief." In his "Lamentation of the Overflowing Heart of the Red Man of the Forest," he played the role of the "vanishing American." This trope allowed Blackbird to command the reader's attention as the last authentic voice of his people. With his chapter "The Twenty-One Precepts or Moral Commandments of the Ottawa and Chippewa," he took on the role of the "noble savage." In utilizing these timeworn tropes Blackbird donned the rhetorical costume expected of the performing Indian. Eloquence, defiance, and tragedy were the notes expected in all Indian literary productions. Andrew's text both acts out the expected role and co-opts the clichéd structure to fulfill his personal purpose, honoring his family, his people, and asserting his personal worth.[40]

When Blackbird had written the bulk of the text of his book, he began to lecture on the topic of Ottawa history, thereby moving the performative element of his project from the rhetorical to the theatrical. He hoped to raise enough money on the stage to pay for the cost of publication. It is likely that his lectures took him beyond the confines of the Little Traverse resort communities and at least as far east as Ypsilanti, where he had attended the State Normal School thirty years before. In Ypsilanti he won the patronage of the local chapter of the Women's National Indian Association. The group had been founded in 1879 and was dedicated to Christianization and assimilation of Native Americans. Blackbird's commitment to both aims made his book appealing enough that the Ypsilanti auxiliary solicited donations to pay for publication. They regarded the volume as a "most rare and important history" and erroneously believed that it was "the only instance where a native Indian has recorded the story of his people and given a grammar of their language."[41]

One of the leaders of the Ypsilanti Auxiliary, Mrs. G. W. Owen, played an even larger role in the project. According to a 1888 newspaper article she edited "nearly the whole work." Owen's participation does not seem to rise to the level of collaboration or coauthorship that has been raised in the case of other American Indian autobiographies such as *The Narrative of the Life of Black Hawk* or perhaps Simon Pokagon's *Queen of the Woods.* Owen's contributions appear to have been limited to grammar and punctuation. It is also perhaps to Owen that the *History* owes its passages of polite and proper conversation, recorded thirty and forty years after they took place. Owen was enthusiastic about the book project, and it was she who enlisted the aid of the editor of the *Daily Ypsilantian* to edit the grammar section of the volume and to publish the volume at a reduced cost. The perspective of Blackbird's *History* is consistent with his correspondence over more than a half-century and the views expressed in his published pamphlets. His text should not be judged as being significantly, in the jargon of literary scholars, "mediated" by white collaborators. On the other hand, Blackbird's text certainly was shaped by the political context of the late 1880s.[42]

By successfully enlisting the support of the Women's National Indian Association, Blackbird became involved in a small way in the national debate on American Indian policy. In the wake of the Civil War, many evangelical social activists switched their focus from abolitionism to Indian policy. They strongly advocated emancipating Indians from a corrupt federal bureaucracy by putting them on the path to citizenship through education and the allotment of private property. When Blackbird was writing his book in the mid-1880s, Congress was finally moving toward legislation that would revolutionize Indian policy. Since 1855 Blackbird and the Ottawa had walked the path of citizenship and allotment. Yet neither Congress nor the reformers bothered to look at the sobering lesson that could have been learned from Michigan. Andrew Blackbird also failed to grasp the opportunity to use the *Anishnabeg* experience with allotment to inform policy. In the *History,* Blackbird's critique is brief and muted, making the problem of agent corruption seem an individual matter. The collusion of local courts and government in schemes to defraud the Ottawa, which needed a systematic examination, was afforded only a few bitter lines. It is possible that because of the involvement of the Women's National Indian Association, the text of the *History* was altered. Andrew's book was published late in 1887. While it was being edited, Congress, lobbied hard by the Women's National Indian Association, approved the infamous Dawes Act. A critique published in its wake may have seemed like an attempt to undercut a long-sought "reform."[43]

While Blackbird's *History* was not written as a conscious effort to shape Indian policy, he did pen a second publication that had that purpose. In 1900 Andrew Blackbird authored a pamphlet titled *The Indian Problem from the Indian's Standpoint.* The title was similar to that of an essay published two years earlier by Carlos Montezuma, a Yavappai Indian who after being adopted by whites in his youth went on to a career as a physician in Chicago. Montezuma was a fierce critic of the Office of Indian Affairs and he shared Blackbird's commitment to assimilation. In taking the same title Montezuma had earlier used, Blackbird revealed his understanding of the national debate that continued to swirl around federal Indian policy and his desire to participate in that debate. It also appears from his several references to Montezuma that Blackbird was familiar with articles on Indian policy published in the *Red Man,* the newspaper of the Carlisle Indian Industrial School. Andrew's pamphlet was again published with the help of Ypsilanti friends and it was distributed by his old benefactor, the Women's National Indian Association.[44]

In the pamphlet Blackbird returned to the importance of Indian education, a central point in the autobiographical portions of his *History,* and one of the favorite issues of the Women's National Indian Association. On his way to discussing education, Blackbird's polemic briefly touched on other favorite themes such as the native goodness of precontact Indian society, the failure of the judicial system to protect Indian rights, what he saw as the negative influence of the Catholic mission program, and the ineffectiveness of the Office of Indian Affairs. Blackbird lauded the establishment of industrial schools like Carlisle for Indians, but he questioned the efficacy of limiting their programs to a mere five years. Such schools in Blackbird's opinion cost the government a very large outlay of money, and did little beyond teaching basic literacy. Thinking back on his own experience at Twinsburg, Andrew advocated the placement of Indian students in regular public schools and elite boarding schools, where they would sit side by side with white American students. Anticipating that many whites and especially Indians would think that "it would be cruel to take children away from their parents and homes," Blackbird noted that "it is done every where by white people and is not considered cruel." Besides, Andrew called for each child to be assigned "a friend, or kind guardian to give advice and encouragement." Indians would internalize civilization only, Blackbird wrote, when they had "direct association with refined, intelligent, well-cultivated people."[45]

As a policy statement, *The Indian Problem from the Indian's Standpoint* did not offer much that was substantive. As a polemicist, Blackbird did give voice to Indian frustrations over the patronizing and futile civilization programs of the federal bureaucrats and Christian missionaries. The aged advocate for the Ottawa was at least eighty years old when the pamphlet was published; nonetheless he aligned himself with Carlos Montezuma and other new and confident voices coming out of Indian country, speaking back to the white man, and trying to take policymaking into their own hands. In closing his pamphlet, he noted that his lifelong ambition had been to ensure that Indian youths would receive an education that was the equal to that of the leaders of white America: "This plan has been my war-song."

NOTHING IN THE WORLD BUT MY OWN BODY

Blackbird wrote his history in part to raise money. The first edition must have sold well enough because in 1897 a second edition was issued by the Petoskey print shop of Babcock and Darling. Income from the book, however, never was enough to sustain Andrew and Elizabeth. Throughout the last years of his life, a lack of money was a major problem for the Blackbirds. They came to rely upon gifts of cash from friends among the summer visitors, a pittance from appearance fees, and food brought by neighbors.[46]

Ill health also dogged him. By 1900 he was at least eighty years old and suffering from failing eyesight. Andrew was greatly pained with rheumatoid arthritis made worse by reoccurring bouts of what he called "the Grip," an influenza that swelled his joints and resulted in excruciating pain. In the summer when he earned money performing, he could buy patent medicines that provided some relief, but come autumn he did without. As befit a man of his years, he was further plagued by something he delicately called "water trouble." In winter the piercing hyperborean winds made it almost impossible for him to venture out of doors. No longer could he walk up to his barn and groom his horse, let alone race it through the streets of the town. But no matter; he could no longer afford fodder for ponies. Although Elizabeth was considerably younger than Andrew, she was actually less ambulatory than he. At some point in the 1890s she seems to have suffered from an accident and she was often unable to walk. Andrew described her lovingly as "his life companion," but when he was himself ill, he naturally complained to friends about having to "take care of my poor decrepit and helpless woman."[47]

As he grew older Blackbird was gradually replaced as a leader and spokesmen among the Ottawa by younger men. Principal among these was Simon Keshigobenese. Like Andrew, Keshigobenese was from Harbor Springs. Unlike Andrew, Keshigobenese had never worked for the government, and he was willing to act more aggressively. In 1887 Keshigobenese and a small delegation of leaders visited Washington, D.C., to press the Office of Indian Affairs about money owed to the Ottawa. The government contended that there was no money due to the Ottawa under previous treaties, and they pointed to Article 3 of the 1855 treaty that released the United States from all financial obligations stemming from previous agreements. Blackbird vociferously objected to this reasoning. As one of the last living members of the treaty party he stated, "I was there present every day in the Council Hall. I did not hear any such abrogation!" Blackbird made his case in correspondence to Michigan congressional leaders and to the Indian Office. He knew, however, that the government did not approve of uninvited Indian delegations simply showing up in the capital. When Keshigobenese pressed ahead with the visit, Blackbird was angered. He wrote to Congressman Spencer O. Fisher that he feared the delegation would commit "some great blunders" because they had a limited knowledge of the issue. He further undercut Keshigobenese by implying that the men with him were "very apt to get drunk."[48]

Keshigobenese represented a younger faction in the Ottawa community. English literacy and familiarity with the European-American world were no longer unique skills. The young men's growing influence with some of the older, traditional chiefs caused a rupture with Blackbird, who had been accustomed to being the mouthpiece of the Little Traverse Ottawa. Keshigobenese believed that the Ottawa had money due them under the 1836 treaty, and he collected funds in order to hire an attorney to prosecute Ottawa grievances in the Court of Claims. Andrew was unfamiliar with the claims process, although at this time it was also being pursued by the Potawatomi and Chippewa. He advocated dealing directly with the Office of Indian Affairs on the unmet obligations of the 1855 treaty. Blackbird chastised Keshigobenese for getting people's hopes up with talk of a multimillion-dollar settlement. Eventually, in 1905 Keshigobenese, Abraham Petoskey, and others succeeded in winning a $131,000 judgment in the Court of Claims. That case, however, was, as Blackbird advocated, based on the United States' unfilled obligations under Article 2 of the 1855 treaty.[49]

As long as Blackbird could see and hold a pen steady enough to write, he remained an advocate for the Ottawa. While the pace of Indian land loss slowed by the end of the nineteenth century, there always were people who needed to be heard and letters for Andrew to write. Indeed, the most egregious assault on Ottawa land tenure occurred in 1900. In October of that year, a real estate speculator named John McGinn, backed by a sheriff's posse, seized control of an Ottawa village on the shores of Burt Lake. Empowered by a tax deed in his name, McGinn evicted the Indian families into the cold and burned every home to the ground. The dispute over the Burt Lake village had simmered for decades. Blackbird had intervened numerous times in the 1870s and 1890s. The Ottawa, he argued, did not owe taxes on the Burt Lake village because the land had been purchased with annuity money between 1846 and 1849 and formally deeded to the governor of Michigan to hold in trust for the band. The transfer had been sanctioned by the United States Indian agent and the office of the governor. When local officials chose to treat the tract as private land, Blackbird appealed to the governor of Michigan. Unfortunately, the State of Michigan misconstrued its responsibility for the land and McGinn was given the authority to take over the town.[50]

The heartless burning out of a stable, half-century-old community was clearly a miscarriage of justice and within months the action was regretted by state officials.

Governor Haven S. Pingree, who had failed to exercise the trust placed in him by the Ottawa, complained that the incident was "an outrage" and said the state had a "moral obligation" to those who lost their homes. He asked a special December session of the state legislature to provide the victims with financial relief. When this effort failed, Pingree made a second appeal in 1902. Blackbird tried to rally local support for the proposal. He wrote and circulated a petition calling upon the government to purchase back the land and rebuild all homes. He was gratified that every "business man in Harbor Springs & Petoskey—including all county officers sign[ed] the petition." Unfortunately, the best the legislature would do was purchase swampland near Mullet Lake for any victims who sought a new home.[51]

Blackbird had his own personal land crisis in his declining years. In the late 1880s and into the 1890s Andrew fought a running battle with one of the rising businessmen of Harbor Springs, Andrew L. Deuel. The latter was a recent arrival in northern Michigan, active in the Republican Party, and popular with the town's white elite. Deuel used his knowledge of the law to build a profitable business in land speculation, often at the expense of Ottawa landowners. In 1887 Blackbird and another Harbor Springs attorney, B. T. Halstead, attacked Deuel in an article in the *Petoskey Independent Democrat.* Halstead, who later would work on behalf of the Burt Lake

Ottawa, shared Blackbird's belief that while Deuel acted within the law, his actions were hardly in the public interest, particularly after he won control of a broad swath of land along the bay shore between Harbor Springs and Petoskey. Blackbird's exposé, however, seems to have done little to slow Deuel's rise to prominence. Supported by the *Petoskey Record,* Deuel tried to smear Andrew's reputation by implying he used his position of trust among the Ottawa to his financial advantage.[52]

Blackbird was not surprised by Deuel's campaign of public innuendo because he already had personal experience with Deuel's sleazy real estate tactics. Between 1884 and 1886 Blackbird had barely managed to ward off Deuel's direct attack on his land. Adjacent to Blackbird's forty-acre allotment outside Harbor Springs, the family had a second forty-acre parcel in the name of Ogechegumequay. It is possible that Deuel was not aware this was Elizabeth Blackbird's Ottawa name. In any event, he set his sights on securing the land by fraudulent means. Pursuing a common tactic, Deuel went to an *Anishnabeg* village in Canada with the aid of John Deverney, an Ottawa living in Harbor Springs who probably acted as a translator. Deuel told an Indian family there that they were heirs to the property in question. The family was related to the deceased wife a Grand River Ottawa man who was killed fighting in the Civil War, so Deuel's story made sense to them, although they had no idea where the land might be. When Deuel offered to pay them a few dollars to sign over to him a deed that corresponded with the Blackbird land, they accepted.[53]

Deuel got more than he bargained for when he returned. The usual way his gambit worked was to confront the Indian landowners with the fraudulent deed and bluff them off the land. If they contested Deuel's deed, they would have to go to court, where the lawyer held the advantage. Blackbird, however, recognized the defects in Deuel's paperwork and refused to budge. Since Blackbird was not going to be intimidated, Deuel tried a different tactic. The rogue offered to "throw up his claim" if Blackbird would "deed him 6 acres gratis." Outraged, Blackbird called the lawyer "a thief & a liar." Out of pure spite, Deuel then proceeded to do all he could to cloud Blackbird's title and cause him legal difficulties by selling portions of the disputed land to innocent third parties. Andrew was left to fume about the ways of "sharp lawyer thieves" and the fact that in local courts, "an Indian has no chance for justice."[54]

As the years and bills began to accumulate, Blackbird was eventually forced to sell his allotment. The tract's location, overlooking the bay, was among the most attractive in the county. Debts forced him to take a mortgage on the property sometime in the 1890s; then in 1899 he sold off three acres to satisfy the mortgage. Still desperate for funds, Blackbird was approached by the Wequetonsing Association. The resort wanted to add a golf course and Blackbird's land seemed the perfect location. Initially a lease was negotiated that would allow Blackbird to maintain his garden on a few acres; however, over time the golf course was expanded and a green was built where he once grew vegetables. While this action was resented by the Blackbirds, they were dependent on the lease money as one of their few sources of income. This need eventually forced the old couple to deed the land to the golf course, leaving the Blackbirds only with their small lot in town. The land the treaty of 1855 set aside for his "benefit" now became the domain of knickered sports hacking divots in the earth.[55]

Andrew cut a sad figure in his declining years. His carefully brushed high hat and frock coat had long before been worn out and replaced by "castoff garments given him in charity." U. P. Hedrick, who knew Andrew for many years, left a sad account of their last meeting.

> The years had stolen all the fire from his eyes, the strength from his body. I went to ask him about the Ottawa. As he tried to answer my questions, the old Indian steadied his palsied head with his hands, saying to himself before he would answer me: "Be calm, Blackbird! Be calm!"
>
> Even his English, fluent in earlier years, had almost gone, he mumbled in the language of his childhood. Again and again he tapped his forehead, muttering: "So many things gone from here! Gone! Gone!"[56]

On September 7, 1908, Andrew Blackbird died. He passed away not at his Harbor Springs home, but in the Emmet County Poor Farm. Earlier that year he had been declared mentally incompetent and was placed by his wife and sons in the Brutus, Michigan, facility. The old man's health had been poor for many years, with his eyesight in particular deteriorating. It is possible that a stroke or some sudden ailment rendered him incapable of home care. Nonetheless, it was not typical for property owners, former elected officials, let alone fathers with four mature children, to end their days as a ward of the state. The fact that Elizabeth Blackbird herself required care may have made the move a necessity.[57]

At the time of his death Blackbird owned no real estate, the family home being in Elizabeth's name. According to the Probate Court report the only thing of value he had was his per capita share of the payment the Court of Claims had determined the United States owed to the Little Traverse Ottawa. That amounted to $21.16 to be divided among his four children.[58]

Two days after his death his three sons, in their late thirties or early forties, gathered with a "large circle of friends" for a funeral service at the little white clapboarded St. John's Episcopal Church. Most likely missing the service was Janette, Andrew's only daughter, who lived in California, the wife of a prosperous businessman. Bishop Daniel Tuttle officiated, and he no doubt recalled his many conversations with Blackbird about faith and religion. The funeral party then made their way up the steep bluff road to Lakeview Cemetery, where Blackbird was laid to rest in a family plot purchased by his wife Elizabeth. From his tree-shaded gravesite it is just possible to glimpse the blue horizon of Lake Michigan.[59]

Epilogue

ANDREW BLACKBIRD'S HOMETOWN OF HARBOR SPRINGS REMAINS A beautiful place. Walking down the hill from Blackbird's grave in Lakeview Cemetery, the visitor's eye is drawn equally to the sight of the beckoning blue bay and the picture-postcard town, with vintage veranda-graced cottages, the Victorian facades of shops, and the gleaming white steeple of Holy Childhood of Jesus Church. On Main Street, in front of an incongruously modest wood frame house, is an equally incongruous totem pole. The house was Andrew Blackbird's home, and in 2009 it housed the Harbor Springs Chamber of Commerce. Attached to it, in the false-fronted clapboard post office Blackbird so bitterly regretted ever having built, is the Andrew J. Blackbird Museum.

The museum was founded in 1948 after the Blackbird family ceased to live in the house. Elizabeth Blackbird died in 1920. Two of her sons, William and Bert, continued to live in the house until their death. When Bert passed away in 1947, his sister Janette made the long train trip from San Francisco to Harbor Springs. She had not been in the small empty house for several decades. Janette had left home while quite young. Her good looks got her a job as a sales clerk in Detroit's posh Cadillac Hotel, and in 1900 she began a career as an actress. While appearing in a play in New York City, she met the son of a prominent family and became his wife. After twenty-three years of marriage in the Golden State, she returned widowed and obliged to tie up her all but forgotten family's loose ends. Amid the threadbare furniture left by her bachelor brothers were books and papers belonging to her father and mother. When Blackbird published his final pamphlet in 1900 he mentioned, "I have many other things written besides this which I am sending to you, which I hope may be heard by civilized people, long after I am dead." Yet whatever was left in the house, Mrs. Janette B. Scofield burned. She said she did this at the request of her mother, which seems strange since she waited twenty-seven years to carry out the request. Neighbors gossiped that the she destroyed the family papers because "she didn't want to be known as an Indian."[1]

In 1948 the Blackbird home was opened as a museum. The forty years between Andrew's death and the opening of a museum in his honor had been a difficult period for the Little Traverse Ottawa. At the end of the nineteenth century, in spite of a relentless assault on Indian land tenure, they were among the more prosperous native peoples in Michigan. Between their continuing access to traditional resources in the forests and lake, and the seasonal economic opportunities available in the tourist industry and in logging, Ottawa families made ends meet. The decline of logging after 1920 coincided with a downturn in the productivity of the Lake Michigan fishery to put a severe pinch on the already subsistence-level economy of the Ottawa. After World War II new economic opportunities were only found far from Little Traverse Bay, in the industrial cities to the south. Other *Anishnabeg* bands such as the Oceana County Ottawa or the Saginaw Chippewa were located much closer to these well-paying factory jobs, and in comparison even with these poor cousins, the Little Traverse band languished. Faced with the dilemma of work or community, most Little Traverse Ottawa chose low-pay seasonal work near home. By the late twentieth century the Little Traverse Bay Bands Tribal Council estimated that 75 percent of its members lived below the poverty line.[2]

The creation of the Blackbird Museum came in the midst of these economic hard times for the Ottawa and was in a small way planned as a response. The group initially behind the museum called itself the Michigan Indian Foundation. They were a group of white business and professional people, most of them from downstate or out-of-state urban centers, who sought to promote the welfare of Indian people in Michigan and to preserve tribal culture as "a highly valued part of American history." Most of their energy focused on organizing "colorful pageants." Eventually they built in Harbor Springs a 4,000-seat outdoor stadium for their event. The white organizers of the Michigan Indian Foundation reveled in the naming ceremony, which for them occupied the center of the gathering. Begun by band member Fred Ettawageshik, the ceremony featured the bestowing of a special Ottawa name on a white friend of the tribe, followed by the awarding of a large Plains Indian style headdress. The pageants also featured Indian dancing and a gathering of "chiefs" from across Michigan. These features foreshadowed the powwows that would later become popular expressions of *Anishnabeg* pride. Like powwows the pageants also were a wonderful occasion to sell Ottawa crafts to a large gathering of tourists.[3]

Long after the Michigan Indian Foundation's demise, the Blackbird Museum endured, operated at various times by the Harbor Springs Historical Commission, the City of Harbor Springs, and the Little Traverse Bay Bands. The Blackbird Museum, like the man after which it is named, has hung uneasily between the preservation of genuine Ottawa culture and public performance. Outside the museum is a totem pole, a symbol the larger American culture has ripped from its unique Pacific Northwest context and made a universal marker of the American Indian. In the museum's collections, however, are the exquisite birch bark vessels that women like Margaret Boyd made. The quill work done by Andrew's sister was not the same as that done by her mother; rather like all art it evolved, reflecting the inspiration of the maker. Andrew Blackbird's life and work reflect this same dynamic. In the pages of his *History* he honored and preserved tradition, but his life was not limited by the past. He no more wanted to be bound by what the Ottawa were in the past than he accepted late nineteenth-century American limitations on what they could become in the future.

Blackbird's memory endured in a small museum because of his *History.* The book ensured that long after he was gone Blackbird's name would be remembered. His little book has been the indispensable source of American Indian history in northern Michigan, and it has remained in print for most of the 120 years since it was first published. Through his book the story of Mackadepenessy and the Ottawa's program of cultural reinvention has been preserved, not as a tribal memory but as history. Through his book the example of Ottawa people spearheading religious change, managing local governments, and fighting for their land was preserved as a source of inspiration for future generations. Together the book and the little museum remind both resort visitors and white citizens of this privileged corner of the Great Lakes region that before the yachts and beach houses, Little Traverse was Indian country.

Andrew Blackbird was a pioneer for his people. Mackadepenessy and the men and women of his generation marked out a new path for the Ottawa within the uncomfortable confines of American civilization. By adopting Christianity, contracting their subsistence cycle, and building American-style towns, Andrew's father and uncles committed the Ottawa to the American New World. They, however, were too old to explore that world and identify its opportunities and dangers. Andrew Blackbird and a handful of other Ottawa young men took up that challenge. Blackbird journeyed deep into American society. He learned its language, values, and prejudices. Through education he sought to distinguish himself and be a leader of his people. These aspirations were only partially realized.

Mackadepenessy was a conservative revolutionary. He sought to change Ottawa life only so far as was necessary to preserve it in the northwest Michigan homeland. In choosing Catholicism as a vehicle of assimilation, he embraced both a Christian future and the past of French-Canadian association through the middle ground. Andrew was a son of this conservative revolution, and he grew up in an antebellum Michigan in which the hunting camps and war parties of the past were no longer the measures of manhood. He envisioned a future in which the Ottawa would use the legal and economic forms of American society, yet preserve the distinctive cultural core of *Anishnabeg* life. By lobbying for *Anishnabeg* citizenship and negotiating land allotments Blackbird and the other Ottawa leaders of his generation advanced the revolution begun by their fathers. By modeling assimilation Blackbird hoped to make possible the persistence of his people.

More than other Ottawa of his generation Blackbird embraced the promise of American individualism. While his contemporaries were content with the limited literacy program of the local Catholic school, he journeyed east for an Anglo-American education. While most Ottawa helped to nurture a sense of community through the practice of Catholic devotionalism, Blackbird, in very American fashion, asserted the importance of individual conscience and he embraced a minority Protestant denomination. He did not appreciate that while Catholic social life isolated the Ottawa from the Anglo-Protestant American mainstream, it also served as a protective cocoon for core cultural values during a time of profound change. In spite of the fact that most Ottawa leaned toward the Democratic Party, Blackbird very early on became a vocal supporter of the upstart Republicans. While most Ottawa men found comfort and stability marrying *Anishnabe* or mixed-blood women, Blackbird shattered convention and took a white woman for his wife. Each of these were life-shaping decisions and each marked him as an individual determined to live his life as he saw fit. These decisions, however, also isolated him from the mainstream of Ottawa life, and reduced the effectiveness of his leadership. From his adolescence through mature manhood, Blackbird was always a bit of an outsider among the Ottawa. When he died alone in the Emmet County Poor Farm, he ironically completed his American journey from Ottawa communalism to the isolation of rugged individualism.

Yet Blackbird was ever an Ottawa. While he journeyed into the world of Anglo-America for education, he always did so with the intention of returning to Little Traverse, "to be able to do good amongst my own people." As a teacher, elected official, Indian Office employee, and private citizen Blackbird used his education and his experience with American society to help the Ottawa defend their rights as citizens and landowners. That white avarice and racism overrode government good intentions was one of the great disappointments of his life. While not overlooking the inequalities of the government-to-government treaty process, it was not the Office of

Indian Affairs that stole Ottawa land. Individual Americans defrauded and humiliated their newly made fellow citizens. Blackbird's story illustrates that a multicultural nation, then as now, requires a government with the will and the means to protect civil rights. Like African-American freedmen in the Reconstruction South, newly made *Anishnabeg* citizens found legal rights scant protection in an era of laissez-faire government. While that lesson was one the Ottawa would learn again and again in the future, Blackbird's many missives to Washington and Lansing also pointed the way for future band leaders to use the law to their advantage.[4]

In 1948, just as Andrew's old home was being transformed into a museum in his honor, a new generation of Ottawa leaders prepared to force a change in their people's status. Robert and Waunetta Dominic of Petoskey took the lead in organizing the Northern Michigan Ottawa Association with the goal of challenging the federal government's execution of its treaty obligations to the Ottawa. The creation of the Indian Claims Commission a year later simplified the process; nonetheless, it took until 1964 for the Little Traverse bands to win their claims under the 1836 and 1855 treaties. It took even longer, until the twenty-first century, for the government to pay the claims. Nonetheless, the legal process started by the Dominics began a new era of Ottawa political action that culminated in the 1994 when Congress passed legislation renewing government-to-government relations between the United States and the Little Traverse Ottawa. The rebirth of tribal sovereignty brought a return of Ottawa men and women to elected political office and an economic revival, fueled in part by the assertion of historic fishing rights on Lake Michigan and the establishment of a band-owned resort and casino in Petoskey.[5]

The Ottawa endure today as a people in Michigan because of the actions of Mackadepenessy, Andrew Blackbird, and the men and women of their time. Tribal self-government today rests on a leadership of eloquent, educated individuals protective of Ottawa identity but capable and comfortable working within the larger American society. This is the role that Blackbird fulfilled in his lifetime; it is the goal toward which he tried and failed to push both the Ottawa and the United States government. Yet popular culture, both within American Indian communities and especially within the larger society, continues to valorize the warrior as the symbol and protector of Indian identity, when it was and is the men and women who were pathfinders in education and law that have laid the foundation for the rebirth of native America. Even when Blackbird despaired over the theft of Ottawa homesteads in the 1870s and 1880s, he still envisioned a future in which education would be the means by which the promise of citizenship would be redeemed. In the face of "great antipathy and prejudice," he saw "no remedy but to educate the Indians, and permit them to be in the halls of Legislature and in the halls of Congress to protect the rights of their beguile[d] race." Near the end of his life, in the pamphlet *The Indian Problem from the Indian's Standpoint*, Blackbird returned to this hope.

> This plan has been my war song, ever since 1855, but my days are being numbered and soon I will be no more among the living. But I pray to God that somebody may step in my footsteps and continue to sing the same, until every inhabitant, including the government of the United States, would deign to listen to this war-song.[6]

Notes

INTRODUCTION

1. Telling a story out of season was alleged to arouse snakes and frogs. See Gertrude Kurath and Jane Willets Ettawageshik, "Notes on Religious Customs of Modern Michigan Algonquians," draft of an unfinished book, American Philosophical Society, Philadelphia, 1955, part 1, p. 3.
2. Andrew Jackson Blackbird, *History of the Ottawa and Chippewa Indians of Michigan: A Grammar of Their Language, and Personal and Family History of the Author* (Ypsilanti, Mich.: Ypsilantian Job Printing House, 1887), 25. Hereafter cited as Blackbird, *History of the Ottawa and Chippewa.*
3. Among the anthropologists who have left unpublished notes and manuscripts documenting Ottawa culture are Paul Radin, Jane Willets Ettawageshik, and Gertrude Kurath. The best published ethnographic treatment of the Ottawa is the article by Johanna E. Feest and Christian F. Feest published in *Handbook of North American Indians*, vol. 15, *Northeast*, ed. Bruce G. Trigger (Washington, D.C.: Smithsonian Institution, 1978), 772–86.
4. Richard White, *The Middle Ground: Indians, Empires, and Republics in the Great Lakes Region, 1650–1815* (New York: Cambridge University Press, 1991).
5. Quoted from Joseph J. Ellis, *Founding Brothers: The Revolutionary Generation* (New York: Knopf, 2000), 4.
6. Edmund Jefferson Danziger, *Great Lakes Indian Accommodation and Resistance during the Early Reservation Years, 1850–1900* (Ann Arbor: University of Michigan Press, 2009); Rebecca Kugel, *To Be the Main Leaders of Our People: A History of Minnesota Ojibwa Politics, 1825–1898* (East Lansing: Michigan State University Press, 1998); Jane E. Chute, *The Legacy of Shingwaukonse: A Century of Native Leadership* (Toronto: University of Toronto Press, 1998).
7. Roosevelt quoted in Wilma Pearl Mankiller and Michael Wallis, *Mankiller: A Chief and Her People* (New York: St. Martins, 2000), 5; Charles Eastman, *The Essential Charles Eastman (Ohiyesa)* (Bloomington, Ind.: World Wisdom Press, 2007); Sarah Winnemucca, *Life among the Paiutes* (Las Vegas: University of Nevada Press, 1994); Joy Porter and William Fenton, *To Be an*

Indian: The Life of Iroquois-Seneca Arthur Caswell Parker (Norman: University of Oklahoma Press, 2001); Andrew Jackson Blackbird, "The Indian Problem; from the Indian's Standpoint," in *American Indian Nonfiction: An Anthology of Writings, 1760s–1930s,* ed. Bernd C. Peyer (Norman: University of Oklahoma Press, 2007), 250.

8. Andrew Blackbird to Indian Agent George Lee, November 19, 1877, National Archives, RG 75, Letters Received Michigan Superintendency, Box 3; for more on this theme see Siobhan Senier, *Voices of American Indian Assimilation and Resistance: Helen Hunt Jackson, Sarah Winnemucca, and Victoria Howard* (Norman: University of Oklahoma Press, 2003).

CHAPTER ONE. A FOREST YOUTH

1. Robert Ritzenthaler and Pat Ritzenthaler, *The Woodland Indians of the Western Great Lakes* (New York: American Museum of Natural History, 1970), 27–28; Andrew Jackson Blackbird, *History of the Ottawa and Chippewa Indians of Michigan: A Grammar of Their Language, and Personal and Family History of the Author* (Ypsilanti, Mich.: The Ypsilantian Job Printing House, 1887), 32; It is not possible to have an exact translation of Andrew's name. Richard Rhodes, Department of Linguistics, University of California, Berkeley, personal communication, January 21, 2003.
2. *The Traverse Region, Historical and Descriptive, with Illustrations of Scenery and Portraits and Biographical Sketches of Some of Its Prominent Men and Pioneers* (Chicago: H. R. Page and Company, 1884), 145; Andrew Jackson Blackbird, "The Indian Problem, from the Indian's Standpoint," in *American Indian Nonfiction: An Anthology of Writings, 1760s–1930s,* ed. Bernd C. Peyer (Norman: University of Oklahoma Press, 2007), 5, 7.
3. Blackbird, *History of the Ottawa and Chippewa,* 33; Alexander Henry, *Travels and Adventures in Canada and the Indian Territories Between the Years 1760 and 1776* (Edmonton: M.G. Hurtig, 1969), 148.
4. Blackbird, *History of the Ottawa and Chippewa,* 25; Helen Hornbeck Tanner, *Atlas of Great Lakes Indian History* (Norman: University of Oklahoma Press, 1987), 4.
5. Blackbird, *History of the Ottawa and Chippewa,* 26; Nehemiah Matson, "Sketch of Shaubena, Pottowattamie Chief," in *Collections of the State Historical Society of Wisconsin* (Madison: State Historical Society of Wisconsin, 1888–1931), 7:415–22(hereafter *Wisconsin Historical Collections*); Lewis Cass to George Boyd, August 30, 1820, *Wisconsin Historical Collections,* 20:182; Aura P. Stewart, "Recollections of Aura P. Stewart, of St. Clair County, of

Things Relating to the Early Settlement of Michigan," in Michigan Historical Commission/Pioneer Society of Michigan, *Michigan Pioneer and Historical Collections*, 40 vols. (Lansing: Michigan Historical Commission/ Pioneer Society of Michigan, 1877–1929), 4:345 (hereafter *MPHC*); Henry R. Schoolcraft, *Personal Memoirs of a Residence of Thirty Years With the Indian Tribes of the American Frontiers* (Philadelphia: Lippincott, Grambo and Co., 1851), 446.

6. Blackbird, *History of the Ottawa and Chippewa,* 33.
7. Ibid., 45.
8. Antoine de la Mothe Cadillac, quoted in W. Vernon Kinietz, *The Indians of the Western Great Lakes, 1615–1760* (Ann Arbor: University of Michigan Press, 1965), 242.
9. Blackbird, *History of the Ottawa and Chippewa,* 46.
10. Ibid., 10–11.
11. Ibid., 11.
12. Ibid., 11–12.
13. Ibid., 10–11.
14. Tanner, *Atlas of Great Lakes Indian History,* 46, 172–73; Richard White, *The Middle Ground: Indians, Empires, and Republics in the Great Lakes Region, 1650–1815* (New York: Cambridge University Press, 1991), 246; Baron Longueuil to French Minister of State, October 1, 1751, *Wisconsin Historical Collections,* 18, 116.
15. Francis Parkman, *The Conspiracy of Pontiac* (New York: Collier, 1962), 249; 297; Blackbird, *History of the Ottawa and Chippewa,* 9; William W. Warren, *History of the Ojibway People* (St. Paul: Minnesota Historical Society, 1984), 260; for more analysis of this story see Helen Jaskoski, "A Terrible Sickness Among Them: Smallpox and Stories of the Frontier," in *Early Native American Writing: New Critical Essays,* ed. Helen Jaskoski (New York: Cambridge University Press, 1996), 136–56; Jaskoski, "Andrew Blackbird's Smallpox Story," in *Native American Perspectives on Literature and History* (Norman: University of Oklahoma Press, 1995), 26–35.
16. James M. McClurken, "We Wish To Be Civilized: Ottawa-American Political Contests on the Michigan Frontier," PhD diss., Michigan State University, 1988, 79, 91.
17. Claude Charles Le Roy, Bacqueville de la Potherie, *Histore de l'Amerique septentrionale,* ed. and trans. Emma Helen Blair as *The Indian Tribes of the Upper Mississippi and region of the Great Lakes* (Lincoln: University of Nebraska Press, 1996), 282.
18. Speech of the Outaouacs of Missilmackinac, June 16, 1742, ed. Reuban Gold Thwaites, *Wisconsin Historical Collections,* 17:372; Charles de la Boische de Beauharnois to Outaouacs of Missilimackinac, July 8, 1741, *Wisconsin*

Historical Collections, 17:351–52; Beauharnois to Minister, October 5, 1741, *Wisconsin Historical Collections,* 17:368.

19. Blackbird, *History of the Ottawa and Chippewa,* 27.
20. Peter Fidler, Journal of a Journey from Red Deers Lake to the mouth of Slave Indian River, 1799, *Saskatchewan Journals and Correspondence: Edmonton House, 1795–1800, Chesterfield House, 1800–1802,* ed. Alice M. Johnson (London: Hudson's Bay Record Society, 1967), 228–29.
21. Laura Peers, *The Ojibwa of Western Canada, 1780 to 1870* (St. Paul: Minnesota Historical Society Press, 1994), 31, 43.
22. Blackbird, *History of the Ottawa and Chippewa,* 27–29.
23. Blackbird to Mr. Bodley, March 18, 1901, Indians of North America Collection, Burton Collection, Detroit Public Library.
24. Harold A. Innis, *The Fur Trade in Canada* (Toronto: University of Toronto Press, 1965) 195.
25. Peers, *Ojibwa of Western Canada,* 32–33.
26. Blackbird, *History of the Ottawa and Chippewa,* 27–28.
27. Ibid., 28.
28. Peers, *Ojibiwa of Western Canada,* 40–41.
29. Blackbird, *History of the Ottawa and Chippewa,* 28–29.
30. John Tanner, *A Narrative of the Captivity and Adventures of John Tanner,* ed. Edwin James (New York: Garland, 1975), 161.
31. Ibid.; Blackbird, *History of the Ottawa and Chippewa,* 27.
32. R. David Edmunds, *Tecumseh and the Quest for Indian Leadership* (Boston: Little, Brown, 1984), 73–78.
33. White, *The Middle Ground,* 486.
34. Tanner, *Narrative,* 145–48.
35. John Askin, Jr., to John Askin, Sr., September 1, 1807, in *The John Askin Papers,* ed. Milo M. Quaife, vol. 2 (Detroit: Detroit Library Commission, 1931), 568–69.
36. R. David Edmunds, *The Shawnee Prophet* (Lincoln: University of Nebraska Press, 1983), 51–52; Warren, *History of the Ojibway People,* 322–23.
37. Edmunds, *The Shawnee Prophet,* 76; Warren, *History of the Ojibway People,* 323.
38. Edmuds, *The Shawnee Prophet,* 77.
39. Blackbird, *History of the Ottawa and Chippewa,* 29–30.
40. Ibid.; Jedidiah Morse, *A Report to the Secretary of War of the United States on Indian Affairs* (New Haven: Davis & Force, 1822), 92, appendix E, 25.
41. Treaty With the Ottawa, 1807, Treaty With the Chippewa, 1808, in *Indian Treaties, 1778–1883,* ed. Charles J. Kappler (New York: Interland Publishing, 1972), 92–95, 99–100.

42. Fred Landon, *Lake Huron* (New York: Bobbs-Merrill, 1944), 78–80.
43. The identification of Wing as Mackadepennesy's older brother is based on Andrew Blackbird's statement that he was "one of my father's own brothers" and Schoolcraft's report that in 1833 Wing was about "seventy-six years of age." See Schoolcraft, *Personal Memoirs,* 446.
44. "Ne-gwa-gon, the Little Wing," *Wisconsin Historical Collections,* 3:328–30; Treaty With the Ottawa, Kappler, *Indian Treaties,* 454.
45. J. Grath Taylor, "Assiginac's Canoe," *The Beaver*, October–November 1986, 50–52; Lieut. Col. Robert McDonall to Capt. A. Bulger, May 2, 1815, *MPHC,* 23:512–13.
46. Taylor, "Assiginac's Canoe," 51.
47. Alec R. Gilpin, *The War of 1812 in the Old Northwest* (East Lansing: Michigan State University Press, 1958), 248–57.
48. Taylor, "Assiginac's Canoe," 50.
49. David Lavender, *The Fist in the Wilderness* (Albuquerque: University of New Mexico Press, 1979), 225.
50. Colonel Robert McDonall to Captain A. Bulger, May 2, 1815, *MPHC,* 23:512–13.
51. Proceedings of a Court of Inquiry held by order of His Excellency Major General Sir F. P. Robinson, Fort Drummond, Oct. 1815, *MPHC,* 16:332.
52. Janet E. Chute, *The Legacy of Shingwaukonse* (Toronto: University of Toronto Press, 1998), 30–31; Schoolcraft, *Personal Memoirs,* 631–32.

CHAPTER TWO. THE CRISIS

1. Andrew Jackson Blackbird, *History of the Ottawa and Chippewa Indians: A Grammar of Their Language, and Personal and Family History of the Author* (Ypsilanti, Mich.: The Ypsilantian Job Printing House, 1887), 50–51.
2. Ibid., 51.
3. Historians Susan Sleeper-Smith and Keith R. Widder both take issue with this periodization. See Sleeper-Smith, *French Men and Indian Women: Rethinking Cultural Encounter in the Western Great Lakes* (Amherst: University of Massachusetts Press, 2001) and Widder, *Battle for the Soul: Metis Children Encounter Evangelical Protestants at Mackinaw Mission, 1823–1837* (East Lansing: Michigan State University Press, 1999).
4. Widder, *Battle for the Soul,* 50–51; Theresa M. Schenck, "The Cadottes: Five Generations of Fur Traders on Lake Superior," in *The Fur Trade Revisited: Selected Papers of the Sixth North American Fur Trade Conference, Mackinac*

Island, Michigan, 1991, ed. Jennifer S. H. Brown, W. J. Eccles, and Donald P. Heldman (East Lansing: Michigan State University Press, 1994), 197.

5. Elizabeth Therese Baird, "Reminiscences of Early Days on Mackinac Island," in *Wisconsin Historical Collections,* 14:42–43.
6. Marjorie Cahn Brazer, *Harps Upon the Willows: The Johnston Family of the Old Northwest* (Ann Arbor: Historical Society of Michigan, 1993), 162, 225.
7. George Boyd to Lewis Cass, June 20, 1822, *Wisconsin Historical Collections,* 20:261; John Harold Humins, "George Boyd: Indian Agent of the Upper Great Lakes, 1819–1842," PhD diss., Michigan State University, 1975, 85.
8. J. Grath Taylor, "Assiginac's Canoe," *The Beaver* (October–November 1986): 50.
9. Andrew J. Blackbird, *The Indian Problem from the Indian's Standpoint* (Ypsilanti, Mich.: Scharf Label, Tag, and Box Company, 1900), 7.
10. Taylor, "Assiginac's Canoe," 50; Charles Cleland, *Rites of Conquest: The History and Culture of Michigan's Native Americans* (Ann Arbor: University of Michigan Press, 1992), 146–74.
11. John Long, *Voyages and Travels of an Indian Interpreter and Trader* (London: Robson, Debrett, and Egerton, 1791), 104–5, 111–12.
12. Frederic Baraga to Leopoldine Foundation, February 1, 1834, Bishop Baraga Papers, University of Notre Dame Archives, South Bend, Indiana.
13. Paul Kane, *Wanderings of an Artist Among the Indians of North America* (London: Longman, Brown, Green, Longman & Roberts, 1859), 7–8.
14. Ibid.
15. Anna Jameson, *Winter Studies and Summer Rambles in Canada* (London: Saunder and Otley, 1838), 298.
16. Douglas Leighton, "Jean Baptist Assiginack," *Dictionary of Canadian Biography Online,* http://www.biographi.ca/009004–119.01-e.php?&id_nbr=4269&&PHPSESSID=ychzfqkvzape.
17. Richard White, *The Middle Ground: Indians, Empires, and Republics in the Great Lakes Region, 1650–1815* (New York: Cambridge University Press, 1991), 485.
18. Jedidiah Morse, *A Report to the Secretary of War of the United States on Indian Affairs* (New Haven: Davis & Force, 1822), appendix, 8–9.
19. Treaty with the Ottawa and Chippewa, 1820, in *Indian Treaties, 1778–1883,* ed. Charles J. Kappler (New York: Interland Publishing, 1972), 188.
20. Ibid., 187–88.
21. Morse, *Report to the Secretary of War,* 9–10.
22. Ibid., 23–24.
23. Ibid., 24–25,
24. Ibid., 9–11.
25. Ibid., 12–14.

26. Henry R. Schoolcraft, *Personal Memoirs of a Residence of Thirty Years With the Indian Tribes of the American Frontiers* (Philadelphia: Lippincott, Grambo and Co., 1851), 483.
27. Lewis Cass to John C. Calhoun, February 1, 1822, Ohio River–Great Lakes Ethnohistory Archive, Ottawa File, Glenn Black Archaeological Laboratory, Indiana University, Bloomington, Indiana.
28. Ibid.
29. Treaty with the Ottawa, 1821, in Kappler, *Indian Treaties, 1778–1883*, 199–201.
30. Isaac McCoy, *History of the Baptist Indian Missions* (New York: Johnson Reprint Corporation, 1970), 193; John S. Schenck, *History of Ionia and Montcalm Counties, Michigan* (Philadelphia: D. W. Ensign, 1881), 29.
31. John C. Shea, *Catholic Missions Among the Indian Tribes of the United States* (New York: E. Dunigan & Brother, 1854), 383.
32. William H. Puthuff to Governor Lewis Cass, May 14 1816, *Wisconsin Historical Collections*, 19:413.
33. Puthuff to Cass, August 20, 1817, *Wisconsin Historical Collections*, 19:473.
34. Morse, *Report to the Secretary of War*, appendix E, 13.
35. Shea, *Catholic Missions*, 361–79.
36. Ibid., 383.
37. Andrew Blackbird actually estimates the event as occurring "about 1824." I think the date of 1822 would more likely be right. All of the dates used in this portion of the history are qualified by the word "about"; however, Blackbird's narrative of the sequence of events that brought Christianity to the Ottawa is very plausible and it is generally supported by other documentation,
38. Blackbird describes Andowish having resided "among the Stockbridge Indians somewhere near Montreal." The Stockbridge Mahicans, however, were based at that time in New York state. A smaller branch of the Mahicans settled with the western Abenaki early in the eighteenth century and converted to Catholicism. For more see T. J. Brasser, "Mahican," in *Handbook of North American Indians*, vol. 15, *Northeast*, ed. Bruce G. Trigger (Washington, D.C.: Smithsonian Institution, 1978), 206.
39. Blackbird, *History of the Ottawa and Chippewa*, 46.
40. Ibid.; Widder, *Battle for the Soul*, 64–65.
41. Humins, "George Boyd," 164.
42. Francis Pierz, "Indians of North America," trans. and ed. Eugene Hagedorn, *Social Justice Review* 40 (November 1947): 245.
43. Shea, *Catholic Missions*, 383–84. The name "Hawk" appears first among names affixed to the August 1823 memorial to the president. Black Hawk, according to Andrew Blackbird, was the proper translation of his father's name. His name appeared on the 1820 treaty as "Black Hawk." Blackbird,

History of the Ottawa and Chippewa, 31; Petition of the Chiefs of the Ottawa Indians, Arbre Croche, August 12, 1823, Chronological File, Manuscripts Division, State Historical Society of Wisconsin.

44. An English text of the letter can be found in P. Chrysostomus Verwyst, *Life and Labors of Rt. Rev. Fréderic Baraga* (Milwaukee: M.H. Wiltzius, 1900), 57.
45. *Annales De L'Association De La Propagation De La Foi*, vol. 9 (Paris: La Librairie Ecclésiastique De Rusand, November 1826), 121–35.
46. Ibid.
47. Ibid.
48. Blackbird, *History of the Ottawa and Chippewa*, 46–47.
49. *Annales De L'Association De La Propagation De La Foi*, vol. 21 (Paris: La Librairie Ecclésiastique De Rusand, July 1830), 476.
50. *Annales De L'Association De La Propagation De La Foi*, 9:121–131.
51. Shea, *Catholic Missions*, 385; Willis F. Dunbar and George S. May, *Michigan: A History of the Wolverine State* (Grand Rapids, Mich.: William Eerdmans, 1995), 186.
52. *Annales De L'Association De La Propagation De La Foi*, 9:129–30; J. B. Assiginack to T. G. Anderson, September 22, 1827, *Michigan Pioneer and Historical Collections* 23 (1895):140.
53. Blackbird, *History of the Ottawa and Chippewa*, 46.
54. Ibid., 46–47.
55. Ibid., 31–32, 47.
56. James A. Clifton, *The Prairie People: Continuity and Change in Potawatomi Indian Culture, 1665–1965* (Lawrence: University of Kansas Press, 1977), 445; personal communication, Richard Rhodes, Department of Linguistics, University of California, Berkeley, June 10, 2003.
57. Gertrude P. Kurath and Jane Willets Ettawageshik, "Notes on Religious Customs of Modern Michigan Algonquians," part 1, n.p., American Philosophical Society, Philadelphia.
58. Shea, *Catholic Missions*, 385.
59. Francis Assikinack, "Legends and Traditions of the Odahwah Indians," *Canadian Journal of Industry, Science, and Art* .3, no. 14 (1858): 115.
60. Blackbird, *History of the Ottawa and Chippewa*, 35; Father John DeBruyn to Bishop Frederic Rese, June 17, 1836, Papers of the Diocese of Detroit, University of Notre Dame Archives (hereafter cited as Diocese of Detroit Papers).
61. Blackbird, *History of the Ottawa and Chippewa*, 33–34.
62. Ibid., 34–35.
63. M. Inez Hilger, "Chippewa Child Life and its Cultural Background," *Smithsonian Institution, Bureau of American Ethnology, Bulletin* 146 (1951): 39–44; Blackbird, *History of the Ottawa and Chippewa*, 35.
64. Blackbird, *History of the Ottawa and Chippewa*, 35.

65. Ibid., 35, 43–44; Verwyst, *Life and Labors*, 107, 467.
66. J. B. Assiginack to T. G. Anderson, September 22, 1827, *MPHC*, 23:140.
67. Thomas G. Anderson to Col. McKay, July 22, 1828, *MPHC*, 23:150–51.
68. Ibid.
69. Ibid.; Thomas Anderson to William McKay, November 29, 1828, *MPHC*, 23:156.
70. Shea, *Catholic Missions*, 386; *Annales De L'Association De La Propagation De La Foi*, 21 :486–89.
71. Samuel Mazzuchelli, *The Memoirs of Father Samuel Mazzuchelli, O.P.* (Chicago: Priory Press, 1967), 77–78.
72. John Tanner, *A Narrative of the Captivity and Adventures of John Tanner*, ed. Edwin James (New York: Garland, 1975), 162.
73. Ibid., 161. During the 1930s Joseph Shomin, a descendent of one of the first Catholic Ottawa, told the anthropologist Paul Radin a variation on the story. In Shomin's version the conclusion that many Indians drew from being shut out of the white man's heaven was that it was best to "believe in their own ways," which Shomin explained was the reason "why the Indians are so poor." Journey to Spirit-land, Paul Radin, Ojibwe-Ottawa Notes, American Philosophical Society, Philadelphia.
74. This village was often referred to simply as Arbre Croche. Later in the mid-nineteenth century it was known as Little Traverse and today the town is known as Harbor Springs, Michigan. *Annales De L'Association De La Propagation De La Foi*, 21:481–83; Shea, *Catholic Missions*, 386; Blackbird, *History of the Ottawa and Chippewa*, 47.
75. Blackbird, *History of the Ottawa and Chippewa*, 47–48.
76. William H. Puthuff to Governor Lewis Cass, May 14, 1816, *Wisconsin Historical Collections*, 19:413.
77. Petition of the Chippewa Indians of Michilimackinac, October 15, 1834, National Archives, RG 75, M-234, Roll 421, frames 475–78.
78. Blackbird, *History of the Ottawa and Chippewa*, 53.
79. Ibid., 53.
80. Ibid., 42.
81. Andrew Jackson Blackbird to Samuel Bissell, n.d., Box 1, Folder 5, Samuel Bissell Papers, Western Reserve Historical Society, Cleveland, Ohio. Hereafter referred to as the Bissell Papers.
82. Blackbird, *History of the Ottawa and Chippewa*, 53.
83. Ibid., 54; Father J. DeBruyn to Bishop Rese, November 2, 1835, Diocese of Detroit Papers.
84. Blackbird, *History of the Ottawa and Chippewa*, 49; Verwyst, *Life and Labors*, 136–44; for Baraga's educational philosophy see Baraga to Bishop Peter Paul Lefevere, May 24, 1848, Diocese of Detroit Papers.

85. Blackbird, *History of the Ottawa and Chippewa*, 53.
86. Douglas Leighton, "Jean Baptist Assiginack," *Dictionary of Canadian Biography Online*, http://www.biographi.ca/009004–119.01-e.php?&id_nbr=4269&&PHPSESSID=ychzfqkvzape.
87. Chiefs and headmen of Arbre Croche to Bishop Fenwick, n.d., in Verwyst, *Life and Labors*, 128–9.
88. Blackbird, *History of the Ottawa and Chippewa*, 35–38.
89. Letter to Mons. Frederic Rese, July 13, 1833, Verwyst, *Life and Labors*, 463–64.
90. Blackbird, *History of the Ottawa and Chippewa*, 36–37.
91. Ibid., 40–43.
92. Ibid., 42–44; Cardinal Carolo M. Pedicini to Bishop Rese, July 13, 1833; Cardinal Pedicini to Bishop Rese, April 3, 1836, Diocese of Detroit Papers.
93. Blackbird, *History of the Ottawa and Chippewa*, 42.
94. It is important to note that removal was by no means championed by all whites interested in the good of the Indians. The act was opposed by many missionaries who worked with American Indians, but the coalition between those who wanted Indian land and those sought a refuge for Indians in the West was too strong to be overcome.
95. Francis Paul Prucha, *American Indian Policy in the Formative Years: The Indian Trade and Intercourse Acts, 1790–1834* (Lincoln: University of Nebraska Press, 1962), 213–26.
96. Willard Carl Klunder, *Lewis Cass and the Politics of Moderation* (Kent, Ohio: Kent State University Press, 1996), 48–53.
97. Dunbar and May, *Michigan*, 165.
98. Susan E. Gray, *The Yankee West: Community Life on the Michigan Frontier* (Chapel Hill: University of North Carolina Press, 1996), 44.
99. R. David Edmunds, *The Potawatomis: Keepers of the Fire* (Norman: University of Oklahoma Press, 1978), 246–50; Father Simon Saenderl to Bishop Frederic Rese, June 9, 1834, (translated from German), Diocese of Detroit Papers; Schoolcraft, Personal *Memoirs*, 483–84.
100. Henry Rowe Schoolcraft to Governor George Porter, November 21, 1833, National Archives, Letters Sent by the Agent, Mackinac,1833–1836, Records of the Michigan Superintendency, 1814–1851, RG 75, M-1, Roll 69, frame 018; Baraga to the Leopoldine Foundation, March 7, 1834, Baraga to Bishop Frederic Rese, November 27, 1833, Baraga Papers.
101. Commissioner of Indian Affairs Elbert Herring to Governor Porter, April 16, 1834, National Archives, Letters Received from the Office of Indian Affairs, Michigan Superintendency, RG 75, M-1, Roll 34, frame 113.
102. Schoolcraft, *Personal Memoirs*, 465.

103. Schoolcraft to Stevens Mason, Governor of Michigan, August 18, 1834, National Archives, Letters sent by the Agent, Mackinac, RG 75, M-1, Roll 69, frame 77.
104. Speech of Pabanmitabi of L'Arbre Croche, August 18, 1834, National Archives, Letters Sent by the Agent, Mackinac, RG 75, M-1, Roll 69, frame 79.
105. Ibid.
106. Baraga to Leopoldine Foundation, June 26, 1834, Baraga Papers.
107. James McClurken, "We Wish To Be Civilized: Ottawa-American Political Contests on the Michigan Frontier," PhD diss., Michigan State University, 1988, 166.
108. Schoolcraft, *Personal Memoirs*, 486–87.
109. Schoolcraft to Elbert Herring, June 20, 1835, National Archives, Letters Sent by the Agent, Mackinac, 1833–1836, RG 75, M-1, Roll 69, frame 105; Commissioner Herring to Schoolcraft, August 29, 1835, Letters Received by the Office of Indian Affairs, Michigan Superintendency, National Archives, RG 75, M-1, Roll 72, frame 108; Schoolcraft to Major Cobbs, September 23, 1835, RG 75, M-1, Roll 69, p. 121.
110. Widder, *Battle for the Soul*, 91–101.
111. Speech [of Augustin Hamlin] reported by Chabwawee, Bubenesu, and Baubewegeick, November 24, 1835, National Archives, Letters Received by the Office of Indian Affairs, Michigan Superintendency, RG 75, M-1, Roll 72, frames 159–60.
112. Appointment of Augustin Hamelin, *MPHC*, 12:622.
113. Paul Radin, Ojibwa-Ottawa Notes II, American Philosophical Society, Philadelphia.
114. Father Simon Saendrel to Bishop Rese, July 20, 1835, Diocese of Detroit Papers.
115. McClurken, ""We Wish To Be Civilized," 168.
116. Speech [of Augustin Hamlin] reported by Chabwawee, et al., November 24, 1835.
117. Memorial of the Ottawa delegation by A. Hamlin, Jr., December 5, 1835, National Archives, Letters Received by the Office of Indian Affairs, Michigan Superintendency, RG 75, M-234, Roll 421, frames 722–25.
118. Ibid.; Simon Saendrel to Bishop Rese, July 20, 1835, Diocese of Detroit Papers.
119. Memorial of the Ottawa delegation, December 5, 1835.
120. Ibid.
121. Blackbird, *History of the Ottawa and Chippewa*, 51.

CHAPTER THREE. A NEW WORLD

1. Mary Holiday to Ramsay Crooks, March 17, 1836, American Fur Company Papers, New York Historical Society, New York, microfilm at Clarke Historical Library, Central Michigan University, Roll 23, frame 1385.
2. Ibid.; *Democratic Free Press* (Detroit), April 6, 1836.
3. For more on Schoolcraft see Richard G. Bremer, *Indian Agent and Wilderness Scholar: The Life of Henry Rowe Schoolcraft* (Mount Pleasant, Mich.: Clarke Historical Library, 1987); and Philip P. Mason ed., *Schoolcraft's Expedition to Lake Itasca: The Discovery of the Source of the Mississippi* (East Lansing: Michigan State University Press, 1993).
4. *Democratic Free Press* (Detroit), April 20, 1836.
5. *Democratic Free Press* (Detroit), April 20, 1836.
6. Records of a Treaty concluded with the Ottawa and Chippewa Nations at Washington, D.C., March 28, 1836, Papers of Henry Rowe Schoolcraft, Library of Congress, Washington, D.C.
7. Two other hotels that were sometimes used by Indian delegations at this time were the Washington Hotel, located just east of the White House, and Williamson's Hotel, which was nearby. See Herman J. Viola, *Diplomats in Buckskins: A History of Indian Delegations in Washington City* (Washington, D.C.: Smithsonian Institution Press, 1981), 122–23.
8. Records of a Treaty, March 28, 1836.
9. Ibid.; Rix Robinson to Ramsay Crooks, March 23, 1836, American Fur Company Papers, microfilm at Central Michigan University, Roll 23, frame 1411.
10. Records of a Treaty, March 28, 1836.
11. Ibid.
12. Ibid.
13. Ibid.
14. Henry Rowe Schoolcraft, *Personal Memoirs of a Residence of Thirty Years With the Indian Tribes of the American Frontiers* (Philadelphia: Lippincott, Grambo and Co., 1851), 534.
15. *Army Navy Chronicle,* April, 7, 1836, 223.
16. Father John DeBruyn to Bishop Frederic Rese, June 17, 1836, Diocese of Detroit Papers. It is tempting to ascribe the rumor to Henry Rowe Schoolcraft. As the individual charged with obtaining Indian consent to a treaty greatly altered by the Senate it would have served his purpose to raise the fear of imminent removal. Schoolcraft was in Washington when the revisions took place but returned to Mackinac on June 15, well after the Father DeBruyn reported the rumor.

17. Treaty with the Ottawa, etc. 1836, *Indian Treaties, 1778–1883*, ed. Charles J. Kappler (New York: Interland Publishing, 1972), 451–53.
18. Schoolcraft, *Personal Memoirs*, 538.
19. Schoolcraft to Cass, July 18, 1836, National Archives, Records of the Mackinac Agency, RG 75, M-1, Roll 37, pp. 3–5.
20. Treaty with the Ottawa, 450–55.
21. John Tanner, *A Narrative of the Captivity and Adventures of John Tanner*, ed. Edwin James (New York: Garland, 1975), 163–64.
22. Wakaso to President of the United States & the Senate and House of Representatives in Congress Assembled, National Archives, Letters Received by the Office of Indian Affairs, Michigan, RG 75, M-1, Roll 72, frames 229–30.
23. Ibid.
24. James McClurken, "We Wish to Be Civilized: Ottawa-American Political Contests on the Michigan Frontier," PhD diss., Michigan State University, 1988, 21–23.
25. Articles of Assent to the Amendments of the Resolution of the Senate of the United States, July 12, 1836, National Archives, RG 11, M-668, Roll 8, frame 106.
26. Gabriel Franchere to Lyman Warren, February 2, 1836, American Fur Company Letterbook, Saulte Ste. Marie Outfit, 1835–1837, Bayliss Library, Sault Ste. Marie; Franchere to Ramsay Crooks, July 21, 1836, AFC Letterbook, Bayliss Library.
27. *Michigan State Register* (Detroit), November 1, 1836.
28. Schoolcraft, *Personal Memoirs*, 543.
29. Blackbird, *History of the Ottawa and Chippewa Indians of Michigan: A Grammar of Their Language, and Personal and Family History of the Author* (Ypsilanti, Mich.: The Ypsilantian Job Printing House, 1887), 51.
30. Schoolcraft, *Personal Memoirs*, 543.
31. Fr. Francois Pierz to Bishop Lefevere, January 28, 1850, Diocese of Detroit Papers.
32. Fr. Pierz to Bishop Lefevere, November 17, 1843, Diocese of Detroit Papers.
33. Fr. Pierz to Bishop Lefevere, July 9, 1845, Diocese of Detroit Papers.
34. Pierz to Lefevere, November 17, 1843, September 26, 1850, Diocese of Detroit Papers.
35. Pierz to Lefevere, September 26, 1850, November 5, 1848, Diocese of Detroit Papers.
36. "Ottawas in Michigan," *Baptist Missionary Magazine*, June 1839, 19, 6, 124–25.
37. Father John DeBruyn to Bishop Frederic Rese, November 2, 1835, June 17, 1836, Diocese of Detroit Papers.

38. Ibid.; Delia Cook to Andrew J. Blackbird, June 1, 1847, Bissell Papers, Box 1, Folder 2; Keith R. Widder, *Battle for the Soul: Metis Children Encounter Evangelical Protestants at Mackinac Mission, 1823–1837* (East Lansing: Michigan State University Press, 1999), 120.
39. DeBruyn to Rese, June 17, 1836.
40. Blackbird, *History of the Ottawa and Chippewa*, 53.
41. Ibid.
42. Log of the schooner *Gazelle*, 1838, Justice Bailey master, State Historical Society of Wisconsin, Madison; Log of the schooners *Mary Elizabeth* and *Hero*, Henry B. Ketcham, master, c. 1844–46, State Historical Society of Wisconsin, Green Bay Area Research Center, University of Wisconsin, Green Bay.
43. For more on the life of lake mariners see Theodore J. Karamanski, *Schooner Passage: Sailing Ships and the Lake Michigan Frontier* (Detroit: Wayne State University Press, 2000).
44. Blackbird, *History of the Ottawa and Chippewa*, 54.
45. Ibid.
46. Ibid.
47. The identity of the blacksmith at Mission Point in 1840 is not certain. Isaac George was the blacksmith when the agency was created in 1839. Andrew Blackbird never mentions the blacksmith's name. For more on the founding of the agency see S. E. Waite, *Old Settlers of the Grand Traverse Region* (Traverse City, Mich.: S. E. Waite, 1918), 17.
48. For more on the Johnston family see Marjorie Cahn Brazer's admirable *Harps upon the Willows: The Johnston Family of the Old Northwest* (Ann Arbor: Historical Society of Michigan, 1993).
49. Grace Walz, "Andrew Jackson Blackbird of L'Arbre Croche," M.A. thesis, Western Michigan University, 1964, 16.
50. Blackbird, *History of the Ottawa and Chippewa*, 56.
51. Peter Dougherty was a native of New York State. When he first came to Michigan he was thirty-two years of age and a graduate of Rutgers and Princeton Theological Seminary. He would devote the next thirty-three years of his life to evangelizing the Chippewa. For more information see Peter Dougherty, "The Diaries of Peter Dougherty," ed. Charles A. Anderson, *Journal of the Presbyterian Historical Society* 30 (1952): 95–253; and Ruth Craker, *First Protestant Mission in the Grand Traverse Region* (Omena, Mich.: privately printed, 1931).
52. Peter Dougherty to Walter Lowrie, May 4, 1839, Peter Dougherty Papers, Reel 1, Bentley Historical Library, University of Michigan, Ann Arbor.
53. Brazer, *Harps upon the Willows*, 300–304.

54. U.S. Office of Indian Affairs, *Annual Report of the Commissioner of Indian Affairs, 1840* (New York: AMS Press, 1976), 341–43; Dougherty to Wells, February 6, 1841, Dougherty Papers, Reel 1.
55. Dougherty to Wells, February 6, 1841, Dougherty Papers, Reel 1.
56. Akosa to Robert Stuart, February 15, 1841, National Archives, Letters Received by the Agent at Mackinac, RG 75, M-1, Roll 50.
57. U.S. Office of Indian Affairs, *Annual Report of the Commissioner of Indian Affairs, 1844* (New York: AMS Press, 1976), 486–87; for more on the work of a blacksmith shop see Leonard E. Fisher, *The Blacksmiths* (New York: Franklin Watts, 1976).
58. Dougherty, "Diary," 252; Walz, "Blackbird of L'Arbre Croche," 16; Deborah Beaumont, *History of Brown County, Wisconsin* (Chicago: S.J. Clarke, 1913), 240.
59. Blackbird, *History of the Ottawa and Chippewa*, 95–96.
60. Minutes of the Old Mission and New Mission (Grove Hill) Church, http://members.aol.com//vwilson5771mission.html; Walz, "Blackbird of L'Arbre Croche," 17.
61. Petition of the Ottawa and Chippewa to the President, August 12, 1840, National Archives, Letters Received by the Office of Indian Affairs, Michigan, RG 75, M-234, Roll 424, frames 0050–53; Alvin Coe to President of the United States, October 27, 1841, Letters Received by the Office of Indian Affairs, Michigan, RG 75, M-234, Roll 424, frames 0694–96; Dougherty to Wells, May 26, 1841, Dougherty Papers, Reel 1; U.S. Office of Indian Affairs, *Annual Report, 1844*, 481–82.
62. McClurken, "We Wish to Be Civilized," 255.
63. U.S. Office of Indian Affairs, *Annual Report, 1843*, (New York: AMS Press, 1976), 321; U.S. Office of Indian Affairs, *Annual Report, 1844*, (New York: AMS Press, 1976), 485.
64. Walz, "Blackbird of L'Arbre Croche," 17.
65. Blackbird, *History of the Ottawa and Chippewa*, 56.

CHAPTER FOUR. WE NOW WISH TO BECOME MEN

1. This was the village known some times as New L'Arbre Croche or Little Traverse. It is known today as Harbor Springs, Michigan.
2. Blackbird to Unknown, n.d. [1847–48], Samuel Bissell Papers, Western Reserve Historical Society, Cleveland, Ohio.

3. Andrew Jackson Blackbird, *History of the Ottawa and Chippewa Indians of Michigan: A Grammar of Their Language, and Personal and Family History of the Author* (Ypsilanti, Mich.: The Ypsilantian Job Printing House, 1887), 57.
4. Ibid., 57.
5. Ibid., 58–59.
6. Lena M. Carter, *Centennial of Twinsburg, Ohio 1817–1917* (Twinsburg, Ohio: Bissell Memorial Library Association, 1917), 9–18.
7. Samuel Bissell, Autobiography, n.d., Box 2, Folder 1, Bissell Papers.
8. Samuel Bissell, "They were Strangers & we took them in," undated manuscript, Bissell Papers.
9. George B. Herttinger, "Samuel Bissell, Humanitarian and Educator, 1797–1895," PhD diss., University of Akron, 1981, 116–18; Blackbird, *History of the Ottawa and Chippewa*, 59.
10. Blackbird, *History of the Ottawa and Chippewa*, 59.
11. Samuel Bissell, *Indian Youth in Search of An Education*, broadsheet published in Philadelphia, 1847, Bissell Papers; J. B. Mansfield, *History of the Great Lakes*, vol. 1 (Chicago: B. H. Beers, 1899), 797.
12. Lewis Cass to Samuel Bissell, February 16, 1846; Invoice of Samuel Bissell to the United States, March 31, 1846, Bissell Papers.
13. Andrew Blackbird to William Medill, n.d., Bissell Papers.
14. Twinsburg Institute Receipts & Expenditures of Indian Youth, 1847–1850, Bissell Papers; A. J. Maccadabenasbi or Blackbird to unknown, n.d., Bissell Papers.
15. Samuel Bissell, *Indian Youth*; A. J. Maccadabenasbi or Blackbird, An Appeal for Money for Education, n.d., Bissell Papers.
16. Blackbird, *History of the Ottawa and Chippewa*, 59; Craker, *First Protestant Mission in the Grand Traverse Region,* 20.
17. Twinsburg Institute Receipts and Expenditures of Indian Youth, 1847–1850, Bissell Papers.
18. A. J. Maccadabenasbi or Blackbird to unknown, n.d., Bissell Papers.
19. Maureen Konkle, *Writing Indian Nations: Native Intellectuals and the Politics of Historiography, 1827–1863* (Chapel Hill: University of North Carolina Press, 2004), 40; Bernd C. Peyer, *The Tutor'd Mind: Indian Missionary-Writers in Antebellum America* (Amherst: University of Massachusetts Press, 1997), 245–47.
20. George Smith to Samuel Bissell, October 4, 1850; Louis Martin to Samuel Bissell, January 26, 1849; Alvin Coe to My Friend, March 28, 1848, Bissell Papers.
21. Simon Pokagon, "Simon Pokagon on Naming the Indians," *American Monthly Review of Reviews* 16 (September 1897): 320–21.

22. *Catalogue of the Instructors and Students of the Twinsburg Institute For the Academic Year Commencing April 13, 1846 and Ending March 13, 1847 Together with Studies, Condition* (Cleveland: Younglove's Steam Press, 1847).
23. J. H. Perrault to Samuel Bissell, January 10, 1847, Bissell Papers; William H. Perrin, *History of Summit County, Ohio* (Chicago: Baskin & Battey, 1881); *Marion* (Ohio) *Daily Star,* June 27, 1914; Blackbird to Unknown, March 14, 1849, Bissell Papers.
24. George David Smith to Bissell, November 17, 1851, Bissell Papers.
25. Herttinger, "Samuel Bissell," 110–17.
26. Blackbird to Bissell, November 15, 1850, Bissell Papers; Blackbird to Unknown, March 24, 1849, Bissell Papers.
27. Blackbird to Unknown, n.d. [1847–48], Bissell Papers.
28. Blackbird to Unknown, n.d. [1849], Bissell Papers.
29. Blackbird to Unknown, March 24, 1849; Blackbird to Bissell, October 28, 1850; Blackbird to Unknown, n.d. [1849], Bissell Papers.
30. Blackbird to Bissell, October 28, 1850; Blackbird to Bissell, November 21, 1850, Bissell Papers.
31. Jeremy W. Kilar, *Michigan's Lumbertowns: Lumbermen and Laborers in Saginaw, Bay City, and Muskegon* (Detroit: Wayne State University Press, 1990) 43–44; Theodore J. Karamanski, *Schooner Passage: Sailing Ships and the Lake Michigan Frontier* (Detroit: Wayne State University Press, 2000), 56–58; Barbara Benson, "Logs and Lumber: The Development of the Lumber Industry in Michigan's Lower Peninsula, 1837–1870," PhD diss., Indiana University, Bloomington, 1976, 110–12.
32. Peter Dougherty to Walter Lowrie, May 1, 1849, Reel 1, Dougherty Papers; L. L. Hamling to Secretary of War, October 12, 1849, National Archives, RG 75, M-234, roll 771, p. 306; Pierz to Lefevere, May 17, 1849, June 12, 1849, Diocese of Detroit Papers.
33. Edmund J. Danziger, *The Chippewas of Lake Superior* (Norman: University of Oklahoma Press, 1979), 84–90; James M. McClurken, "We Wish to Be Civilized: Ottawa-American Political Contests on the Michigan Frontier," PhD diss., Michigan State University, 1988, 316–23.
34. Jan Morley, ed., *Harbor Springs: A Collection of Historical Essays* (Clarksville, Tenn.: Harbor Springs Historical Commission, 1981), 5; Pierz to Lefevere, November 21, 1851, Pierz to Lefevere, October 12, 1849, Pierz to Lefevere, November 25, 1847, Pierz to Lefevere, October 10, 1851, Diocese of Detroit Papers; Blackbird, *History of the Ottawa and Chippewa,* 59.
35. Blackbird to Bissell, October 28, 1850; Smith to Bissell, November 17, 1851, Bissell Papers.

36. Pierz to Lefevere, October 22, 1844, October 25, 1844, Pierz to Stuart, no month/no day 1843, Diocese of Detroit Papers; Robert Stuart to Pierz, November 30, 1844, National Archives, Letters Sent by the Agent at Mackinac, RG 75, M-1, Roll 39.
37. McClurken, "We Wish to Be Civilized," 266–69; Pierz to Lefevere, January 28, 1850, December 23, 1850, Diocese of Detroit Papers.
38. Treaty with the Ottawa, 1836, in *Indian Treaties, 1778–1883,* ed. Charles J. Kappler (New York: Interland Publishing, 1972), 452; Blackbird to Bissell, November 18, 1850, Bissell Papers.
39. Ottawa Chiefs to President Millard Fillmore, February 19, 1851, National Archives, RG 75, M-234, Roll 403, frames 584–88. Blackbird's authorship of the petition is based on the content of the document and his role as the sole witness to its signing by the head chiefs.
40. Augustin Hamlin to Charles Babcock, September 9, 1850, National Archives, RG 75, M-1, Roll 64, p. 367.
41. *Michigan Statutes Annotated,* vol. 1, p. 220.
42. Blackbird, *History of the Ottawa and Chippewa,* 60; Blackbird to Bissell, November 21, 1850.
43. Blackbird, *History of the Ottawa and Chippewa,* 60.
44. Patrick J. Comer, Dennis A. Albert, et al., *Michigan's Native Landscape: As Interpreted from the General Land Office Surveys, 1816–1856* (Lansing: Michigan Natural Features Inventory, 1995), 37–41; Erminie Wheeler-Voegelin, "An Anthropological Report on Indian Use and Occupancy of Northern Michigan," in *Chippewa Indians*, vol. 5 (New York: Garland Press, 1974), 13–14, 62; Blackbird, *History of the Ottawa and Chippewa,* 60.
45. Blackbird, *History of the Ottawa and Chippewa,* 60.
46. Ibid., 60–61.
47. Michigan Supreme Court Historical Society, "Warner Wing, 7th Justice," http://www.micourthistory.org/resources/wwing.php; Blackbird, *History of the Ottawa and Chippewa,* 61.
48. Blackbird to Bissell, August 1, 1851, Bissell Papers; Blackbird, *History of the Ottawa and Chippewa*, 61.
49. Ibid.; *Acts of the Legislature of the State of Michigan* (Lansing: R. W. Ingalls, 1851), 258–59.
50. Blackbird, *History of the Ottawa and Chippewa*, 60; Memorial of the Ottawa delegation by A. Hamlin Jr., December 5, 1835, National Archives, RG 75, M-234, Roll 421, frames 722–25; Pierz to President of the United States, July 20, 1843, National Archives, RG 75, M-234, Roll 425, frame 292; Ruben Turner to J. Spencer, February 28, 1842, National Archives, RG 75, M-234, Roll 425, frame 220.

51. Oshawanah, Waubojeg, et al., to Commissioner of Indian Affairs, November 1, 1853, National Archives, RG 75, M-234; Blackbird, *History of the Ottawa and Chippewa*, 61.
52. *Report of the Proceedings and Debates in the Convention to Revise the Constitution of Michigan, 1850* (Lansing: R. W. Ingalls, 1850), 420; for the best discussion of Indian citizenship in Michigan see Barbara Rosen, *American Indians and State Law: Sovereignty, Race, and Citizenship, 1790–1880* (Lincoln: University of Nebraska Press, 2007), 131–36, 143–49.
53. Blackbird to Bissell, August 1, 1851, Bissell Papers.
54. Ibid.; Actually it was Elias Murray's son, Harvey Murray, who made the trip of inspection to northern Michigan; see Elias Murray to Luke Lea, September 2, 1851, National Archives, RG 75, M-234, Roll 598, frame 41.
55. Blackbird to Bissell, November 21, 1850, Blackbird to Bissell, November 15, 1850, Bissell Papers.
56. Blackbird to Bissell, November 18, 1850, Bissell Papers.
57. Blackbird to Bissell, n.d. [enclosed in Bissell to unknown, December 14, 1853], Bissell Papers; Blackbird, *History of the Ottawa and Chippewa*, 59–60.
58. *Catalogue of the Twinsburg Institute*, 16; Blackbird, *History of the Ottawa and Chippewa*, 64.
59. Blackbird to Bissell, August 1, 1851, Bissell Papers.
60. Blackbird to Bissell, n.d. [in Bissell to Unknown, December 14, 1853], Bissell Papers.
61. Pierz to Lefevere, September 12, 1844, Diocese of Detroit Papers; Pierz to Reverend Dean, May 1, 1836, "Historical Studies and Notes: Letters of Father Franz Pierz, Pioneer Missionary," *Central-Blatt and Social Justice*, May 1934, 55.
62. William P. Furlan, *In Charity Unfeigned: The Life of Father Francis Xavier Pierz* (St. Cloud, Minn.: St. Anthony Press, 1952), 17, 176.
63. Francis Pierz, "The Indians of North America," trans. and ed. Eugene Hagedorn, *Social Justice Review* 40 (March 1948): 388.
64. Ibid., 130; George David Smith to Bissell, October 4, 1850, Bissell Papers.
65. Smith to Bissell, February 14, 1851, Bissell Papers.
66. Pierz, "Indians of North America," 130; Pierz to Lefevere, July 3, 1845, July 28, 1846, September 9, 1844, July 17, 1851, Diocese of Detroit Papers; Blackbird to Bissell, n.d., Bissell Papers.
67. Blackbird to Bissell, n.d. [enclosed in December 14, 1853], Bissell Papers.
68. Dougherty to Lowrie, October 23, 1851, Dougherty Papers, Bentley Historical Library, University of Michigan, Ann Arbor; L. Morgan Leach, *A History of the Grand Traverse Region* (Traverse City, Mich.: Grand Traverse Herald, 1903), 29.

69. Blackbird to Bissell, August 1, 1851, Bissell Papers; Leach, *History of Grand Traverse*, 29.
70. Leach, *History of Grand Traverse*, 29; Blackbird, *History of the Ottawa and Chippewa*, 64.

CHAPTER FIVE. CITIZEN BLACKBIRD

1. Blackbird to Bissell, August 1, 1851, June 24, 1852, Bissell Papers.
2. George W. Manypenny to Secretary of the Interior, R. McClelland, May 21, 1855, National Archives, RG 75, M-234, Roll 404, frames 844–51.
3. Blackbird to Unknown, n.d. [1849], Bissell Papers.
4. Blackbird to Bissell, November 18, 1850, Bissell Papers.
5. *Detroit Free Press,* July 26, 1855; Treaty with the Ottawa and Chippewa, 1855,in *Indian Treaties, 1778–1883,* ed. Charles J. Kappler (New York: Interland Publishing, 1972), 730.
6. Proceedings of a Council with the Chippewas and Ottawas of Michigan held at the City of Detroit by the Hon. George W. Manypenny [*sic*] & Henry C. Gilbert, Commissioner of the United States, July 25, 1855, typescript, p. 5, original in National Archives, microfilm series T497, reel 123, p. 57 (hereafter cited as Proceedings of Council, 1855).
7. Ibid., 29–30.
8. Ibid., 38–39.
9. Ibid., 24, 28, 42, and 46–47.
10. Ibid., 31.
11. Ibid., 54; Treaty with the Ottawa and Chippewa, 1855, 728.
12. Proceedings of Council, 1855, 60.
13. Blackbird, *History of the Ottawa and Chippewa*, 62.
14. Proceedings of Council, 1855, 70; Manypenny to Acting Commissioner, Charles E. Mix, August 7, 1855, National Archives, Letters Received by the Office of Indian Affairs, Michigan Superintendency, RG 75, M-234, Roll 404; Kappler, *Indian Treaties*, 726–31.
15. Andrew J. Blackbird, *Education of Indian Youth, Letter of Rev. Samuel Bissell and Appeal of A.J. Blackbird, A Chippewa Indian* (Philadelphia: William F. Geddes, 1856), 13.
16. Ibid., 9–10.
17. Roger Daniels, *Coming to America: A History of Immigration and Ethnicity in American Life* (New York: Harper, 1990), 266–67.
18. Blackbird, *Education of Indian Youth*, 11.

19. Ibid., 13–15.
20. Andre Jackson Blackbird et al. to George W. Manypenny, November 22, 1855, National Archives, Letters Received by the Office of Indian Affairs, RG 75, M-234, Roll 405.
21. "Emmet County History and Information," http.mymichigangenealogy.com; Roger Van Noord, *King of Beaver Island* (Urbana: University of Illinois Press, 1988), 195–99, 215–19.
22. Emmet County Supervisor's Journal, 1859–1863 and Statement of Votes, 1855–1869, Office of Emmet County Clerk, Petoskey, Michigan; Henry Gilbert to Commissioner Manypenny, December 26, 1856, National Archives, RG 75, Letters Received by the Michigan Superintendency, M-234, Roll 405, p. 226.
23. Willis F. Dunbar and George S. May, *Michigan: A History of the Wolverine State* (Grand Rapids, Mich.: William Eerdmans, 1995), 308–10; Bruce Alan Rubenstein, "Justice Denied: An Analysis of American Indian–White Relations in Michigan, 1855–1889," PhD diss., Michigan State University, 1974, 159–60.
24. Blackbird, *History of the Ottawa and Chippewa*, 65.
25. Emmet County Supervisor's Journal, Statement of Votes, 1855–1869; Blackbird, *History of the Ottawa and Chippewa*, 66.
26. Blackbird, *History of the Ottawa and Chippewa*, 65–66.
27. Ibid., 66; D. Thomas to G. Manypenny, December 11, 1856, National Archives, Letters Received by the Office of Indian Affairs, Mackinac Agency, RG 75, M-234, Roll 405; Rubenstein, "Justice Denied," 141–44.
28. Gilbert did go on to give a good account of himself in the American Civil War. He raised the Nineteenth Michigan Infantry and served as its colonel until 1864 when he died of wounds suffered in the Battle of Resaca. Henry C. Gilbert Papers, Clements Library, University of Michigan; Rubenstein, "Justice Denied," 143–44.
29. Blackbird, *History of the Ottawa and Chippewa*, 66.
30. For Cass's career see Willard Carl Klunder, *Lewis Cass and the Politics of Moderation* (Kent, Ohio: Kent State University Press, 1996); Proceedings of Council, 1855, 26.
31. Blackbird, *History of the Ottawa and Chippewa*, 67.
32. Ibid.
33. "A Historic Tour of Eastern Michigan University: Buildings That No Longer Exist," http://www.emu/walkingtour/oldbuildings.htm; Blackbird, *History of the Ottawa and Chippewa*, 68.
34. Blackbird, *History of the Ottawa and Chippewa*, 68.
35. Blackbird to Bissell, June 18, 1858, Bissell Papers; Blackbird, *History of the Ottawa and Chippewa*, 69.

36. "A Historic Tour of Eastern Michigan University: A Brief History of EMU," http://www.emu/walkingtour/history.htm.
37. Student Register, October 1858–1861, Michigan State Normal School, Eastern Michigan University Archives, Ypsilanti, Michigan; *Catalogue of the Officers and Students of the Michigan State Normal School for the School Year 1857–1858* (Detroit: Tribune Printing Office, 1858); *Daily Enquirer Herald* (Grand Rapids), July 13, 1858; to Bissell, June 18, 1858, Bissell Papers.
38. Andrew Blackbird to Lewis Cass, October 30, 1857, Archives and Records Department, Little Traverse Bay Bands of Odawa, Harbor Springs, Mich.; Blackbird, *History of the Ottawa and Chippewa*, 69.
39. Blackbird to Bissell, October 11, 1858, Bissell Papers; Blackbird, *History of the Ottawa and Chippewa*, acknowledgment.
40. During her life Elizabeth Blackbird freely exercised a woman's right to lie about her age. She may have been as young as seventeen at the time of her marriage or as old as twenty-six. See the 1860, 1870, and 1880 U.S. censuses, Emmet County, Michigan; Janette Scofield to Will Hampton, September 21, 1956, Hampton Papers, Bentley Historical Library, University of Michigan, Ann Arbor; U. P. Hedrick, *The Land of the Crooked Tree* (1948; Detroit: Wayne State University Press, 1986), 27; Will E. Hampton, "Memoirs of Harbor Springs," 5, Hampton Papers; Blackbird to Bissell, September 13, 1858, Bissell Papers; Blackbird to Bissell, October 11, 1858, Bissell Papers.
41. Blackbird, *History of the Ottawa and Chippewa*, 70; *Daily Enquirer Herald* (Grand Rapids), May 6, 1859.
42. "Lamentation of the Overflowing Heart of the Red Man of the Forest," in Blackbird, *History of the Ottawa and Chippewa*, 102.

CHAPTER SIX. DOING GOOD AMONGST MY PEOPLE

1. Blackbird, *History of the Ottawa and Chippewa Indians of Michigan: A Grammar of Their Language, and Personal and Family History of the Author* (Ypsilanti, Mich.: The Ypsilantian Job Printing House, 1887), 101.
2. Blackbird to Bissell, June 1858, Bissell Papers; Blackbird, *History of the Ottawa and Chippewa*, 70.
3. U.S. Census, 1860, Little Traverse Township; Blackbird to Bissell, October 11, 1858; Blackbird to Bissell, September 13, 1858, Bissell Papers; Blackbird, *History of the Ottawa and Chippewa*, 70.
4. Blackbird to Bissell, April 4, 1861, Bissell Papers; Emmet County Supervisor's Journal, 1859–63, Emmet County Courthouse, Petoskey, Michigan, 42.

5. Blackbird to George W. Lee, Indian Agent, February 2, 1882, National Archives, Letters Received by the Office of Indian Affairs, 1881–1907, RG 75, Box 63, File 3334, Blackbird, *History of the Ottawa and Chippewa*, 53.
6. Mary Sagatoo, *Thirty-Three Years Among the Indians: The Story of Mary Sagatoo,* ed. Donna Winters (1897; Caledonia, Mich.: Bigwater Classics, 1994), 52, 62–63; Record of Deed, Andrew Blackbird and Elizabeth Blackbird, alias Oge che gume quay to Northrup & Trask, August 25, 1879, Emmet County Record of Deeds, Liber I, p. 307.
7. Grace Walz, "Andrew Jackson Blackbird of L'Arbre Croche," M.A. thesis, Western Michigan University, 1964, 36–37.
8. Ibid., 33–34.
9. U. P. Hedrick, *Land of the Crooked Tree* (1948; Detroit: Wayne State University Press, 1986), 27–28; Janette Scofield to Will Hampton, September 21, 1956, Hampton Papers, Bentley Historical Library, University of Michigan, Ann Arbor.
10. Fr. Pierz to Bishop Lefevere, October 22, 1844, October 25, 1844, Pierz to David Stuart, no month/no day 1843, Diocese of Detroit Papers; Proceedings of a Council, 1855, 56–71; G. J. Wendell, Memorandum of Terms of Survey, August 31, 1857, National Archives, Letters Received by the Office of Indian Affairs, RG 75, M-234, Roll 406, frame 1041.
11. Bruce Alan Rubenstein, "Justice Denied: An Analysis of American Indian–White Relations in Michigan, 1855–1889," PhD diss., Michigan State University, 1974, 7–8.
12. Blackbird to Bissell, April 4, 1861, Bissell Papers.
13. Barbara Rosen, *American Indians and State Law: Sovereignty, Race, and Citizenship, 1790–1880* (Lincoln: University of Nebraska Press, 2007), 135.
14. Rubenstein, "Justice Denied," 10.
15. James M. McClurken, "Augustin Hamlin, Jr.: Ottawa Identity and Politics of Ottawa Persistence," in *Being and Becoming an Indian: Biographical Studies of North American Frontiers*, ed. James A. Clifton (Chicago: Dorsey Press, 1989), 82–111.
16. Emmet County Land Entries, 1844–1858, Michigan Land Entry Data Base, Historical Research Associates, Missoula, Mont.
17. Ely Parker, Commissioner of Indian Affairs to James Long, Indian Agent, July 30, 1869, National Archives, Letters Sent by the Office of Indian Affairs, RG 75, M-21, Roll 91; D. C. Leach to William Dole, Commissioner of Indian Affairs, May 9, 1861, National Archives, Letters Received by the Office of Indian Affairs, RG 75, M-234, Roll 406, frames 0952–53.
18. Ibid.; U.S. Office of Indian Affairs, *Annual Report of the Commissioner of Indian Affairs, 1864* (Washington, D.C.: U.S. Government Printing Office, 1864), 589–90.

19. Parker to Long, July 30, 1869.
20. U.S. Office of Indian Affairs, *Annual Report of the Commissioner of Indian Affairs, 1863* (Washington, D.C.: Government Printing Office, 1863), 499; H. J. Alvord to L. V. Bogy, Commissioner of Indian Affairs, November 16, 1866, National Archives, Letters Received by the Office of Indian Affairs, RG 75, M-234, Roll 407, frames 852–65.
21. H. J. Alvord to L. V. Bogy, Commissioner of Indian Affairs, November 16, 1866, National Archives, Letters Received by the Office of Indian Affairs, RG 75, M-234, Roll 407, frames 852–65.
22. U.S. Office of Indian Affairs, *Annual Report, 1863*, 496.
23. Ibid.; 499; U.S. Office of Indian Affairs, *Annual Report, 1864,* 590, 593.
24. Blackbird, *History of the Ottawa and Chippewa*, 70.
25. Thomas Slaughter, Special Agent to William P. Dole, Commissioner of Indian Affairs, October 27, 1861, National Archives, Letters Received by the Office of Indian Affairs, RG 75, M-234, Roll 406, frames 1053–62.
26. U.S. Office of Indian Affairs, *Annual Report, 1863*, 494.
27. U.S. Office of Indian Affairs, *Annual Report, 1864*, 444–47; Leach to Dole, July 24, 1863, National Archives, Letters Received by the Office of Indian Affairs, RG 75, M-234, Roll 406, frames 718–19.
28. U.S. Office of Indian Affairs, *Annual Report, 1864*, 447; Leach to Charles Eddie, Acting Commissioner of Indian Affairs, September 13, 1862, National Archives, Letters Received by the Office of Indian Affairs, RG 75, M-234, Roll 407, frames 130–31.
29. Leach to Dole, October 4, 1864, National Archives, Letters Received by the Office of Indian Affairs, RG 75, M-234, Roll 514; Rev. George Bradley to H. J. Alvord, Special Agent, Office of Indian Affairs, December 13, 1864, Roll 407, frames 6363–64.
30. Andrew Blackbird to Rev. Bissell, May 1, 1865, Bissell Papers; Joseph Wakazoo, http://freepages.genealogy.rootsweb.ancestry.com/~Waukazoo/joseph_waukazoo.html.
31. Laurence M. Hauptman, *Between Two Fires: American Indians and the Civil War* (New York: Free Press, 1995), 127–29; Gravereat, http://genealogy.com/users/w/e/l/Terry-Weller/FILE/0017page.html.
32. Hauptman, *Between Two Fires*, 127–29.
33. Ibid., 136–43.
34. Claudia Linares, "Civil War Pension Law," Center for Population Economics Working Paper, 2001–6, University of Chicago, November 2001, http://www.cpe.uchicago.edu/publication/publication/html, 19–21; Declaration for Invalid Pension, James M. Doyle, U.S. Pension Office, April 15, 1905, National Archives, Civil War Pension No. 1334541.

35. Raymond J. Herek, *These Men Have Seen Hard Service: The First Michigan Sharpshooters in the Civil War* (Detroit: Wayne State University Press, 1998), 346.
36. Charles E. Mix to John Usher, Secretary of the Interior, January 26, 1865, National Archives, Letters Received by the Office of Indian Affairs, RG 75, M-234, Roll 407, frame 0638; Captain Robert Strickland to Col. B. H. Hill, February 23, 1865, Roll 407, frame 0645; Captain R. C. Denison to Col. B. H. Hill, February 28, 1865, Roll 407, frame 0644.
37. Andrew Blackbird to Rev. Bissell, May 1, 1865; U.S. Office of Indian Affairs, *Annual Report of the Commissioner of Indian Affairs, 1865* (Washington, D.C.: Government Printing Office, 1865), 636; Andrew Blackbird to Committee of Arrangements, November 9, 1864, Bissell Papers.
38. Earl DeLaVergne and Stephen Graham, "Early History," in *Harbor Springs: A Collection of Historical Essays*, ed. Jan Morley (Harbor Springs, Mich.: Harbor Springs Historical Commission, 1986), 5–8.
39. Willis F. Dunbar and George S. May, *Michigan: History of the Wolverine State* (Grand Rapids, Mich.: William Eerdmans, 1995), 331, 339.
40. The Five Bands of Ottawas and Chippewas to Commissioner of Indian Affairs, 1866, National Archives, Letters Received by the Office of Indian Affairs, RG 75, M-234, Roll 408, frame 0608; Richard Smith to D. N. Cooley, Commissioner of Indian Affairs, February 12, 1866, Roll 407, frame 1061.
41. Ibid.
42. Ibid.
43. Proceedings of a Treaty, 1855, 7; Five Bands of Ottawas and Chippewas to Commissioner of Indian Affairs, 1866.
44. D. C. Leach to William Dole, Commissioner of Indian Affairs, January 23, 1863, National Archives, Letters Received by the Office of Indian Affairs, RG 75, M-234, Roll 407, frame 0223, Richard M. Smith to Commissioner Cooley, February 12, 1866, Roll 407, frame 1061.
45. Richard Smith to Commissioner of Indian Affairs, October 29, 1868, National Archives, Letters Received by the Office of Indian Affairs, RG 75, M-234, Roll 408, frames 574–75; Commissioner of Indian Affairs to Secretary of the Interior, January 27, 1869, Roll 408, frames 489–97.
46. *Portrait and Biographical Album of Isabella County, Michigan* (Chicago: Chapman Brothers, 1884), 513–14.
47. U.S. Office of Indian Affairs, *Annual Report of the Commissioner of Indian Affairs, 1869* (Washington, D.C.: Government Printing Office, 1869), 434; Ely Parker, Commissioner of Indian Affairs to Major James Long, July 30, 1869, National Archives, Letters Sent by the Office of Indian Affairs, RG 75, M-21, Roll 91.

48. U.S. Office of Indian Affairs, *Annual Report, 1869*, 435.
49. Rubenstein, "Justice Denied," 111; U.S. Office of Indian Affairs, *Annual Report of the Commissioner of Indian Affairs, 1870* (Washington, D.C.: Government Printing Office, 1870), 317.
50. Rubenstein, "Justice Denied," 19; U.S. Office of Indian Affairs, *Annual Report of the Commissioner of Indian Affairs, 1871* (Washington, D.C.: Government Printing Office, 1871), 925.
51. S.1035, A Bill for the Restoration to Market of Certain Lands in Michigan, 42nd Congress, 2nd Session, June 10, 1872, A Century of Law Making for a New Nation: U.S. Congressional Documents and Debates, 1774–1875, http://memory.loc.gov/cgi-bin/ampage?collId=llsb&fileName=042/llsb042.db&recNum=3251; "The Michigan Indians," *Chicago Daily Tribune*, July 16, 1873, 7.
52. Rubenstein, "Justice Denied," 110–11; James Long to Commissioner of Indian Affairs, Ely Parker, July 5, 1871, National Archives, Letters Received by the Office of Indian Affairs, RG 75, M-234, Roll 409.
53. Kenneth E. Lewis, *West to Far Michigan: Settling the Lower Peninsula, 1815–1860* (East Lansing: Michigan State University Press, 2002), 55.
54. Hedrick, *Land of the Crooked Tree,* 3–7.
55. 1870 and 1880 Michigan County Population, United States Census, University of Virginia Historical Census Browser, http://fisher.lib.virginia.edu/collections/states/histcensus/php/county.php.
56. Ibid.; Father Edward Jacker to anonymous, June 21, 1877, Jacker Papers, Burton Collection, Detroit Public Library; Hedrick, *Land of the Crooked Tree,* 21, 138, 258.
57. Hedrick, *Land of the Crooked Tree,* 18–20.
58. Ibid., 12, 201, 252–55.
59. Ibid., 7, 27–28.
60. Richard Smith to Andrew Blackbird, March 9, 1866, July 5, 1866, National Archives, Letters Sent by Richard Smith, Mackinac Agency, 1865–1868 (letter press volume), RG 75, Box 1, PI-163; Columbus Delano to Smith, M-234, Roll 409, frame 639.
61. Dennis T. Downing to Commissioner of Indian Affairs, January 22, 1869, National Archives, RG 75, M-234, Roll 408, frame 0088.
62. Andrew Blackbird to James W. Long, February 20, 1871, National Archives, Letters Received by the Michigan Superintendency, 1870–74, RG 75, Box 2.
63. Andrew Keewakendo to Richard Smith, June 26, 1871, National Archives, Letters Received by the Office of Indian Affairs, RG 75, Box 2, PI-163,; Blackbird to Smith, August 1, 1871, Box 2.
64. Walz, "Blackbird of L'Arbre Croche," 40; Emmet County Supervisor's Journal, vol. 2, pp. 35, 84; *The Traverse Region, Historical and Descriptive, with*

Illustrations of Scenery and Portraits and Biographical Sketches of Some of Its Prominent Men and Pioneers (Chicago: H.R. Page, 1884), 149.

65. Emmet County Supervisor's Journal, 1859–1873; *Grand Traverse Herald,* April 16, 1874.
66. Walz, "Blackbird of L'Arbre Croche," 38–39; Blackbird to Congressman O. D. Conger, May 18, 1884, Letters Received, Office of Indian Affairs, Box 197; Blackbird, *History of the Ottawa and Chippewa,* 70–71. Blackbird also served his postal clients as a notary, *Grand Traverse Herald,* February 25, 1869. One of those who complained about Blackbird's postal administration was Martha Tanner, the daughter of John Tanner, the famous white captive who lived his life as an Indian. Martha Tanner had a deep antipathy to both Andrew and his sister Margaret. See Martha Tanner to Rev. Edward Jacker, January 31, 1876, Jacker Papers, Burton Collection, Detroit Public Library.
67. Blackbird, *History of the Ottawa and Chippewa,* 71.
68. George W. Lee, Indian Agent to J. Smith, Commissioner of Indian Affairs, January 20, 1876, National Archives, Letters Received by the Office of Indian Affairs, RG 75, M-234, Roll 412, frame 0158; Blackbird to Lee, July 17, 1876, Letters Received, 1877–79, Box 3.
69. Martha Tanner to George Lee, July 12, 1876, National Archives, Letters Received, 1877–1879, RG 75, Box 3; Emmet County Census Report, State Census of Emmet County, 1884, State Library of Michigan, Lansing; U.S. Census 1870, Agricultural Schedule, Emmet County; *Grand Traverse Herald,* January 22, 1874; Emmet County Record of Deeds, Liber L, pp. 184, 390, Emmet County Courthouse, Petoskey, Mich.; According to a commercial history published in 1884 "A.J. Blackbird" is listed among five local residents who "carried on extensively" the real estate business. Emmet County Deed records, however, do not support rating him a major player in real estate speculation. The reference may in fact have alluded to the fact Blackbird was involved in many legal disputes trying to protect Ottawa property rights.
70. Edwin J. Brooks to Ezra A. Hayt, Commissioner of Indian Affairs, January 12, 1878, National Archives, Letters Received Office of Indian Affairs, RG 75, M-234, Roll 413, frame 0105.
71. Andrew Blackbird to George W. Lee, Indian Agent, May 12, May 18, May 21, 1877, National Archives, Letters Received by Michigan Superintendency, 1877–79, RG 75, Box 3; Rubenstein, "Justice Denied," 119–20.
72. Edwin Brooks, Complaints of Indian Grievances Relative to Homesteads, Grant Traverse Land District, February 1877, National Archives, Letters Received, RG 75, M-234, Roll 412, frame 0207; John O. Shomin to George Lee, January 4, 1877, M-234, Roll 412, frame 0133; Blackbird to Lee, January 12, 1880, Letters Received Michigan Superintendency, 1877–79, Box 4; Blackbird to Lee, February 27, 1879, Box 3; Rubenstein, "Justice Denied," 118–19.

73. Blackbird to Lee, August 22, November 19, 1877, National Archives, Letters Received Michigan Superintendency, 1877–79, RG 75, Box 3.
74. Margaret Ogabejigokwe to President Grant, January 7, 1877, National Archives, Letters Received, RG 75, M-234, Roll 412, frame 0469; W. W. Upton, Comptroller to E. A. Hayt, Commissioner of Indian Affairs, October 10, 1877, Roll 412, frame 0058; Margaret Ogabejigokwe or Boyd to Great Father, June 1877, M-234, Roll 412, frame 0024. A white account of the meeting has Grant listening to Margaret with "utmost respect" and assuring her that "everything would be made right." See S. E. Waite, *Old Settlers of the Grand Traverse Region* (Traverse City, Mich.: S.E. Waite, 1918), 51. It is interesting that Margaret used her Ottawa name, not Boyd, her married name, on this trip. Her husband's father was related by marriage to former President John Q. Adams; such a connection might have helped her in Washington.
75. Edwin Brooks to Commissioner Hayt, January 4, January12, 1878, National Archives, Letters Received by the Office of Indian Affairs, RG 75, M-234, Roll 413, frame 0054.
76. As a special interpreter Blackbird received less than half the salary he earned when he held a regular appointment, although having official status again no doubt helped to get Ottawa grievances heard. George Lee to Commissioner of Indian Affairs J. Smith, March 31, 1877, National Archives, RG 75, M-234, Roll 412, frame 0288; Blackbird to Agent George Lee, November 19, 1877, National Archives, Letters Received Michigan Superintendency, Box 3; Land Entries By Indians in Michigan, Letter From the Secretary of the Interior, April 30, 1878, 45th Congress, 2nd Session, House of Representatives, Executive Document No. 82, pp. 1–5; Rubenstein, "Justice Denied," 113–14.
77. Margaret Ogabeqyigokwe to President Grant, January 7, 1877; Blackbird to Lee, January 7, 1879, Letters Received, Box 3; Brooks to Hayt, January 12, 1878; Tax Assessment Rolls of Little Traverse Township, Emmet County, 1859, Augustin Hamlin Papers, Burton Historical Collection, Detroit Public Library.
78. Blackbird to Lee, November 19, 1877.
79. Brooks, Report of Complaints, 1877, Roll 412; Blackbird to Lee, January 20, 1879, Letters Received, Box 3; Blackbird to Lee, February 6, 1880, Letters Received, Box 4; Rubenstein, "Justice Denied," 121.
80. Blackbird to Lee, February 2, 1882, Letters Received Michigan Superintendency, 1881–1907, Box 63; United States Census, Emmet County, 1870, 1880; Blackbird, *History of the Ottawa and Chippewa*, 44.
81. Agent George Lee to J. Smith, Commissioner of Indian Affairs, January 4, 1877, M-234, Roll 412, frame 0144.
82. Blackbird to Lee, February 27, 1879, Letters Received, Box 3; Blackbird to Lee, October 4, 1879, Letters Received, Box 3.

83. Blackbird to Lee, April 12, 1881, Letters Received, Box 4; Blackbird and wife, alias Ogechegemequay to Northrup and Trask, August 25, 1878, Emmet County Book of Deeds, Liber I, p. 307; E. M. Blackbird to G. Kwetchio, February 21, 1880, Emmet County Book of Deeds, Liber G.
84. Rubenstein, "Justice Denied," 121–22.
85. Blackbird to Lee, September 6, October 14, 1881, Letters Received, Box 4; Blackbird to Lee, February 10, 1879, Letters Received, Box 3; Residents of Emmet County to Commissioner of Indian Affairs, June 3, 1877, M-234, Roll 44, frame 0065; Hedrick, *The Land of the Crooked Tree,* 252–55.
86. Emmet County Book of Deeds, Liber L, pp. 184, 390.

CHAPTER SEVEN. LIGHT AND SHADOWS

1. "An Aged Indian Chief," *Detroit Free Press,* September 8, 1895.
2. Andrew Blackbird to Congressman O. D. Conger, May 18, 1884, National Archives, Letters Received by the Office of Indian Affairs, RG 75, Box 197.
3. D. C. Leach to Commissioner of Indian Affairs, March 8, 1889, National Archives, Letters Received by the Office of Indian Affairs, RG 75, Box 511; Hyacinth Sacco to Senator Palmer, March 6, 1889, National Archives, Letters Received by the Office of Indian Affairs, RG 75, Box 511; G. W. Owen to Commissioner of Indian Affairs, April 2, 1889, National Archives, Letters Received by the Office of Indian Affairs, RG 75, Box 511; "Blackbird Disgusted: Chief's Failure to Secure Indian Office," March 9, 1889, newspaper clipping from unnamed newspaper [probably the *Northern Independent* (Harbor Springs)], National Archives, Letters Received by the Office of Indian Affairs, Letters[0] Received, RG 75, Box 511; Blackbird to Governor Luce, February 13, 1889, State Archives of Michigan, Office of Executive Records, RG 44, Box 37, File 28.
4. Sacco to Palmer, March 6, 1889, Box 511.
5. "Blackbird Disgusted." The Dawes Act passed in 1887 called for breaking up tribal lands into family allotments, preparing individual Indians for citizenship, and putting "excess" Indian lands on the real estate market. This law remained the center piece of U.S. Indian policy until 1934.
6. "Blackbird Disgusted."
7. Blackbird to Commissioner of Indian Affairs, March 15, 1893, June 26, 1893, quoted in Grace Walz, "Andrew Jackson Blackbird of L'Arbre Croche," M.A. thesis, Western Michigan University, 1964, 45–46.
8. U. P. Hedrick, *Land of the Crooked Tree* (1948; Detroit: Wayne State University Press, 1986), 45–47.

9. Walz, "Blackbird of L'Arbre Croche," 37; Hedrick, *Land of the Crooked Tree,* 28.
10. Hampton, "Memoirs of Harbor Springs," 7–9; Nettie Scofield to Will Hampton, September 21, 1956, Hampton Papers, Bentley Historical Library, University of Michigan, Ann Arbor.
11. Walz, "Blackbird of L'Arbre Croche," 38.
12. Blackbird, *History of the Ottawa and Chippewa,* 25; Walz, "Blackbird of L'Arbre Croche," 58; Susan Shagonaby, interview, March 2, 1974, Bentley Historical Library, University of Michigan.
13. James M. McClurken, *Gah-baeh-Jhagwah-buk = The Way It Happened: A Visual Culture History of the Little Traverse Bay Bands of Odawa* (East Lansing: Michigan State University Museum, 1991), 91; Gertude P. Kurath, Jane Willets Ettawageshik, and Fred Ettawageshik, "Religious Customs of Modern Michigan Algonquians," part 2, Field Report of the American Philosophical Society, June 23, 1955, 5.
14. For more on the role of the parish as a social institution see Jay Dolan, *The American Catholic Experience: A History from Colonial Times to the Present* (New York: Doubleday, 1985), *The American Catholic Parish: A History from 1850 to the Present* (New York: Paulist Press, 1987); Eileen M. McMahon, *What Parish Are You From? A Chicago Irish Community and Race Relations* (Lexington: University of Kentucky Press, 1985).
15. Kurath, J. Ettawageshik, and F. Ettawageshik, "Religious Customs," 5.
16. Blackbird-Greensky Correspondence, Andrew J. Blackbird Museum, Harbor Springs, Michigan; Hedrick, *Land of the Crooked Tree,* 28; William Baker, "Churches," *Harbor Springs: A Collection of Historical Essays* (Clarksville, Tenn.: Jostens for the Harbor Springs Historical Commission, 1986), 27–37; *Detroit Free Press,* September 8, 1895.
17. Willis F. Dunbar and George S. May, *Michigan: History of the Wolverine State* (Grand Rapids, Mich.: William Eerdmans, 1995), 372–73.
18. Judy Rogers, "Resorts," *Harbor Springs,* 65–74; Russell Carpenter, "The Development of Tourist Industry in the Little Traverse Bay Region," M.A. essay, Loyola University Public History Program, 1994; Russell McKee, "It Was a Very Stylish Age," in *Mackinac: The Gathering Place* (Lansing: Michigan Natural Resources Magazine, 1981), 19–23.
19. Frank Ettawageshik, "My Father's Business," in *Unpacking Culture: Art and Commodity in Colonial and Post-Colonial Worlds,* ed. Ruth B. Phillips and Christopher B. Steiner (Berkeley: University of California Press, 1999), 20–24; *Detroit Free Press,* September 8, 1895; Blackbird to George Lee, April 12, 1881, National Archives, Letters Received by the Office of Indian Affairs, RG 75, Box 4.

20. Blackbird, *History of the Ottawa and Chippewa*, 100–102.
21. Ibid.; *Detroit Free Press*, September 8, 1895.
22. Paul Radin, Ojibwe-Ottawa Notes, No. 2, Radin Papers, American Philosophical Society; Edith Knaul, "Petoskey at the Turn of the Century," *Michigan History*, September 1952, 226.
23. Hedrick, *Land of the Crooked Tree*, 27; J. G. Inglis, *Northern Michigan Handbook for Travelers, 1898* (Petoskey, Mich.: Geo. Spring, 1898).
24. Twentieth-century newspapers also later claimed that Blackbird's uncle, Assiginack, participated in the 1812 capture of Fort Mackinac and the destruction of Fort Dearborn. Edward Clark, *The Indian Encampment At Lincoln Park, Chicago, September 26 to October 1, 1903: In Honor of the City's Centennial Anniversary* (Chicago: Chicago Centennial Committee, 1903); "Indians Invade City At Dawn," *Chicago Daily Tribune*, September, 27 1903; "Indians Again Invade City," *Chicago Record Herald*, September 26, 1903. Also see Roy Fleming, "Chief Black Bird Who Led Raid on Ft. Dearborn Manitoulin Isle Figure," *Owen Sound Sun-Times*, November 8, 1952.
25. Clark, *Indian Encampment.*
26. Michael McNally, "The Indian Passion Play: Contesting the Real Indian in the *Song of Hiawatha* Pageants, 1901–1965," *American Quarterly* 58 (2006): 105–36; Alan Trachtenberg, *Shades of Hiawatha: Staging Indians, Making Americans, 1880–1930* (New York: Hill & Wang, 2004), 91–97.
27. Blackbird to Bissell, June 18, 1858, September 7, 1884, Bissell Papers; *Detroit Advertiser*, May 6, 1859.
28. Blackbird to Bissell, September 18, 1884, Bissell Papers.
29. Francis Assikinack, "Legends and Traditions of the Odahwah Indians," *Canadian Journal of Industry, Science, and Art* 3, no. 14 (1858): 115–25; "Social and Warlike Customs of the Odahwah," *Canadian Journal* 3, no. 14 (1858): 297–308; "The Odahwah Indian Language," *Canadian Journal* 3, no. 14 (1858): 481–85.
30. Bernd C. Peyer, *The Tutor'd Mind: Indian Missionary Writers in Ante-Bellum America* (Amherst: University of Massachusetts Press, 1997), 224–48.
31. J. Fletcher Williams, "Memoir of William W. Warren," in *History of the Ojibway People* (St. Paul: Minnesota Historical Society Press, 1885), 7–20.
32. Blackbird, *History of the Ottawa and Chippewa*, 25.
33. Ibid., 7–14; Francis Parkman, *The Conspiracy of Pontiac and the Indian War*, vol. 2 (Boston: Little, Brown, 1891), 39–41.
34. Blackbird, *History of the Ottawa and Chippewa*, 19–22, 72–73; for more on this analysis see Helen Jaskoski, "Andrew Blackbird's Smallpox Story," in *Native American Perspectives on Literature and History* (Norman: University of Oklahoma Press, 1995), 30–31.

35. Blackbird, *History of the Ottawa and Chippewa,* 28, 42, 43, 46–48.
36. Ibid., 72–74, 97; Richard White, *"It's Your Misfortune and None of My Own": A History of the American West* (Norman: University of Oklahoma Press, 1991), 439.
37. Blackbird, *History of the Ottawa and Chippewa,* 11–13.
38. Ibid., 13, 50; Peyer, *The Tutor'd Mind.*
39. Blackbird, *History of the Ottawa and Chippewa,* 98.
40. Ibid., 100–106; Lucy Maddox, *Citizen Indians: Native American Intellectuals, Race, and Reform* (Ithaca, N.Y.: Cornell University Press, 2005), 5–7; Michael A. Elliott, *Custerology: The Enduring Legacy of the Indian Wars and George Armstrong Custer* (Chicago: University of Chicago Press, 2007), 198–99.
41. Blackbird, *History of the Ottawa and Chippewa,* acknowledgment.
42. *The Ypsilantian,* February 9, 1888; Simon Pokagon, *O-gi-maw-kwe mit-i-gwa-ki: Queen of the woods* (Hartford, Mich.: C. H. Engle, 1899); for more on Black Hawk's autobiography and the problem of "mediation" in Indian autobiography see Arnold Krupat, *Native American Autobiography: An Anthology* (Madison: University of Wisconsin Press, 1994); also see David J. Carlson, *Sovereign Selves: American Indian Autobiography and the Law* (Urbana: University of Illinois Press, 2006), 10–11.
43. Frederick E. Hoxie, *A Final Promise: The Campaign to Assimilate the Indians, 1880–1920* (Lincoln: University of Nebraska Press, 1984), 11, 44–50.
44. Andrew J. Blackbird, *The Indian Problem from the Indian's Standpoint* (Ypsilanti, Mich.: Scharf, Tag, Label, and Box Company, 1900); Carlos Montezuma, "The Indian Problem from the Indian's Standpoint," *Red Man* February 1898, 1–2; Bernd C. Peyer, ed., *American Indian Nonfiction: Two Centuries of Indian Political Writings* (Norman: University of Oklahoma Press, 2007), 244–53.
45. Blackbird, *Indian Problem,* 3–5.
46. Andrew Blackbird to "Friend" Bodley, February 26, March 18, 1901, Indians of North America Collection, Burton Collection, Detroit Public Library.
47. Ibid.
48. Blackbird to Honorable Spencer O. Fisher, December 13, 1887, National Archives, Letters Received Office of Indian Affairs, RG 75, Box 436; Fisher to Commissioner of Indian Affairs, December 17, 1887, Box 436.
49. McClurken, *Gah-baeh-Jhagwah-buk,* 81–82; Blackbird to Secretary of the Interior, May 25, 1891, Letters Received, Box 736; Blackbird to Commissioner of Indian Affairs, March 24, 1905, Letters Received, Box 2751; Treaty with the Ottawa and Chippewa, 1855, in *Indian Treaties, 1778–1883,* ed. Charles J. Kappler (New York: Interland Publishing, 1972), 729.
50. Richard White, "The Burt Lake Band: An Ethnohistorical Report on the Trust Lands of Indian Village," unpublished report, n.d. on file, Office of the

Attorney General of Michigan, Lansing, 67–88; Blackbird to Governor, April 10, 1894, State Archives of Michigan, Executive Office Records, RG 44, Box 139, Folder 1; Burton Parker to John T. Rich, Governor, May 19, 1894, Executive Office, RG 44, Box 176, Folder 6.

51. White, "The Burt Lake Band," 93–94; Blackbird to Bodley, n.d., February 1903, Burton Collection; "White Man's Treachery recalled," *Detroit News,* October 12, 1969.
52. *Petoskey Record,* May 18, 1887; *Directory of the City of Petoskey and Adjacent Summer Resort* (Petoskey, Mich.: Independent Democrat, 1899), 71; Sophia Sawgawnawquaudequay to Andrew Deuel, Emmet County Record of Deeds, Liber J, p. 338; Peter Wabegona, Jr. et al. to Andrew Deuel, Emmet County Book of Deeds, Liber J, p. 403; Walz, "Blackbird of L'Arbre Croche," 59.
53. Blackbird to Commissioner of Indian Affairs, October 27, 1885, National Archives, Correspondence of the BIA, 1880–1907, Box 240.
54. Ibid.; Blackbird to Commissioner of Indian Affairs, March 29, 1886, National Archives, Correspondence of the BIA, 1880–1907, Box 298.
55. Blackbird to Mr. Bodley, September 1, 1900, February 26, March 18, 1901, Indians of North America Collection, Burton Collection.
56. Hedrick, *Land of the Crooked Tree,* 29–30.
57. Emmet County, Michigan Probate Court Calendar, 1881–1909, Petoskey, Mich.; *Daily Resorter and Petoskey Evening News,* September 9, 1908.
58. Petition for the Appointment of a Special Administrator, Probate Court of Emmet 16 County, August 1910, Emmet County Probate Court, Petoskey, Mich.
59. *Daily Resorter and Petoskey Evening News,* September 9, 1908.

EPILOGUE

1. Andrew J. Blackbird, *The Indian Problem from the Indian's Standpoint* (Ypsilanti, Mich.: Scharf, Tag, Label, and Box Company, 1900), 5; Janette Scofield to Will Hampton, August 14, September 21, 1956, Hampton Papers, Bentley Historical Library; Grace Walz, "Andrew Jackson Blackbird of L'Arbre Croche," M.A. thesis, Western Michigan University, 1964, 50.
2. Margaret Beattie Bogue, *Fishing the Great Lakes: An Environmental History* (Madison: University of Wisconsin Press, 2000), 330–37; James McClurken, "Wage Labor in Two Michigan Ottawa Communities," in *Native Americans and Wage Labor: Ethnohistorical Perspectives,* ed. Alice Littlefield and Martha C. Knack (Norman: University of Oklahoma Press, 1996), 65–99.

3. Michigan Indian Foundation, Inc., *Annual Review, 1949–1950* (Harbor Springs, Mich.: Michigan Indian Foundation, 1950); Tara Brower, *Heartbeat of the People: Music and Dance of the Northern Pow-Wow* (Urbana: University of Illinois Press, 2004), 34–42. The practice of naming ceremonies is deeply rooted in Ottawa culture. According to James M. McClurken in *Gah-baeh-Jhagwah-buk = The Way It Happened: A Visual Culture History of the Little Traverse Bay Bands of Odawa* (East Lansing: Michigan State University Museum, 1991), 95–98, the practice was revived as a public celebration in 1935 by the Michigan Indian Defense Association in conjunction with the Holy Childhood of Jesus church picnic. The naming ceremonies included traditional dances. After cooperating for several years the white-led Michigan Indian Foundation and the Ottawa community had a falling out and the pageants were ended.
4. Blackbird to Bissell, n.d., June 1858, Bissell Papers.
5. A Tribal History of the Little Traverse Bay Bands of Odawa Indians, http://www.ltbbodawa-nsn.gov/TribalHistoryhtml.
6. For an excellent account of the success of modern Indian leadership see Charles Wilkinson, *Blood Struggle: The Rise of Modern Indian Nations* (New York: Norton, 2005); Blackbird, *Indian Problem,* 17.

Bibliography

ARCHIVES

American Fur Company Saulte Ste. Marie Outfit Papers, Bayliss Library, Sault Ste. Marie, Michigan.

American Fur Company Papers, New York Historical Society, New York, New York.

Frederic Baraga Papers, University of Notre Dame Archives, South Bend, Indiana.

Samuel Bissell Papers, Western Reserve Historical Society, Cleveland, Ohio.

Andrew Blackbird Materials, Archives and Records Department, Little Traverse Bay Bands of Odawa, Harbor Springs, Michigan.

Diocese of Detroit Papers, University of Notre Dame Archives, South Bend, Indiana.

Peter Dougherty Papers, Bentley Historical Library, University of Michigan, Ann Arbor.

Emmet County, Office of Emmet County Clerk, Petoskey, Michigan.

Executive Office Records, State Archives of Michigan, Lansing, Michigan.

Great Lakes Ethnohistory Archive, Glenn Black Archeological Laboratory, Indiana University, Bloomington.

Augustin Hamlin Papers, Burton Historical Collection, Detroit Public Library.

William Hampton Papers, Bentley Historical Library, University of Michigan, Ann Arbor.

Indians of North America Papers, Burton Collection, Detroit Public Library.

Edward Jacker Papers, Burton Collection, Detroit Public Library.

Gertrude Kurath Papers, American Philosophical Society, Philadelphia, Pennsylvania.

Log of the Schooner *Gazelle*, 1838. State Historical Society of Wisconsin, Madison.

Log of the Schooners *Mary Elizabeth* and *Hero*, Henry B. Ketcham, master, c. 1844–46, State Historical Society of Wisconsin, Green Bay Area Research Center, University of Wisconsin, Green Bay.

Michigan State Normal School records, Eastern Michigan University Archives, Ypsilanti, Michigan.

National Archives, Record Group 11, M-668, General Records of the United States, State Department Ratified Treaties.

National Archives, Record Group 75, Letters sent by Richard Smith, Mackinac Agency, 1865-1868 (Letter press volume).

National Archives, Record Group 75, unmicrofilmed records, Letters Received by the Office of Indian Affairs, 1881-1908.

National Archives, Record Group 75, M-1, Letters Received by the Agent at Mackinac.

National Archives, Record Group 75, M-1, Records of the Mackinac Agency.

National Archives, Record Group 75, M-1, Records of the Michigan Superintendency of Indian Affairs, 1814-1851.

National Archives, Record Group 75, M-234, Letters Received by the Office of Indian Affairs, 1824-1881.

National Archives, Record Group 75, T-494, Documents Relating to the Negotiation of Ratified and Unratified Treaties with Various Indian Tribes, 1801-1869.

National Archives, United States Pension Office, Civil War Pension Records, Washington, D.C.

Native Americans in Michigan Collection, Clarke Historical Library, Central Michigan University, Mount Pleasant, Michigan.

Paul Radin Papers, American Philosophical Society, Philadelphia, Pennsylvania.

Henry Rowe Schoolcraft Papers, Library of Congress, Washington, D.C.

Susan Shagonaby Interview, Bentley Historical Library, University of Michigan.

PUBLISHED SOURCES

Acts of the Legislature of the State of Michigan. Lansing: R.W. Ingalls, 1851.

Anderson, Gary Clayton. *Kinsmen of Another Kind: Dakota-White Relations in the Upper Mississippi Valley, 1650–1862.* St. Paul: Minnesota Historical Society Press, 1997.

Annales De L'Association De La Propagation De La Foi. Paris: La Librairie Ecclésiastique De Rusand, 1824–1831.

Assikinack, Francis. "Legends and Traditions of the Odahwah Indians." *Canadian Journal of Industry, Science, and Art* 3, no. 14 (1858): 115–25.

———. "The Odahwah Indian Language." *Canadian Journal of Industry, Science and Art* 3, no. 14 (1858): 481–85.

———. "Social and Warlike Customs of the Odahwah." *Canadian Journal of Industry, Science and Art* 3, no. 14 (1858): 297–308.

Beaumont, Deborah. *History of Brown County, Wisconsin.* Chicago: S.J. Clark, 1913.

Benson, Barbara. "Logs and Lumber: The Development of the Lumber Industry in Michigan's Lower Peninsula, 1837–1870." PhD diss., Indiana University, Bloomington, 1976.

Bissell, Samuel. *Indian Youth in Search of An Education.* Philadelphia, 1847.

Blackbird, Andrew Jackson. *Education of Indian Youth, Letter of Rev. Samuel Bissell and Appeal of A.J. Blackbird, A Chippewa Indian*. Philadelphia: William F. Geddes, 1856.

———. *History of the Ottawa and Chippewa Indians of Michigan: A Grammar of Their Language, and Personal and Family History of the Author.* Ypsilanti, Mich.: The Ypsilantian Job Printing House, 1887.

———. *The Indian Problem from the Indian's Standpoint.* Ypsilanti, Mich.: Scharf, Tag, Label, and Box Company, 1900.

Blair, Emma Helen, ed. *The Indian Tribes of the Upper Mississippi Valley and Region of the Great Lakes.* Lincoln: University of Nebraska Press, 1996.

Bleasdale, Ruth. "Manitowaning: An Experiment in Indian Settlement." *Ontario History* 66 (1974): 147–57.

Bogue, Margaret Beattie. *Fishing the Great Lakes: An Environmental History.* Madison: University of Wisconsin Press, 2000.

Brasser, T. J. "Mahican." In *Handbook of North American Indians,* vol. 15, *Northeast,* edited by Bruce G. Trigger. Washington, D.C.: Smithsonian Institution, 1978), 198–212.

Brazer, Marjorie Cahn. *Harps upon the Willows: The Johnston Family of the Old Northwest.* Ann Arbor: Historical Society of Michigan, 1993.

Bremer, Richard G. *Indian Agent and Wilderness Scholar: The Life of Henry Rowe Schoolcraft.* Mount Pleasant, Mich.: Clarke Historical Library, 1987.

Brower, Tara. *Heartbeat of the People: Music and Dance of the Northern Pow-Wow.* Urbana: University of Illinois Press, 2004.

Brown, Jennifer S. H. "Linguistic Solitudes and Changing Social Categories." In *Old Trails and New Directions: Papers of the Third North American Fur Trade Conference.* Toronto: University of Toronto Press, 1980.

———. *Strangers in the Blood: Fur Trade Company Families in Indian Country.* Vancouver: University of British Columbia Press, 1980.

Carpenter, Russell. "The Development of Tourist Industry in the Little Traverse Bay Region." M.A. essay, Loyola University Public History Program, 1994.

Carter, Clarence, ed. *Territorial Papers of the United States.* Washington, D.C.: United States Government Printing Office, 1934.

Carter, Lena M. *Centennial of Twinsburg, Ohio, 1817–1917.* Twinsburg, Ohio: Bissell Memorial Library Association, 1917.

Catalogue of the Instructors and Students of the Twinsburg Institute for the Academic Year Commencing April 13, 1846 and Ending March 13, 1847 Together with Studies, Condition. Cleveland: Younglove's Steam Press, 1847.

Catalogue of the Officers and Students of the Michigan State Normal School for the School Year 1857–1858. Detroit: Tribune Printing Office, 1858.

Chute, Jane E. *The Legacy of Shingwaukonse.* Toronto: University of Toronto Press, 1998.

Clark, Edward. *The Indian Encampment at Lincoln Park, Chicago, September 26 to October 1, 1903: In Honor of the City's Centennial Anniversary.* Chicago: Chicago Centennial Committee, 1903.

Cleland, Charles. *Rites of Conquest: The History and Culture of Michigan's Native Americans.* Ann Arbor: University of Michigan Press, 1992.

Clifton, James A. *The Prairie People: Continuity and Change in Potawatomi Indian Culture, 1665–1965.* Lawrence: University of Kansas Press, 1977.

Collections of the State Historical Society of Wisconsin Madison: State Historical Society of Wisconsin, 1888–1931.

Comer, Patrick J., Dennis A. Albert, et al. *Michigan's Native Landscape: As Interpreted from the General Land Office Surveys, 1816–1856.* Lansing: Michigan Natural Features Inventory, 1995.

Copway, George. *Life, Letters, and Speeches of George Copway (Kahgegagahbowh),* edited by A. LaVonne Brown Ruoff and Donald B. Smith. Lincoln: University of Nebraska Press, 1997.

Craker, Ruth. *First Protestant Mission in the Grand Traverse Region.* Omena, Mich.: privately printed, 1931.

Daniels, Roger. *Coming to America: A History of Immigration and Ethnicity in American Life.* New York: Harper, 1990.

Danziger, Edmund J. *Great Lakes Indian Accommodation and Resistance during the Early Reservation Years, 1850–1900.* Ann Arbor: University of Michigan, 2009.

———. *The Chippewas of Lake Superior.* Norman: University of Oklahoma Press, 1979.

Day, Gordon M. and Bruce G. Trigger, "Algonquin." In *Handbook of North American Indians, Northeast.* Washington, D.C.: Smithsonian Institution, 1979.

DeLaVergne, Earl and Stephen Graham. "Early History." In *Harbor Springs: A Collection of Historical Essays,* ed. Jan Morley. Harbor Springs, Mich.: Harbor Springs Historical Commission, 1986.

Deloria, Philip J. *Playing Indian.* New Haven: Yale University Press, 1999.

Densmore, Frances. *Chippewa Customs.* Washington, D.C.: Bureau of American Ethnology, U.S. Government Printing Office, 1929.

Directory of the City of Petoskey and Adjacent Summer Resort. Petoskey, Mich.: Independent Democrat, 1899.

Dougherty, Peter. "Diaries of Peter Dougherty," ed. Charles A. Anderson. *Journal of the Presbyterian Historical Society* 30 (1952): 95–253 Dunbar, Willis F. and George S. May. *Michigan: A History of the Wolverine State.* Grand Rapids, Mich.: William Eerdmans, 1995.

Eastman, Charles. *The Essential Charles Eastman (Ohiyesa).* Bloomington, Ind.: World Wisdom Press, 2007.

Edmunds, R. David. *The Potawatomi's: Keepers of the Fire.* Norman: University of Oklahoma Press, 1978.

———. *The Shawnee Prophet.* Lincoln: University of Nebraska Press, 1983.

———. *Tecumseh and the Quest for Indian Leadership.* Boston: Little Brown, 1984.

Elliott, Michael A. *Custerology: The Enduring Legacy of the Indian Wars and George Armstrong Custer.* Chicago: University of Chicago Press, 2007.

Ellis, Joseph J., *Founding Brothers: The Revolutionary Generation.* New York: Knopf, 2000.

Emmet County Land Entries, 1844–1858, Michigan Land Entry Data Base, Historical Research Associates, Missoula, Mont.

Emmet County Supervisor's Journal, 1859–1863. Petoskey, Mich.: Emmet County Courthouse.

Ettawageshik, Frank. "My Father's Business." In *Unpacking Culture: Art and Commodity in Colonial and Post-Colonial Worlds,* ed. Ruth B. Phillips and Christopher B. Steiner. Berkeley: University of California Press, 1999.

Feest, Johanna E., and Christian F. Feest. "Ottawa." In *Handbook of North American Indians,* vol. 15, *Northeast,* edited by Bruce G. Trigger. Washington D.C.: Smithsonian Institution, 1978.

Fisher, Leonard E. *The Blacksmiths.* New York: Franklin Watts, 1976.

Furlan, William P. *In Charity Unfeigned: The Life of Father Francis Xavier Pierz.* St. Cloud, Minn.: St. Anthony Press, 1952.

Gates, Charles M, ed. *Five Fur Traders of the Northwest.* St. Paul: Minnesota Historical Society Press, 1965.

Gilpin, Alec R. *The War of 1812 in the Old Northwest.* East Lansing: Michigan State University Press, 1958.

Gray, Susan E. *The Yankee West: Community and Life on the Michigan Frontier.* Chapel Hill: University of North Carolina Press, 1996.

Hauptman, Lawrence M. *Between Two Fires: American Indians and the Civil War.* New York: Free Press, 1995.

Hedrick, U. P. *The Land of the Crooked Tree.* Detroit: Wayne State University Press, 1986.

Henry, Alexander. *Travels and Adventures in Canada and the Indian Territories Between the Years 1760 and 1776.* Edmonton: M.G. Hurtig, 1969.

Herek, Raymond J. *These Men Have Seen Hard Service: The First Michigan Sharpshooters in the Civil War.* Detroit: Wayne State University Press, 1998.

Herttinger, George B. "Samuel Bissell, Humanitarian and Educator, 1797–1895." PhD diss., University of Akron, 1981.

Hickerson, Harold. *The Chippewa and Their Neighbors.* New York: Holt, Rinehart, 1970.

Hilger, M. Inez. "Chippewa Child Life and Its Cultural Background." *Smithsonian Institution, Bureau of American Ethnology, Bulletin 146* (1951).

"Historical Studies and Notes: Letters of Father Franz Pierz, Pioneer Missionary." *Central-Blatt and Social Justice* (May 1934): 51–65.

Hoxie, Frederick E. *A Final Promise: The Campaign to Assimilate the Indians, 1880–1920.* Lincoln: University of Nebraska Press, 1984.

Hubbard, Gurdon Saltonstall. *The Autobiography of Gurdon Saltonstall Hubbard.* New York: Citadel Press, 1969.

Humins, John Harold. "George Boyd: Indian Agent of the Upper Great Lakes, 1819–1842." PhD dissertation, Michigan State University, East Lansing Michigan, 1975.

Inglis, J.G. *Northern Michigan Handbook for Travelers, 1898.* Petoskey, Mich. Geo. Spring, 1898.

Innis, Harold A. *The Fur Trade in Canada.* Toronto: University of Toronto Press, 1965.

Jameson, Anna. *Winter Studies and Summer Rambles.* London: Saunder and Otley, 1838.

Jaskoski, Helen, "Andrew Blackbird's Smallpox Story." In *Native American Perspectives on Literature and History*, ed. Alan R. Velie. Norman: University of Oklahoma Press, 1995.

———. "A Terrible Sickness Among Them: Smallpox and Stories of the Frontier." In *Early Native American Writing: New Critical Essays,* ed. Helen Jaskoski. New York: Cambridge University Press, 1996.

Johnson, Alice M., editor, *Saskatchewan Journals and Correspondence: Edmonton House, 1795–1802.* London: Hudson's Bay Company Record Society, 1967.

Kane, Paul. *Wanderings of an Artist Among the Indians of North America.* London: Longman, Brown, Green, 1859.

Kappler, Charles J., ed. *Indian Treaties, 1778–1883.* New York: Interland Publishing, 1972.

Karamanski, Theodore J. *Schooner Passage: Sailing Ships and the Lake Michigan Frontier.* Detroit: Wayne State University Press, 2000.

Kilar, Jeremy W. *Michigan's Lumbertowns: Lumbermen and Laborers in Saginaw, Bay City, and Muskegon.* Detroit: Wayne State University Press, 1990.

Kinietz, W. Vernon. *The Indians of the Western Great Lakes, 1615–1760.* Ann Arbor: University of Michigan Press, 1965.

Klunder, Willard Carl. *Lewis Cass and the Politics of Moderation.* Kent, Ohio: Kent State University Press, 1996.

Knaul, Edith, "Petoskey at the Turn of the Century." *Michigan History* 36, no. 3 (September 1952): 224–30.

Kohl, Johann Georg. *Kitchi-Gami: Life Among the Lake Superior Ojibway.* St. Paul: Minnesota Historical Society Press, 1985.

Konkle, Maureen. *Writing Indian Nations: Native Intellectuals and the Politics of Historiography, 1827–1863.* Chapel Hill: University of North Carolina Press, 2004.

Kugel, Rebecca. *To Be the Main Leaders of Our People: A History of Minnesota Ojibwa Politics, 1825–1898.* East Lansing: Michigan State University Press, 1998.

Kurath, Gertrude P., Jane Willets Ettawageshik, and Fred Ettawageshik. "Religious Customs of Modern Michigan Algonquians." Field Report of the American Philosophical Society, June 23, 1955.

Landon, Fred. *Lake Huron.* New York: Bobbs-Merrill, 1944.

Lavender, David. *The Fist in the Wilderness.* Albuquerque: University of New Mexico Press, 1979.

Leach, L. Morgan. *A History of the Grand Traverse Region.* Traverse City, Mich.: Grand Traverse Herald, 1903.

Le Roy, Claude Charles. *The Indian Tribes of the Upper Mississippi and region of the Great Lakes,* edited and translated by Emma Helen Blair. Lincoln: University of Nebraska Press, 1996.

Lewis, Kenneth E. *West to Far Michigan: Settling the Lower Peninsula, 1815–1860.* East Lansing: Michigan State University Press, 2002.

Long, John. *Voyages and Travels of an Indian Interpreter and Trader.* London: Robson, Debrett, and Egerton, 1791.

Maddox, Lucy. *Citizen Indians: Native American Intellectuals, Race, and Reform.* Ithaca, N.Y.: Cornell University Press, 2005.

Mankiller, Wilma Pearl, and Michael Wallis. *Mankiller: A Chief and Her People.* New York: St. Martins, 2000.

Mansfield, J. B. *History of the Great Lakes.* Chicago: B.H. Beers, 1899.

Mason, Philip P., ed. *Schoolcraft's Expedition to Lake Itasca: The Discovery of the Source of the Mississippi River.* East Lansing: Michigan State University Press, 1993.

Mazzuchelli, Samuel. *The Memoirs of Father Samuel Mazzucheli, O.P.* Chicago: Priory Press, 1967.

McClurken, James. "Augustin Hamlin, Jr.: Ottawa Identity and Politics of Ottawa Persistence." In *Being and Becoming an Indian: Biographical Studies of North American Frontiers,* ed. James A. Clifton. Chicago: Dorsey Press, 1989.

———. *Gah-baeh-Jhagwah-buk = The Way It Happened: A Visual Culture History of the Little Traverse Bay Bands of Odawa.* East Lansing: Michigan State University Museum, 1991.

———. "Wage Labor in Two Michigan Indian Communities." In *Native Americans and Wage Labor: Ethnohistorical Perspectives,* edited by Alice Littlefield and Martha C. Knack. Norman: University of Oklahoma Press, 1996.

———. "We Wish to be Civilized: Ottawa-American Political Contests on the Michigan Frontier." PhD dissertation, Michigan State University, 1988.

McCoy, Isaac. *History of the Baptist Indian Missions.* New York: Johnson Reprint Corporation, 1970.

McKee, Russell. "It Was a Very Stylish Age." *Mackinac: The Gathering Place.* Lansing: Michigan Natural Resources Magazine, 1981.

McNally, Michael. "The Indian Passion Play: Contesting the Real Indian in the *Song of Hiawatha* Pageants, 1901–1965." *American Quarterly* 58 (2006): 105–36.

Michigan Indian Foundation, *Annual Review, 1949–1950.* Harbor Springs, Mich.: Michigan Indian Foundation, 1950.

Michigan Statutes Annotated, vol. 1. Chicago: Callaghan, 1882.

Montezuma, Carlos. "The Indian Problem from the Indian's Standpoint." *Red Man* 15 (February 1898): 1–2.

Morley, Jan, ed. *Harbor Springs: A Collection of Historical Essays.* Clarksville, Tenn.: Harbor Springs Historical Commission, 1981.

Morse, Jedidiah. *A Report to the Secretary of War of the United States on Indian Affairs.* New Haven, Conn.: Davis & Force, 1822.

Neumeyer, Elizabeth A. Indian Removal in Michigan, 1833–1855. M.A. Thesis, Central Michigan University, Mount Pleasant, 1968.

Nute, Grace Lee. *Lake Superior.* New York: Bobbs-Merrill, 1944.

"Ottawas of Michigan." *Baptist Missionary Magazine,* 2 November 1835.

Parkman, Francis. *The Conspiracy of Pontiac and the Indian War,* vol. 2. New York: Collier, 1962.

Peers, Laura. *The Ojibwa of Western Canada, 1780 to 1870.* St. Paul: Minnesota Historical Society Press, 1994.

Perrin, William H. *History of Summit County, Ohio.* Chicago: Baskin & Battey, 1881.

Peyer, Bernd C. *The Tutor'd Mind: Indian Missionary-Writers in Antebellum America.* Amherst: University of Massachusetts Press, 1997.

———, ed. *American Indian Nonfiction: Two Centuries of Indian Political Writings.* Norman: University of Oklahoma Press, 2007.

Pierz, Francis. *Die Indianer in Nord Amerika, Ihre Lebensweise, Siten und Gebrauche.* St. Louis: Franz Saler, 1855.

Pierz, Francis. "Indians of North America," trans. and ed. Eugene Hagedorn. *Social Justice Review* 40 (1947–1948): 24–390.

Pokagon, Simon. *O-gi-maw-kwe mit-i-gwa-ki: Queen of the Woods.* Hartford, Mich.: C.H. Engle, 1899.

———. "Simon Pokagon on Naming the Indians." *American Monthly Review of Reviews* 16 (September 1897): 320–21.

Porter, Joy, and William Fenton. *To Be an Indian: The Life of Iroquois-Seneca Arthur Caswell Parker.* Norman: University of Oklahoma Press, 2001.

Portrait and Biographical Album of Isabella County, Michigan. Chicago: Chapman Brothers, 1884.

Prucha, Francis Paul. *American Indian Policy in the Formative Years: The Indian

Trade and Intercourse Acts, 1790–1834. Lincoln: University of Nebraska Press, 1962.

Quaife, Milo M., ed. *The John Askin Papers.* Detroit: Detroit Library Commission, 1931.

Report of the Proceedings and Debates in the Convention to Revise the Constitution of Michigan, 1850. Lansing: R.W. Ingalls, 1850.

Ritzenthaler, Robert, and Pat Ritzenthaler. *Woodland Indians of the Western Great Lakes.* New York: American Museum of Natural History, 1970.

Rorabaugh, W. R. *The Alcoholic Republic: An American Tradition.* New York: Oxford University Press, 1979.

Rosen, Barbara. *American Indians and State Law: Sovereignty, Race, and Citizenship, 1790–1880.* Lincoln: University of Nebraska Press, 2007.

Rubenstein, Bruce Alan. "Justice Denied: An Analysis of American Indian-White Relations in Michigan, 1855–1889." PhD diss., Michigan State University, 1974.

Sagatoo, Mary. *Thirty-Three Years Among the Indians: The Story of Mary Sagatoo,* ed. Donna Winters. Caledonia, Mich.: Bigwater Classics, 1994.

Schenck, John. *History of Ionia and Montcalm Counties.* Philadelphia: D.W. Ensign, 1881.

Schenck, Theresa M. "The Cadottes: Five Generations of Fur Traders on Lake Superior." In *The Fur Trade Revisited: Selected Papers of the Sixth North American Fur Trade Conference, Mackinac Island, Michigan, 1991*, edited by Jennifer S. H. Brown, W. J. Eccles, and Donald P. Heldman. East Lansing: Michigan State University Press, 1994), 189–197.

Schoolcraft, Henry Rowe. *Personal Memoirs of a Residence of Thirty Years With the Indian Tribes of the American Frontiers.* Philadelphia: Lippincott, Grambo and Co., 1851.

Senier, Siobhan. *Voices of American Indian Assimilation and Resistance: Helen Hunt Jackson, Sarah Winnemucca, and Victoria Howard.* Norman: University of Oklahoma Press, 2003.

Shea, John C. *Catholic Missions Among the Indian Tribes of the United States.* New York: E. Dunigan & Brother, 1854.

Sleeper-Smith, Susan. *French Men and Indian Women: Rethinking Cultural Encounter in the Western Great Lakes.* Amherst: University of Massachusetts Press, 2001.

Sugden, John. *Tecumseh: A Life.* New York: Holt, 1999.

Tanner, Helen Hornbeck. *Atlas of Great Lakes Indian History.* Norman: University of Oklahoma Press, 1987.

Tanner, John. *Narrative of the Adventures of John Tanner (U.S. Interpreter at the Sault Ste. Marie) During Thirty Years Residence Among the Indians in the Interior of North America.* Minneapolis: Ross & Haines, Inc., 1956.

———. *A Narrative of the Captivity and Adventures of John Tanner,* ed. Edwin James. New York: Garland, 1975.

Taylor, J. Garth. "Assiginac's Canoe." *The Beaver* (October,ÄíNovember 1986): 50–53.

Trachtenberg, Alan. *Shades of Hiawatha: Staging Indians, Making Americans, 1880–1930.* New York: Hill & Wang, 2004.

Traverse Region: Historical and Descriptive, with Illustrations of Scenery and Portraits and Biographical Sketches of Some of Its Prominent Men and Pioneers. Chicago: H.R. Page, 1884.

U.S. Office of Indian Affairs, *Annual Report of the Commissioner of Indian Affairs, 1840–1895.* New York: AMS Press, 1976.

Van Kirk, Sylvia. *Many Tender Ties: Women in Fur Trade Society, 1670–1870.* Norman: University of Oklahoma Press, 1980.

Van Noord, Roger. *King of Beaver Island.* Urbana: University of Illinois Press, 1988.

Verwyst, P. Chrysostomus. *Life and Labors of Rt. Rev. Frederic Baraga.* Milwaukee: M.H. Wiltzius, 1900.

Viola, Herman J. *Diplomats in Buckskins: A History of Indian Delegations in Washington City.* Washington, D.C.: Smithsonian Institution Press, 1981.

Waite, S. E. *Old Settlers of the Grand Traverse Region.* Traverse City, Mich.: S.E. Waite, 1918.

Walz, Grace. Andrew Jackson Blackbird of L'Arbre Croche. M.A. thesis, Western Michigan University, 1964.

Warren, William W. *History of the Ojibway People.* St. Paul: Minnesota Historical Society, 1984.

Wheeler-Voegelin, Erminie. "An Anthropological Report on Indian Use and Occupancy of Northern Michigan." In *Chippewa Indians,* vol. 5. New York: Garland Press, 1974.

White, Richard. *The Middle Ground: Indians, Empires, and Republics in the Great Lakes Region, 1650–1815.* New York: Cambridge University Press, 1991.

———. *"It's Your Misfortune and None of My Own": A History of the American West.* Norman: University of Oklahoma Press, 1991.

Widder, Keith R. *Battle for the Soul: Metis Children Encounter Evangelical Protestants at Mackinac Mission, 1823–1837.* East Lansing: Michigan State University Press, 1999.

Williams, J. Fletcher. "Memoir of William W. Warren." In *History of the Ojibway People.* St. Paul: Minnesota Historical Society Press, 1885.

Winnemucca, Sarah. *Life among the Paiutes.* Las Vegas: University of Nevada Press, 1994.

Index

C

S

T

U